Aggression
Theoretical and Empirical Reviews

Volume 1

Theoretical and Methodological Issues

Contributors

Albert Bandura
Leonard Berkowitz
H. S. Bertilson
M. K. Covey
H. A. Dengerink
Tamara J. Ferguson
D. W. Rajecki
Brendan Gail Rule
James T. Tedeschi
Dolf Zillmann

Aggression

Theoretical and Empirical Reviews

Volume 1
Theoretical and Methodological Issues

Edited by

Russell G. Geen

Department of Psychology
University of Missouri
Columbia, Missouri

Edward I. Donnerstein

Department of Communication Arts
The University of Wisconsin–Madison
Madison, Wisconsin

 1983

ACADEMIC PRESS
A Subsidiary of Harcourt Brace Jovanovich, Publishers
New York   London
Paris   San Diego   San Francisco   São Paulo   Sydney   Tokyo   Toronto

ACADEMIC PRESS, INC.
111 Fifth Avenue, New York, New York 10003

United Kingdom Edition published by
ACADEMIC PRESS, INC. (LONDON) LTD.
24/28 Oval Road, London NW1 7DX

Library of Congress Cataloging in Publication Data
Main entry under title:

Aggression, theoretical and empirical reviews.

Bibliography: p.
Includes index.
1. Aggressiveness (Psychology) 2. Violence.
I. Geen, Russell G., Date   II. Donnerstein,
Edward I. [DNLM: 1. Agression. BF 575.A3 A266]
BF575.A3A525 1983   155.2'32   82-24348
ISBN 0–12–278801–X (v. 1)

PRINTED IN THE UNITED STATES OF AMERICA

83 84 85 86   9 8 7 6 5 4 3 2 1

To Barbara and Debbie

Contents

one

Psychological Mechanisms of Aggression   1

Albert Bandura

two

An Attributional Perspective on Anger and Aggression   41

Tamara J. Ferguson and Brendan Gail Rule

three

Arousal and Aggression 75

Dolf Zillmann

four

The Experience of Anger as a Parallel Process in the Display of Impulsive, "Angry" Aggression 103

Leonard Berkowitz

five

Social Influence Theory and Aggression 135

James T. Tedeschi

six
Implications of an Escape–Avoidance Theory of Aggressive Responses to Attack   **163**
H. A. Dengerink and M. K. Covey

seven
Animal Aggression: Implications for Human Aggression   **189**
D. W. Rajecki

eight
Methodology in the Study of Aggression   **213**
H. S. Bertilson

A Concluding Comment   **247**

Contributors

Numbers in parentheses indicate the pages on which the authors' contributions begin.

Albert Bandura (1), Department of Psychology, Stanford University, Stanford, California 94305

Leonard Berkowitz (103), Department of Psychology, University of Wisconsin, Madison, Wisconsin 53706

H. S. Bertilson (213), Department of Psychology, Weber State College, Ogden, Utah 84408

M. K. Covey[1] (163), Department of Psychology, Washington State University, Pullman, Washington 99164

H. A. Dengerink (163), Department of Psychology, Washington State University, Pullman, Washington 99164

Tamara J. Ferguson (41), Psychologisch Laboratorium der Katholieke Universiteit, Montessorilaan 6500 HE, Nijmegen, The Netherlands

D. W. Rajecki (189), Department of Psychology, IUPUI, Indianapolis, Indiana 46205

Brendan Gail Rule (41), Department of Psychology, University of Alberta, Edmonton, Alberta, T6H 2E9 Canada

James T. Tedeschi (135), Department of Psychology, State University of New York at Albany, Albany, New York 12222

Dolf Zillmann (75), Institute for Communication Research, Indiana University, Bloomington, Indiana 47405

[1]PRESENT ADDRESS: Department of Psychology, University of Idaho, Moscow, Idaho 83843

Preface

Concern over the problems of aggression and violence continues to dominate a large amount of our individual and collective lives. Individual citizens, the actual or potential victims of violence, demand that the problem be controlled. Scientists, legislators, and law officers seek the causes and solutions. These two issues—cause and control—have always been at the heart of the efforts of psychologists to study the phenomenon of aggression. As scientists, psychologists have generally sought first the causes, reasoning that efforts at control would not be effective unless based on knowledge of why people often behave so aggressively. During the 1960s, when the study of aggression began in earnest, American society sought the causes of aggression within either social structures or the underlying characteristics of human personality. Under the pressure of mounting levels of violence in our society during the 1970s, however (e.g., crime in the streets, drug-related crime, crime among adolescents), people demanded needed controls, and interest in probing for causes receded.

However, as the chapters in this volume will show, the quest for causation is more intense and is proceeding at a higher level of refinement than was the case 20 or 10 years ago. The reviews presented here show that we have developed considerably more sophisticated theoretical models to account for data than we had even a few years ago. This volume represents an attempt to review a number of these theoretical viewpoints that psychologists now use to explain aggression, as well as the principal methods of research used to test these views.

In the first chapter, "Psychological Mechanisms of Aggression," Bandura notes that any theory needs to account for many aspects of aggression from individual to institutional sanctions. In his social learning theory of aggression, Bandura discusses how aggressive behaviors are developed (e.g., biological factors, observational learning), how they are instigated (e.g., aversive conditions, modeling), and how they are maintained (e.g., reinforcement, disengagement of internal control).

The next three chapters represent the current debate over the roles of anger, arousal, and attributional processes in the formation of human aggressive behavior. In the first of these chapters, "An Attributional Perspective on Anger and Aggression," Ferguson and Rule elaborate on the cognitive processes that influence anger and subsequent aggression. In their analysis they discuss the attributions made about harmful behavior. Is a harm doer responsible for the harm? Is he or she morally culpable? A model for the instigation of anger, the assignment of blame, and the subsequent retaliation are presented in light of judgments of causal responsibility and perceived assessment of what "ought" to have happened in a harmful situation. Considerations for future research and unresolved issues in the model are considered.

In the second chapter, "Arousal and Aggression," Zillmann addresses the issue of the relationship between arousal and human aggression. As he notes, arousal is *not* always a facilitator of aggression, but rather depends on a number of circumstances, particularly cognitive influences. The cognitive processes that facilitate and maintain aggression are examined, as well as conditions that do not link or modify the arousal–aggression relationship. Considerations of arousal in impulsive aggression and various types of physiological arousal are examined in regard to future research in this area.

In the final chapter on this topic, "The Experience of Anger as a Parallel Process in the Display of Impulsive, 'Angry' Aggression," Berkowitz presents a model somewhat different than the preceding two chapters. While noting that cognitions can play a role in aggression, they are not necessary for the expression of aggressive behavior. Based on current theories of emotion and a research program on the effects of aversive stimulation, Berkowitz argues that the "sort of analyses envisioned by the cognitive–attributional theories of emotion" do not adequately explain impulsive aggression.

In the chapter by Tedeschi, "Social Influence Theory and Aggression," a rather different approach is presented. In his theory of coercive power, Tedeschi attempts to redefine the entire concept of aggression. The issue of why an individual uses coercion and when such behaviors are "defined" as aggression are developed. A critique of other major theoretical explanations of aggression as well as experimental study are considered in light of his social influence theory.

Another explanation of aggression, that which is instigated by attack, is offered by Dengerink and Covey in their chapter, "Implications of an Escape–Avoidance Theory of Aggressive Responses to Attack." The authors present evidence to suggest that aggressive behavior may be an instrumental attempt to terminate or avoid aversive behaviors from another individual. Their model relies on predictions from negative reinforcement theory as well as social learning theory. The role that this model plays in other aggression-related phenomena, like attribution of intent, aggressive cues, aggressive escalation, and control of aggression are considered.

A clear and informative explanation of the relationship of animal to human aggression is presented by Rajecki in his chapter, "Animal Aggression: Implications for Human Aggression." Rajecki discusses the notions of homology, analogy, and model in social behavior and shows how these various approaches can be used as a framework to incorporate both nonhuman and human aggression research in our general understanding of aggression.

In the final chapter, "Methodology in the Study of Aggression," Bertilson discusses the major methodological issues (e.g., internal and external validity) as well as the various ways in which research on aggression in humans has been conducted (e.g., case studies, laboratory and field experiments). The chapter offers an overview of the many ways we can conduct studies on the causes and prevention of aggression.

Contents of Volume 2

one

Psychological Mechanisms of Aggression[1]

ALBERT BANDURA

Analysis of the determinants and mechanisms of aggression requires prior consideration of the phenomena the concept composes. Differing conceptions of what constitutes aggression produce different lines of theorizing and research. Psychological theories of aggression have been largely concerned with individual physically injurious acts that are aversively motivated. In most of these accounts, not only is aggression attributed to a narrow set of instigators but the purposes it presumably serves are limited. Inflicting injury and destruction is considered to be satisfying in its own right and hence the major aim of aggressive behavior. In actuality, aggression is a multifaceted phenomenon that has many determinants and serves diverse purposes. Therefore, theoretical formulations couched in terms of frustrating instigators and injurious aims have limited explanatory power (Bandura, 1973). A complete theory of aggression must be sufficiently broad in scope to encompass a large set of variables governing diverse facets of aggression, whether individual or collective, personally or institutionally sanctioned.

[1]The preparation of this paper and research by the author reported here was facilitated by Public Health Research Grant M-5162 from the National Institute of Mental Health and by the James McKeen Cattell Award. This chapter is reprinted by permission from M. von Cranach, K. Foppa, W. Lepenies and D. Ploog (Eds.), *Human ethology: Claims and limits of a new discipline.* Cambridge: Cambridge University Press, 1979.

1

ISBN 0-12-278801-X

SOCIAL LABELING PROCESSES

Aggression is generally defined as behavior that results in personal injury and physical destruction. The injury may be physical, or it may involve psychological impairment through disparagement and abusive exercise of coercive power. Not all injurious and destructive acts are judged aggressive, however. Although injury is a major defining property, in fact, aggression refers to complex events that include not only injurious behavior but judgmental factors that lead people to attach aggression labels to some forms of harmful conduct but not to others.

Whether injurious behavior will be perceived as aggressive or otherwise depends heavily on subjective judgments of intentions and causality. The greater the attribution of personal responsibility and injurious intent to the harm doer, the higher the likelihood that the behavior will be judged as aggressive (Bandura, 1973; Rule & Nesdale, 1976b). The same harmful act is perceived differently depending on the sex, age, attractiveness, status, socioeconomic level, and ethnic background of the performer. As a general rule, people judge the harmful acts of favored individuals and groups as unintended and prompted by situational circumstances, but they perceive the harmful acts of the disfavored as intentional and personally initiated. Value orientations of the labelers also influence their judgments of activities that cause harmful effects.

There are few disagreements over the labeling of direct assaultive behavior that is performed with explicit intent to injure or destroy. But people ordinarily do not aggress in conspicuous direct ways that reveal causal responsibility and carry high risk of retaliation. Rather, they tend to harm and destroy in ways that diffuse or obscure responsibility for detrimental actions, to reduce self-reproof and social reprisals. Most of the injurious consequences of major social concern are caused remotely, circuitously, and impersonally through social practices judged aggressive by the victims but not by those who benefit from them. Students of aggression examine direct assaultive behavior in minute detail, whereas remote circuitous acts, which produce widespread harm, receive comparatively little attention.

Disputes over the labeling of aggressive acts assume special significance in the case of collective behavior involving dissident and institutionally sanctioned aggression. Agencies of government are entrusted with considerable rewarding and coercive power. Either of these sources of power can be misused to produce detrimental social effects. Punitive and coercive means of control may be employed to maintain inequitable systems, to suppress legitimate dissent, and to victimize disadvantaged segments of society. People can similarly be harmed both physically and socially by arbitrary denial or discriminative administration of beneficial resources to which they are entitled.

Just as not all individual acts that produce injury are necessarily aggressive, neither are all institutional practices that cause harm expressions of aggression.

Some social practices instituted with well-meaning intent create detrimental consequences that were unforeseen. Others are performed routinely and thoughtlessly through established custom. Judgments of institutional aggression are likely to be made in terms of indicants of injurious intent, deliberate negligence, and unwillingness to rectify detrimental conditions.

Dissident aggression is also judged in large part on the basis of factors external to the behavior. Some of these include the perceived legitimacy of the grievances, the appropriateness of coercive tactics, the professed aims and credibility of the challengers, and the ideological allegiances of the judges (Bandura, 1973). People vary markedly in their perceptions of aggression for social control and for social change (Blumenthal et al., 1972). The more advantaged citizenry tend to view even extreme levels of violence for social control as lawful discharges of duty, whereas disadvantaged members regard such practices as expressions of institutional aggression. Conversely, aggression for social change, and even group protest without injury, is judged as violence by patriots of the system but not by dissidents. Thus, in conflicts of power, one person's violence is another person's benevolence. Whether a particular form of aggression is regarded as adaptive or destructive depends on who bears the consequences. As this brief review suggests, factors influencing the social labeling of different forms of injurious behavior merit more systematic investigation than they have received to date.

A complete theory of aggression must explain how aggressive patterns are developed, what provokes people to behave aggressively, and what sustains such actions after they have been initiated. Figure 1 summarizes the determi-

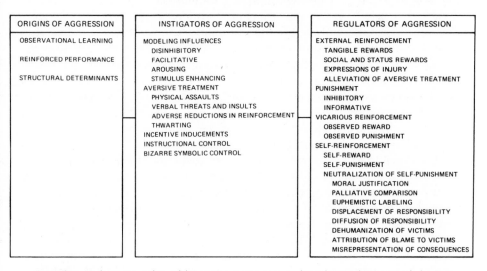

SOCIAL LEARNING ANALYSIS OF AGGRESSION

ORIGINS OF AGGRESSION	INSTIGATORS OF AGGRESSION	REGULATORS OF AGGRESSION
OBSERVATIONAL LEARNING	MODELING INFLUENCES	EXTERNAL REINFORCEMENT
	DISINHIBITORY	TANGIBLE REWARDS
REINFORCED PERFORMANCE	FACILITATIVE	SOCIAL AND STATUS REWARDS
	AROUSING	EXPRESSIONS OF INJURY
STRUCTURAL DETERMINANTS	STIMULUS ENHANCING	ALLEVIATION OF AVERSIVE TREATMENT
	AVERSIVE TREATMENT	PUNISHMENT
	PHYSICAL ASSAULTS	INHIBITORY
	VERBAL THREATS AND INSULTS	INFORMATIVE
	ADVERSE REDUCTIONS IN REINFORCEMENT	VICARIOUS REINFORCEMENT
	THWARTING	OBSERVED REWARD
	INCENTIVE INDUCEMENTS	OBSERVED PUNISHMENT
	INSTRUCTIONAL CONTROL	SELF-REINFORCEMENT
	BIZARRE SYMBOLIC CONTROL	SELF-REWARD
		SELF-PUNISHMENT
		NEUTRALIZATION OF SELF-PUNISHMENT
		MORAL JUSTIFICATION
		PALLIATIVE COMPARISON
		EUPHEMISTIC LABELING
		DISPLACEMENT OF RESPONSIBILITY
		DIFFUSION OF RESPONSIBILITY
		DEHUMANIZATION OF VICTIMS
		ATTRIBUTION OF BLAME TO VICTIMS
		MISREPRESENTATION OF CONSEQUENCES

FIGURE 1 Schematic outline of the origins, instigators, and regulators of aggressive behavior in social learning theory.

nants of these three aspects of aggression within the framework of social learning theory.

ACQUISITION MECHANISMS

People are not born with preformed repertoires of aggressive behavior. They must learn them. Some of the elementary forms of aggression can be perfected with minimal guidance, but most aggressive activities—whether they be dueling with switchblade knives, sparring with opponents, military combat, or vengeful ridicule—entail intricate skills that require extensive learning.

Biological Factors

New modes of behavior are not fashioned solely through experience. Biological factors, of course, set limits on the types of aggressive responses that can be developed and influence the rate at which learning progresses. In addition to biological constraints on behavior, evolved biological systems predispose organisms to perceive and to learn critical features of their immediate environment.

The orchestration of aggressive actions, like other forms of visceral and motor responsiveness, depends on neurophysiological mechanisms. Research conducted with animals has identified subcortical structures, principally the hypothalamus and the limbic system, that mediate aggressive behavior (Goldstein, 1974). But these neural systems are selectively activated and controlled by central processing of environmental stimulation. Research by Delgado (1967) illustrates how social learning factors influence the types of responses that are likely to be activated by stimulating the same neural structure. Hypothalamic stimulation of a dominant monkey in a colony prompted him to attack subordinate males but not the females with whom he was on friendly terms. In contrast, hypothalamic stimulation elicited submissiveness in a monkey when she occupied a low hierarchical position, but increased aggressiveness toward subordinates as her social rank was elevated by changing the membership of the colony. Thus, electrical stimulation of the same anatomical site produced markedly different behavior under different social conditions.

It is valuable to know how neurophysiological systems operate internally, but from the standpoint of explaining aggression, it is especially important to understand how they are socially activated for different courses of action. In everyday life, biological systems are roused in humans by provocative external events and by ideational activation. A remark interpreted as an insult will generate activity in the hypothalamus, whereas the same comment viewed innocuously will leave the hypothalamus unperturbed. Given a negative interpretation, social and cognitive factors are likely to determine the nature of the response.

In the social learning view, people are endowed with neurophysiological mechanisms that enable them to behave aggressively, but the activation of these mechanisms depends on appropriate stimulation and is subject to cognitive control. Therefore, the specific forms that aggressive behavior takes, the frequency with which it is expressed, the situations in which it is displayed, and the specific targets selected for attack are largely determined by social learning factors. As we shall see, these factors are varied and complex.

The role played by biological factors in aggression will vary across species, circumstances, and types of aggressive behavior. In infrahuman organisms, genetic and hormonal factors that affect neural organization and structural development figure prominently in aggressive responsiveness. Aggression in animals is largely determined by combat successes that depend on a robust physical build. The more powerfully developed members generally become belligerent fighters through victories; the physically less well endowed become submissive through defeats. Because genetic and hormonal factors affect physical development, they are related to aggressiveness in animals.

People's capacity to devise and use destructive weapons greatly reduces their dependence on biological structure to succeed in aggressive encounters. A puny person with a gun can easily triumph over powerfully built opponents who are unarmed. People's proclivity for social organization similarly reduces the importance of structural characteristics in aggressive attainments. At the social level, aggressive power derives from organized collective action. The chance of victory in aggressive confrontation is enhanced by the force of numbers acting in concert, and the physical stature of individual challengers does not much matter.

Structural characteristics related to aggressiveness also have different evolutionary and survival consequences for animals and humans. In many animal species, physical strength determines which males do the mating. Combat victors gain possession of females so that the most dominant males have the highest reproduction rates. In humans, mate selection is based more on such qualities as attractiveness, intelligence, parental arrangement, religious affiliation, and financial standing than on fighting prowess. Societal sanctions prohibit the brawny members of a social group from impregnating at will whomever they desire. Differential reproduction rates are primarily determined by religious beliefs, ideological commitments, socioeconomic factors, and birth control practices. For these reasons, one would not expect variations in human aggressiveness to be reflected in differential reproduction rates.

Observational Learning

Psychological theories have traditionally assumed that learning can occur only by performing responses and experiencing their consequences. In fact, virtually all learning phenomena resulting from direct experience can occur on a vicarious basis by observing the behavior of others and its consequences for them. The capacity to learn by observation enables organisms to acquire large, integrated patterns of behavior without having to form them gradually by tedious trial and error.

The abbreviation of the acquisition process through observational learning is vital for both development and survival. Because errors can produce costly or even fatal outcomes, the prospects of survival would be slim indeed if organisms could learn solely by the consequences of their actions. The more costly and hazardous the possible mistakes, the heavier is the reliance on observational learning from competent models. This is particularly true of aggression, where the dangers of crippling or fatal consequences limit the value of learning through trial and error. By observing the aggressive conduct of others, one forms a conception of how the behavior is performed, and on later occasions, the symbolic representation can serve as a guide for action.

Learning by observation is governed by four interrelated subprocesses (Bandura, 1977a). *Attentional* processes regulate exploration and perception of modeled activities. Organisms cannot be much influenced by observation of modeled behavior if they have no memory of it. Through coding into images, words, or other symbolic modes, transitory modeling influences are transformed for *memory representation* into enduring performance guides. The capacity for observational learning, whether assessed across species or over the course of development, increases with increasing capability to symbolize experience. Symbolic representations must eventually be transformed into appropriate actions. *Motor production* processes, the third component of modeling, govern the integration of constituent acts into new response patterns.

Social learning theory distinguishes between acquisition of behaviors that have destructive and injurious potential and factors that determine whether individuals will perform what they have learned. This distinction is important because not all the things learned are enacted. People can acquire, retain, and possess the capability to act aggressively, but the behavior may rarely be expressed if it has no functional value for them or is negatively sanctioned. Should appropriate inducements arise on later occasions, individuals put into practice what they have learned (Bandura, 1965; Madsen, 1968). *Incentive and motivational* processes regulate the performance of observationally learned responses.

Findings of numerous studies show that children can acquire entire repertoires of novel aggressive behavior from observing aggressive models and can retain such response patterns over extended periods (Bandura 1973; Hicks 1968). Factors that affect the four component processes influence the level of observational learning. In many instances, the behavior being modeled is learned in essentially the same form. But models teach more general lessons as well. From observing the behavior of others, people can extract general tactics and strategies of behavior that enable them to go beyond what they have seen

or heard. By synthesizing features of different modeled patterns into new amal-
gams, observers can evolve new forms of aggression.

In a modern society, aggressive styles of behavior can be adopted from three
principal sources. One prominent origin is the aggression modeled and reinforced by family members. Studies of familial determinants of aggression show
that parents who favor aggressive solutions to problems have children who
tend to use similar aggressive tactics in dealing with others (Bandura & Walters,
1959; Hoffman, 1960). That familial violence breeds violent styles of conduct
is further shown by similarities in child abuse practices across several generations (Silver, Dublin, & Lourie, 1969).

Although familial influences play a major role in setting the direction of
social development, the family is embedded in a network of other social systems. The subculture in which people reside, and with which they have repeated contact, provides a second important source of aggression. Not surprisingly,
the highest incidence of aggression is found in communities in which aggressive models abound and fighting prowess is regarded as a valued attribute
(Short, 1968; Wolfgang & Ferracuti, 1967).

The third source of aggressive conduct is the abundant symbolic modeling
provided by the mass media. The advent of television has greatly expanded the
range of models available to a growing child. Whereas their predecessors
rarely, if ever, observed brutal aggression in their everyday life, both children
and adults today have unlimited opportunities to learn the whole gamut of
violent conduct from televised modeling within the comfort of their homes.

A considerable amount of research has been conducted in recent years on
the effects of televised influences on social behavior. The findings show that
exposure to televised violence can have at least four different effects on viewers: (a) It teaches aggressive styles of conduct; (b) it alters restraints over aggressive behavior; (c) it desensitizes and habituates people to violence; and (d) it
shapes people's images of reality upon which they base many of their actions.
Let us review briefly each of these effects.

Television is an effective tutor. Both laboratory and controlled field studies in
which young children and adolescents are repeatedly shown either violent or
nonviolent fare disclose that exposure to filmed violence shapes the form of
aggression and typically increases interpersonal aggressiveness in everyday life
(Bandura, 1973; Leyens et al., 1975; Liebert, Neale, & Davidson, 1973; Parke
et al., 1977; Friedrich & Stein, 1973; Steuer, Applefield, & Smith, 1971).
Adults who pursue a life of crime improve their criminal skills by patterning
their behavior after the ingenious styles portrayed in the mass media (Hendrick,
1977). Being an influential tutor, television can foster humanitarian qualities as
well as injurious conduct. Programs that portray positive attitudes and social
behavior foster cooperativeness, sharing, and reduce interpersonal aggression
(Leifer, Gordon, & Graves, 1974).

Another line of research has examined how inhibitions over aggression are affected by exposure to televised violence. Several characteristics of televised presentations tend to weaken people's restraints over behaving aggressively. Physical aggression is often shown to be the preferred solution to interpersonal conflicts. It is portrayed as acceptable, unsullied, and relatively successful. Superheroes do most of the killing. When good triumphs over evil by violent means, viewers are more strongly influenced than when aggressive conduct is not morally sanctioned by prestigious figures. In experimental tests, adults generally behave more punitively after they have seen others act aggressively than if they have not been exposed to aggressive modeling. This is especially true if the modeled aggressive conduct is legitimized by social justifications (Berkowitz, 1970).

Desensitization and habituation to violence are reflected in decreases in physiological reactions to repeated exposure to displays of violence. Heavy viewers of television respond with less emotion to violence than do light viewers (Cline, Croft, & Courrier, 1973). In addition to emotional desensitization, violence viewing can create behavioral indifference to human aggression. In studies demonstrating the habituation effect, children who have had prior exposure to interpersonal violence are less likely to intervene in escalating aggression between children they are overseeing (Drabman & Thomas, 1974; Thomas & Drabman, 1975; Thomas et al., 1977).

During the course of their daily lives, people have direct contact with only a small sector of the physical and social environment. In their daily routines, they travel the same routes, visit the same places, and see essentially the same group of friends and work associates. Consequently, people form impressions of the social realities with which they have little or no contact partly from televised representations of society. Because the world of television is heavily populated with villainous and unscrupulous people, it can distort knowledge about the real world. Indeed, communications researchers have found that heavy viewers of television are less trustful of others and overestimate their chances of being criminally victimized than do light viewers (Gerbner & Gross, 1976). Heavy viewers see the society at large as more dangerous regardless of their educational level, sex, age, and amount of newspaper reading.

Many of the misconceptions that people develop about certain occupations, nationalities, ethnic groups, sex roles, social roles, and other aspects of life are cultivated through modeling of stereotypes by the media. Too often their actions are based on such misconceptions.

Symbolic modeling plays an especially significant role in the shaping and rapid spread of collective aggression. Social diffusion of new styles and tactics of aggression conforms to the generalized pattern of most other contagious activities: New behavior is introduced by a salient example; it spreads rapidly in a contagious fashion; and it then either stabilizes or is discarded depending on its functional value.

Modeled solutions to problems that achieve some success are not only adopted by people facing similar difficulties but tend also to spread to other

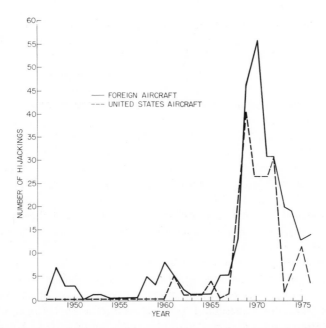

FIGURE 2 Incidence of hijackings over a span of 30 years. The rise in foreign hijackings during 1948–1950 occurred in Slavic countries during the Hungarian uprisings, and the second flare-up, in 1958–1961, comprised almost entirely Cuban hijackings to Miami. A sudden widespread diffusion of hijackings occurred in 1969–1970, involving airliners from 71 different countries. (Data from Federal Aviation Administration.)

troublesome areas. The civil rights struggle, which itself was modeled after Gandhi's crusades of nonviolent resistance, in turn provided the example for other protest campaigns aimed at eliminating injustices and undesired social practices. The model of collective protest is now widely used as a means of forcing change.

Airline hijacking provides another example of the rapid diffusion and decline of aggressive tactics. Air piracy was unheard of in the United States until an airliner was hijacked to Havana in 1961. Prior to that incident, Cubans were hijacking planes to Miami. These incidents were followed by a wave of hijackings both in the United States and abroad, eventually involving 71 different countries (see Figure 2). Just as aggressive strategies are widely modeled, so are the countermeasures that prove effective in controlling modeled aggression.

Learning by Direct Experience

People rarely teach social behaviors that are never exemplified by anyone in their environment. Therefore, in behavior acquired under natural conditions, it is often difficult to determine whether reinforcing experiences create the new responses or activate what was already partly learned by observation. Although modeling influences are universally present, patterns of behavior can be shaped through a more rudimentary form of learning relying on the consequences of trial-and-error performance.

Until recently, learning by reinforcement was portrayed as a mechanistic process in which responses are shaped automatically by their immediate consequences. In more recent theoretical analyses, learning from response consequences is conceived of largely as a cognitive process, especially in humans. Consequences serve as an unarticulated way of informing performers what they must do to gain beneficial outcomes and to avoid punishing ones. By observing the differential effects of their actions, individuals discern which responses are appropriate in which settings and behave accordingly. Although the empirical issue is not yet fully resolved, evidence that human behavior is not much affected by consequences until the point at which the contingencies are discerned raises serious questions concerning the automaticity of reinforcement.

Viewed from the cognitive framework (Bandura, 1977a), learning from differential outcomes becomes a special case of observational learning. In this mode of conveying response information, the conception of the appropriate behavior is gradually constructed from observing the effects of one's actions rather than from the synthesized examples provided by others. A vast amount of evidence lends validity to the view that reinforcement serves principally as an informative and motivational operation rather than as a mechanical response shaper.

There have been few experimental attempts to fashion novel forms of aggression by differential reinforcement alone. It would be foolhardy to instruct novices how to use lethal weapons or to fight dangerous opponents by selectively reinforcing trial-and-error efforts. Where the consequences of mistakes can be dangerous or fatal, demonstration rather than unguided experience is the best tutor.

Learning through combat experience has been explored to a limited extent in experiments with lower species designed to train docile animals into ferocious fighters (Ginsburg & Allee, 1942; Scott & Marston, 1953). This is achieved by arranging a series of bouts with progressively more experienced fighters under conditions where trainees can win fights without being hurt. As fighting skills are developed and reinforced through repeated victories, formerly noncombative animals become more and more vicious in their aggressive behavior. Whereas successful fighting produces brutal aggressors, severe defeats create enduring submissiveness (Kahn, 1951).

Patterson, Littman, and Bricker (1967) report a field study illustrating how passive children can be shaped into aggressors through a process of victimization and successful counteraggression. Passive children who were repeatedly victimized but occasionally succeeded in halting attacks by counteraggression, not only increased defensive fighting over time, but began to initiate attacks of their own. Passive children who were seldom maltreated because they avoided others, and those whose counteraggression proved unsuccessful, remained submissive.

Modeling and reinforcement influences operate jointly in the social learning of aggression in everyday life. Styles of aggression are largely learned through observation and refined through reinforced practice. The effects of these two determinants on the form and incidence of aggression are graphically revealed in ethnographic reports of societies that pursue a warlike way of life and those that follow a pacific style. In cultures lacking aggressive models and devaluing injurious conduct, people live peaceably (Alland, 1972; Denton, 1968; Levy, 1969; Mead, 1935; Turnbull, 1961). In other societies that provide extensive training in aggression, attach prestige to it, and make its use functional, people spend a great deal of time threatening, fighting, maiming, and killing each other (Bateson, 1936; Chagnon, 1968; Gardner & Heider, 1969; Whiting, 1941).

INSTIGATION MECHANISMS

A theory must explain not only how aggressive patterns are acquired but also how they are activated and channeled. Social learning theory distinguishes between two broad classes of motivators of behavior. First, there are the biologically based motivators. These include internal aversive stimulation arising from tissue deficits and external sources of aversive stimulation that activate behavior through their painful effects. The second major source of response inducement involves cognitively based motivators. The capacity to represent future consequences in thought provides one cognitively based source of motivation. Through cognitive representation of future outcomes, individuals can generate current motivators of behavior. The outcome expectations may be material (e.g., consummatory, physically painful), sensory (e.g., novel, enjoyable, or unpleasant sensory stimulation), or social (e.g., positive and negative evaluative reactions). Another cognitively based source of motivation operates through the intervening influences of goal setting and self-evaluative reactions. Self-motivation involves standards against which performances can be evaluated. By making positive self-evaluation conditional on attaining a certain level of behavior, individuals create self-inducements to persist in their efforts until their performances match self-prescribed standards.

As will be shown shortly, some aggressive acts are motivated by painful stimulation. However, most of the events that lead people to aggress, such as insults, verbal challenges, status threats, and unjust treatment, gain this activating capacity through learning experiences. People learn to dislike and to attack certain types of individuals either through direct unpleasant encounters with them or on the basis of symbolic and vicarious experiences that conjure up hatreds. Because of regularities in environmental events, antecedent cues come to signify future events and the outcomes particular actions are likely to produce. Such uniformities create expectations about what leads to what. When aggressive behavior produces different results depending on the times, places, or persons toward whom it is directed, people use cues predictive of probable consequences in regulating their behavior. They tend to aggress toward persons and in contexts where it is relatively safe and rewarding to do so, but they are disinclined to act aggressively when it carries a high risk of punishment. The different forms that aggression elicitors take are discussed separately in the sections that follow.

Aversive Instigators

It has been traditionally assumed that aggressive behavior is activated by an aggressive drive. According to the instinct doctrine, organisms are innately endowed with an aggressive drive that automatically builds up and must be discharged periodically through some form of aggressive behavior. Despite intensive study, researchers have been unable to find an inborn autonomous drive of this type.

For years, aggression was viewed as a product of frustration. In this conception, frustration generates an aggressive drive, that in turn motivates aggressive behavior. Frustration replaced instinct as the activating source, but the two theories are much alike in their social implications. Since frustration is ever present, in both approaches people are continuously burdened with aggressive energy that must be drained from time to time.

The frustration–aggression theory was widely accepted until its limited explanatory value became apparent from growing evidence. Frustration has varied effects on behavior; aggression does not require frustration. Frustration subsumes such a diverse set of conditions—physical assault, deprivation, insult, thwarting, harassment, and defeat—that it no longer has any specific meaning. As new instigators of aggression were identified, the definition of frustration was stretched to accommodate them. Not only is there great heterogeneity on the antecedent side of the relationship, but the consequence part of the formula, the aggressive behavior, also embraces a vast array of activities sifted through value judgments. One cannot expect a generalizable relationship to emerge from such a wide assortment of antecedents and behaviors.

The diverse events subsumed under the omnibus term *frustration* do have one feature in common—they are all aversive. In social learning theory, rather than frustration generating an aggressive drive that is reducible only by injurious behavior, aversive stimulation produces a general state of emotional arousal that can facilitate any number of responses (see Figure 3). The type of behavior elicited will depend on how the source of arousal is cognitively appraised, the modes of response learned for coping with stress, and their relative effectiveness. When distressed, some people seek help and support; others increase achievement efforts; others display withdrawal and resignation;

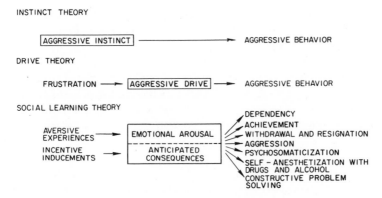

FIGURE 3 Schematization of alternative motivational analyses of aggression.

some aggress; others experience heightened somatic reactivity; still others anesthetize themselves against a miserable existence with drugs or alcohol; and most intensify constructive efforts to overcome the source of distress.

Several lines of evidence, reviewed in detail elsewhere (Bandura, 1973), lend greater validity to the *arousal-prepotent response* formulation than to the *frustration–aggression* view. Different emotions appear to have a similar physiological state (Ax, 1953). The same physiological state can be experienced phenomenologically as different emotions, depending on what people see as the incitements and how they interpret them (Hunt, Cole, & Reis, 1958; Mandler, 1975). In individuals who are prone to behave aggressively, different sources of emotional arousal can heighten their aggression (Rule & Nesdale, 1976a; Tannenbaum & Zillman, 1975).

In drive theories, the aroused aggressive drive presumably remains active until discharged by some form of aggression. Actually, anger arousal dissipates rapidly, but it can be easily regenerated on later occasions through rumination on anger-provoking incidents. By thinking about past insulting treatment, people can work themselves into a rage long after their emotional reactions have subsided. Persistence of elevated anger stems from thought-produced arousal, rather than from an undischarged reservoir of aggressive energy. Consider the example of a person who becomes angered by an apparent exclusion from an important meeting only to receive the notice in the next day's mail. The person will show an immediate drop in anger arousal and aggressiveness without having to assault or denounce someone to drain a roused drive. Anger arousal decreased through cognitive means will reduce aggression as much as, or even more than, will acting aggressively (Mallick & McCandless, 1966). When anticipated consequences are varied, the same aggressive acts can raise or lower physiological arousal (Hokanson, Willers, & Koropsak, 1968).

Frustration or anger arousal is a facilitative, rather than a necessary, condition for aggression. Frustration tends to provoke aggression mainly in people who have learned to respond to aversive experiences with aggressive attitudes and conduct. Thus, after being frustrated, aggressively trained children behave more aggressively, whereas cooperatively trained children behave more cooperatively (Davitz, 1952).

There exists a large body of evidence that painful treatment, deprivation or delay of rewards, personal insults, failure experiences, and obstructions, all of which are aversive, do not have uniform behavioral effects (Bandura, 1969). Some of these aversive antecedents convey injurious intent more clearly than others and therefore have greater aggression-provoking potential.

PHYSICAL ASSAULTS

If one wished to provoke aggression, one way to do so would be simply to hit another person, who is likely to oblige with a counterattack. To the extent that counteraggression discourages further assaults, it is reinforced by pain reduction and thereby assumes high functional value in social interactions. Although naturally occurring contingencies favor the development of a pain–aggression relationship, there is some dispute over whether it is innate or acquired.

Azrin (1967) and Ulrich (1966) were major proponents of the nativistic view that pain-induced aggression is an unlearned reflexive behavior. As the determinants of pain–attack reactions were examined more closely, however, they began to lose their reflexive status. Young animals rarely, if ever, fight when shocked unless they have had some fighting experience, and in some studies, shocks produce little or no fighting in 20–30% of mature animals (Hutchinson, Ulrich, & Azrin, 1965; Powell & Creer, 1969). If aggression is an unlearned dominant response to pain, then initial shocks should produce attack, which is not generally the case (Azrin, Hutchinson, & Hake, 1963). Contrary to the reflexive elicitation hypothesis, when combative responses are shocked the pain reduces and eliminates rather than provokes fighting (Azrin, 1970; Baenninger & Grossman, 1969). The most striking evidence that pain–aggression reactions are determined more by situational factors than by innate organization is the finding that in a small enclosure approximately 90% of the shocks provoke fighting, whereas in a larger chamber animals ignore each other and only 2% of the shocks elicit attack (Ulrich & Azrin, 1962). As environmental constraints to fight are removed, avoidance and flight responses to painful stimulation take priority over attack (Knutson, 1971; Logan & Boice, 1969; Sbordone, Garcia, & Carder, 1977). Physically painful experiences may be facilitative but clearly not sufficient to provoke aggression in animals.

Pain stimulation is even a less consistent elicitor of aggression in humans. Nonsocial sources of pain rarely lead people to attack bystanders. Whether or not they counteraggress in the face of physical assaults depends on their combat skill and the power of their assailant. Those who possess fighting prowess escalate counterattacks to subdue assailants (Edwards, 1968; Peterson, 1971). Given other alternatives, low aggressors are easily dissuaded from counterattacks under retaliative threats.

VERBAL THREATS AND INSULTS

Social interchanges are typically escalated into physical aggression by verbal threats and insults. In analyzing dyadic interchanges of assault-prone individuals, Toch (1969) found that humiliating affronts and threats to reputation and manly status emerged as major precipitants of violence. High sensitivity to devaluation was usually combined with deficient verbal skills for resolving disputes and restoring self-esteem without having to dispose of antagonists physically. The counterattacks evoked by physical assaults are probably instigated more by humiliation than by physical pain. Indeed, it is not uncommon for individuals, groups, and even nations to pay heavy injury costs in efforts to save face by combat victory.

Insult alone is less effective in provoking attack in those who eschew aggression, but it does heighten their aggressiveness given hostile modeling and other disinhibitory influences (Hartmann, 1969; Wheeler & Caggiula, 1966). In subcultures in which social ranking is determined by fighting prowess, status threats from challengers within the group or rival outsiders are quick to provoke defensive aggression (Short, 1968).

The most plausible explanation of how insults acquire aggression-eliciting potential is in terms of foreseen consequences. Affronts that are not counteracted can have far-reaching effects for victims. Not only do they become easy targets for further victimization, but they are apt to forfeit the rewards and privileges that go with social standing. To the extent that punishment of insults reduces the likelihood of future maltreatment, the insult—aggression reaction becomes well established.

ADVERSE REDUCTIONS IN CONDITIONS OF LIFE

Aversive changes in the conditions of life can also provoke people to aggressive action. Explanations of collective aggression usually invoke impoverishment and discontent arising from privations as principal causal factors. However, since most impoverished people do not aggress, the view that discontent breeds violence requires qualification. This issue is well illustrated in interpretations of urban riots in ghetto areas. Despite condemnation of their degrading and exploitive conditions of life, comparatively few of the disadvantaged took active measures to force warranted changes. Even in cities that experienced civil disturbances, only a small percentage of ghetto residents actively participated in the aggressive activities (Lieberson & Silverman, 1965; McCord & Howard, 1968; Sears & McConahay, 1969).

The critical question for social scientists to answer is not why some people who are subjected to aversive conditions aggress, but rather why a sizable majority of them acquiesce to dismal living conditions in the midst of affluent styles of life. To invoke the frustration—aggression hypothesis, as is commonly done, is to disregard the more striking evidence that severe privation generally produces feelings of hopelessness and massive apathy. People give up trying when they lack a sense of personal efficacy and no longer expect their efforts to produce any beneficial results in an environment that is unresponsive or is consistently punishing (Bandura, 1977b, 1982; Maier & Seligman, 1976).

In accord with self-efficacy theory, comparative studies indicate that discontent produces aggression, not in those who have lost hope, but in the more successful members whose assertive efforts at social and economic betterment have been periodically reinforced. Consequently, they have some reason to expect that they can effect change by coercive action (Caplan, 1970; Crawford & Naditch, 1970).

More recent explanations of violent protest emphasize relative deprivation rather than the actual level of aversive conditions as the instigator of collective aggression. In an analysis of conditions preceding major revolutions, Davies (1969) reports that revolutions are most likely to occur when a period of social and economic advances that instills rising expectations is followed by a sharp reversal. People judge their present gains not only in relation to those they secured in the past; they also compare their lot in life with the benefits accruing to others (Bandura, 1977a). Inequities between observed and experienced outcomes tend to create discontent, whereas individuals may be satisfied with limited rewards as long as they are as good as what others are receiving.

Since most people who feel relatively deprived do not resort to violent action, aversive privation, like other forms of aversive treatment, is not in itself a sufficient cause of collective aggression. Additional social learning factors must be considered that determine whether discontent will take an aggressive form or some other behavioral expression. Using such a multideterminant approach, Gurr (1970) examined the magnitude of civil disorder in Western nations as a function of three sets of factors. The first is the level of social discontent arising from economic decline, oppressive restrictions, and social inequities. The second factor is the traditional acceptance of force to achieve social change. Some societies disavow aggressive tactics, whereas others regard mass protests and coups d'etat as acceptable means of change. The third factor is the balance of coercive power between the system and the challengers as measured by the amount of military, police, industrial, labor, and foreign support the protagonists can marshal on their side. The analysis reveals that when aggressive tactics are considered acceptable and challengers possess coercive power, they will use less extreme forms of collective aggression without requiring much discontent. Revolutionary violence, however, requires widespread discontent and strong coercive power by challengers, while tactical traditions are of less importance.

Although aggression is more likely to be provoked by relative than by absolute privation, clarification of the role of relative deprivation requires greater consideration of the multifaceted bases of comparative evaluation. People judge their life circumstances in relation to their aspirations, to their past conditions, and to the life situations of others whom they select for social comparison. Discontent created by raised aspirations, by reduction or rewards and privileges from accustomed levels, and by deceleration in the rate of one's own improvement compared to that of others undoubtedly has variant effects. Different sources of inequity (social, economic, policital) may have differential aggression-activating potential. Response to inequitable deprivation is further influenced by mollifying social justifications and promise of social reforms. Considering the complex interplay of influences, it is hardly surprising that level of deprivation alone, whether defined in absolute or in relative terms, is a weak predictor of collective aggression (McPhail, 1971).

THWARTING OF GOAL-DIRECTED BEHAVIOR

Proponents of the frustration—aggression theory define frustration in terms of interference or blocking of goal-seeking activities. In this view, people are provoked to aggression when obstructed, delayed, or otherwise thwarted from getting what they want. Research bearing on this issue shows that thwarting can lead people to intensify their efforts, which, if sufficiently vigorous, may be construed as aggressive. However, thwarting fails to provoke forceful action in people who have not experienced sufficient success to develop reward expectations and in those who are blocked far enough from the goal that it appears unattainable (Bandura & Walters, 1963; Longstreth, 1966).

When thwarting provokes aggression, it is probably attributable more to personal affront than to blocking of behavior. Consistent with this interpretation, people report more aggression to thwartings that appear unwarranted or suggest hostile intent than to those for which excusable reasons exist, even though both involve identical blocking of goal-directed behavior (Cohen, 1955; Pastore, 1952).

The overall evidence regarding the different forms of aversive instigators supports the conclusion that aversive antecedents, though they vary in their activating potential, are facilitative rather than necessary or sufficient conditions for aggression.

Incentive Instigators

The preceding discussion was concerned solely with aversive instigators of aggression, which traditionally occupied a central role in psychological theorizing, often to the neglect of more important determinants. The cognitive capacity of humans to represent future consequences enables them to guide their behavior by outcomes extended forward in time. A great deal of human aggression, in fact, is prompted by anticipated positive consequences. Here, the instigator is the pull of expected benefits, rather than the push of painful treatment. This positive source of motivation for aggression represents the second component of social learning theory in the motivational analyses depicted schematically in Figure 3.

The consequences that people anticipate for their actions are derived from, and therefore usually correspond to, prevailing conditions of reinforcement. The anticipatory activation and incentive regulation of aggression receive detailed consideration later. Expectation and actuality do not always coincide because anticipated consequences are also partly inferred from the observed outcomes of others, from what one reads or is told, and from other indicators of likely consequences. Because judgments are fallible, aggressive actions are sometimes prompted and temporarily sustained by erroneous anticipated consequences. Habitual offenders, for example, often err by overestimating the chances of success for transgressive behavior (Claster, 1967). In social interchanges and collective protest, coercive actions are partly sustained, even in the face of punishing consequences by expectations that continued pressure may eventually produce desired results.

Modeling Instigators

Of the numerous antecedent cues that influence human behavior at any given moment, none is more common than the actions of others. Therefore, a reliable way to prompt people to aggress is to have others do it. Indeed, both children and adults are more likely to behave aggressively and with greater intensity if they have seen others act aggressively than if they have not been exposed to aggressive models (Bandura, 1973; Liebert, Neale, & Davidson, 1973). The activation potential of modeling influences is enhanced if observers are angered (Berkowitz, 1965; Hartmann, 1969; Wheeler, 1966), if the modeled aggression is socially justified (Berkowitz, 1965; Meyer, 1972) or shown to be successful in securing rewards (Bandura, Ross, & Ross, 1963), and if the victim invites attack through prior association with aggression (Berkowitz, 1970).

Social learning theory distinguishes four processes by which modeling influences can activate aggressive behavior. One mode of operation is in terms of the *directive function* of modeled actions. In many instances, behaving like others is advantageous because the prevalent modes have proven functional, whereas divergent courses of action may be less effective. After modeling cues acquire predictive value through correlated consequences, they come to serve as informative prompts for others to behave in a similar fashion.

Aggressive behavior, especially when harsh and lacking justification, is socially censured if not self-condemned. Anticipated punishment exerts a restraining influence on injurious conduct. Seeing people respond approvingly or even indifferently toward aggressors conveys the impression that such behavior is an acceptable or normative mode of response. The same modeled aggression is much more effective in reducing restraints if it is socially legitimated than if it is portrayed as unjustified (Goranson, 1970). In aggressive conduct that is unencumbered by restraints because it is regarded as emulative, aggressive modeling is primarily instigational, whereas it serves a *disinhibitory function* in injurious behavior that is fear or guilt provoking. Since physical aggression usually incurs some negative effects, both instigational and disinhibitory processes are likely to be involved.

Seeing others aggressive generates *emotional arousal* in observers. For individuals who are prone to behave aggressively, emotional arousal can enhance their aggressive response. Some of the instigative effects of modeling may well reflect the emotional facilitation of aggressive behavior.

Aggressive modeling can additionally increase the likelihood of aggressive behavior through its *stimulus-enhancing effects*. Modeled activities inevitably direct observers' attention to the particular implements being used. This attentional focus may prompt observers to use the same instruments to a greater extent, though not necessarily in an imitative way. In one experiment (Bandura, 1962), for example, children who had observed a model pummel a plastic figure with a mallet spent more time pounding other objects with a mallet than those who did not see it used for assaultive purposes. In sum, the combined evidence reveals that modeling influences, depending on their form and content, can function as teachers, elicitors, disinhibitors, stimulus enhancers, and emotion arousers.

Instructional Instigators

During the process of socialization, people are trained to obey orders. By rewarding compliance and punishing disobedience, directives issued in the form of authoritative commands elicit obedient aggression. After this form of social control is established, legitimate authorities can secure obedient aggression from others, especially if the actions are presented as justified and necessary, and the issuers possess strong coercive power. As Snow (1961) has perceptively observed, "When you think of the long and gloomy history of man, you will find more hideous crimes have been committed in the name of obedience than in the name of rebellion [p. 24]."

In studies of obedient aggression, Milgram (1974) and others (Kilham & Mann, 1974; Mantell & Panzarella, 1976) have shown that well-meaning adults will administer increasingly severe shocks on command despite their victims' desperate pleas. Adults find it difficult to resist peer pressures calling for increasingly harmful actions, just as they are averse to defying legitimized authority. Seeing others carrying out punitive orders calmly likewise increases obedient aggression (Powers & Geen, 1972).

It is less difficult to hurt people on command when their suffering is not visible and when causal actions seem physically or temporally remote from their deleterious effects. Mechanized forms of warfare, where masses of people can be put to death by destructive forces released remotely, illustrate such depersonalized aggression. When the injurious consequences of one's actions are fully evident, vicariously aroused distress and self-censure serve as restraining influences over aggressive conduct that is otherwise authoritatively sanctioned. Obedience declines as the harmful consequences of destructive acts become increasingly more salient and personalized (Milgram, 1974). As the results of these and other studies to be cited later show, it requires conducive social conditions rather than monstrous people to produce heinous deeds.

Delusional Instigators

In addition to the various external instigators, aggressive behavior can be prompted by bizarre beliefs. Every so often tragic episodes occur in which individuals are led by delusional beliefs to commit acts of violence. Some follow divine inner voices commanding them to murder. There are those who resort to self-protective attacks on paranoid suspicions that others are conspiring to harm them (Reich & Hepps, 1972). Others kill for deranged sacrificial purposes. And still others are prompted by grandiose convictions that it is their heroic responsibility to eliminate evil individuals in positions of influence.

A study of American presidential assassins (Weisz & Taylor, 1970) shows that, almost without exception, the murderous assaults were delusionally instigated. Assassins tend to be loners who are troubled by severe personal failure. They acted either under divine mandate, through alarm that the president was in conspiracy with treacherous foreign agents to overthrow the government, or on the conviction that their own adversities resulted from presidential persecution. Being unusually seclusive, the assassins barred themselves from the type of confiding relationships needed to correct erroneous beliefs and to check autistically generated resentments.

MAINTAINING MECHANISMS

So far, we have discussed how aggressive behavior is learned and activated. The third major feature of the social learning formulation concerns the conditions that sustain aggressive responding. It is amply documented in psychological research that behavior is extensively regulated by its consequences. This principle applies equally to aggression. Injurious modes of response, like other forms of social behavior, can be increased, eliminated, and reinstated by altering the effects they produce.

People aggress for many different reasons. Similar aggressive actions may thus have markedly different functional value for different individuals and for the same individual on different occasions. Traditional behavior theories conceptualize reinforcement influences almost exclusively in terms of the effects of external outcomes impinging directly upon performers. But external consequences, as influential as they often are, are not the only kind of outcomes that regulate human behavior. People guide their actions partly on the basis of observed consequences and partly by consequences they create for themselves. These three forms of outcomes—external, vicarious, and self-produced—not only serve as separate sources of influence but also interact in ways that weaken or enhance their effects on behavior (Bandura, 1977a).

External Reinforcement

As we have previously noted, consequences exert effects on behavior largely through their informative and incentive functions. For the most part, response consequences influence behavior antecedently by creating expectations of similar outcomes on future occasions. The likelihood of particular actions is increased by anticipated benefits and reduced by anticipated punishment.

Aggression is strongly influenced by its consequences. Extrinsic rewards assume special importance in interpersonal aggression because such behavior, by its very nature, usually produces some costs among its diverse effects. People who get into fights, for example, will suffer pain and injury even though they eventually triumph over their opponents. Under noncoercive conditions, positive incentives are needed to overcome inhibitions arising from the aversive concomitants of aggression. The positive incentives take a variety of forms.

TANGIBLE REWARDS

Aggression is often used by those lacking better alternatives because it is an effective means of securing desired tangible rewards. Ordinarily docile animals will fight when aggressive attacks produce food or drink (Azrin & Hutchinson, 1967; Ulrich et al., 1963). Observation of children's interactions reveals that most of the assaultive actions of aggressors produce rewarding outcomes for them (Patterson, Littman, & Bricker, 1967). Given this high level of positive reinforcement of aggressive behavior, there is no need to invoke an aggressive drive to explain the prevalence of such actions. Aggressive behavior is especially persistent when it is reinforced only intermittently, which is usually the case under the variable conditions of everyday life (Walters & Brown, 1963).

There are other forms of aggression that are sustained by their material consequences, though for obvious reasons, they are not easily subject to systematic analysis. Delinquents and adult transgressors can support themselves on income derived from aggressive pursuits; protesters can secure through forceful collective response social reforms that affect their lives materially; governments that rule by force are rewarded in using punitive control by the personal gains it brings to those in power and to supporters who benefit from the existing social arrangements; and nations are sometimes able to gain control over prized territories by military force.

SOCIAL AND STATUS REWARDS

Aggressive styles of behavior are often adopted because they win approval and status rewards. When people are commended for behaving punitively, they become progressively more aggressive, whereas they display a relatively low level of aggression when it is not treated as praiseworthy (Geen & Stonner, 1971; Staples & Walters, 1964). Approval not only increases the specific aggressive responses that are socially reinforced but tends to enhance other forms of aggression as well (Geen & Pigg, 1970; Loew, 1967; Slaby, 1974).

Analyses of social reinforcement of aggressive behavior in natural settings are in general agreement with results of laboratory studies. Parents of assaultive children are generally nonpermissive for aggressive behavior in the home, but condone, actively encourage, and reinforce provocative and aggressive actions toward others in the community (Bandura, 1960; Bandura & Walters, 1959).

In aggressive gangs, members not only gain approval but achieve social status through their skills in fighting (Short, 1968). In status rewards, performance of valued behavior gains one a social rank that carries with it multiple benefits as long as the position is occupied. A rank-contingent system of reward is more powerful than one in which specific responses are socially rewarded. If failure to behave aggressively deprives one of a specific reward, the negative consequence is limited and of no great importance. A demotion in rank, however, results in forfeiture of all the social and material benefits that go with it. The pressure for aggressive accomplishments is especially strong when status positions are limited and there are many eager competitors for them.

During wartime, societies offer medals, promotions, and social commendations on the basis of skill in killing. When reinforcement practices are instituted that favor inhuman forms of behavior, otherwise socialized people can be led to behave brutally and to take pride in such actions.

REDUCTION OF AVERSIVE TREATMENT

People are often treated aversively by others from which they seek relief. Coercive action that is not unduly hazardous is the most direct and quickest means of alleviating maltreatment, if only temporarily. Defensive forms of aggression are frequently reinforced by their capacity to terminate humiliating and painful treatment. Reinforcement through pain reduction is well documented in studies cited earlier showing that children who are victimized but terminate the abuse by successful counteraggression eventually become highly aggressive in their behavior (Patterson, Littman, & Bricker, 1967).

Patterson's (1978) analysis of familial interactions of hyperaggressive children further documents the role of negative reinforcement in promoting aggressive styles of behavior. In such families, children are inadvertently trained to use coercive behavior as the means of commanding parental attention or terminating social demands. The children's antagonistic behavior rapidly accelerates parental counteraggression in an escalating power struggle. By escalating reciprocal aggression, each member provides aversive instigation for each other, and each member is periodically reinforced for behaving coercively by overpowering the other through more painful counteractions. Mutual coercion is most likely to appear as a prominent factor in families that find their children's control techniques painful and therefore seek relief from clinics. However, intrafamilial coercion is not a significant factor in families of predelinquent children who are forced to consult clinics because of legal threats rather than mutual torment (Reid & Patterson, 1976).

A quite different view of aggression emerges if hyperaggressive children are selected from the population at large rather than from clinics. In one study (Bandura, 1960), the most hyperaggressive children in an entire community were identified in school settings and their social behavior was systematically observed. Despite the fact that these children were highly belligerent, assaultive, and destructive of property, few of these families had ever consulted a clinic. This was because their training in aggression did not produce torment in the home. The parents modeled aggressive attitudes and, while nonpermissive and punitive for aggression toward themselves, they actively encouraged and rewarded aggression directed at others outside the home. As a result of this differential training, the children were reasonably well behaved at home but readily assaultive toward others. If their youngsters misbehaved, the parents believed it was because others were at fault. Not only did the parents of these hyperaggressive children see little reason to consult clinics, but many of them considered aggression to be a valued attribute. In these families the development of aggression is better explained in terms of a positive, rather than a negative, reinforcement model. Samples of hyperaggressive children drawn from different sources may thus yield different theories on the familial determinants of aggression.

In the social learning analysis, defensive aggression is sustained to a greater extent by anticipated consequences than by its instantaneous effects. People will endure the pain of reprisals on expectations that their aggressive efforts will eventually remove deleterious conditions. Aggressive actions may also be partly maintained in the face of painful counterattack by anticipated costs of timidity. In aggression-oriented circles, failure to fight back can arouse fear of future victimization and humiliation. A physical pummeling may, therefore, be far less distressing than repeated social derision or increased likelihood of future abuse. In other words, humans do not behave like unthinking servomechanisms directed solely by immediate response feedback. Under aversive conditions of life, people will persist, at least for a time, in aggressive behavior that produces immediate pain but prospective relief from misery.

EXPRESSIONS OF INJURY

In the view of drive theorists, the purpose of aggression is infliction of injury. Just as eating relieves hunger, hurting others presumably discharges the aggressive drive. It has therefore been widely assumed that aggressive behavior is reinforced by signs of suffering in the victim. According to Sears, Maccoby, and Levin (1957), pain cues become rewarding because the pain produced by aggressive acts is repeatedly associated with tension relief and removal of frustrations. Feshbach (1970) interprets the rewarding value of pain expression in terms of self-esteem processes. Perception of pain in one's tormentors is experienced as satisfying because it signifies successful retaliation and thus restores the aggressor's self-esteem.

A contrasting view is that signs of suffering ordinarily function as inhibitors rather than as positive reinforcers of aggressive behavior. Because of the dangers of intragroup violence, all societies establish strong prohibitions against cruel and destructive acts, except under special circumstances. In the course of socialization, most people adopt for self-evaluation the standard that ruthless aggression is morally reprehensible. Consequently, aggression that produces evident suffering in others elicits both fear of punishment and self-censure, which tend to inhibit injurious attacks.

Studies on how pain expressions affect assaults on suffering victims support the inhibitory effects. Aggressors behave less punitively when their victims express anguished cries than when they do not see or hear them suffer (Baron, 1971a, 1971b; Sanders & Baron, 1977). Contrary to the effect attributed to them in drive theory, pain cues reduce aggression regardless of whether assailants are angered or not (Geen, 1970; Rule & Leger, 1976). People are even less inclined to behave cruelly when they see their suffering victims than when they merely hear the distress they have caused them (Milgram, 1974).

The scope of the experimental treatments and the populations studied are too limited to warrant the strong conclusion that pain expressions never enhance aggressive behavior. A gratuitous insult from a stranger in a laboratory may not create sufficient animosity for the victim to derive satisfaction from injurious retaliation. It is a quite different matter when an antagonist repeatedly tyrannizes others or wields power in ways that make life miserable for them. In such instances, news of the misfortune, serious illness, or death of an oppressor is joyfully received by people who ordinarily respond more compassionately to the adversities befalling others. However, the alleviation of aversive treatment from injured oppressors rather than their suffering may be the primary source of satisfaction. In experimental investigations, pain expressions occur without the other extraneous rewards accompanying victory over antagonists.

From the standpoint of social learning theory, suffering of one's enemy is most apt to augment aggression when hurting them lessens maltreatment or benefits aggressors in other ways. When aggressors suffer reprisals or self-contempt for harming others, signs of suffering function as negative reinforcers that deter injurious attacks.

Findings of studies with infrahuman subjects are sometimes cited as evidence that fighting is inherently rewarding. Animals will perform responses that produce an attackable target, especially if they have been trained for aggression and are subjected to aversive stimulation. However, because of inadequate controls, this line of experimentation failed to clarify whether the animals were seeking combat, escape, or social contact (Bandura, 1973). Studies including conditions in which animals perform responses to gain contact without opportunity to fight (Kelsey & Cassidy, 1976) demonstrate that social contact rather than combat is the source of reward.

Under certain conditions pain expressions may assume reward value. Examples can be cited of societal practices in which brutal acts are regarded as praiseworthy by those in positions of power. Inhumane reinforcement contingencies can breed people who take pleasure in inflicting pain and humiliation. Additionally, clinical studies of sexual perversion have disclosed cases in which pain cues acquire powerful reward value through repeated association with sexual gratification. As a result, erotic pleasure is derived from inflicting pain on others or on oneself.

There are no conceptual or empirical grounds for regarding aggression maintained by certain effects as more genuine or important than others. A comprehensive theory must account for all aggressive actions, whatever purposes they serve. To restrict analysis of aggression to behavior that is supposedly reinforced by expressions of injury is to exclude from consideration some of the most violent activities where injury is an unavoidable concomitant rather than the major function of the behavior.

One might also question the distinction traditionally drawn between instrumental aggression, which is supposedly aimed at securing extraneous rewards, and hostile aggression, the sole purpose of which is presumably to inflict suffering (Feshbach, 1970). Since, in all instances, the behavior is instrumental in producing certain desired outcomes, be they pain, approval, status, or material gain, it is more meaningful to differentiate aggressive behaviors in terms of their functional value rather than whether or not they are instrumental.

Punishing Consequences

Restraints over injurious behavior arise from two different sources. *Social restraints* are rooted in threats of external punishment. *Personal restraints* operate through anticipatory self-condemning reactions toward one's own conduct. In developmental theories, these two sources of restraint are traditionally characterized as fear control and guilt control, respectively. Punishing consequences that are observed or experienced directly convey information about the circumstances under which aggressive behavior is safe and those under which it is hazardous. Aggressive actions are therefore regulated partly on the basis of anticipated negative consequences. Being under cognitive and situational control, restraints arising from external threats vary in durability and in how widely they generalize beyond the prohibitive situations.

The effectiveness of punishment in controlling behavior is determined by a number of factors (Bandura, 1969; Campbell & Church, 1969). Of special importance are the benefits derived through aggressive actions and the availability of alternative means of securing desired goals. Other determinants of the suppressive power of punishment include the likelihood that aggression will be punished and the nature, severity, timing, and duration of aversive consequences. In addition, the level of instigation to aggression and the characteristics of the prohibitive agents influence how aggressors will respond under threat of punishment.

When alternative means are available for people to get what they seek, aggressive modes of behavior that carry a high risk of punishment are rapidly discarded. Aggression control through punishment becomes more problematic when aggressive actions are socially or tangibly rewarded and alternative means of securing desired outcomes are either unavailable, less effective in producing results, or not within the capabilities of the aggressor. Here, punishment must be applied with considerable force and consistency to outweigh the benefits of aggression. Even then it achieves, at best, temporary selective control in the threatening situation. Functional aggression is reinstated when threats are removed, and it is readily performed in settings in which the chance of punishment is low (Bandura & Walters, 1959). Not only is punishment precarious as an external inhibitor of intermittently rewarded behavior, but its frequent use can inadvertently promote aggression by modeling punitive modes of control (Hoffman, 1960).

Punishment, whether direct or observed, is informative as well as inhibitory. People can profit from witnessing the failures of others or from their own mistakes. Given strong instigation to aggression and limited options, threats lead people to adopt safer forms of aggression or to refine the prohibited behavior to improve its chances of success. For this reason, antisocial aggression is best prevented by combining deterrents with the cultivation of more functional alternatives. Most law-abiding behavior relies more on deterrence through preferable prosocial options than on threats of legal sanctions.

Under certain conditions aggression is escalated through punishment, at least in the short run. Individuals who recurrently engage in aggressive behavior have experienced some success in controlling others through force. In interpersonal encounters, they respond to counterattacks with progressively more punitive reactions to force acquiescence (Edwards, 1968; Patterson, 1977; Toch, 1969). The use of punishment as a control technique also carries risks of escalating collective aggression when grievances are justifiable and challengers possess substantial coercive power (Bandura, 1973; Gurr, 1970).

Under these circumstances, continued aggressive behavior eventually succeeds in changing social practices that lack sufficient justification to withstand concerted protest.

Vicarious Reinforcement

In the course of everyday life, there are numerous opportunities to observe the actions of others and the circumstances under which they are rewarded, ignored, or punished. Observed outcomes influence behavior in much the same way as directly experienced consequences. People can profit from the successes and mistakes of others as well as from their own experiences. As a general rule, seeing aggression rewarded in others increases, and seeing it punished decreases, the tendency to behave in similar ways (Bandura, 1965; Bandura, Ross & Ross, 1963). The more consistent the observed response consequences, the greater are the facilitatory and inhibitory effects on viewers (Rosekrans & Hartup, 1967).

Vicarious reinforcement operates primarily through its informative function. Since observed outcomes convey different types of information, they can have diverse behavioral effects. Response consequences accruing to others convey contingency information about the types of actions likely to be rewarded or punished and the situations in which it is appropriate to perform them. A number of factors that enter into the process of social comparison can alter the customary effects of observed consequences. Models and observers often differ in distinguishable ways so that behavior considered approvable for one may be punishable for the other, depending on discrepancies in sex, age, and social status. When the same behavior produces unlike consequences for different members, observed reward may not enhance the level of imitative aggressiveness (Thelen & Soltz, 1969).

When observed outcomes are judged personally attainable, they create incentive motivation. Seeing others' successes can function as a motivator by arousing in observers expectations that they can gain similar rewards for analogous performances. Some of the changes in responsiveness may also reflect vicarious acquisition or extinction of fears through the affective consequences accruing to models. Indeed, the legal system of deterrence rests heavily on the restraining function of exemplary punishment (Packer, 1968; Zimring, 1973). But observed outcomes also reduce the deterrent efficacy of threatened legal consequences. The chance of being caught and punished for criminal conduct is relatively low. In locales in which transgressions are common, people have personal knowledge of countless crimes being committed without detection. Such exposure to unpunished transgressions tends to reduce the force of legal deterrents.

In addition to the aforementioned effects, valuation of people and activities can be significantly altered on the basis of observed consequences. Ordinarily, observed punishment tends to devalue the models and their behavior, whereas the same models become a source of emulation when their actions are admired. However, aggressors may gain, rather than lose, status in the eyes of their peers when they are punished for a style of behavior valued by the group or when they aggress against institutional practices that violate the professed values of society. It is for this reason that authoritative agencies are usually careful not to discipline challengers in ways that might martyr them.

Observed consequences can change observers' valuation of those who exercise power as well as of the recipients. Restrained and principled use of coercive power elicits respect. When societal agents misuse their power to reward and punish, they undermine the legitimacy of their authority and arouse opposition. Seeing inequitable punishment, rather than securing compliance, may foster aggressive reprisals. Indeed, activists sometimes attempt to rally supporters to their cause by selecting aggressive tactics calculated to provoke authorities to excessive countermeasures.

The manner in which aggressors respond to the consequences of their behavior can also influence how observers later react when they themselves are rewarded for displaying similar responses. In one such study (Ditrichs, Simon, & Greene 1967), children who observed models express progressively more hostility for social approval later increased their own output of hostile responses that brought praise. However, when models appeared oppositional by reducing hostile responses that brought them praise, or reacted in a random fashion as though they were uninfluenced, observers did not increase their expression of hostility even though they were praised whenever they did so. Thus, susceptibility to direct reinforcement was increased by observed willing responsiveness, but reduced by observed resistance.

Observed outcomes introduce comparative processes into the operation of reinforcement influences. The observed consequences accruing to others provide a standard for judging whether the outcomes one customarily receives are equitable, beneficent, or unfair. The same external outcome can function as a reward or as a punishment depending on the observed consequences used for comparison. Relational properties of reinforcement affect not only behavior but the level of personal satisfaction or discontent as well. Equitable treatment tends to promote a sense of well-being, whereas inequitable reinforcement generates resentments and dissatisfactions. The effects of perceived inequity on aggression were reviewed earlier in the discussion of relative deprivation.

Self-Regulatory Mechanisms

The discussion thus far has analyzed how behavior is regulated by external consequences that are either observed or experienced firsthand. People are not simply reactors to external influences. Through self-generated inducements and self-produced consequences, they can exercise some influence over their own behavior. In this self-regulatory process, people adopt through tuition and modeling certain standards of behavior and respond to their own actions in self-rewarding or self-punishing ways. An act therefore includes among its determinants self-produced influences.

A detailed account of self-regulatory processes, which is presented elsewhere (Bandura, 1976, 1978), falls beyond the scope of this chapter. In social learning theory, a self-system is not a psychic agent that controls behavior. Rather, it refers to cognitive structures that provide the referential standards against which behavior is judged and a set of subfunctions for the perception, evaluation, and regulation of action. Figure 4 presents a diagrammatic representation of three main subfunctions in the self-regulation of behavior by self-produced incentives. The first component concerns the selective observation of one's own behavior in terms of a number of relevant dimensions. Behavior produces self-reactions through a judgmental function relying on several subsidiary processes, that include referential comparisons of perceived conduct to internal standards, valuation of the activities in which one is engaged, and cognitive appraisal of the determinants of one's behavior. Performance appraisals set the occasion for self-produced consequences. Favorable judgments give rise to rewarding self-reactions, whereas unfavorable appraisals activate negative self-reactions.

Self-regulated incentives are conceptualized as motivational devices rather than as automatic strengtheners of preceding responses. By making self-reward and self-punishment contingent on designated performances, people motivate themselves to expend the effort needed to attain performances that give them self-satisfaction and they refrain from behaving in ways that result in self-

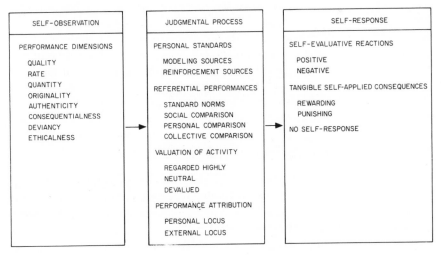

FIGURE 4 Component processes in the self-regulation of behavior by self-produced consequences.

censure. Because of self-reactive tendencies, aggressors must contend with themselves as well as with others when they behave in an injurious manner.

SELF-REWARD FOR AGGRESSION

One can distinguish several ways in which self-generated consequences enter into the self-regulation of aggressive behavior. At one extreme are individuals who have adopted behavioral standards and codes that make aggressive feats a source of personal pride. Such individuals readily engage in aggressive activities and derive enhanced feelings of self-worth from physical conquests (Bandura & Walters, 1959; Toch, 1969; Yablonsky, 1962). Lacking self-reprimands for hurtful conduct, they are deterred from cruel acts mainly by reprisal threats. Idiosyncratic self-systems of morality are not confined to individuals or fighting gangs. In aggressive cultures where prestige is closely tied to fighting prowess, members take considerable pride in aggressive exploits.

SELF-PUNISHMENT FOR AGGRESSION

After ethical and moral standards of conduct are adopted, anticipatory self-condemning reactions for violating personal standards ordinarily serve as self-deterrents against reprehensible acts. Results of the study by Bandura and Walters (1959) reveal how anticipatory self-reproach for repudiated aggression serves as a motivating influence to keep behavior in line with adopted standards. Adolescents who were compassionate in their dealing with others responded with self-disapproval, remorse, and attempts at reparation even when their aggressive activities were minor in nature. In contrast, assaultive boys experienced relatively few negative self-reactions over serious aggressive activities. These differential self-reactive patterns are corroborated by Perry and Bussey (1977) in laboratory tests. Highly aggressive boys reward themselves generously for inflicting suffering on another child, whereas those who display low aggressive tendencies react with self-denial for behaving injuriously. In studies of aggressive modeling, the more reprehensible children judge aggressive actions to be, the less likely they are to adopt them when they are later exemplified by a peer model (Hicks, 1971).

DISENGAGEMENT OF INTERNAL CONTROL

Theories of internalization generally portray incorporated entities in the form of a conscience, superego, and moral codes as continuous internal overseers of conduct. Such theories encounter difficulties in explaining the variable operation of internal control and the perpetration of gross inhumanities by otherwise humane, compassionate people. Such concepts as superego lucunae, islands of superego, and various mental defense mechanisms have been proposed as the explanatory factors.

In the social learning analysis, moral people perform culpable acts through processes that disengage evaluative self-reactions from such conduct, rather than because of defects in the development or the structure of their superegos (Bandura, 1973). Acquisition of self-regulatory capabilities does not create an invariant control mechanism within a person. Self-evaluative influences do not operate unless activated, and many situational dynamics influence their selective activation.

Self-deterring consequences are likely to be activated most strongly when the causal connection between conduct and the detrimental effects it produces is unambiguous. There are various means, however, by which self-evaluative consequences can be dissociated from censurable behavior. Figure 5 shows the several points in the process at which the disengagement can occur.

One set of disengagement practices operates at the level of the behavior. People do not ordinarily engage in reprehensible conduct until they have justified to themselves the morality of their actions. What is culpable can be made honorable through cognitive restructuring. In this process, reprehensible conduct is made personally and socially acceptable by portraying it in the service of moral ends. Over the years, much destructive and reprehensible conduct has been perpetrated by decent, moral people in the name of religious principles and righteous ideologies. Acting on moral or ideological imperative reflects, not an unconscious defense mechanism, but a conscious offense mechanism.

Self-deplored acts can also be made righteous by contrasting them with flagrant inhumanities. The more outrageous the comparison practices, the more likely are one's reprehensible acts to appear trifling or even benevolent. Euphemistic language provides an additional convenient device for disguising

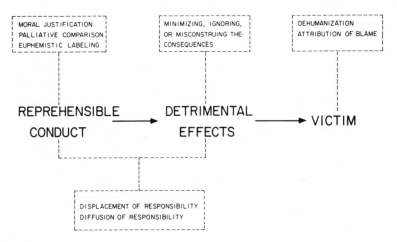

FIGURE 5 Mechanisms through which behavior is disengaged from self-evaluative consequences at different points in the behavioral process.

reprehensible activities and according them a respectable status. Through convoluted verbiage, pernicious conduct is made benign and those who engage in it are relieved of a sense of personal agency (Gambino, 1973). Moral justifications and palliative characterizations are especially effective disinhibitors because they not only eliminate self-generated deterrents but engage self-reward in the service of injurious behavior. What was morally unacceptable becomes a source of self-pride.

Another set of dissociative practices operates by obscuring or distorting the relationship between actions and the effects they cause. People will behave in highly punitive ways they normally repudiate if a legitimate authority acknowledged responsibility for the consequences of the conduct (Diener et al., 1975; Milgram, 1974). By displacing responsibility, people do not see themselves as personally accountable for their actions and are thus spared self-prohibiting reactions. Nor is self-censure activated when the link between conduct and its consequences is obscured by diffusing responsibility. Through division of labor, diffusion of decision making, and collective action, people can behave injuriously without anyone feeling personally responsible for culpable behavior. They therefore act more aggressively when responsibility is obscured by a collective instrumentality (Bandura, Underwood, & Fromson, 1975).

Additional ways of weakening self-deterring reactions operate by disregarding or obscuring the consequences of actions. When people embark on a self-disapproved course of action for personal gain, or because of other inducements, they avoid facing the harm they cause. Self-censuring reactions are unlikely to be activated as long as the detrimental effects of conduct are disregarded, minimized, or misjudged (Brock & Buss, 1962, 1964).

The final set of disengagement practices operate at the level of the recipients of injurious effects. The strength of self-evaluative reactions partly depends on how the people toward whom actions are directed are viewed. Maltreatment of individuals who are regarded as subhuman or debased is less apt to arouse self-reproof than if they are seen as human beings with dignifying qualities (Bandura, Underwood, & Fromson, 1975; Zimbardo, 1969). Analysis of the cognitive concomitants of injurious behavior reveals that dehumanization fosters a variety of self-exonerating maneuvers (Bandura, Underwood, & Fromson, 1975). People strongly disapprove of cruel behavior and rarely excuse its use when they interact with humanized individuals. By contrast, people seldom condemn punitive conduct and generate self-disinhibiting justifications for it when they direct their behavior toward individuals divested of humanness.

Many conditions of contemporary life are conducive to dehumanization. Bureaucratization, automation, urbanization, and high social mobility lead people to relate to each other in anonymous, impersonal ways. In addition, social practices that divide people into in-group and out-group members produce human estrangement that fosters dehumanization. Strangers can be more easily cast as unfeeling beings than can personal acquaintances.

Psychological research tends to focus on the disinhibiting effects of social practices that divest people of human qualities. This emphasis is understandable considering the prevalence and the serious consequences of people's inhumanities toward each other. Of equal theoretical and social significance is the power of humanization to counteract injurious conduct. Studies examining this process reveal that, even under conditions that ordinarily weaken self-deterrents, it is difficult for people to behave cruelly toward others when they are characterized in ways that personalize and humanize them (Bandura, Underwood, & Fromson, 1975).

Attributing blame to one's victims is still another expedient that can serve self-exonerative purposes. Detrimental interactions usually involve a series of reciprocally escalative actions in which the victims are rarely faultless. One can always select from the chain of events an instance of defensive behavior by the adversary and view it as the original instigation. Victims then get blamed for bringing suffering on themselves, or extraordinary circumstances are invoked to vindicate irresponsible conduct. By blaming others, one can excuse one's own actions. People are socially aided in dehumanizing and blaming groups held in disfavor by pejorative stereotyping and indoctrination.

GRADUALISM AND DISINHIBITION

The aforementioned practices will not instantaneously transform a gentle person into a brutal aggressor. Rather, the change is usually achieved through a gradual disinhibition process in which participants may not fully recognize the marked changes they are undergoing. Initially, individuals are prompted to perform aggressive acts they can tolerate without excessive self-censure. After their discomfort and self-reproof are diminished through repeated performance, the level of aggression is progressively increased in this manner until eventually gruesome deeds, originally regarded as abhorrent, can be performed without much distress.

As is evident from the preceding discussion, the development of self-regulatory functions does not create a mechanical servocontrol system wherein behavioral output is accurately monitored, compared against an internal standard and, if judged deviant, is promptly brought in line with the referent standard. Nor do situational influences exercise mechanical control. Personal judgments operating at each subfunction preclude the automaticity of the process. There is leeway in judging whether a given behavioral standard is applicable. Because of the complexity and inherent ambiguity of most events, there is even greater leeway in the judgment of behavior and its effects. To add further to the variability of the self-control process, most activities are performed under collective arrangements that obscure responsibility, thus permitting leeway in judging the degree of personal agency in the effects that are socially produced. In short, considerable latitude exists for personal judgmental factors to affect whether or not self-regulatory influences will be engaged in any given activity.

Differing Perspectives on
Disengagement of Internal Restraints

The preceding discussion analyzed reduction of internal control within the framework of social learning theory. Other researchers have addressed this issue from a different conceptual perspective. Zimbardo (1969) explains reduction of restraints over aggression in terms of deindividuation. Deindividuation is an internal state characterized by a loss of self-consciousness and self-evaluation coupled with a diminished concern for negative evaluation from others. According to this view, the altered perception of self and others weakens cognitive control over behavior, thus facilitating intense impulsive actions.

People can be deindividuated by a variety of external conditions, including anonymity, immersion in a group, diffusion of responsibility, high emotional arousal, intense sensory stimulation, and physiological factors that alter states of consciousness. Many of the postulated determinants of deindividuation remain to be investigated. However, the conditions that have been examined empirically, such as group presence, anonymity, and emotional arousal, have variable effects on behavior depending on the presence of other personal and situational factors conducive to aggression (Bandura, 1973; Diener, 1977; Zimbardo, 1969). Verification of the deindividuation link in the causal process is a much more complicated matter because it requires independent assessment of the internal state. The initial attempts to link the indicants of deindividuation either to the situational conditions or to the disinhibited behavior have so far produced inconclusive results (Diener, 1977).

It should be recognized that this line of research presents especially difficult methodological problems. One cannot keep interrupting unrestrained aggressors for their perceptions of themselves and others without aborting the disinhibitory process. To measure the cognitive concomitants of external disinhibitory conditions prior to performance is to alter the very phenomenon being studied. Judgments of the promise of a theory in this field must therefore rest heavily on its success in identifying determinants of behavioral disinhibition and in bringing order among diverse findings. In view of the important role played by self-justification processes in disinhibition, a full explanation of how aggression is freed from internal restraints must consider the self-regulatory mechanisms discussed earlier.

Although deindividuation and social learning theory posit some overlapping determinants and processes of internal disinhibition, they differ in certain important respects. Deindividuation views intense aggression as resulting mainly from loss of cognitive control. Social learning encompasses a broad range of disinhibitory factors designed to provide a unified theory for explaining both impulsive and principled aggressive conduct. As shown earlier, people frequently engage in violent activities not because of reduced self-control but because their cognitive skills and self-control are enlisted all too well through moral justifications and self-exonerative devices in the service of destructive causes. The massive threats to human welfare are generally brought about by deliberate acts of principle rather than by unrestrained acts of impulse. It is the principled resort to aggression that is of greatest social concern but most ignored in psychological theorizing and research.

REFERENCES

Alland, A., Jr. *The human imperative*. New York: Columbia University Press, 1972.

Ax, A. F. The physiological differentiation between fear and anger in humans. *Psychosomatic Medicine*, 1953, 15:433–442.

Azrin, N. H. Pain and aggression. *Psychology Today*, 1967, 1:27–33.

Azrin, N. H. Punishment of elicited aggression. *Journal of the Experimental Analysis of Behavior*, 1970, 14:7–10.

Azrin, N. H., & Hutchinson, R. R. Conditioning of the aggressive behavior of pigeons by a fixed-interval schedule of reinforcement. *Journal of the Experimental Analysis of Behavior*, 1967, 10:395–402.

Azrin, N. H., Hutchinson, R. R., & Hake, D. F. Pain-induced fighting in the squirrel monkey. *Journal of the Experimental Analysis of Behavior*, 1963, 6:620.

Baenninger, R., & Grossman, J. C. Some effects of punishment on pain-elicited aggression. *Journal of the Experimental Analysis of Behavior*, 1969, 12:1017–1022.

Bandura, A. *Relationship of family patterns to child behavior disorders*. Progress Report, Stanford University Project no. M–1734, United States Public Health Service, 1960.

Bandura, A. Social learning through imitation. In M. R. Jones (Ed.), *Nebraska symposium on motivation*. Lincoln: University of Nebraska Press, 1962.

Bandura, A. Influence of models' reinforcement contingencies on the acquisition of imitative responses. *Journal of Personality and Social Psychology*, 1965, 1:589–595.

Bandura, A. *Principles of behavior modification*. New York: Holt, Rinehart and Winston, 1969.

Bandura, A. *Aggression: A social learning analysis*. Englewood Cliffs, New Jersey: Prentice-Hall, 1973.

Bandura, A. Self-reinforcement: theoretical and methodological considerations. *Behaviorism*, 1976, 4:135–155.

Bandura, A. *Social learning theory*. Englewood Cliffs, New Jersey: Prentice-Hall, 1977. (a)

Bandura, A. Self-efficacy: toward a unifying theory of behavioral change. *Psychological Review*, 1977, 84:191, 215. (b)

Bandura, A. The self system in reciprocal determinism. *American Psychologist*, 1978, 33:344–358.

Bandura, A. Self-efficacy mechanism in human agency. *American Psychologist*, 1982, 37, 122–147.

Bandura, A. Ross, D., & Ross, S. A. Vicarious reinforcement and imitative learning. *Journal of Abnormal and Social Psychology*, 1963, 67:601–607.

Bandura, A., Underwood, B., & Fromson, M. E. Disinhibition of aggression through diffusion of responsibility and dehumanization of victims. *Journal of Research in Personality*, 1975, 9:253–269.

Bandura, A., & Walters, R. H. *Adolescent aggression*. New York: Ronald, 1959.

Bandura, A., & Walters, R. H. *Social learning and personality development*. New York: Holt, Rinehart and Winston, 1963.

Baron, R. A. Magnitude of victim's pain cues and level of prior anger arousal as determinants of adult aggressive behavior. *Journal of Personality and Social Psychology*, 1971, 17:236–243. (a)

Baron, R. A. Aggression as a function of magnitude of victim's pain cues, level of prior anger arousal, and aggressor-victim similarity. *Journal of Personality and Social Psychology*, 1971, *18*:48–54. (b)

Bateson, G. *The naven.* Stanford, California: Stanford University Press, 1936.

Berkowitz, L. The concept of aggressive drive: Some additional considerations. In L. Berkowitz (Ed.), *Advances in experimental social psychology* (Vol. II.). New York: Academic Press, 1965.

Berkowitz, L. The contagion of violence: An S-R mediational analysis of some effects of observed aggression. In W. J. Arnold and M. M. Page (Eds.), *Nebraska symposium on motivation.* Lincoln: University of Nebraska Press, 1970.

Blumenthal, M., Kahn, R. L., Andrews, F. M., & Head, K. B. *Justifying violence: the attitudes of American men.* Ann Arbor: Institute for Social Research, 1972.

Brock, T. C., & Buss, A. H. Dissonance, aggression, and evaluation of pain. *Journal of Abnormal and Social Psychology*, 1962, *65*:197–202.

Brock, T. C., & Buss, A. H. Effects of justification for aggression and communication with the victim on postaggression dissonance. *Journal of Abnormal and Social Psychology*, 1964, *68*:403–412.

Campbell, B. A., & Church, R. M. *Punishment and aversive behavior.* New York: Appleton-Century-Crofts, 1969.

Caplan, N. The new ghetto man: a review of recent empirical studies. *Journal of Social Issues*, 1970, *26*:59–73.

Chagnon, N. *Yanomamo: the fierce people.* New York: Holt, Rinehart and Winston, 1968.

Claster, D. S. Comparison of risk perception between delinquents and non-deliquents. *Journal of Criminal Law, Criminology, and Police Science*, 1967, *58*:80–86.

Cline, V. B., Croft, R. G., & Courrier, S. Desensitization of children to television violence. *Journal of Personality and Social Psychology*, 1973, *27*:360–365.

Cohen, A. R. Social norms, arbitrariness of frustration, and status of the agent of frustration in the frustration-aggression hypothesis. *Journal of Abnormal and Social Psychology*, 1955, *51*:222–226.

Crawford, T., & Naditch, M. Relative deprivation, powerlessness, and militancy: the psychology of social protest. *Psychiatry*, 1970, *33*:208–223.

Davies, J. C. The J-curve of rising and declining satisfactions as a cause of some revolutions and a contained rebellion. In H. D. Graham and T. R. Gurr (Eds.), *Violence in America: Historical and comparative perspectives* Vol. 2. Washington, DC: US Government Printing Office, 1969.

Davitz, J. R. The effects of previous training on postfrustration behavior. *Journal of Abnormal and Social Psychology*, 1952, *47*:309–315.

Delgado, J. M. Social rank and radio-stimulated aggressiveness in monkeys. *Journal of Nervous and Mental Disease*, 1967, *144*:383–390.

Dentan, R. K. *The Semai: a nonviolent people of Malaya.* New York: Holt, Rinehart and Winston, 1968.

Diener, E. Deindividuation: Causes and characteristics. *Social Behavior and Personality*, 1977, *5*:143–156.

Diener, E., Dineen, J., Endresen, K., Beaman, A. L., & Fraser, S. C. Effects of altered responsibility, cognitive set, and modeling on physical aggression and deindividuation. *Journal of Personality and Social Psychology*, 1975, *31*:328–337.

Ditrichs, R., Simon, S., & Greene, B. Effect of vicarious scheduling on the verbal conditioning of hostility in children. *Journal of Personality and Social Psychology*, 1967, *6*:71–78.

Drabman, R. S., & Thomas, M. H. Does media violence increase children's toleration of real-life aggression? *Developmental Psychology*, 1974, *10*:418–421.

Edwards, N. L. Aggressive expression under threat of retaliation. *Dissertation Abstracts*, 1968, *28*:3470B.

Feshbach, S. Aggression. In P. H. Mussen (Ed.), *Carmichael's manual of child psychology* (vol. 2. 2 vols.) New York: Wiley, 1970.

Friedrich, L. K., & Stein, A. H. Aggressive and prosocial television programs and the natural behavior of preschool children. *Monographs of the Society for Research in Child Development,* 1973, *38*(4), serial no. 151.

Gambino, R. Watergate lingo: a language of non-responsibility. *Freedom at Issue,* 1973, 22.

Gardner, R., & Heider, K. G. *Gardens of war.* New York: Random House, 1969.

Geen, R. G. Perceived suffering of the victim as an inhibitor of attack-induced aggression. *Journal of Social Psychology,* 1970, *81*:209–216.

Geen, R. G., & Pigg, R. Acquisition of an aggressive response and its generalization to verbal behavior. *Journal of Personality and Social Psychology,* 1970, *15*:165–170.

Geen, R. G., & Stonner, D. Effects of aggressiveness habit strength on behavior in the presence of aggression-related stimuli. *Journal of Personality and Social Psychology,* 1971, *17*:149–153.

Gerbner, G., & Gross, L. Living with television: the violence profile. *Journal of Communication,* 1976, *26*:173–199.

Ginsburg, B., & Allee, W. C. Some effects of conditioning on social dominance and subordination in inbred strains of mice. *Physiological Zoology,* 1942, *15*:485–506.

Goldstein, M. Brain research and violent behavior. *Archives of Neurology,* 1974, *30*:1–34.

Goranson, R. E. Media violence and aggressive behavior: A review of experimental research. In L. Berkowitz (Ed.), *Advances in experimental social psychology* (vol. V). New York: Academic Press, 1970.

Gurr, T. R. Sources of rebellion in Western societies: some quantitative evidence. *Annals of the American Academy of Political and Social Science,* 1970. *391*:128–44.

Hartmann, D. P. Influence of symbolically modeled instrumental aggression and pain cues on aggressive behavior. *Journal of Personality and Social Psychology,* 1969, *11*:280–288.

Hendrick, G. When television is a school for criminals. *TV Guide,* 1977, 29 January: 4–10.

Hicks, D. J. Short- and long-term retention of affectively varied modeled behavior. *Psychonomic Science,* 1968, *11*:369–370.

Hicks, D. J. Girls' attitudes toward modeled behaviors and the content of imitative private play. *Child Development,* 1971, *42*:139–47.

Hoffman, M. L. Power assertion by the parent and its impact on the child. *Child Development,* 1960, *31*:129–143.

Hokanson, J. E., Willers, K. R., & Koropsak, E. The modification of autonomic responses during aggressive interchange. *Journal of Personality,* 1968, *36*:386–404.

Hunt, J. M., Cole, M. W., & Reis, E. E. S. Situational cues distinguishing anger, fear, and sorrow. *American Journal of Psychology,* 1958, *71*:136–51.

Hutchinson, R. R., Ulrich, R. E., & Azrin, N. H. Effects of age and related factors on the pain-aggression reaction. *Journal of Comparative and Physiological Psychology,* 1965, *59*:365–369.

Kahn, M. W. The effect of severe defeat at various age levels on the aggressive behavior of mice. *Journal of Genetic Psychology,* 1951, *79*:117–130.

Kelsey, J. E., & Cassidy, D. The reinforcing properties of aggressive vs. nonaggressive social interactions in isolated male ICR mice (*Mus Musculus*). *Aggressive Behavior,* 1976, *2*:275–284.

Kilham, W., & Mann, L. Level of destructive obedience as a function of transmitter and executant roles in the Milgram obedience paradigm. *Journal of Personality and Social Psychology,* 1974, *29*:696–702.

Knutson, J. The effects of shocking one member of a pair of rats. *Psychonomic Science,* 1971, *22*:265–266.

Leifer, A. D., Gordon, N. J., & Graves, S. B. Children's television: more than mere entertainment. *Harvard Educational Review,* 1974, *44*:213–245.

Levy, R. I. On getting angry in the Society Islands. In W. Caudill and T. Y. Lin (Eds.), *Mental health research in Asia and the Pacific*. Honolulu: East-West Center Press, 1969.

Leyens, J. P., Camino, L., Parke, R. D., & Berkowitz, L. Effects of movie violence on aggression in a field setting as a function of group dominance and cohesion. *Journal of Personality and Social Psychology*, 1975, *32*:346–360.

Lieberson, S., & Silverman, A. R. The precipitants and underlying conditions of race riots. *American Sociological Review*, 1965, *30*:887–898.

Liebert, R. M., Neale, J. M., & Davidson, E. S. *The early window: effects of television on children and youth*. New York: Pergamon, 1973.

Loew, C. A. Acquisition of a hostile attitude and its relationship to aggressive behavior. *Journal of Personality and Social Psychology*, 1967, *5*:335–341.

Logan, F. A., & Boice, R. Aggressive behaviors of paired rodents in an avoidance context. *Behaviour*, 1969, *34*:161–183.

Longstreth, L. E. Distance to goal and reinforcement schedule as determinants of human instrumental behavior. *Proceedings of the 74th Annual Convention of the American Psychological Association*, 1966, 39–40.

McCord, W., & Howard, J. Negro opinions in three riot cities. *American Behavioral Scientist*, 1968, *11*:24–27.

McPhail, C. Civil disorder participation: a critical examination of recent research. *American Sociological Review*, 1971, *36*:1058–1072.

Madsen, C., Jr. Nurturance and modeling in preschoolers. *Child Development*, 1968, *39*:221–236.

Maier, S. F., & Seligman, M. E. Learned helplessness: theory and evidence. *Journal of Experimental Psychology*, 1976, *105*:3–46.

Mallick, S. K., & McCandless, B. R. A study of catharsis of aggression. *Journal of Personality and Social Psychology*, 1966, *4*:591–596.

Mandler, G. *Mind and emotion*. New York: Wiley, 1975.

Mantell, D. M., & Panzarella, R. Obedience and responsibility. *British Journal of Social and Clinical Psychology*, 1976, *15*:239–246.

Mead, M. *Sex and temperament in three savage tribes*. New York: Morrow, 1935.

Meyer, T. P. Effects of viewing justified and unjustified real film violence on aggressive behavior. *Journal of Personality and Social Psychology*, 1972, *23*:21–29.

Milgram, S. *Obedience to authority: An experimental view*. New York: Harper and Row, 1974.

Packer, H. L. *The limits of the criminal sanction*. Stanford, California: Stanford University Press, 1968.

Parke, R. D., Berkowitz, L., Leyens, J. P. West, S. G., & Sebastian, R. J. Some effects of violent and nonviolent movies on the behavior of juvenile delinquents. In L. Berkowitz (Ed.), *Advances in experimental social psychology* (Vol. X). New York: Academic Press, 1977.

Pastore, N. The role of arbitrariness in the frustration-aggression hypothesis. *Journal of Abnormal and Social Psychology*, 1952, *47*:728–731.

Patterson, G. R. A performance theory for coercive family interaction. In R. Cairns (Ed.), *Social interaction: Methods, analysis, and illustration. Monographs of the Society for Research in Child Development*, 1979. (in press)

Patterson, G. R., Littman, R. A., & Bricker, W. Assertive behavior in children: a setp toward a theory of aggression. *Monographs of the Society for Research in Child Development*, 1967, *32*(5), Serial No. 113.

Perry, D. G., & Bussey, K. Self-reinforcement in high- and low-aggressive boys following acts of aggression. *Child Development*, 1977, *48*:653–657.

Peterson, R. A., Aggression level as a function of expected retaliation and aggression level of target and aggressor. *Developmental Psychology*, 1971, *5*:161–166.

Powell, D. A., & Creer, T. L. Interaction of developmental and environmental variables in shock-elicited aggression. *Journal of Comparative and Physiological Psychology,* 1969, 69:219–225.

Powers, P. C., & Geen, R. G. Effects of the behavior and the perceived arousal of a model on instrumental aggression. *Journal of Personality and Social Psychology,* 1972, *23*:175–183.

Reich, P., & Hepps, R. B. Homicide during a psychosis induced by LSD. *Journal of the American Medical Association,* 1972, *219*:869–871.

Reid, J. B., & Patterson, G. R. The modification of aggression and stealing behavior of boys in the home setting. In E. Ribes-Inesta and A. Bandura (Eds.), *Analysis of delinquency and aggression.* Hillsdale, New Jersey: Erlbaum, 1976.

Rosekrans, M. A., & Hartup, W. W. Imitative influences of consistent and inconsistent response consequences to a model and aggressive behavior in children. *Journal of Personality and Social Psychology,* 1967, *7*:429–434.

Rosenthal, T. L., & Zimmerman, B. J. *Social learning and cognition.* New York: Academic Press, 1978.

Rule, B. G., & Leger, G. L. Pain cues and differing functions of aggression. *Canadian Journal of Behavioural Science,* 1976, *8*:213–223.

Rule, B. G., & Nesdale, A. R. Emotional arousal and aggressive behavior. *Psychological Bulletin,* 1976, *83*:851–63. (a)

Rule, B. G., & Nesdale, A. R. Moral judgments of aggressive behavior. In R. G. Geen and E. O'Neal (Eds.), *Perspectives on aggression,* New York: Academic Press, 1976. (b)

Sanders, G. S., & Baron, R. S. Pain cues and uncertainty as determinants of aggression in a situation involving repeated instigation. *Journal of Personality and Social Psychology,* 1977, *32*:495–502.

Sbordone, R., Garcia, J., & Carder, B. Shock-elicited aggression: its displacement by a passive social orientation avoidance response. *Bulletin of the Psychonomic Society,* 1977, *9*:272–274.

Scott, J. P., & Marston, M. Nonadaptive behavior resulting from a series of defeats in fighting mice. *Journal of Abnormal and Social Psychology,* 1953, *48*:417–428.

Sears, D. O., & McConahay, J. B. Participation in the Los Angeles riot. *Social Problems,* 1969, *17*:3–20.

Sears, R. R., Maccoby, E. E. & Levin, H. *Patterns of child rearing.* Evanston, Ill.: Row, Peterson, 1957.

Short, J. F., Jr (Ed.) *Gang delinquency and delinquent subcultures.* New York: Harper and Row, 1968.

Silver, L. B., Dublin, C. C., & Lourie, R. S. Does violence breed violence? Contributions from a study of the child abuse syndrome. *American Journal of Psychiatry,* 1969, *126*:404–407.

Slaby, R. Verbal regulation of aggression and altruism. In J. De Wit and W. Hartup (Eds.), *Determinants and origins of aggressive behavior.* The Hague: Mouton Press, 1974.

Snow, C. P. Either-or. *Progressive,* 1961, *25*:24–25.

Staples, F. R., & Walters, R. H. Influence of positive reinforcement of aggression on subjects differing in initial aggressive level. *Journal of Consulting Psychology,* 1964, *28*:547–552.

Steuer, F. B., Applefield, J. M., & Smith, R. Televised aggression and the interpersonal aggression of preschool children. *Journal of Experimental Child Psychology,* 1971, *11*:442–447.

Tannenbaum, P. H., & Zillmann, D. Emotional arousal in the facilitation of aggression through communication. In L. Berkowitz (Ed.), *Advances in experimental social psychology* (Vol. VIII). New York: Academic Press, 1975.

Thelen, M. H., & Soltz, W. The effect of vicarious reinforcement on imitation in two social racial groups. *Child Development,* 1969, *40*:879–887.

Thomas, M. H., & Drabman, R. S. Toleration of real life aggression as a function of exposure to televised violence and age of subject. *Merrill-Palmer Quarterly of Behavior and Development,* 1975, *21*:227–232.

Thomas, M. H., Horton, R. W., Lippincott, E. C., & Drabman, R. S. Desensitization to portrayals of real-life aggression as a function of exposure to television violence. *Journal of Personality and Social Psychology,* 1977, *35*:450–458.

Toch, H. *Violent men.* Chicago: Aldine, 1969.

Turnbull, C. M. *The forest people.* New York: Simon and Schuster, 1961.

Ulrich, R. Pain as a cause of aggression. *American Zoologist,* 1966, *6*:643–662.

Ulrich, R. E., & Azrin, N. H. Reflexive fighting in response to aversive stimulation. *Journal of the Experimental Analysis of Behavior,* 1962, *5*:511–520.

Ulrich, R., Johnston, M., Richardson, J., & Wolff, P. The operant conditioning of fighting behavior in rats. *Psychological Record,* 1963, *13*:465–470.

Walters, R. H., & Brown, M. Studies of reinforcement of aggression: III. Transfer of responses to an interpersonal situation. *Child Development,* 1963, *34*:563–571.

Weisz, A. E., & Taylor, R. L. American presidential assassination. In D. N. Daniels, M. F. Gilula and F. M. Ochberg (Eds.), *Violence and the struggle for existence.* Boston: Little, Brown, 1970.

Wheeler, L. Toward a theory of behavioral contagion. *Psychological Review,* 1966, *73*:179–192.

Wheeler, L., & Caggiula, A. R. The contagion of aggression. *Journal of Experimental Social Psychology,* 1966, *2*:1–10.

Whiting, J. W. M. *Becoming a Kwoma.* New Haven: Yale University Press, 1941.

Wolfgang, M. E., & Ferracuti, F. *The subculture of violence.* London: Tavistock, 1967.

Yablonsky, L. *The violent gang.* New York: Macmillan, 1962.

Zimbardo, P. G. The human choice: individuation, reason, and order vs. deindividuation, impulse, and chaos. In W. J. Arnold and D. Levins (Eds.), *Nebraska symposium on motivation.* Lincoln: University of Nebraska Press, 1969.

Zimring, F. *Deterrence: the legal threat in crime control.* Chicago: Chicago University Press, 1973.

two

An Attributional Perspective on Anger and Aggression[1]

TAMARA J. FERGUSON
BRENDAN GAIL RULE

INTRODUCTION

The ubiquity and diversity of human aggressive behavior has attracted considerable speculation about its nature. Observation in everyday life shows that, while aggression is often disapproved of and punished, it may also be condoned and admired. The multifaceted nature of aggression has also been recognized in many theories proposed to account for it. Aggression has been viewed as reflecting innate reactions to releasing stimuli, expressive reactions to anger-inducing stimuli, a learned motivation to eliminate frustrating stimuli, as well as a desire to uphold societal norms and expectations (Feshbach, 1964). These various characterizations are reflected, of course, in existing theories of aggression, which span a wide range, from those that stress the learned nature of aggression (e.g., Bandura, 1973), to those stressing its innate nature (e.g., Freud, 1925), to those emphasizing the role of anger as a powerful instigator of aggression (Konečni, 1975; Zillmann, 1978).

The purpose of this chapter is to specify the cognitive processes that contribute to anger and its expression. Early analyses of the anger–aggression relationship have often treated anger-induced aggression as an unthinking and uncontrolled process, but questions have been raised about whether anger-induced

[1]Preparation of this manuscript was facilitated by a research grant to B. G. Rule from the Social Sciences and Humanities Research Council of Canada.

41

aggression necessarily reflects noncognitive or uncontrolled reactions to the receipt of harm. While there are many instances in which anger and aggression may be characterized as an unthinking and uncontrolled response to harm, there are also many instances in which anger and its subsequent expression reflect the perceiver's attributions for why harm occurred and his or her interpretations of whether harm was justified. We are interested in those instances of anger and aggression that are mediated by the perceiver's attributions for the harm doer's behavior.

Examination of the research literature on aggression highlights the important role that attributions play in influencing anger and retaliation. Hostile aggression (defined as an intentionally committed act designed to interfere with another's psychological or physical welfare) is instigated by such anger-inducing stimuli as insult, attack, or frustration (e.g., Berkowitz, 1962; Buss, 1971). But the degree of anger and subsequent hostile retaliation in response to insult, attack, or frustration depend less on the magnitude of these types of provocation than on whether they can be attributed more to something about the provocateur's personal characteristics than to characteristics of the situation. More specifically, anger and its subsequent behavioral expression are greater when the provocation is seen as intentional rather than unintentional, foreseeable rather than unforeseeable, or perpetrated for socially unacceptable rather than socially acceptable reasons (e.g., Dyck & Rule, 1978; Greenwell & Dengerink, 1973; Nickel, 1974; Pastore, 1952). Findings such as these prompted several investigators to incorporate attributionally based constructs in their conceptualizations of hostile retaliation (e.g., Averill, 1979; Buss, 1971; Feshbach, 1964; Pepitone, 1975; Rule & Nesdale, 1976; Zillmann, 1978).

Despite recognition of the importance of these processes (e.g., Bandura, 1973; Berkowitz, 1962; Kelley, 1972; Zillmann, 1978), no concerted attempt has been made to identify the factors likely to determine a perceiver's attributions about harm or to specify why attributions for harm affect anger and retaliation. Moreover, the hypotheses underlying attributionally based aggression research have been derived unsystematically from attributional perspectives and have focused mainly on the viewpoint that internal or personal attributions for harm instigate greater anger and retaliation than external or situational attributions for harm. While the evidence is consistent with this general notion, we have found that attributional discriminations finer than those captured by the personal–situational dichotomy are necessary to account for relations among attributions, anger, and aggression. Thus, considering the underdeveloped nature of research and theory on the cognitive determinants of anger and aggression, we have attempted to explicate further the factors that affect both recipients' and observers' attributions for harm and to indicate how these attributions are reflected in blame ascriptions, anger, and hostile retaliation.

Our analysis focuses on specifying the processes that determine perceptions of causal responsibility as well as perceptions of how the actor should have behaved in the harmful situation. Central to our analysis is the proposition that retaliation, anger reactions, and blame ascriptions are each (among other factors) a function of the perceived discrepancy between the actor's causal responsibility for harm (i.e., the "what is") and what the perceiver believes should have occurred (i.e., the "what ought to be"). As the perceived "is–ought" discrepancy increases, anger, blame, and the desire to retaliate or punish the actor may be elevated. However, while blame, anger, and retaliation are affected by common processes, each of these reactions may be governed by other processes not common to all of them. Therefore, anger, blame, and retaliation may be, but are not necessarily, isomorphic to one another.

Our model is comprised of several elements:

1. The perceiver of harm may appraise the situation to determine the way in which the actor is causally responsible for harm. To assess the actor's causal responsibility for harm, the perceiver attempts to discern whether harm was intended or unintended by the actor; if unintended, whether the harmful consequences of the action were foreseeable or unforeseeable; and, if intended, whether the actor's motives for harm were malevolent or nonmalevolent. Assessments of causal responsibility are based on information available in the harmful situation and on target-based and category-based expectancies about the actor. Having made these assessments, the actor's behavior is thereby causally classified as accidental, foreseeable, nonmalevolently intended, or malevolently intended.

2. The perceiver of harm may also assess the actor's moral culpability for harm. Judgments of moral culpability are a function of the relationship between the perceiver's assessment of what ought to have happened in the situation and what actually happened. Assigned moral culpability increases as the actor's causal responsibility for harm deviates from what ought or ought not to have happened.

3. Judgments of what actually happened are reflected in the perceiver's causal responsibility assignment.

4. Judgments of what ought to have happened are, however, multiply determined. These judgments may be specified for the perceiver by someone else (as in the legal system) or may reflect the perceiver's own value system. The "oughts" relevant to harmful behavior can be described in terms of Heider's types of personal responsibility. An actor may be held morally culpable for harm, because (a) one ought not to cause harm; (b) one ought not to be careless or not try to do one's best; (c) one ought not to intentionally harm another no matter what the circumstances; or (d) one ought not to intentionally harm another unless harm was a necessary means to fulfill a more valuable ought.

5. Anger is a function of several factors, including the arousal engendered by harm and other factors. Anger is also a function of the magnitude of the perceived is–ought discrepancy. Anger increases as arousal increases and may increase as the magnitude of the is–ought discrepancy increases.

6. The perceiver's desire to express hostile retaliation is a function of anger. As anger increases, the likelihood of hostile retaliation increases unless inhibitory factors prevail. Inhibition is greater to the extent that hostile retaliation could result in actual social disapproval and to the extent that the ought governing the perceiver's anger response prohibits harm.

We elaborate on these elements of the model in the following sections. In the next section, we define the different types of causal responsibility and discuss those factors that affect assignments of causal responsibility. In the third section, we define the different oughts that may be used in morally evaluating harmful behavior and indicate how blame assignments, anger, and retaliation are influenced by causal responsibility assignment and perceived "oughtness" requirements. Finally, in the fourth section, we suggest several directions for future research and address issues as yet unresolved by our analysis.

CAUSAL RESPONSIBILITY ASSIGNMENT

Types of Causal Responsibility

In any situation, there are likely to be several effects or consequences of an actor's behavior. At least one or more of these consequences may have been intended by the actor—that is, the actor may have actually wanted to achieve these consequences. However, other effects may have been unintended by-products of behavior, some or all of which may not even have been foreseen by the actor. In order to understand the actor, form an impression, or predict the actor's future behavior, the perceiver is presumably interested in discerning whether a given effect (e.g., harm) was intended by the actor; if intended, what reasons or motives guided the intent; and if unintended, whether the target effect was or was not foreseen by the actor. In this section, we elucidate the functional role of these attributionally relevant considerations in judgments of causal responsibility. In doing this, we rely on the attributional perspectives of Heider (1958), Jones and Davis (1965), Jones and McGillis (1976), and Kelley (1972).

In the situations we are discussing, the harmful consequences of an actor's behavior are the grist for the attributional mill. The terms *harmful outcome* and *harm* are used in a generic sense to refer to those consequences that the perceiver values negatively and would prefer to avoid. These terms encompass many consequences, including physical injury, psychological damage, a perceived affront to the recipient's values or self-esteem, as well as a perceived blocking of deserved rewards or desired outcomes. In contrast, *nonharmful outcomes* are those that are valued positively and that the perceiver would wish to achieve rather than avoid. Either harmful or nonharmful consequences can be the result of the commission or omission of an act.

Heider (1958) noted the various questions that the perceiver of harm may attempt to answer in determining the way in which an actor is causally responsible for a harmful outcome. The perceiver may ask, for example, "Did the actor actually cause harm?" "Was the actor trying to harm the recipient (me)?" and "Why was the actor trying to harm the recipient (me)?" The perceiver's answers to these questions determine the way in which the actor is linked causally with the harmful consequences of action. More formally, based on Heider's analysis, we distinguish four types of causal responsibility.[2] That is, an actor may be linked causally with the harmful consequences of action, because the harmful outcome was:

1. *Accidental*—that is, while it was the actor's behavior that caused the harmful outcome, the actor could not have been aware of, and therefore could not have avoided, the harmful consequences of his or her behavior.

2. *Foreseeable*—that is, it was the actor's behavior that caused the harmful outcome and the actor either (a) could have been but was not or (b) actually was aware of the potential harmful consequences of his or her actions, even though these consequences were not what the actor wanted to produce.

3. *Nonmalevolently intentional*—that is, the actor produced, foresaw, and wanted to produce the harmful outcome as a means to achieving a further nonharmful end.

4. *Malevolently intentional*—that is, the actor produced, foresaw, and wanted to produce the harmful outcome either as an end in itself or as a means to achieve a further harmful end.

Our adapted version of Heider's types of personal responsibility indicates that three judgments are involved in discerning the way in which an actor is causally responsible for the harmful consequences of his or her actions. One judgment concerns whether the actor produced harm intentionally or unintentionally. A second judgment concerns whether harm produced intentionally was motivated by acceptable or unacceptable goals. A third judgment concerns whether unintentional harm was foreseeable or unforeseeable. Before elaborating in the next section how each of these judgments is affected by characteristics of the harmful situation itself and by characteristics independent

[2]These types of causal responsibility are adaptations of Heider's (1958, pp. 113–114) stages of personal responsibility. We have omitted Heider's first stage, in which the actor is held responsible for any effect with which he or she is associated but that he or she did not actually produce. This association stage has been omitted because most of the aggression research has not examined anger and retaliation in response to associational types of responsibility. Moreover, the reader should note that our responsibility types (3) and (4) are not identical to Heider's descriptions of his last two stages; for example, Heider did not incorporate nonmalevolent and malevolent motives in his last two stages of personal responsibility, respectively. Moreover, although we assume that the four levels describe the ways in which the actor is causally associated with an event, we do not adopt Heider's notion that responsibility as culpability increases linearly with increases in personal causation. The levels do, however, describe the different evaluative standards or oughts that *could* be applied in assigning responsibility as culpability.

of the harmful situation, we would like to indicate the assumptions underlying the attributional aspects of our model.

As will become clear in subsequent sections, there is no need to assume that the three attributional judgments occur in a particular sequence. Instead, because these judgments are nested within one another, it is more reasonable to assume that the judgments may be made in a more parallel manner. Moreover, we need not assume that these judgments are made consciously (i.e., with awareness) or that they are time consuming to make. It is primarily when the harmful outcome is unexpected or extreme that we would expect the perceiver to try to make these judgments consciously. In addition, certain factors may short-circuit the attribution process altogether or lead the perceiver to weigh differentially the available attributionally relevant information and/or to reach attributional conclusions based more on the perceiver's a priori assumptions than on the available information. Factors that may engage a less than rational assessment include the arousal engendered by harm itself or by other factors, and the perceiver's mood or cognitive set prior to observing harm. Where possible, we will review research that indicates how these factors influence the attribution process.

Factors Affecting Causal Responsibility Assignment

Our purpose in this section is to (a) identify those constructs that existing models of attribution indicate underlie perceivers' perceptions of foreseeability, intent, and motives; (b) indicate the range of manipulations that could be used to operationalize these constructs; and (c) review research within and outside the area of aggression that illustrates how the identified factors affect perceptions of foreseeability, intent, and motives.

INFERENCES OF INTENTIONALITY

Several conditions must be met before the perceiver can conclude that the actor intended to cause the harmful consequences of his or her behavior. These conditions include knowledge that the actor actually had the ability to produce the observed harm, knowledge that the actor was aware of the harmful consequences of action, and knowledge that the actor was free to engage in the behavior resulting in harm (Heider, 1958; Jones & Davis, 1965; Jones & McGillis, 1976).

Inferences of ability, awareness, and behavioral freedom will enhance the perception that harm was intended. However, since it is usually clear that the actor had the ability to produce harm, we will forgo a description of the factors affecting perceptions of ability (see Frieze, 1976, for an illustration of these factors). Moreover, the factors affecting inferences of awareness and inferences of choice are discussed in later sections. We will simply assume for now that the perceiver thinks the actor had ability, awareness, and choice so that we may discuss those factors critical to the inference of intent.

Knowledge that the actor had the ability to produce, was aware of, and was free to choose the behavior resulting in harm are necessary but not sufficient conditions to establish intent (Jones & Davis, 1965), because there may have been other consequences of behavior (in addition to harm) that the actor may have actually been trying to produce. Such a perception would be enhanced were these other consequences desirable. Thus, to discern the actor's true intent, the perceiver must consider what action alternatives were available to the actor, what consequences would have resulted from each action, how desirable each consequence was, which consequences were unique to the chosen behavior, and finally, the relative desirability of these unique consequences. The presence of desirable consequences in addition to harm reduces the perception that harm was intended. This perception would be offset only if the harmful outcome itself were unique (i.e., noncommon) to the enacted behavior and/or if other behaviors available to the actor would have been just as likely to result in the desirable consequences.

Some research has examined and confirmed the hypotheses of Jones and Davis that intent inferences are greater when the target effect is unique to the behavior performed by the actor, when the performed behavior has few other consequences, and when the target effect is desirable (Ajzen, 1971; Newtson, 1974; Lowe & McConnell, Note 1). These hypotheses have not been directly tested using aggression as the target behavior. It is nonetheless easy to see how these notions may be applied to interpret the results of some aggression research. For example, several aggression studies have found that anger and retaliation are greatest in those conditions supporting perceptions that (a) harm was unique to the chosen behavior; (b) there were no other possible desirable reasons for (i.e., effects of) producing harm; and (c) the alternative behaviors available actually had more desirable consequences (e.g., Epstein & Taylor, 1967; Fishman, 1965; Gentry, 1970).

In addition to subjecting these hypotheses to a more direct test, other questions remain regarding the influence of effect uniqueness and relative desirability on inferences of harmful intent. These pertain to elucidating exceptions to the line of attributional reasoning elaborated by Jones and Davis. For example, we suspect that perceivers may view harm as unintended primarily when there were actually more undesirable consequences associated with the nonchosen compared to the chosen course of action. Moreover, we need to examine how inferences of harmful intent are affected by each of the several criteria available for assessing the desirability of the observed and potential consequences. For example, perceived desirability may be inferred according to one or more of several criteria, including (a) the perceiver's knowledge regarding the specific actor's likes and dislikes; (b) the perceiver's knowledge regarding the likes and dislikes of people similar to the actor; (c) the perceiver's own likes and dislikes; and/or (d) the perceiver's more global assessment of what the culture would find likable or dislikable. Obviously, then, the perceiver's assessment of the total package of effects associated with the actual and possible actions may differ depending on which of these four criteria is used. This will in turn differentially affect perceptions of intent.

Inferences that harm was intended will also be affected by effort and other less stable characteristics, such as nonverbal aspects of the actor's behavior (e.g., his or her facial expressions). Very little research has examined how intent inferences are affected by aspects of the action situation itself, such as perceived effort, persistence in trying to produce harm, or the actor's emotional expression. A few examples are, however, available from the literature. Even children as young as kindergarten age use emotional expression cues to infer whether transgressions were intended or not intended. Both Nelson (1980) and Rybash, Roodin, and Hallion (1979) found that transgressors' happy or sad facial expressions while perpetrating harm affected whether children classified the transgression as intentional or not intentional. Other research has shown that adults' perceptions of harmful intent are greater when the actor expended high rather than low effort in harming another (e.g., Joseph, Kane, Gaes, & Tedeschi, 1976). Unfortunately, however, the factors that reduce or enhance perceptions of effort are more difficult to specify, but these may include knowledge that the actor had very high versus low ability to produce the harmful consequence, that there were few versus many environmental obstacles to overcome in producing harm, and that, of the several opportunities the actor had to cause harm, he or she did so on only one or a few, as opposed to many, of them. In this respect, it is interesting to note that many manipulations of attack vary such factors as the frequency and duration of aversive stimulation, which may be an indirect indication to the victim of effort expended in trying to harm him or her. For example, a condition leading to high anger and aggression in Epstein and Taylor's (1967) study was one in which the actor persistently set the most aversive shock despite the possibility that this could have interfered with the actor's own performance. This type of behavior was undoubtedly a clear indication of harmful intent.

A biased inference of intent may be made depending on (a) whether the harmful effects are more disappointing for the perceiver than other effects that could have occurred (i.e., was hedonically relevant, Jones & Davis, 1965); (b) whether the perceiver is involved as only an observer or as an actual recipient; and (c) whether the perceiver's prior expectations of the actor are consistent or inconsistent with the inference of harmful intent. There are no data reagrding whether the hedonic relevance of harm differentially affects inferences of intent. However, several studies have found either stronger affective reactions (e.g., Chaiken & Cooper, 1973; Enzle, Harvey, & Wright, 1980) or more extreme evaluations of the actor (e.g., Lowe & McConnell, Note 1) when the conditions facilitated hedonic relevance by, for example, manipulating the perceiver's observer versus recipient role. We assume that such reactions reflect perceptions of high intent. On the basis of other attribution research, moreover, we suspect that several conditions will increase the hedonic relevance of harm, which should thereby increase inferences of intent even by observers who are not affected immediately by observed harm. These conditions include increasing the dependency of the perceiver's future outcomes on the actor's behavior (e.g., Berscheid, Graziano, Monson, & Dermer, 1976), increasing the expectancy of future interaction (e.g., Miller, Norman, & Wright, 1978), increasing the actor's similarity to the perceiver (e.g., Nesdale & Rule, 1974), and basing the harmful event on a belief, attitude, or value dimension that is personally important to the perceiver. Interesting questions stemming from these methods of enhancing hedonic relevance are, for example, whether and why the negative comment of a liked other may actually have more sting than that of a less familiar or disliked other and yet reduce our perception of intent. This and other examples indicate that hedonic relevance may inconsistently influence affective reactions and intent ascriptions.

Attention also needs to be given to how preexisting knowledge about the actor may affect intentionality inferences. In many situations, we have prior knowledge about the actor's attitudes, beliefs, personality characteristics, and typical behaviors because we know the actor personally and/or have stereotypes about the group(s) to which the actor belongs. Such knowledge of the actor personally and stereotypically is referred to as target-based and category-based expectancies, respectively (see Jones & McGillis, 1976). Both types of expectancies are likely to provide a basis for judging whether harmful behavior is consistent or inconsistent with the actor's attitudes, beliefs, personality characteristics, and behavior. Moreover, the perceived consistency between harmful behavior and target-based and category-based expectancies is likely to affect inferences regarding whether harm was intended or unintended.

In our view, any preexisting knowledge about the actor that is consistent with the view that the actor would intentionally cause a harmful outcome will lead perceivers to infer that harmful behavior was intended. Conversely, any preexisting knowledge about the actor that is inconsistent with the view that the actor would cause harm intentionally will lead perceivers to infer that harm was unintended. Thus, target- and category-based expectancies may *bias* perceivers' use of information directly available in the situation to infer whether harm was or was not intended. Such biases may operate to cause the perceiver to weigh heavily information available in the situation that is consistent with prior expectations or to discount information that is inconsistent with prior expectations. However, the extent to which directly available information is attenuated or amplified in its usage will also depend on the perceiver's involvement in the situation and affective relationship with the actor. There are likely occasions in which, therefore, the inferences made by perceivers who have prior knowledge about the actor will be no different from those made by perceivers who do not have such information. More importantly, however, is the idea that behavior disconfirming a prior expectation of the actor may lead to skepticism about the actor's causal responsibility and to a greater search for information that would disambiguate the actor's causal responsibility (Jones & McGillis, 1976). Some data bear on these notions.

Although not interpreted in this way by Rosenfield and Stephan (1977), their results indicate that target-based and category-based expectancies consistent with intentionally causing harm lead to greater personal attributions for hostile behavior than expectancies inconsistent with the intentional production of harm (see also Bell, Wicklund, Manko, & Larkin, 1976). Target-based expectancies were manipulated by providing information about the actor's personality characteristics (e.g., kind versus hostile) and/or by providing information regarding the actor's voluntary group membership (e.g., member of the high school band and choir versus the boxing and football teams). Category-based expectancies were established by informing observers that the majority versus the minority of group members approved of open expressions of hostility. Although Rosenfield and Stephan did not measure perceived intent, their results revealed that target-based expectancies were stronger determinants of attribution than were category-based expectancies. This suggests that violation of target- compared to category-based expectancies may result in skepticism regarding the actor's presumed causal responsibility and to a search for information that would support a causal assignment consistent, or at least not inconsistent, with the original expectation. That is, compared to violations of category-based expectancies, harmful behavior disconfirming a target-based expectancy is least likely to lead to the ascription of malevolent intent. Harmful behavior confirming a target-based expectancy is most likely to lead to the ascription of malevolent intent. For example, harm by a liked other may not even be perceived as nonmalevolently intended: instead, harm is more likely to be perceived as foreseeable or perhaps as purely accidental. We suspect, however, that there must be some ambiguity regarding the causes of the liked other's behavior for this type of bias to occur.

In addition to knowledge of group membership,[3] information regarding the similarity between the actor and perceiver may also lead to category-based expectancies regarding a person's tendency to behave aggressively. Perceived similarity has usually been manipulated by varying actor–perceiver attitude similarity on social and political issues (see Byrne, 1971). Manipulations of attitude similarity may be viewed as establishing either a target- or a category-based expectancy. When attitude similarity only is manipulated, we suggest that it is better viewed as an indirect manipulation of a category-based expectancy. Nevertheless, regardless of the nature of this expectation, attitudinally

---

[3]Although Jones and McGillis (1976) restrict category-based expectancies to involuntary group membership, we claim that both voluntary and involuntary group membership may serve as a basis for such expectancies.

similar relative to dissimilar persons are viewed by observers and recipients as more well intentioned and as more justified when they cause harmful behavior (e.g., McKillip & Posovac, 1972; Nesdale, Rule, & Hill, 1978; Seligman, Paschall, & Takata, 1974; Turkat & Dawson, 1976; Veitch & Piccione, 1978).

Several studies of observers' and recipients' reactions also indicate that category-based expectancies formed on the basis of involuntary group membership differentially affect perceptions of the actor's behavior. Actors who are physically or personally unattractive, black, male, or who have unpopular first names are viewed more negatively and seen as more likely to behave aggressively than actors who are physically or personally attractive, white, female, or who have popular first names (e.g., Landy & Aronson, 1969; Lerner, 1969; Lerner & Korn, 1972; McDavid & Harari, 1966; Nesdale & Rule, 1974; Nesdale, Rule, & McAra, 1975; Rule, Dyck, McAra, & Nesdale, 1975; Shepherd & Bagley, 1970; Staffieri, 1967, 1972; Steele & Woods, 1977; Walker, 1962). For example, Duncan (1976) found that white adults viewed the act of shoving by a black actor as more violent than the same act by a white actor. Such biases persist even when the intentional nature of the act is unambiguous. For example, Dion (1972) found that adults rated an unattractive compared to an attractive child's intentional aggression less positively.

While few of these studies measured perceived intent, the results considered together suggest that target-based expectancies and stereotypes based on another's involuntary or voluntary group membership may positively or negatively affect perceptions of intent. Such expectations appear to bias the attribution of intent process; otherwise, such characteristics as personal likability and similarity affect perceivers' reactions even when there is low causal ambiguity regarding the actor's intentions. Nevertheless, these perceptions probably have some basis in reality. For example, parents who bless their children with strange names may also socialize their children in strange ways.

In this section, we proposed numerous factors that are likely to affect as well as to bias the inference that harm was intended rather than unintended. First, if the perceiver assumes that the actor had ability, awareness, and choice, he or she will consider harm intended, especially if the harm is unique to the chosen behavior, if there are no other possible desirable reasons for producing harm and if the alternative behaviors available had desirable consequences. We suggested several criteria, however, that may affect the perceiver's assessment of the various effects associated with the actual actions. Second, inferences that harm is intended are also derived from characteristics of the actor related to the situation, such as his or her effort and nonverbal cues. The inference of intent may actually be *biased* by motivational and expectancy factors. These include the hedonic relevance of the behavior, the perceiver's involvement, and the perceiver's prior expectations about the actor. Despite some empirical support for our various conjectures, they await direct confirmation.

PERCEPTIONS OF FORESEEABILITY

We have just reviewed several factors that are likely to affect perceivers' assessments of whether a harmful outcome was intended or unintended. In this section, we will identify those factors affecting perceptions of whether unintentionally produced harm was accidental or foreseeable. A similar emphasis will be placed in this section on how the harmful circumstances themselves and prior knowledge about the actor affect perceptions of whether harm was produced accidentally or with some element of foreseeability.

Potential or actual awareness of the harmful consequences of action distinguishes between events labeled as accidental or foreseeable. The harmful outcome is considered accidental when the actor was a productive cause of harm but did not have the ability to foresee and therefore could not have avoided producing the harmful outcome. If there were no uncontrollable personal or environmental forces interfering with the actor's ability to foresee (and therefore to avoid) the outcome, harm is classified as foreseeable.

In addition to this general definition of foreseeability, we would like to make explicit the different types of foreseeability that were implicit in Heider's (1958, p. 113) definition. An outcome may be seen as foreseeable because of the actor's negligence, by which it is meant that carelessness or inattentiveness on the actor's part prevented him or her from foreseeing and therefore avoiding the outcome. An outcome may also be viewed as foreseeable because of the actor's moral weakness or ruthlessness, by which it is meant that the actor actually was aware that harm could result from his or her actions but engaged in the harm-dependent behavior because of the actor's interest in achieving another goal. We refer to these as *negligent foreseeability and ruthless foreseeability,* respectively, and make this distinction because these two types of foreseeability may elicit differentially negative evaluations of the actor's behavior. Moreover, we believe that characteristics of the perceiver (e.g., his or her involvement and expectations of the actor) will affect the particular type of foreseeability imputed to the actor.

In order to assess whether harm was accidental or foreseeable, the perceiver must be able to answer several questions (Brewer, 1977). The perceiver must be able to assess whether harm was more probable with than without the actor's specific intervention, because we view attributed awareness as greater when harm is perceived as more probable with than without the actor's intervening behavior and its associated causes. The perceiver must also be able to assess whether the immediate or prior cause of harm was controllable by the actor (Brickman, Ryan, & Wortman, 1975). Regardless of whether the actor actually foresaw the consequences, attributed awareness will be greater when either the immediate or prior cause of harm is perceived as controllable. Moreover, the perceiver must be able to discern whether the immediate or prior cause of harm was internal or external (Brickman et al., 1975). While perhaps irrational, greater awareness will be attributed when the immediate or prior cause of harm is internal rather than external. Moreover, even external causes actually not controllable by the actor may wrongly fail to reduce perceptions of foreseeability when these external causes themselves were due to voluntary human intervention (Fincham & Jaspars, 1979). Although incomplete, the results of several studies illustrate the basis for these various conjectures about the factors affecting judgments of foreseeability.

The results of Brickman et al.'s (1975) study, for example, indicate greater judgments of foreseeability for automobile accidents when the cause of the accident was internal (e.g., not looking at the road) rather than external (e.g., a steering failure). Although confounded with causal locus, prior controllable (e.g., daydreaming) compared to uncontrollable (e.g., an inept mechanic) causes also increased foreseeability judgments (see also Arkkelin, Oakley, & Mynatt, 1979). Their study also illustrates the importance of distinguishing negligent from ruthless foreseeability judgments. Although foreseeability did not differ, judgments of responsibility were higher in the case where the driver knew about the mechanical fault and simply had not had the car looked at in over a year compared to the case in which the driver was daydreaming. This probably reflects the observers' perceptions that both drivers were negligent but that the former was also morally weak because he simply ignored the possibly fatal consequences of a faulty steering mechanism. Consistent with these results are the combined findings of Nickel (1974) and Dyck and Rule (1978) that actors who could not have been aware of the harm they caused to another were rated as less able to foresee these consequences.

Brickman et al. employed manipulations of immediate and prior internal and external causes that were specific to a given event (e.g., an automobile accident). In other research, however, several classes of variables that are not event specific have been identified as influencing judgments of foreseeability. For example, severe compared to mild positive or negative outcomes are perceived as more foreseeable, even though the outcomes were clearly unintentional (e.g., Shaver, 1970a, Experiment 3; Ugwuegbu & Hendrick, 1974; Walster, 1966). Moreover, several studies found that observers of unintended outcomes reported that they would have been more likely to foresee and to have taken actions to avoid severe relative to mildly harmful outcomes. Chaikin and Darley (1973) also found that severe relative to mildly harmful outcomes were attributed less to chance by potential victims of the outcome, which indirectly indicates that they saw severe outcomes as more foreseeable.

A second body of research has shown that the situational or personal similarity between the observer and perpetrator of the action affects judgments of foreseeability. Chaiken and Darley demonstrated that observers who were potential perpetrators of a negative outcome attributed the outcome more to chance than did observers who were potential victims of the outcome. Shaver (1970a, Experiment 3) also demonstrated that observers of events that could happen to them thought the perpetrator of an accident would have been less able to foresee the consequences of action than did observers of events that could not happen to them. Similar findings have been reported in other studies (e.g., Hill, 1975; McKillip & Posovac, 1975). In addition, Shaver (1970a, Experiment 2) found that attitudinally similar others were perceived as having taken greater precautions to avoid a negative outcome and were seen as more conscientious and clear in their thinking relative to dissimilar others.

This research has several implications. First, we are likely as perpetrators of harm to try to excuse our transgressions by appeals to a lack of ability to foresee or avoid the outcome, thereby arguing that the outcome was produced accidentally (Horai, 1977; Scott & Lyman, 1968). Second, as recipients of a transgression, we are unlikely to accept or believe the actor's excuses nor are we likely to make up excuses for the actor. We may believe instead that the actor should have foreseen the action's consequences. However, third, observers' tendencies to accept or construct excuses will likely depend on their relationship to the actor and on their prior experience with events like the one in question, both of which may bias perceptions of whether the actor could have avoided producing the outcome. Observers who have an affectively positive relationship with the actor may be more convinced that the actor could not have foreseen and therefore could not have avoided producing the outcome. Observers who have a negative relationship with the actor may be less convinced regarding avoidability and, even if they are convinced, may nevertheless argue that the actor should have avoided it. Moreover, prior experience in the target environment will provide the perceiver with a better idea of what level of ability is necessary to overcome environmental constraints. This information may be used to either the actor's advantage or disadvantage vis-à-vis perceptions of foreseeability. For example, a common strategy in jury selection is for lawyers to select potential jurors on the basis of these very two factors—that is, jurors whose own prior experience and similarity (e.g., on the basis of sex, race, nationality) to the defendant will best facilitate the lawyer's desired interpretation of the "objective" evidence.

Several studies also indirectly support our expectation that the actor's perceived ability to foresee the consequences of his or her actions may be reduced by involuntary group membership characteristics of the actor or other stable characteristics of the actor's personality. For example, Jones, Hester, Farina, and Davis (1959) found that recipients of a negative evaluation rated a maladjusted person less negatively than a well-adjusted person for his derogatory comments (see also Phares & Wilson, 1973), presumably because the maladjusted other was less able to foresee the consequences of his behavior. Similarly, Gergen and Jones's (1963) study shows that participants changed their evaluations of a maladjusted person more when that person was judged as able to control his or her thwarting behavior. Other characteristics of the actor seem to affect the perception of whether he or she could, should, or did foresee the consequences of his or her actions. The age of the aggressor is one noteworthy characteristic. Savitsky, Czyzewski, Dubord, and Kaminsky (1976) have shown that adults evaluate children's transgressions less harshly than they do adults' transgressions, perhaps because children are seen as less able than adults to control the consequences of their action. The perceived intelligence of the aggressor may also affect perceptions of foreseeability. For example, Horai and O'Rourke (Note 2) have shown that dull transgressors are punished less than intelligent transgressors. And, as verified by Brickman et al.'s (1975) results, perceptions of the ability to control one's behavior are positively correlated with perceptions of foreseeability. Thus, all these results may reflect perceivers' reasoning that children relative to adults and dull relative to bright people are more helpless and less able to withstand or control environmental pressures.

As in the case of distinguishing intended versus unintended harm, the judgment of whether harm is foreseeable or accidental is affected by circumstances surrounding the harm and prior knowledge about the actor. The perception that harm was foreseeable rather than accidental is greater to the extent that the actor was aware of the consequences and could potentially have controlled them, or to the extent that harm was internally produced. These judgments are determined by event-specific factors, the severity of the harm, the similarity between the observer and harm doer, and prior expectations about characteristics related to negligence, moral weakness, or uncontrollability. Our conjectures about the factors that are encompassed especially by hedonic relevance and expectancy notions require a priori verification in subsequent research.

Very little research has examined systematically the factors contributing to perceptions of foreseeability. Nonetheless, it is clear from the available data that we are more likely to observe biases in perceptions of harm as foreseeable rather than accidental as the information about the actor's ability to foresee the outcome becomes more indirect. In these more ambiguous situations, there is less constraint on the perceiver to discern objectively the causal antecedents of the actor's behavior and there is more opportunity for the operation of such biases as the false consensus bias (Ross, 1977) or the tendency to explain events in terms of controllable factors (Kelley, 1972).

MOTIVE INFERENCES

The variety of motives for inflicting harm may be viewed in terms of the functions of aggression outlined by Feshbach (1964) and Rule (1975). Harmful behavior may be designed to fulfill a personally based or instrumentally based motive of the actor. Alternatively, harmful behavior may be designed to fulfill prosocial motives—that is, to achieve a nonharmful end. As an example, consider an actor who hits a recipient to retrieve a lost wallet from the recipient (see Nesdale et al., 1975). In one case, the hitting occurs so that the actor can retrieve the wallet and keep it for himself. This is an example of personal–instrumental aggression, because the harm was intended as a means to achieve a further harmful end. In a second condition, the hitting occurs so that the actor can retrieve the wallet to return it to its rightful owner. This is an example of prosocial aggression because, while harm was intended, it was intended to achieve a nonharmful end. As expected, the perceivers' assessments of the actor's moral reprehensibility were more negative in the former compared to the latter condition.

In the Nesdale et al. (1975) study, participants were given rather clear-cut information regarding the actor's motives in both conditions. To infer the actor's motives in most situations, however, the perceiver must rely on knowledge of the actor's characteristic motives for negative behavior or on the perceiver's own assessment of whether and when harm is used to achieve nonharmful ends. Because of the perceiver's reliance on these cues, this aspect of the inference process is quite apt to break down. In particular, we suspect that there is a tendency to associate like motives with like outcomes—that is, to infer that malevolent rather than nonmalevolent reasons guided the intentional production of harm. How often do we as parents remind our children before spanking "This is going to hurt me more than it hurts you"? The perceiver may simply not try to detect the presence of nonmalevolent motives, assuming instead that the actor malevolently intended harm. Alternatively, the perceiver's prior positive or negative expectations of the actor may not easily allow for the inference of malevolent intent or nonmalevolent intent. For example, when a dispositionally acerbic person behaves aggressively, we are more likely to attribute harmful behavior to something about the acerbic person's personality and we may even ascribe to him or her more malevolent intent. The hostile behavior of a nice person, on the other hand, is apt to be attributed more to something about the situation and is less likely to result in an inference of malevolent intent. Similarly, if people prefer to think the best of others, inferences of nonmalevolent intent are more likely. Alternatively, cues regarding another's nonmalevolent intent may have to be especially strong to convince perceivers who believe or expect the worst of others of the nonharmful nature of the motive.

Although little research has focused on isolating the factors contributing to perceptions that the actor's intent was malevolent or nonmalevolent, the results of several studies suggest that the presence of potential positive effects of harm reduces the ascription of malevolent intent. For example, harm in response to prior provocation (e.g., Harvey & Rule, 1978), harm designed to punish a recipient for poor performance (e.g., Fishman, 1965; Gentry, 1970), and harm as an attempt to right some wrong perpetrated by the recipient against a third party (e.g., Nesdale et al., 1975) each reduces the extent to which anger is aroused and/or blame is assigned and/or retaliation is expressed. We have also found studies where, while the investigators expected their "provocation" or "no provocation" manipulations to induce or reduce anger, they did not (see Baron, 1977). Our view is that such a reduction or enhancement did not occur because aspects of their procedures inadvertently introduced possible nonharmful or harmful motives for harm production (e.g., Fishman, 1965; Gentry, 1970). Thus, in any event where the harm is a response to external facilitory factors (such as poor as opposed to good performance, threat of punishment for not inflicting harm) or is reactive, the perception of nonmalevolent intent will be enhanced. Harm committed in the presence of inhibitory factors (such as threat for producing harm) will increase the perception of malevolent intent.

For example, manipulations of choice to perform a given behavior presumably have a large impact on the perceiver's perceptions that the actor intended to cause the target outcome. Low choice (in the form of command by a superior or threatened punishment for not enacting the target behavior) presumably reduces the perceiver's inference that the actor even wanted to achieve the target outcome. The absence of command or fear of punishment, on the other hand, would strengthen (or at least not weaken) the perceiver's belief that the actor wanted the target effect. According to this view, harm resulting from command or low choice would not even be perceived as intended. Instead, it will be perceived as foreseeable and as reflecting perhaps on the actor's moral weakness or ruthlessness.

However, explicit choice manipulations such as these may not have their primary effect on inferences regarding whether the target outcome (in our case, harm) was intended. Rather, such choice manipulations may have their effects on perceptions of the actor's motives. When an actor is commanded to aggress, he or she may comply with this request, however distasteful, in order to achieve yet another nonharmful end (e.g., obeying one's superiors, self-preservation). In this case, therefore, we suspect that perceivers would see harm as intended but for nonmalevolent reasons. Conversely, freely produced harm is likely to enhance the perception of malevolent intent. Moreover, there is likely to be a strong tendency for observers to see even commanded harm as malevolently intended unless the observer were convinced that he or she too could not have disobeyed the external agent's orders. Instructive in this respect is Milgram's (1965) well-known study where observers derogated actors commanded to hurt another, on the basis that they (the observers) would have defied the experimenter because they were not the kind of people who would hurt people for the sake of science (see also Hamilton, 1978). And, of course, the extensive literature on attitude attribution also indicates that perceivers are very resistant to "no-choice" manipulations despite repeated attempts to weaken such resistance (see Jones & McGillis, 1976). Such resistance may be particularly difficult to undercut, for example, as the severity of the observed harm increases and as the perceiver becomes more negatively motivationally involved (e.g., as a recipient as opposed to a loved one of the actor). It is clear, however, that these are simply general guidelines regarding motive perception and that they are in need of further elaboration, both empirically and conceptually.

EFFECTS OF CAUSAL ASSIGNMENT AND NORMATIVE CONSIDERATIONS ON BLAME ASCRIPTION, ANGER, AND AGGRESSION

We have identified several factors that affect whether harm is perceived as accidental, foreseeable, nonmalevolently intended, or malevolently intended. In addition to establishing the type of causal responsibility for harmful behavior, we suggest that the perceiver may consider the relationship between the actor's causal responsibility for harm and what the perceiver believes ought to have occurred in the harmful situation. In this section, we will indicate how causal responsibility assignment and the perceived "oughtness" requirements of the situation affect blame ascriptions, anger, and the desire to retaliate.

We assume that evaluations of, and reactions to, harmful behavior are affected partly by that set of norms, or oughts, that the perceiver has learned are important from the perspective of his or her culture and that the perceiver views as applicable to the situation in question. An ought is defined as a belief expressing the imperativeness aspect of the obligation to act, think, or feel in a certain way (Heider, 1958; Hollingworth, 1949). While the terms *values* or *norms* have been used interchangeably with the term *ought*, we prefer the term *ought* because it more clearly connotes the belief that people should or should not act, think, or feel in certain ways (Kelley, 1971; Pepitone, 1975)—a belief that is conveyed when we credit or blame someone for behaving in a particular way.

The production of harm, of course, violates an important ought—that of respecting another's physical or psychological welfare. In regard to this ought requirement, there is no difference among behaviors independently classified as accidental, negligently foreseeable, ruthlessly foreseeable, malevolently intended, or nonmalevolently intended. These types of causal responsibility differ, however, with respect to perceptions relevant to other ought requirements. For example, foreseeably harmful events represent those in which the actor has not tried to do his or her best or has not tried to be as careful as possible, and in this process, has violated respect for another. Accidentally harmful events also violate respect for the individual but, by virtue of our definition, the outcome would have occurred regardless of the person's effort. Therefore, unlike foreseeable events, accidental events do not violate ought-related perceptions regarding carefulness and trying to do one's best. Malevolently intended events intentionally violate respect for the individual and possibly, in addition, a series of other ought-related perceptions, such as being fair, sharing, and respecting others' property, life, and liberty. Finally, in the case of nonmalevolently intended harm, the production of harm although intentional was presumably motivated by the desire to achieve a nonharmful end, describable, for example, in terms of ought-related perceptions such as doing unto others as you would have them do unto you, helping or bearing the infirmities of the weak, being loyal, keeping one's promises, respecting contracts, obeying superiors, and being loyal.

Thus, the types of causality we have described differ not only according to the degree of personal causation involved in producing harm (Heider, 1958, pp. 113–114) but also according to the oughts that have been violated or fulfilled by them. Unlike the implications of Heider's (1958) analysis of degrees of personal causation, therefore, our theory does not assume that ascriptions or blame are necessarily isomorphic with degrees of personal causality. According to Heider's analysis and the research stimulated by this analysis (see Fincham & Jaspars, 1979), the degree of personal causality assigned increases from what we have labeled as Type 1 (accidental) to Type 4 (malevolent intent) events. In a parallel manner, the actor should receive increasing blame proceeding from Type 1 to Type 4. We subscribe to such blame-degrees of personal causality isomorphism, however, only in those instances in which the same outcome is described by the same ought in two or more situations. For example, severe harm produced intentionally would be assigned more blame than severe harm produced with foreseeability. Consistent with previous suggestions (e.g., Harvey & Rule, 1978; Pepitone, 1975), however, we can think of different situations in which blame will not covary positively with the degree of personal causation assigned. An actor who only foreseeably caused severe harm may be blamed more than an actor who intentionally caused minor harm. In this example, the actor is being judged not according to his or her causal responsibility, but according to the *seriousness* with which the two different oughts have been violated. A similar and more compelling case can be made comparing two intentionally produced outcomes (both of which violate the same ought), one of which is severe and the other of which is mild. Thus, the actor is judged to deserve blame not only (if at all) according to his or her degree of personal responsibility for the outcome but also according to (a) the seriousness with which ought-related requirements in the situation have been violated and (b) the relative importance to the perceiver of the oughts violated. Reflected in this suggestion is the assumption that perceivers have a norm or ought hierarchy, by which we mean that the fulfillment (or violation) of certain norms is more important to the perceiver than the fulfillment (or violation) of other norms or oughts.

Also reflected in this suggestion is the idea that there may be intra- and interperceiver differences in the ought standard that will be applied in evaluating the actor's moral culpability for harm. Such differences may result in a complete lack of differentiation among the different types of causal responsibility when evaluating the actor's moral culpability (Fishbein & Ajzen, 1973). A complete lack of differentiation might occur, for example, when the perceiver believes the relevant ought to be "one ought not to cause harm." In this case, blame is assigned when the perceiver simply establishes that the actor caused harm. Whether the actor foresaw, intended, or had nonmalevolent reasons would be irrelevant from this perceiver's perspective. At the other extreme may be the perceiver who believes the relevant ought to be "one ought not to intentionally cause harm, unless harm is a necessary means to achieve a more valuable ought." Accordingly, only malevolently intended harm would lead to extreme judgments of blame, and accidental, foreseeable, and nonmalevolently intended harm would not receive high judgments of blame.

Of course, adopting Fishbein and Ajzen's (1973) suggestion raises the question of what factors affect the ought standard adopted by the perceiver in evaluating another's moral culpability for harmful behavior. Some general guidelines are offered in this respect. First, the perceiver's characteristic level of moral reasoning may be influential. The sophistication of this reasoning will be related to the perceiver's age, intelligence, socioeconomic status, and personality characteristics (e.g., reflection–impulsivity, cognitive complexity, authoritarianism). Second, the perceiver's degree of involvement in the situation is also likely to have an effect on the ought standard adopted by the perceiver. A perceiver who is an actual or potential victim of the harm may be more likely than an uninvolved observer to adopt a lower causal responsibility criterion. Thus, accidental causal responsibility alone may be sufficient to produce negative evaluation by a victim. The same perceiver asked to take the perspective of an uninvolved observer may adopt a more stringent ought standard, such as that embodied by foreseeability or intentionality. However, even observers who are uninvolved as actual or potential victims of harm may adopt differing ought standards depending on, for example, their relation to the actor or actual victim(s). If a loved one is the actor (victim), the observer may adopt spontaneously a higher (lower) causal responsibility criterion. If the actor (victim) is someone the observer dislikes, a lower (higher) causal responsibility criterion may be adopted. Similar derivations can be made even in cases where the perceiver is personally unfamiliar with the actor and/or the victim based, for example, on their group membership or status. For example, a white perceiver (especially the victim) may adopt a lower causal responsibility criterion if the actor is black rather than white. In this respect, any factor that plays on prejudice or ingroup and outgroup animosities can raise or lower the causal responsibility criterion employed by the perceiver. The extent to which any of these factors modifies the causal responsibility criterion likely depends, however, on the perceiver's expectations of being criticized or punished for being overly lenient or overly harsh.

The characteristics mentioned thus far have ignored how factors in the situation (such as the seriousness of the observed harm) affect the adopted causal responsibility criterion. Generally speaking, we would suggest that any factor raising rather than lowering the perceiver's level of arousal, enhancing a negative mood, and reducing empathy for the actor but enhancing empathy with the victim would lower the adopted responsibility criterion (Ross & DiTecco, 1975). The observer may more harshly evaluate the actor and may require less information about causal responsibility to the extent that his or her affective set prior to or after observing harm is negative rather than positive.

Incorporating these notions helps us disambiguate the findings that (a) non-malevolently intended actions are sometimes blamed as little as accidental actions (e.g., Ferguson & Rule, 1980) and (b) foreseeable actions are sometimes blamed more than nonmalevolently intended actions (Harvey & Rule, 1978). These results are not at all surprising from the perspective that blame judgments should not be viewed as isomorphic with degrees of personal causality. Rather, blame judgments should be viewed as reflecting the perceived discrepancy between what the perceiver believes ought to have happened and the perceiver's assessment of what actually happened (as reflected in his or her causal responsibility assignment).

We suggest that these results also occur because actions classified as non-malevolently intentional sometimes will and sometimes will not be seen as justified. While the process of causal responsibility assignment facilitates the detection of nonmalevolent intent, a further discrimination is made regarding the justification of the actor's nonmalevolently intended behavior when evaluating blameworthiness. Whether the perceiver accepts nonharmful or altruistic motives as justifying intentional harm may depend on three considerations. First, the perceiver must agree that these nonharmful or altruistic concerns fulfilled an equally more valued ought than that violated by producing harm. Second, the perceiver must agree that harm was a necessary means to achieve the desired nonharmful outcome—that is, that less harmful or nonharmful alternative means to achieve the nonharmful goal were not available in the situation. Third, the perceiver must agree that the negative consequences of harm were not too great to question the ends justifying the means.

Thus, even a harmful act committed for presumably nonmalevolent reasons may be viewed as justified or unjustified depending on (a) whether the ought or norm sacrificed by producing harm (e.g., respect for another's welfare) is coupled with an equally or more valued ought; (b) whether there were no other means of achieving the nonharmful goal; and (c) whether the harmful outcome is perceived as so extreme as to override the positive consequences embodied by the nonharmful motive. For example, we consider provoked retaliation to be nonmalevolently intended aggression and to be justified (see Tedeschi, Smith, & Brown, 1974). We do not consider it to be malevolently intended, because provoked retaliation is not simply an end in itself or a means to another harmful end. Rather, it is an expression of "an eye for an eye" or a callous "do unto others as you would have them do unto you" norm. However, some observers may disagree with us, perceiving instead that "one ought to forgive others who trespass against us." A perceiver adopting this perspective would view provoked retaliation as unjustified and may blame the retaliator to the same extent as he or she would blame an actor who malevolently intended harm. We, on the other hand, would blame the retaliator to the same extent as we would blame someone who accidentally produced harm. We might change our minds on this, however, if we could detect other nonharmful means of positive goal achievement or if the harmful consequences were perceived as too extreme.

Moreover, whether the end in question is seen as justifying the harmful means will depend on questions of (a) the nature of the end (e.g., defense of one's own or another's life, defense of property, punishment for poor performance) relative to (b) the nature of the means used to achieve this end (e.g., killing, maiming, hitting, restraining, yelling). For example, any of these means (including killing) may be seen as quite justified in cases of self- or other-defense. On the other hand, killing someone for poor performance will be seen as quite unjustified; in this case, yelling might be perceived as a more acceptable means.

As another example, consider the perpetrator whose action is classified as foreseeably ruthless compared with the retaliator who was provoked. These two events differ in a variety of ways, but to us the ruthless perpetrator manifests more stable moral weakness than the provoked retaliator. Hence, we would expect the former to be blamed more than the latter both by us and our more seminarian observers. This last example highlights the idea that Heider's continuum when viewed as reflecting an ought hierarchy is best viewed in terms of at least two dimensions—intentionality–nonintentionality and what we call personal avoidability–personal unavoidability. By the latter, we mean the perception that some stable characteristic of the actor (e.g., high versus low ability, or high versus low moral weakness) and/or stable characteristic of the situation (e.g., its ought requirements) should have or should not have limited the actor's ability to avoid the outcome (Hamilton, 1978). For example, someone who has broken a law because he or she was ignorant of the law is held responsible nevertheless, since the behavior was considered avoidable.

Apart from the studies mentioned that bear on the analysis, the detailed conjectures that we have offered have not been examined empirically. Nonetheless, there are some studies that bear on some of the assertions presented in this section. These studies have provided some comparisons among conditions presumed to yield causal assignment according to the components that we have specified, and they have examined the impact of these conditions on one or two of the several measures that we consider important. The studies are reviewed to illustrate at least rudimentary support for our model.

Blame

A substantial body of literature demonstrates that attribution of responsibility is differentiated for actions that are clearly accidental compared to those that are foreseeable. Specifically, actors are held less responsible (i.e., are seen as less blameworthy) for accidental relative to foreseeable negative consequences. This result occurs in studies where information about the situation provided a direct indication of the foreseeability of the outcome. For example, Whitehead and Smith (1976) directly manipulated an actor's expectancy of a negative outcome. They found that the actor was viewed as more responsible, more blameworthy, and more able to foresee the consequences of his actions as the expectancy of the negative outcome increased and the actor was aware of this (see also Wortman & Linder, 1973). Similar results have been obtained (although statistical tests are not reported in some studies) when the foreseeable versus accidental nature of the outcome had to be inferred by the observer (e.g., Aderman, Archer, & Harris, 1975; Schroeder & Linder, 1976; Shaw & Reitan, 1969; Shaw & Schneider, 1969; Shaw & Sulzer, 1964).

Moreover, the effects of the mild versus serious nature of the outcome on responsibility attributions is restricted to outcomes in which some element of control is present rather than absent. Specifically, uninvolved observers or actual victims of negative outcomes blame perpetrators more for severe relative to mild outcomes particularly if the actor could have avoided the harmful outcome by being more careful (e.g., Lowe & Medway, 1976; Phares & Wilson, 1972; Walster, 1966; Wortman & Linder, 1973). If the element of foreseeability is lacking or is ambiguous, the highly controversial severity-dependent responsibility attribution effect does not occur (cf. Schroeder & Linder, 1976; Shaver, 1970a,b). That is, responsibility attributions are not greater for severe relative to mild outcomes (e.g., Phares & Wilson, 1972; Walster, 1967; Shaver, 1970a,b). Moreover, foreseeable harm is sometimes blamed less than clearly malevolently intended harm (e.g., Ferguson & Rule, 1980; Fincham & Jaspars, 1979; Harris, 1977; Shaw & Iwawaki, 1972; Shaw & Reitan, 1969; Shaw & Sulzer, 1964), except in some studies examining personality differences in responsibility attribution (e.g., Shaw & Schneider, 1969; Sulzer & Burglass, 1968).

The research on responsibility clearly shows that malevolently intended outcomes are most negatively evaluated. Studies with young children and adolescents (e.g., Ferguson & Rule, 1980; Fincham & Jaspars, 1979; Harris, 1977; Shaw & Sulzer, 1964) and young adults (reviewed by Rule & Nesdale, 1976) have revealed that malevolently intended negative events yield the highest judgments of wrongness, blameworthiness, and punishment. On the other hand, intentionally harmful acts perpetrated as a means to produce an otherwise helpful outcome are viewed as right and not deserving of blame or punishment (e.g., Pepitone & Sherberg, 1957). For example, uninvolved observers rated other people as less good when they delivered high shocks to a person who had behaved passively rather than aggressively (Stapleton, Joseph, & Tedeschi, in press). In another study, participants who read descriptions of a man who hit another man in order to (a) return a wallet to its rightful owner or (b) keep it for himself rated the former as less reprehensible than the latter (Rule et al. 1975). Brown and Tedeschi (1976) presented situations in which one man threatened or attempted to strike another man in a barroom. The defensive man intentionally used counterforce by striking the instigator in the stomach. Although the instigator was considered very aggressive, the defensive man, who both intended and actually harmed the instigator, was not judged as aggressive. Along similar lines, Carpenter and Darley (1978) found that observers rated a fight as morally illegitimate when they saw only the fight; but not when they saw it in response to provocation (see also Harvey & Enzle, 1978).

Finally, some studies provide comparisons between accidental and nonmalevolently intended events. Although there is one exception (Fincham & Jaspars, 1979), this research indicates that nonmalevolently intended and accidental events are similarly rated in terms of responsibility (e.g., Ferguson & Rule, 1980; Harris, 1977; Shaw & Iwawaki, 1972; Shaw & Reitan, 1969; Shaw & Sulzer, 1969; Sulzer & Burglass, 1968). However, Shaw and Reitan (1969) found this result only for mildly but not seriously negative outcomes.

Unfortunately, the lack of differentiation in these studies may not reflect perceivers' beliefs that nonmalevolently intended harm is as blameless as accidental harm. In several of these studies, it was unclear whether the actor actually intended the harm necessary to achieve the altruistic or nonharmful goal. Scenarios supposedly depicting nonmalevolently intended harm may have been functionally equivalent to scenarios depicting accidental harm in terms of the actors' perceived causal responsibility. Nevertheless, assuming that such a lack of differentiation is reliable, it may be construed as support for our position that Heider's levels are best viewed in terms of their joint values on the intent, avoidability, and motive acceptability dimensions. Failure to differentiate among types of causal responsibility may then reflect differential weighing of the three dimensions. In this case, subjects may have been weighing avoidability more than intent or motive.

In summary, malevolently intentional acts are evaluated the most negatively and accidental acts the least negatively. Although in some cases, the accidental, foreseeable, and nonmalevolently intended acts are not differentiated (e.g., Shaw & Schneider, 1969), the accidental and nonmalevolently intended are most reliably not differentiated. However, because the stimulus stories vary unsystematically on the oughts or norms and avoidability, it is not possible to ascertain the contributions of these components to the results. Further studies must isolate and compare the impact of the various components on causal assignment and blame.

Anger and Aggression

Because very little research has examined the effects of different bases of causal assignment on anger and aggression, we cannot make systematic comparisons across the various conditions. Nonetheless, some research bears on some aspects of our assumptions.

Averill (1979) asked people to think about a recent incident that made them feel very angry. Of the four categories made available to participants, incidents arousing anger were associated 7.5% with accidental harm, 30% with potentially avoidable harm (reflecting negligence, carelessness, or lack of foresight), 50% with voluntary (the instigator was fully aware of the consequences of action) and unjustified (the instigator had no right to perpetrate the action) harm, and 12.5% with a voluntary and justified act. Anger and the desire to retaliate thus seems most closely associated with instigations that can be attributed to factors that are potentially avoidable and unjustified.

While Averill's data suggest that affective reactions differ according to the causal basis of harm, an important question is whether distinctions among events that may be differentially causally classified are dampened by the arousal engendered by the actual receipt of harm. Several studies provide comparisons among some of the relevant conditions. For example, some data show that malevolently intended harm most facilitates anger and aggression. When people receive information that another person deliberately intended harm, they become angrier than if the other person did not intend harm but could have foreseen the harmful consequence, and they retaliate by increasing aversive stimulation to their partner (Epstein & Taylor, 1967; Greenwell & Dengerink, 1973; Nickel, 1974).

Although perceived intent was not measured in this research, several studies have documented the role of justification on aggression. Arbitrary thwarting (operationalized as illegitimate or unexpected) yields more anger and/or aggression than does nonarbitrary thwarting (Burnstein & Worchel, 1962; Cohen, 1955; Fishman, 1965; Kregarman & Worchel, 1961; Kulik & Brown, 1979; Pastore, 1952; Rothaus, & Worchel, 1960; Rule, Dyck, & Nesdale, 1978). For example, Kulik and Brown (1979) examined aggressive behavior that occurred naturally in response to frustration induced by lack of success in persuading a confederate to donate money to charity. Intended and inadequately justified thwarting increased attributions of blame, anger, and aggression compared to intentional but adequately justified thwarting.

Dyck and Rule (1978) conducted two experiments designed to examine the impact of attributionally relevant information on anger and aggression. In these two experiments, men were defeated on either 17%, 50%, or 83% of the trials in a reaction-time contest, received aversive noise from their partners, and were ostensibly permitted to retaliate by delivering shocks to their partners. In the first study, the noise level was described as typical of most people (high consensus) or atypical of most other people (low consensus); in Study 2 it was described as coming from a partner who knew or did not know the kind and level of noise controlled by the levers that he pushed. When the actor did not know the harmful consequences of his behavior or when there was high consensus, the other attributionally relevant information (defeat level, which indirectly manipulated the partner's nonmalevolent or malevolent motives for delivering noise) had minimal effects on the subjects' responses. When the actor knew the consequences of his lever presses or when there was low consensus for his behavior, more anger and retaliation occurred when he was defeated on 50% rather than on 17% or 83% of the trials. Although the impact of the combined awareness and consensus with defeat conditions was not significant on each of the attribution items, a consistent pattern of results emerged. The perceived intent to help by delivering noise was greater when the actor had been defeated on 50% or 83% of trials. Harm was also viewed as least justified in the 50% than in the other two defeat conditions. These results show that intended attack instigates anger and aggression more than does unintended (in this case, accidental) aggression (see also Nickel, 1974) and that justification for intended attack also mitigates anger and retaliation.

Very little research has specifically examined how different types of causality concomitantly influence anger, blame, and aggression. Consequently, it is difficult to specify with confidence that the relations we have identified have been supported. Nevertheless, it can be seen that the results of two independent lines of research (i.e., that concerned with responsibility attribution and that concerned with anger and aggression) converge on the idea that anger, aggression, and blame are at least in part a function of the perceived is–ought discrepancy. At the same time, it is important for future research to assess these relations in at least two different ways. First, we should ascertain whether information directly available in the situation (e.g., outcome severity, consensus, choice, control) reliably affects causal classification, blame, anger, and retaliation as we have suggested. Second, the boundary conditions on the relation among blame, anger, and aggression must be addressed. It has been suggested (Lowe, Note 3) that the same transgression (e.g., a malevolently intended one) may lead to the same degree of blame but less anger and retaliation for a loved one than for someone we dislike. Such an effect may occur, but we suspect that the harmful event may be classified differently according to the relationship between the recipient and the aggressor. People might discount malevolent intent by a loved one but accept the malevolent intent of a disliked person, thereby leading to less blame, anger, and retaliation for the loved one. Conjectures such as these and their theoretical underpinnings need empirical validation.

DIRECTIONS FOR FUTURE RESEARCH

Although each of our assertions require investigation, general issues related to our analysis bear scrutiny. Two types of studies are needed with regard to the model per se. First, it is important to examine which of the three components (intentionality, avoidability, and motive) of responsibility accounts for the greatest percentage of variance in ascriptions of blame. In so doing, we must ensure that the same harmful incident is being evaluated and does not differ in the perceived ought requirement. This requires holding constant some of the factors that presumably affect causal assignment. Second, it is important to verify our conjectures about the factors affecting causal assignment and blame. Moreover, we should assess whether the criteria for causal assignment or blame differ depending on the relation between the recipient and actor, as well as the age, sex, and personality characteristics of the recipient.

Third, we question whether causal assignment and blame differentially affect either instigation or the willingness to express aggression. Implicit in our analysis is the assumption that anger is differentially instigated by attributionally relevant considerations in relation to the perceived oughtness requirements. Consistent with this, Rule et al. (1978) found that mitigating circumstance information affected instigation but not inhibition of aggression. Yet, there may be occasions when apparently justifiable or accidental harm elicits as much anger as does malevolently intended harm. One might find, however, less retaliation in the former than in the latter case because of the recipient's knowledge that hostile retaliation would be viewed as inappropriate in this case (Zillmann, 1978). Despite several attempts to determine whether nonarbitrary versus arbitrary frustration affects instigation or inhibition, a satisfactory resolution of the question has apparently not been achieved. When the evidence is considered, it is clear that attributionally relevant information does differentially arouse anger, which is in turn reflected in different degrees of retaliation. At the same time, it is also clear that recipients evaluate the appropriateness of their own harmful behavior in the same way (if only more conservatively) as they evaluate the initial provocation, which is reflected in somewhat less retaliation under public rather than private conditions. It is interesting to question whether provocation associated with certain types of causal responsibility might actually elicit more anger and retaliation in public compared to private conditions. There are several instances in which this might occur, such as when the initial provocation causes the actor to lose face in the eyes of his or her reference group (Goffman, 1959).

Whether attributionally relevant information arouses or reduces anger and retaliation as a function of when it is available should also be further investigated. The studies reviewed thus far have presented attributionally relevant information before the harm-producing event and have found the expected increase or decrease in anger and retaliation according to the available attributionally relevant information. As noted earlier, however, the arousal engendered by harm itself or other arousing stimuli may reduce a perceiver's use of attributionally relevant information in much the same way that negative mood inductions facilitate memory for affectively negative stimuli but inhibit memory for affectively positive stimuli (Bower, 1981). A study by Zillmann and Cantor (1976) bears on this point. In their study, physiological measures indicated lower arousal in subjects who received information mitigating an experimenter's insulting behavior either before or after the insult compared to subjects who never received mitigating circumstance information. This result indicates that the anger-arousing or -reducing potential of attributionally relevant information is independent of the time at which it is presented. Surprisingly, however, evaluative measures of retaliation revealed high retaliation in both the group that received no mitigating information and the group that received mitigating information after the insult compared to the group that received mitigating circumstance information before the insult. This result, indicating that retaliation is not simply a function of arousal, also shows that the relations we have described may obtain only if attributionally relevant information is available prior to or concurrent with provocation.

Despite the equivocal nature of these results, they demonstrate several possibilities relevant to our analysis that warrant further investigation. First, they indicate how the availability of attributionally relevant information before or after provocation may differentially set the perceiver to interpret the actor's behavior. In the Zillmann and Cantor study, for example, the mitigating circumstance information may have actually been perceived differently by "before" and "after" subjects. "Being upset about an upcoming exam" could have been perceived by subjects receiving information before insult as the cause of the actor's insulting behavior; he was simply so uptight that he could not control himself. The same statement could have been perceived as an excuse by subjects receiving information after insult. They may have assumed that the experimenter realized only later that he had behaved inappropriately and was trying to make up for it through another person. While each perception may reduce arousal, they may make differentially salient to subjects the inappropriateness of this type of conduct by a presumed responsible experimenter. This was subsequently reflected in the poorer recommendations given by "after" subjects regarding rehiring the experimenter.

Second, the results also indicate the need to examine the impact of attributionally relevant information over more extended periods of time. Assuming that subjects receiving information before and after insult actually encoded information about the experimenter's behavior differently, we would expect such differences in encoding to have an effect on interpretations of the hostile experimenter's subsequent behavior. Subjects receiving information after rather than before the attack may subsequently access negative information about the experimenter more easily, which in turn may influence their use or interpretation of attributionally relevant information regarding subsequent negative or positive behavior. This point emphasizes the need for future research to examine the effects of set or prior impressions (such as those embodied by target-based or category-based expectancies) on the storage, retrieval, and use of attributionally relevant information in an aggressive exchange.

Another possibility is that because of our prior experience in similar situations, the availability of a script (Langer, 1978; Schank & Abelson, 1977) induces anger even in the absence of obvious attributionally relevant information. Being banged by a shopping cart in the grocery may automatically elicit anger. We assume that such careless behavior can be avoided, and anger is elicited by a short-circuiting of the attributional information processing. While the subsequent provision of causally relevant information might reduce or exacerbate the anger, it must be recognized of course that, at high levels of excitation, attributionally relevant information may not be processed. For example, Zillmann and Cantor (1976) have shown that mitigating circumstance information affects anger only when the person is moderately but not highly aroused.

The temporal stability of the effects of causal assignment and blame on our later reactions to the harm doer must be examined. Previous attributional analyses of aggression have been restricted to one moment in time. The effects causal assignment and blame have on our impressions of the harm doer may have long-term repercussions, biasing memory and hence later interpretations of that person's behavior.

Finally, the recipient of harm and the observer may be able to, but may not, process information about the actor's behavior in the same way. The impact of the actor's behavior on the observer may vary according to the observer's involvement. For example, whether the perceiver is involved as the recipient or observer of harm undoubtedly affects the extent to which the perceiver is physiologically aroused by harmful behavior. This, in turn, may limit the perceiver's capacity or willingness to attend to all the potentially available information (Easterbrook, 1959). Consequently, it is important to verify results obtained from uninvolved observers in studies including both involved and uninvolved observers.

ACKNOWLEDGMENTS

The authors wish to thank Michael Enzle, Charles Lowe, Julie Grenier, Michael Katzko and Andrew Nesdale for helpful and significant comments on an earlier version.

REFERENCE NOTES

1. Lowe, C. A., & McConnell, H. K. Intent, dispositional attribution, and correspondent inferences. Paper presented at American Psychological Association, San Francisco, Calif. 1977.
2. Horai, J., & O'Rourke, A. You should have known better than to do that: Attributed IQ and the evaluation of children's transgressions. Paper presented at the meeting of the Eastern Psychological Association, New York, April 1975.
3. Lowe, C. Personal communication, December 1980.

REFERENCES

Aderman, D., Archer, R. L., & Harris, J. L. Effect of emotional empathy on attribution of responsibility. *Journal of Personality*, 1975, *43*, 156–167.
Ajzen, I. Attribution of dispositions to an actor: Effects of perceived decision freedom and behavioral utilities. *Journal of Personality and Social Psychology*, 1971, *18*, 144–156.

Arkkelin, D., Oakley, T., & Mynatt, C. Effects of controllable versus uncontrollable factors on responsibility attributions: A single-subject approach. *Journal of Personality and Social Psychology*, 1979, *37*, 110–115.

Averill, J. R. Anger. In H. Howe & R. Dienstbier (Eds.), *Nebraska symposium on motivation*, 1978, Lincoln: Univ. of Nebraska Press, 1979.

Bandura, A. *Aggression: A social learning analysis.* Englewood Cliffs, N.J.: Prentice-Hall, 1973.

Baron, R. A. *Human aggression.* New York: Plenum, 1977.

Bell, L. G., Wicklund, R. A., Manko, G., & Larkin, C. When unexpected behavior is attributed to the environment. *Journal of Research in Personality*, 1976, *10*, 316–327.

Berkowitz, L. *Aggression: A social psychological analysis.* New York: McGraw-Hill, 1962.

Berscheid, E., Graziano, W., Monson, T., & Dermer, M. Outcome dependency: Attention, attribution, and attraction. *Journal of Personality and Social Psychology*, 1976, *34*, 978–989.

Bower, G. H. Mood and memory. *American Psychologist*, 1981, *36*, 129–148.

Brewer, M. B. An information-processing approach to attribution of responsibility. *Journal of Experimental Social Psychology*, 1977, *13*, 58–69.

Brickman, P., Ryan, K., & Wortman, C. B. Causal chains: Attribution of responsibility as a function of immediate and prior causes. *Journal of Personality and Social Psychology*, 1975, *32*, 1060–1067.

Brown, R. C., Jr., & Tedeschi, J. T. Determinants of perceived aggression. *Journal of Social Psychology*. 1976, *100*, 77–87.

Burnstein, E., & Worchel, P. Arbitrariness of frustration and its consequences for aggression in a social situation. *Journal of Personality*, 1962, *30*, 528–540.

Buss, A. H. Aggression pays. In J. L. Singer (Ed.), *The control of aggression and violence: Cognitive and physiological factors.* New York: Academic Press, 1971.

Byrne, D. *The attraction paradigm.* New York: Academic Press, 1971.

Carpenter, B., & Darley, J. M. A naive psychological analysis of counteraggression. *Personality and Social Psychology Bulletin*, 1978, *4*, 68–72.

Chaikin, A. L., & Cooper, J. Evaluation as a function of correspondence and hedonic relevance. *Journal of Experimental Social Psychology*, 1973, *9*, 257–264.

Chaikin, A. L., & Darley, J. M. Victim or perpetrator?: Defensive attribution of responsibility and the need for order and justice. *Journal of Personality and Social Psychology*, 1973, *25*, 268–275.

Cohen, A. R. Social norms, arbitrariness of frustration, and status of the agent of frustration in the frustration–aggression hypothesis. *Journal of Abnormal and Social Psychology*, 1955, *51*, 222–226.

Dion, K. K. Physical attractiveness and evaluation of children's transgressions. *Journal of Personality and Social Psychology*, 1972, *24*, 207–213.

Duncan, B. L. Differential social perception and attribution of intergroup violence: Testing the lower limits of stereotyping of blacks. *Journal of Personality and Social Psychology*, 1976, *34*, 590–598.

Dyck, R. J., & Rule, B. G. Effect on retaliation of causal attributions concerning attack. *Journal of Personality and Social Psychology*, 1978, *36*, 521–529.

Easterbrook, J. A. The effect of emotion on cue utilization and the organization of behavior. *Psychological Review*, 1959, *66*, 183–201.

Enzle, M. E., Harvey, M. D., & Wright, E. F. Personalism and distinctiveness. *Journal of Personality and Social Psychology*, 1980, *39*, 542–552.

Epstein, S., & Taylor, S. P. Instigation to aggression as a function of degree of defeat and perceived aggressive intent of the opponent. *Journal of Personality*, 1967, *35*, 265–289.

Ferguson, T. J., & Rule, B. G. Effects of inferential set, outcome severity, and basis for responsibility on children's evaluations of aggressive acts. *Developmental Psychology*, 1980, *16*, 141–146.

Feshbach, S. The function of aggression and the regulation of aggressive drive. *Psychological*

Review, 1964, *71*, 257–272.

Fincham, F., & Jaspars, J. Attribution of responsibility to the self and other in children and adults. *Journal of Personality and Social Psychology*, 1979, *37*, 1589–1602.

Fishbein, M., & Ajzen, I. Attribution of responsibility: A theoretical note. *Journal of Experimental Social Psychology*, 1973, *9*, 148–153.

Fishman, C. G. Need for approval and the expression of aggression under varying conditions of frustration. *Journal of Personality and Social Psychology*, 1965, *2*, 809–816.

Freud, S. Instincts and their viscissitudes. In J. Riviere (sup.), *Collected papers of Sigmund Freud* (Vol. 4). London: Hogarth Press, 1925.

Frieze, I. H. The role of information processing in making causal attributions for success and failure. In J. S. Carroll & J. W. Payne (Eds.), *Cognition and social behavior*. Hillsdale, N.J.: Erlbaum, 1976.

Gentry, W. D. Effects of frustration, attack, and prior aggressive training on overt aggression and vascular processes. *Journal of Personality and Social Psychology*, 1970, *16*, 718–725.

Gergen, K. J., & Jones, E. E. Mental illness, predictability, and affective consequences as stimulus factors in person perception. *Journal of Abnormal and Social Psychology*, 1963, *67*, 95–104.

Goffman, E. *The presentation of self in everyday life*. Garden City, N.Y.: Doubleday, 1959.

Greenwell, J., & Dengerink, H. A. The role of perceived versus actual attack in human physical aggression. *Journal of Personality and Social Psychology*, 1973, *26*, 66–71.

Hamilton, V. L. Obedience and responsibility: A jury simulation. *Journal of Personality and Social Psychology*, 1978, *36*, 126–146.

Harris, B. Developmental differences in the attribution of responsibility. *Developmental Psychology*, 1977, *13*, 257–265.

Harvey, M. D., & Enzle, M. E. Effects of retaliation latency and provocation level on judged blameworthiness for retaliatory aggression. *Personality and Social Psychology Bulletin*, 1978, *4*, 579–582.

Harvey, M. D., & Rule, B. G. Moral evaluations and judgments of responsibility. *Personality and Social Psychology Bulletin*, 1978, *4*, 583–588.

Heider, F. *The psychology of interpersonal relations*. New York: Wiley, 1958.

Hill, F. A. Attribution of responsibility in a campus stabbing incident. *Social Behavior and Personality*, 1975, *3*, 127–131.

Hollingworth, H. L. *Psychology and ethics: A study of the sense of obligation*. New York: Ronald Press, 1949.

Horai, J. Attributional conflict, *Journal of Social Issues*, 1977, *33*, 88–100.

Jones, E. E., & Davis, K. E. From acts to dispositions: The attribution process in person perception. In L. Berkowitz (Ed.), *Advances in experimental social psychology* (Vol. 2). New York: Academic Press, 1965.

Jones, E. E., Hester, S. L., Farina, A., & Davis, K. E. Reactions to unfavorable personal evaluations as a function of the evaluator's perceived adjustment. *Journal of Abnormal and Social Psychology*, 1959, *59*, 363–370.

Jones, E. E., & McGillis, D. Correspondent inferences and the attribution cube: A comparative reappraisal. In J. H. Harvey, W. J. Ickes, & R. F. Kidd (Eds.), *New directions in attribution research* (Vol. 1). Hillsdale, N.J.: Erlbaum, 1976.

Joseph, J. M., Kane, T. R., Gaes, G. G., & Tedeschi, J. T. Effects of effort on attributed intent and perceived aggressiveness. *Perceptual and Motor Skills*, 1976, *42*, 706.

Kelley, H. H. Moral evaluation. *American Psychologist*, 1971, *26*, 293–300.

Kelley, H. H. *Causal schemata and the attribution process*. Morristown, N.J.: General Learning Press, 1972.

Konečni, V. J. Annoyance, type and duration of postannoyance activity, and aggression: The "Cathartic Effect." *Journal of Experimental Psychology: General*, 1975, *104*, 76–102.

Kregarman, J. J., & Worchel, P. Arbitrariness of frustration and aggression. *Journal of Abnormal and Social Psychology*, 1961, *63*, 183–187.

Kulik, J. A., & Brown, R. Frustration, attribution of blame, and aggression. *Journal of Experimental Social Psychology,* 1979, *15,* 183–194.

Landy, D., & Aronson, E. The influence of the character of the criminal and his victim on the decisions of simulated jurors. *Journal of Experimental Social Psychology,* 1969, *5,* 141–152.

Langer, E. J. Rethinking the role of thought in social interaction. In J. Harvey, W. J. Ickes, & R. F. Kidd (Eds.), *New directions in attribution research* (Vol. 2). Hillsdale, N.J.: Erlbaum, 1978.

Lerner, R. M. The development of stereotyped expectancies of body build–behavior relations. *Child Development,* 1969, *40,* 137–141.

Lerner, R. M., & Korn, S. J. The development of body build stereotypes in males. *Child Development,* 1972, *43,* 908–920.

Lowe, C. A., & Medway, F. J. Effects of valence, severity, and relevance on responsibility and dispositional attribution. *Journal of Personality,* 1976, *44,* 518–538.

McDavid, J. W., & Harari, H. Stereotyping of names and popularity in grade–school children. *Child Development,* 1966, *37,* 453–459.

McKillip, J., & Posavac, E. J. Attribution of responsibility for an accident: Effects of similarity to the victim and severity of consequences. *Proceedings 80th Annual Convention, American Psychological Association,* 1972.

McKillip, J., & Posavac, E. J. Judgments of responsibility for an accident. *Journal of Personality,* 1975, *43,* 248–265.

Milgram, S. Liberating effects of group pressure. *Journal of Personality and Social Psychology,* 1965, *1,* 127–134.

Miller, D. T., Norman. S. A., & Wright, E. Distortion in person perception as a consequence of the need for effective control. *Journal of Personality and Social Psychology,* 1978, *36,* 598–607.

Nelson, S. A. Factors influencing young children's use of motives and outcomes as moral criteria. *Child Development,* 1980, *51,* 823–829.

Nesdale, A. R., & Rule, B. G. The effects of an aggressor's characteristics and an observer's accountability on judgments of aggression. *Canadian Journal of Behavioral Science,* 1974, *6,* 342–350.

Nesdale, A. R., Rule, B. G., & Hill, K. A. The effect of attraction on causal attributions and retaliation. *Personality and Social Psychology Bulletin,* 1978, *4,* 231–234.

Nesdale, A. R., Rule, B. G., & McAra, M. Moral judgments of aggression: Personal and situational determinants. *European Journal of Social Psychology,* 1975, *5,* 339–349.

Newtson, D. Dispositional inference from effects of actions: Effects chosen and effects forgone. *Journal of Experimental Social Psychology,* 1974, *10,* 489–496.

Nickel, T. W. The attribution of intention as a critical factor in the relation between frustration and aggression. *Journal of Personality,* 1974, *42,* 482–492.

Pastore, N. The role of arbitrariness in the frustration–aggression hypothesis. *Journal of Abnormal and Social Psychology,* 1952, *47,* 728–731.

Pepitone, A. Social psychological perspectives on crime and punishment. *Journal of Social Issues,* 1975, *31,* 197–216.

Pepitone, A., & Sherberg, J. Intentionality, responsibility, and interpersonal attraction. *Journal of Personality,* 1957, *25,* 757–766.

Phares, E. J., & Wilson, K. G. Responsibility attribution: Role of outcome severity, situational ambiguity, and internal–external control. *Journal of Personality,* 1972, *40,* 392–406.

Phares, E. J., & Wilson, K. G. Source and type of wives' problems as related to responsibility attribution, interpersonal attraction and understanding. *Psychological Reports,* 1973, *32,* 923–930.

Rosenfield, D., & Stephan, W. G. When discounting fails: An unexpected finding. *Memory & Cognition,* 1977, *5,* 97–102.

Ross, L. The intuitive psychologist and his shortcomings: Distortions in the attribution process. In L. Berkowitz (Ed.), *Advances in experimental social psychology* (Vol. 10). New York: Academic Press, 1977.

Ross, M., & DiTecco, D. An attribution analysis of moral judgments. *Journal of Social Issues*, 1975, *31*, 91–109.

Rothaus, P., & Worchel, P. The inhibition of aggression under nonarbitrary frustration. *Journal of Personality*, 1960, *28*, 108–117.

Rule, B. G. The hostile and instrumental functions of human aggression. In J. de Wit & W. W. Hartup (Eds.), *Determinants and origins of aggressive behavior*. The Hague: Mouton, 1975.

Rule, B. G., Dyck, R., McAra, M., & Nesdale, A. R. Judgments of aggression serving personal versus prosocial purposes. *Social Behavior and Personality*. 1975, *3*, 55–63.

Rule, B. G., Dyck, R., & Nesdale, A. R. Arbitrariness of frustration: Inhibition or instigation effects on aggression. *European Journal of Social Psychology*, 1978, *8*, 237–244.

Rule, B. G., & Nesdale, A. R. Emotional arousal and aggressive behavior. *Psychological Bulletin*, 1976, *83*, 851–863.

Rybash, J. M., Roodin, P. A., & Hallion, K. The role of affect in children's attribution of intentionality and dispensation of punishment. *Child Development*, 1979, *50*, 1227–1230.

Savitsky, J. C., Czyzewski, D., Dubord, D., & Kaminsky, S. Age and emotion of an offender as determinants of adult punitive reactions. *Journal of Personality*, 1976, *44*, 311–320.

Schank, R. C., & Abelson, R. P. *Scripts, plans, goals and understanding*. Hillsdale, N.J.: Erlbaum, 1977.

Schroeder, D. A., & Linder, D. E. Effects of actor's causal role, outcome severity, and knowledge of prior accidents upon attributions of responsibility. *Journal of Experimental Social Psychology*, 1976, *12*, 340–356.

Scott, M. B., & Lyman, S. M. Accounts. *American Sociological Review*, 1968, *33*, 46–62.

Seligman, C., Paschall, N., & Takata, G. Effects of physical attractiveness on attribution of responsibility. *Canadian Journal of Behavioral Science*, 1974, *6*, 290–296.

Shaver, K. G. Defensive attribution: Effects of severity and relevance on the responsibility assigned for an accident. *Journal of Personality and Social Psychology*, 1970, *14*, 101–113. (a)

Shaver, K. G. Redress and conscientiousness in the attribution of responsibility for accidents. *Journal of Experimental Social Psychology*, 1970, *6*, 100–110. (b)

Shaw, M. E., & Iwawaki, S. Attribution of responsibility by Japanese and Americans as a function of age. *Journal of Cross-Cultural Psychology*, 1972, *3*, 71–81.

Shaw, M. E., & Reitan, H. T. Attribution of responsibility as a basis for sanctioning behaviour. *British Journal of Social and Clinical Psychology*, 1969, *8*, 217–226.

Shaw, M. E., & Schneider, F. W. Negro–white differences in attribution of responsibility as a function of age. *Psychonomic Science*, 1969, *16*, 289–291.

Shaw, M. E., & Sulzer, J. L. An empirical test of Heider's levels in attribution of responsibility. *Journal of Abnormal and Social Psychology*, 1964, *69*, 39–46.

Shepherd, J. W., & Bagley, A. J. The effects of biographical information and order of presentation on the judgment of an aggressive action. *British Journal of Social and Clinical Psychology*, 1970, *9*, 177–179.

Staffieri, J. R. A study of social stereotype of body image in children. *Journal of Personality and Social Psychology*, 1967, *7*, 101–104.

Staffieri, J. R. Body build and behavioral expectancies in young females. *Developmental Psychology*, 1972, *6*, 125–127.

Stapleton, R. E., Joseph, J. H., & Tedeschi, J. T. In the eye of the beholder: When is an actor perceived as aggressive? *Journal of Social Psychology*, in press.

Steele, C. M., & Woods, L. Trait attributions and defense against insult from a dissimilar other. *Journal of Research in Personality*, 1977, *11*, 318–328.

Sulzer, J. L., & Burglass, R. K. Responsibility attribution, empathy, and punitiveness. *Journal of Personality*, 1968, *36*, 272–282.

Tedeschi, J. T., Smith, R. Bob, III., & Brown, R. C., Jr. A reinterpretation of research on aggression. *Psychological Bulletin*, 1974, *81*, 540–562.

Turkat, D., & Dawson, J. Attributions of responsibility for a chance event as a function of sex and physical attractiveness of target individual. *Psychological Reports*, 1976, *39*, 275–279.

Ugwuegbu, D. C., & Hendrick, C. Personal causality and attribution of responsibility. *Social Behavior and Personality,* 1974, *2,* 76–86.

Veitch, R., & Piccione, A. The role of attitude similarity in the attribution process. *Social Psychology Quarterly,* 1978, *41,* 165–169.

Walker, R. N. Body build and behavior in young children: II: Body build and nursery school teacher's ratings. *Monographs of the Society for Research in Child Development,* 1962, *27,* (3, Serial No. 84).

Walster, E. Assignment of responsibility for an accident. *Journal of Personality and Social Psychology,* 1966, *3,* 73–79.

Walster, E. "Second guessing" important events. *Human Relations,* 1967, *20,* 239–250.

Whitehead, I., III, & Smith, S. H. The effect of expectancy on the assignment of responsibility for a misfortune. *Journal of Personality,* 1976, *44,* 69–83.

Wortman, C. B., & Linder, D. E. Attribution of responsibility for an outcome as a function of its likelihood. *Proceedings, 81st Annual Convention, American Psychological ASsociation,* 1973.

Zillmann, D. Attribution and misattribution of excitatory reactions. In J. H. Harvey, W. J. Ickes, & R. F. Kidd (Eds.), *New directions in attribution research* (Vol. 2). Hillsdale, N.J.: Erlbaum, 1978.

Zillmann, D., & Cantor, J. R. Effect of timing of information about mitigating circumstances on emotional responses to provocation and retaliatory behavior. *Journal of Experimental Social Psychology,* 1976, *12,* 38–55.

three

Arousal and Aggression

DOLF ZILLMANN

In this chapter, the emergence of the arousal concept in the study of aggressive behavior is traced and the various ways in which arousal has been conceptualized and operationalized are delineated. The conditions under which arousal facilitates aggressive behavior are discussed, and special attention is given to the interdependencies between cognitive and excitatory processes. The influence that cognitive processes can exert in the evocation and the dissipation of arousal reactions is explored, and the involvement of these processes in the guidance of behavior associated with heightened arousal is investigated. The implications of the loss of cognitive control are considered, and the special role that arousal plays in impulsive aggressive reactions is discussed. Finally, some avenues for future research on the arousal–aggression relationship are indicated.

AROUSAL IN CONCEPTUAL AND OPERATIONAL TERMS

The arousal concept, as it is commonly employed in contemporary research on human aggression (cf. Rule & Nesdale, 1976), has essentially two precursors: the construct of drive and the construct of activation. In order to discuss the relationship between the various concepts, the constructs of drive and activation are briefly introduced.

AGGRESSION
Volume 1

Appetitive Drive and Aggression

Drive has characteristically been conceived of as a noninstinctive motivational force that is induced by depriving the organism of life-supporting
entities or conditions, and that grows in strength with the severity of such
deprivation. This force impels the organism to act toward the termination or, at
least, a reduction of the acute deprivation (cf. Cofer & Appley, 1964). Drive,
then, has been viewed as having appetitive properties.

The construct of appetitive drive translates into a model of specific aggressive drive as follows: Aversive stimulation produces a drive state; this drive
state compels the organism to aggressive action; and the drive state is diminished or terminated after the execution of such consummatory action. According to the model, annoyance always leads to aggression. Drive, once activated, is sustained until a consummatory reaction is performed, and the
consummatory response is necessarily aggressive. This specific-drive model of
aggression has been widely accepted in the form of the original frustration–aggression hypothesis (Dollard, Doob, Miller, Mowrer, & Sears, 1939).
More recently, similar forms of such a model have been espoused by
Berkowitz (1965) and by Feshbach (1970); both investigators have insisted that
aggressive inclinations tend to persist until they find expression in consummatory, aggressive responses. Drive is an entirely hypothetical entity in these
views; bodily manifestations of the presumed persistence of drive have been
neither observed nor suggested.

It was mainly the realization that experiences of annoyance do not necessarily foster aggressive reactions that prompted criticism, modifications, and
eventually the abandonment of models based on the concept of appetitive
drive (e.g., Miller, 1941). With the possible exception of predatory aggression
(cf. Zillmann, 1979), the mechanics of aggressive behavior apparently differ
sharply from those that govern behavior controlled by deprivation. As a result,
the appetitive-drive model, no matter how well it might explain deprivation-
based behaviors, seems more misleading than useful when applied to human
aggression (cf. Bandura, 1973).

Generalized, Diffuse Drive and Aggression

The reasoning on aggressive drive was greatly influenced and altered by
conceptualizations developed in behavior theory. Hull (1943, 1952) had proposed a generalized drive—that is, a nonspecific, undifferentiated drive state
that integrates components of drive from potentially many related or independent sources. The strengths of simultaneously active drives were viewed as
combining into one effective drive state, and the accumulated force of this state
was expected to energize the behavior that, at the time, was prepotent in the

habit structure. Thus, dependent on the prevailing stimulus conditions controlling habit, elements of drive X could be expected to facilitate behavior associated with drive Y, and vice versa. In principle, any behavior could come to be facilitated by *irrelevant drive*—that is, by energy that in the past has not been associated with the behavior in whose energization it participates.

Brown and Farber (1951) applied Hullian drive theory to aggression specifically. In this application, energy mobilized by the instigation to aggression is not viewed as being partial to aggression. It is not considered to have appetitive properties. Rather, this energy is expected to potentiate any behavior—nonaggressive responses as well as aggressive ones—that is evoked by pertinent environmental cues (cf. Geen & O'Neal, 1969; Tannenbaum, 1972; Tannenbaum & Zillmann, 1975).

Activation, Arousal, and Aggression

The measurement of activity in various brain structures led to conceptualizations of behavior energization that closely parallel those advanced in the concept of generalized drive. In activation theory (e.g., Duffy, 1957, 1962; Lindsley, 1951, 1957; Malmo, 1959), attention was focused on activity in the brain stem reticular formation. The ascending reticular activating system had been shown to project diffusely to thalamic, hypothalamic, and cortical regions (e.g., Magoun, 1954; Moruzzi, 1964; Moruzzi & Magoun, 1949). Later modifications and refinements in the delineation of the specific structures involved (cf. Grossman, 1967; Thompson, 1967) did not alter the fact that the projection is not specific, but diffuse. This diffuseness was interpreted as inconsistent with notions of specific, motivating drives. Activation was viewed as a nonspecific, all-encompassing behavior-energizing force.

The concepts of activation and generalized drive, then, have the same implications for the energization of behavior. The critical difference is at the operational level. Whereas drive remained a hypothetical construct assessable only indirectly through such consequences as behavioral vigor and perseverance, states of activation or arousal could be measured directly through the electroencephalogram. Levels of arousal—ranging from coma, deep sleep, light sleep, drowsiness, relaxed wakefulness, and alert attentiveness to strong, excited emotions—could readily be distinguished (e.g., Lindsley, 1957) and mapped onto a continuum. The concept of arousal as a unitary, behavior-energizing force thus virtually followed the operational management of this variable.

Given the high degree of affinity in the concepts of generalized drive and arousal, it should not be surprising that these concepts were treated as interchangeable (e.g., Hebb, 1955). Furthermore, given that drive was an intervening variable (Hull, 1943), whereas arousal could be measured reliably, it also should not be surprising that the possibility of assessing drive through arousal in the reticular formation was considered and widely accepted (e.g., Berlyne, 1960; Bindra, 1959; Brown, 1961).

Most theories of aggression, it seems, have incorporated the arousal concept. Characteristically, however, only a highly qualified version of the concept has been adopted. In Berkowitz's (1965) reasoning, for example, arousal was merely a component of anger that energized aggressive reactions to aggression-eliciting cues. Feshbach (1970) conceptually separated arousal associated with anger from specific aggressive drive and viewed it as "an energizer of ongoing behavior [p. 162]." This ongoing behavior needed not be aggressive. Consequently, whenever frustration and provocation failed to produce aggression and resulted in seemingly intense nonaggressive reactions instead, these reactions could be explained on the basis of the nonspecific arousal component of an otherwise specific drive state. Bandura (1973) also employed the arousal concept to predict the intensity of both aggressive and nonaggressive reactions. According to his reasoning, arousal deriving from the instigation to aggression is likely to energize nonaggressive behaviors as well as aggressive reactions, and analogously, arousal deriving from nonaggressive stimulation may energize aggressive behavior. However, whereas Bandura expects arousal from adverse experiences to energize socially constructive behaviors as well as hostile and aggressive activities, he expects arousal stemming from joyful or rewarding experiences to inhibit rather than facilitate hostile and aggressive reactions. This restriction of the scope of arousal as an energizer is based on the contention that "euphoric arousal" is incompatible with aggression.

In major theories of human aggression, then, arousal has been treated as a behavior-energizing force, but by no means as an entirely diffuse and universal force. The concept of arousal has been selectively applied; it was called upon when it could aid in the preferred projection of outcomes, and it was dismissed or qualified when it could not.

It is of interest to note that in these theories of aggression only the concept of arousal was employed. No commitment to any particular operationalization of arousal, such as activity in the reticular formation, is in evidence. Analogous to generalized drive, arousal was thus treated as a hypothetical construct.

This assessment does not apply to research on the implications of arousal for aggression. Empirical research demands a commitment to operations, and operationalizations of arousal can thus be found in the research literature (e.g., Geen & O'Neal, 1969; Konečni, 1975b).

Sympathetic Excitation and Aggression

Research on the arousal–aggression relationship has been profoundly influenced by the conceptualization of arousal put forth in Schachter's (1964) two-factor theory of emotion. In accord with earlier views (e.g., Duffy, 1962;

Hebb, 1955; Hull, 1952), Schachter held perceptual input from events in the organism's immediate environment accountable for the *direction* of behavior. So-called perception-cognitions (cf. Nisbett & Schachter, 1966) were considered to determine the particular kind of emotion an individual comes to experience. Also in accord with the earlier views, Schachter regarded the *intensity* of behavior to be a simple function of some form of arousal. His proposals concerning this form of arousal differed substantially, however, from earlier conceptualizations. Schachter proposed that emotional experience and emotional behavior derive from intero- and exteroceptive feedback of an arousal reaction. He made the sweeping assumption that arousal is not unique or specific to emotions and that, hence, an arousal state or feedback thereof can not determine the kind of emotion experienced. Schachter nonetheless ascribed a most critical function in the determination of emotion to the feedback from an arousal state. First, such feedback was considered to foster a search for an explanation of the state's induction, a search that was expected to produce a label for the emotion experienced. The search, in other words, was necessary to let the individual understand his or her reaction in terms of an emotional typology (i.e., fear, anger, joy, etc.). Second, such feedback was considered to inform the individual about the magnitude of his or her emotional reaction and to intensify emotional behavior accordingly.

The theoretical focus on intero- and exteroceptive feedback from an arousal reaction directed attention away from the reticular formation and toward peripheral manifestations of arousal. Since activity in the autonomic nervous system is readily accessible through interoception and, in part, through exteroception (cf. Deutsch & Deutsch, 1966), arousal came to be conceived of as sympathetic dominance in the autonomic nervous system (although it was vaguely referred to as "physiological arousal"). The theoretically crucial feedback was expected to derive from such reactions as increased heart rate, increased breathing rate, elevated blood pressure, vasoconstriction, and tremor. All these reactions manifest sympathetic excitation.

At the operational level, attention was similarly focused on sympathetic dominance in the autonomic nervous system. Schachter and his associates (e.g., Schachter & Singer, 1962) employed the subcutaneous administration of epinephrine to increase the level of arousal in subjects. Epinephrine is, of course, a sympathomimetic, and the most characteristic symptoms produced by the injection of this amine are palpitation and tremor—that is, highly obtrusive, attention-demanding manifestations of sympathetic excitation.

Although Schachter's two-factor theory of emotion is patently incomplete in that it presupposes rather than explains the evocation of the arousal reaction that then, according to the theory, produces an emotional state (cf. Zillmann, 1978), and despite evidence that would seem to challenge the broad assumption of nonspecificity of arousal (e.g., Lacey, 1967; Sternbach, 1966), the conceptual separation of excitatory and cognitive processes, as developed in two-factor theory, entered into most contemporary research on the arousal–

aggression linkage in one form or another (e.g., Donnerstein, Donnerstein, & Evans, 1975; Doob & Kirshenbaum, 1973; Geen, 1975; Konečni, 1975b; Zillmann, 1971).

It was generally assumed, explicitly or implicitly, that the level of sympathetic arousal determines the intensity of aggressive action. This assumption of proportionality between arousal and aggression is certainly not unique to two-factor theory. It is consistent with the notion of generalized drive and with activation theory. Additionally, it is apparent in the work of Hokanson and his collaborators, who explored the dissipation of annoyance-associated sympathetic excitation, as measured in peripheral manifestations, after the commission of aggressive and nonaggressive acts (cf. Hokanson, 1970). The research-stimulating impact of the two-factor theory of emotion obviously came from somewhere else. Most probably, it came from the projection of extreme plasticity of emotional experiences and behaviors. If, as Schachter (e.g., 1964) has proposed, emotional states are determined by the causal attribution of arousal to particular inducing conditions, changes in these conditions should lead to different attributions. Even reattributions due to suggestion should lead to genuine changes in emotion (Ross, Rodin, & Zimbardo, 1969). Emotional states such as anger might thus change or be altered without associated changes in arousal (cf. Dienstbier, 1978). Arousal, then, regardless of its particular origin, should potentiate any reaction that, following attributional considerations, is construed as an emotion of a specific kind. Accordingly, in a state of annoyance or anger, arousal from sources that are unrelated to provocation should immerse in the arousal that is produced by the provocation. Any alien arousal should be "misinterpreted" as associated with annoyance and anger, intensify such experiences, and ultimately promote and energize aggressive reactions. Elements of arousal are thus viewed as being "relabeled" (cf. Konečni, 1975b), thereby becoming a part of an emotional reaction associated with dominant or "salient" cognitions (cf. Rule, Ferguson, & Nesdale, 1979).

It should be clear that it is not the proposal of emotional plasticity per se that was novel and that spawned new approaches to aggression. For example, Hebb (1955) and Duffy (1957) had stressed all along that behavior is directed by environmental cues and that arousal blindly energizes the thus guided behavior. Hull (1943, 1952) similarly proposed stimulus-controlled behavior guidance and response energization via generalized drive. There are drastic differences, however, in the conceptualization of the processes presumed to be involved in giving behavior direction. The early proposals were rather vague in this regard, projecting merely a cue function. Behavior theory relied on learned and unlearned stimulus–response connections. Schachter (1964), in contrast, proposed that emotional experiences and the emotional behaviors that these experiences come to guide are the result of highly complex cognitive operations. Specifically, feedback from an arousal reaction (whose origination, as has been said, is left unexplained) is expected to occasion a need for an explanation, which in turn is expected to produce a search for an explanation.

The search is expected to result in the causal attribution of the reaction to an inducer, and the appraisal of this inducer is presumed to furnish a label for the emotion experienced (e.g., anger, fear). Finally, the comprehension of the emotional experience is expected to guide the individual in the selection of appropriate actions (e.g., attack, escape). There can be no doubt, then, that the two-factor theory of emotion projects cognitive operations and decisional processes that are far more complex and specific than those that in earlier models were thought to be involved in giving behavior direction.

These comparatively clear distinctions in the conceptualization of behavior guidance are not at all reflected at the operational level. Attributional processes, in particular, have been assumed, but not demonstrated. Their empirical securement faces, in fact, seemingly insurmountable difficulties. A key problem is that the proposed attributions, misattributions, and reattributions of arousal reactions might not be made spontaneously, but virtually be created in the test situation by directing attention to these processes—such attentional direction being, of course, unavoidable. Arousal attributions have thus maintained a hypothetical status. As a result, the various theoretical models are confounded in the prediction of behavior intensification as a function of arousal. All the models project that arousal intensifies cue-guided behavior, and with the specifics of this guidance unknown, the choice of a theoretical model becomes largely a matter of personal preference. As will be shown later, much research on the arousal–aggression relationship that has been considered supportive of two-factor theory can be considered to support behavior theory or activation theory equally well. In fact, if parsimony of explanation is used as a criterion, the latter models, because of greater simplicity, must be favored over two-factor theory.

Zillmann (1978, 1979) has proposed a three-factor theory of emotion and applied it to the arousal–aggression linkage specifically. This theory has several features that distinguish it sharply from two-factor theory. First of all, the theory explains the evocation of the excitatory reaction associated with emotions, mainly on the basis of learning mechanisms. Second, it similarly entrusts the direction of the incipient motor responses to learning mechanisms. Third, it entails a monitoring function that serves to modify and correct both the direction and the energization of behavior. It is assumed that in this monitoring function, which is considered to be a critical aspect of the *experiential* component of emotion, exteroceptive and/or interoceptive information of the incipient emotional reaction is integrated and that the appropriateness of both overt and covert responses is appraised. This appraisal—which usually involves, among other things, a comprehension of causal relations between actions and events and between events and actions, an appreciation of contingencies of reinforcement, and the ability to anticipate the outcomes of efforts made—may confirm the appropriateness of the reaction. The confirmation assures the continuation of the particular course of action taken. Alternatively, however, the appraisal may foster the recognition that the incipient behavior is inappropriate under the given circumstances. It is assumed that, in this case, the appraisal exerts a degree of control over the emotional behavior, leading either to the inhibition of specific, goal-directed behavior and the dissipation of excitation, or, should the incipient reaction be deemed insufficient to cope with the situation, to increased excitation and stronger goal-directed efforts.

Regarding aggression, it is the endangerment of the individual's well-being that is expected to produce a temporary increase in sympathetic excitation. Endangerment may consist of the immediate experience of pain, discomfort, or debasement; the experience of impending distress of this sort; the vivid anticipation of such distress; the immediate removal or the impediment of a gratifier; or the vivid anticipation of the removal or impediment of a gratifier (cf. Zillmann, 1979). All these endangerments are assumed to trigger an emergency reaction that prepares the organism for "fight or flight," as Cannon (1929) so succinctly put it. In the emergency reaction, the *dispositional* (i.e., response-guiding) and the *excitatory* (i.e., response-energizing) components of emotions are assumed to interact without intrusion of higher-order cognitive functions. A person, for example, who is surprised by a poisonous snake or an assault by a stranger can act quasi-instantaneously to avert the danger. He or she can incapacitate the threatening entity or seek safety through a quick retreat, all without having to rely on elaborate time-consuming deliberations.

The survival value of such a capacity for quick and vigorous action has, of course, been stressed by Cannon (1929, 1932). Much of this survival value, however, has been lost for life in contemporary society. In fact, emergency reactions to endangerments often not only are not adaptive but seem maladaptive. A student, for example, who learns that his girl friend has spent the weekend with someone else may become extremely aroused although there is no apparent course of vigorous action that could "avert" the damage to his well-being. It seems that his excitatory response to the endangerment can only intensify his annoyance and his rage. Such intensely felt negative emotions are devoid of adaptive value and are, if anything, maladaptive. Similarly, being infuriated about or simply scared by the dangers associated with toxic chemical waste will usually not produce a rampage or a rush to a secure place that could have adaptive value for the individual. Potentially maladaptive emotional misreactions can be controlled to some degree, however, by their assessment as inappropriate. Such an assessment is expected to initiate the dissipation of excitation and/or to inhibit motor behavior that is without utility. The monitoring function, then, is viewed as serving adaptation, especially in cases where the emergency reaction lacks adaptive value.

In the three-factor theory of hostility and aggression, Zillmann (1979) has proposed that, while cognitive processes modify excitatory activity, excitatory activity is likely to influence cognitive processes in turn. This influence will be discussed later in connection with impulsive aggressive behavior.

Finally, and in contrast to two-factor theory, the three-factor theory of emotion does not assume that sympathetic excitation is nonspecific. It assumes, instead, that excitation is highly redundant in the various emotions and that interoception of excitation is poorly developed, being practically nonspecific. This conceptualization accommodates reports of differentiated excitatory activity (e.g., Sternbach, 1966). It even accommodates the possibility of some uniqueness in the individual's patterned excitatory response (e.g., Lacey, 1967; Malmo & Bélanger, 1967). At the same time, however, it permits the projection of the summative integration of excitation from different and potentially unrelated sources. This projection is crucial for the paradigm of excitation transfer (Zillmann, 1971, 1978) that predicts the facilitation of an emotional reaction on the basis of residual excitation from any preceding emotional response. The paradigm, which has been extensively used to predict intensification of hostile and aggressive reactions (cf. Tannenbaum & Zillmann, 1975), has also focused attention on the short-lived nature of excitatory reactions in acute emotions (cf. Zillmann, 1978).

AROUSAL FACILITATION OF AGGRESSIVE BEHAVIOR

It might seem that the facilitation of aggressive behavior through arousal, as it is projected by the theoretical models that have been discussed, can be readily examined. The demonstration of a close correspondence between levels of excitation, on the one hand, and aggressiveness, on the other, might be considered supportive evidence. It would, however, be evidence of the least compelling type.

Provocation has been shown to increase sympathetic excitation (e.g., Hokanson & Burgess, 1962; Hokanson & Shetler, 1961). In all probability, this increase is a simple function of the severity of the threat to the individual's well-being that a provocation entails. It appears likely, then, that the stronger the provocation, the higher the level of excitation produced, and in turn, the more intense the aggressive behavior. But such likely correspondence in levels of provocation, arousal, and aggressiveness does not necessarily mean that arousal was causally involved in the intensification of aggression. It is conceivable, for instance, that provocations foster specific retaliatory plans and that stronger provocations call for stronger punitive measures in these plans. Arousal, it could be argued, is a concomitant of the response to provocation that is of little moment in the execution of these retaliatory plans.

To implicate the causal involvement of arousal in the intensification of aggression more decisively than the demonstration of a mere correspondence can, it was necessary to devise techniques that vary the level of arousal while holding the level of provocation constant. Two such techniques have emerged in the research on the arousal–aggression relationship. Both involve the generation of arousal through stimulation unrelated to provocation; but whereas in one approach this additional arousal is produced during the performance of aggressive actions, the other approach utilizes residues of arousal from stimulation preceding the performance of aggressive actions. It should be clear that both approaches are based on the assumption that aggression-intensifying arousal is not specific to aggression but can be increased by adding into it excitatory activity from arousing experiences that have little or no affinity with aggression. (If one were to assume that arousal is highly specific and that only "aggressive arousal" [i.e., appetitive, aggressive drive] facilitates aggressive behavior, the addition of alien arousal should, of course, *not* influence aggressive behavior.)

Geen and O'Neal (1969) conducted the first investigation that explored the facilitation of aggression through simultaneously produced alien arousal. Through exposure to modeling messages and through procedural requirements, male subjects were enticed to behave aggressively. While delivering electric shock to another person, these subjects were exposed to presumably arousing white noise (cf. Kryter, 1970). Aggressiveness, measured in the frequency of shock delivered, was found to be higher in the noise condition than in the control. The investigators attributed this difference in aggressive behavior to the arousal that probably resulted from exposure to noise.

Konečni (1975b) similarly employed exposure to presumably arousing sounds during the performance of aggressive responses to test the arousal–aggression linkage. However, his investigation involved a variation in provocation. Male and female subjects were either provoked or not provoked and then, during the delivery of electric shock to the person with whom they had interacted, exposed to soft or loud sounds. It was observed that, compared to no exposure to sounds, exposure to loud sounds led to more frequent use of electric shock in provoked subjects. Complex but soft sounds had a similar, aggression-enhancing effect on provoked subjects. Simple, soft sounds, in contrast, led to less frequent use of shock in provoked subjects. If, on the basis of earlier research (e.g., Berlyne, Craw, Salapatek, & Lewis, 1963; Bryson & Driver, 1969), it is considered likely that loud and complex sounds increased arousal, whereas soft and noncomplex sounds did not (and may in fact have reduced it), these findings can be interpreted as consistent evidence for the facilitation of motivated aggression through arousal.

Konečni further observed that any arousal differences produced by exposure to sounds had no effect on subjects who had not been provoked. This observation corroborated earlier findings on exertion-induced arousal reported by Zillmann, Katcher, and Milavsky (1972). Arousal, then, appears to have facilitated aggressive behavior only when such behavior was motivated by alternative means.

Donnerstein and Wilson (1976) replicated and extended Konečni's results. In their investigation, male subjects were provoked or not provoked and exposed to noise of low or high intensity while delivering shock. The arousal that was probably produced by exposure to noise of high intensity led to the use of more intense electric shock in subjects who retaliated against their tormentor;

it was of no consequence in subjects who had not been annoyed. Again, arousal appears to have facilitated aggressive behavior only when such behavior was motivated through provocation.

The first investigation that explored the facilitation of aggression through alien residual arousal from preceding stimulation was conducted by Zillmann (1971). Male subjects were provoked, exposed to differently arousing motion pictures, and then provided with an opportunity to retaliate. The excitatory capacity of the motion pictures was assessed in peripheral manifestations of sympathetic excitation, such as increased heart rate, blood pressure, and vasoconstriction. Retaliatory behavior was measured in the intensity of electric shock delivered to the annoyer. Subjects retaliated soon after exposure to one of the motion pictures; that is, they retaliated at a time when excitation was known to be at different levels because of the residues from the differently arousing films. It was found that aggressive behavior was facilitated in proportion to the magnitude of prevailing residual excitation from prior stimulation.

In this investigation, an erotic film had been used as the stimulus with the strongest excitatory potential. The sympathetic component of the sexual arousal that was produced by exposure to this stimulus was apparently capable of intensifying feelings of anger in the subject when he was reconfronted with his annoyer. Ultimately, it proved capable of intensifying aggressive responses as the opportunity for retaliation arose.

The aggression-facilitating effect of highly arousing erotica has been observed in many subsequent investigations (e.g., Donnerstein et al., 1975; Donnerstein & Hallam, 1978; Meyer, 1972; Zillmann, Hoyt, & Day, 1974) and can be considered well established. As was the case for aggression facilitation by noise-generated arousal, the facilitation of aggression through sexual arousal seems to be contingent on provocation and annoyance. Provocation was manipulated in several pertinent investigations (e.g., Cantor, Zillmann, & Einsiedel, 1978; Donnerstein et al., 1975; White, 1979), and only under conditions of provocation was the aggressive behavior of males and females found to be affected by sexual arousal. On occasion, however, aggression facilitation through exposure to erotica has been observed in the absence of deliberate provocation (e.g., Jaffe, Malamuth, Feingold, & Feshbach, 1974).

It has also been shown that residual excitation from exposure to motion pictures that feature violent behaviors is capable of facilitating motivated aggression (e.g., Donnerstein & Hallam, 1978; Geen, 1975; Zillmann, 1971). Doob and Kirshenbaum (1973) presented data suggestive of an additive combination of excitation from provocation and from exposure to violent fare. The aggression-facilitating effect appears to depend on provocation to a large measure (e.g., Donnerstein, Donnerstein, & Barrett, 1976; Geen, 1975; Zillmann & Johnson, 1973), but probably not entirely (e.g., Doob & Climie, 1972), due to the content's suggestive and modeling properties (cf. Bandura, 1973; Berkowitz, 1970). A further qualification seems indicated by the finding that the excitatory response to common, violent fare produces rather modest excitatory reactions in females (Cantor et al., 1978). The aggression-facilitating effect of exposure to violent behaviors thus seems to favor males.

In the earlier indicated extension of Konečni's (1975b) findings on the effects of sounds, Donnerstein and Wilson (1976) observed that exposure to presumably arousing noise prior to provocation and retaliation can also facilitate motivated aggression. Again, as with noise accompanying the performance of aggressive acts, the noise pretreatment had no effect on unprovoked subjects.

In an investigation conducted by Day (1980), the excitatory potential of various musical selections, measured in peripheral manifestations of sympathetic excitation, was determined through pretesting. Male subjects were provoked, exposed to differently arousing music (or were not exposed to music in a control condition), and then provided with an opportunity to retaliate. Arousing music was found to facilitate aggression as measured in the delivery of noxious noise blasts to the annoyer.

Additional investigations demonstrating the facilitation of aggression through exposure to arousing communications have been reviewed by Tannenbaum and Zillmann (1975).

The dependence of the facilitation of aggressive behavior through residual arousal from preceding stimulation on provocation and annoyance (i.e., on aggressive instigation) has been very clearly demonstrated in an investigation by Zillmann et al. (1972). Male subjects were provoked or not provoked; performed highly arousing, strenuous physical exercise or a nonarousing motor task; and were then provided with an opportunity to behave aggressively toward the person with whom they had interacted. Measured in the intensity of electric shock delivered, aggressive behavior was greatly facilitated by residual excitation from exertion when the subjects had been provoked. In sharp contrast, the same residues (assessed in such peripheral manifestations as blood-pressure and heart-rate elevation) had no appreciable effect on unprovoked subjects. These findings are summarized in Figure 1. Investigations by Zillmann and Bryant (1974) and Zillmann, Johnson, and Day (1974) gave further evidence of the basic interaction of provocation and arousal in the facilitation of aggression through arousal.

The available evidence, then, shows with considerable consistency that (a) arousal does not indiscriminately energize behavior—aggressive behavior, in particular—and (b) arousal is likely to intensify aggressive behavior only under conditions in which the individual is predisposed to behave aggressively.

As has been pointed out earlier, the findings cannot be explained on the basis of appetitive drive. They can be accounted for, however, either by a model based on the concept of generalized drive or by any theory of emotion that assigns a guidance function to cognition and a diffuse energization function to arousal. In terms of behavior theory, for instance, it can be argued that only the stimulation associated with provocation will evoke aggressive reactions that then can be energized by generalized drive. In the absence of such

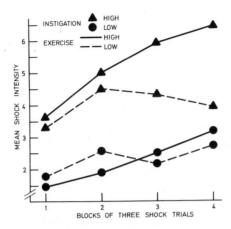

FIGURE 1 Aggression as a joint function of disposition and level of excitation. Excitatory residues from strenuous physical exercise were present during the period of time in which aggressive responses were performed. Residual excitation intensified aggressive behavior when it was motivated through provocation. When aggression was not thus motivated, residual excitation had no appreciable effect on aggression. (Reprinted from Zillmann, Katcher, & Milavsky, 1972, with permission.)

stimulation, drive can only produce general motor restlessness. Theories of emotion project essentially the same situations but tend to replace simple stimulus–response guidance with more complex systems of cognitive response guidance (cf. Zillmann, 1978, 1979).

Some research findings, however, favor emotion theory and are difficult to reconcile with the generalized drive model. These findings concern (a) the duration of the aggression facilitation through arousal and (b) aggressive behavior after the dissipation of arousal.

The fact that sympathetic excitation can be operationalized in unambiguous measures, whereas generalized drive—the hypothetical construct—can not, allows the assessment of the time course of arousal, but not of drive. The dissipation of arousal can readily be measured, and predictions of decreasing aggression facilitation can be based on measured decay gradients. With the dissipation of drive unknown, no such predictions can be made.

Doob and Climie (1972) have shown that arousal produced by exposure to violence in motion pictures is comparatively short lived. About a quarter hour after exposure, the arousal facilitation of aggression observed immediately after exposure had vanished along with residual arousal. Zillmann, Hoyt, and Day (1974) and Day (1976) showed that residual excitation from violent fare vanishes even more rapidly—within a few minutes. Residual excitation from exposure to erotica tends to dissipate somewhat more slowly; still, recovery is usually complete within 5–10 min after cessation of stimulation (Zillmann, Hoyt, & Day, 1974). In both these investigations, it was observed that the arousal facilitation of motivated aggression diminishes in proportion to the dissipation of sympathetic excitation. The findings, then, implicate sympathetic arousal with the facilitatory effect. Generalized drive, unless it is conceived of in terms of sympathetic activity, is simply too vague a notion to account for the indicated correspondence between arousal and facilitation.

In another line of research, it has been demonstrated that residual excitation present during provocation is capable of intensifying aggressive behavior that occurs after the complete dissipation of the residues. Arousal thus functions to intensify the experience of annoyance and anger, not aggression. In an experiment by Zillmann and Bryant (1974), the decay gradients of arousal after a strenuous and a nonstrenuous task were determined, and a provocation treatment was then placed at a time when exertion-produced arousal was either at a high or a low level. Retaliatory opportunities were delayed to a point where these differences had vanished. It was found that arousal that had intensified the experience of annoyance and anger led to increased aggressive behavior at a later time, when arousal levels were comparatively low and probably the same in the two transfer conditions.

Since it can be argued that, although peripheral indexes of excitation showed recovery, some form of arousal may have been maintained and may have directly facilitated aggressive behavior, this investigation led to a follow-up experiment by Bryant and Zillmann (1979) in which the opportunity for aggression was delayed by an entire week. It is conceivable, for instance, that in the first investigation, in which provocation and retaliation were separated by less than 10 min, activity in the sympathetic-adrenal medullary system had ceased at the time of retaliation but that activity in the slower operating pituitary–adrenal cortical system, through the secretion of corticosteroids, had not. Aggression, consequently, might have been energized by this residual activity. The follow-up investigation rules out such an interpretation, however. It was found that the intensity of aggression that was delayed for 1 week was nonetheless proportional with the magnitude of residual excitation transferred into provocation. Incidentally, both these investigations of delayed aggression show once more that arousal is of no consequence in the aggressive behavior of unprovoked persons.

It is difficult to see how a drive model could accommodate such findings. The elicitation of delayed aggressive reactions can readily be explained as a response to salient stimuli, but the model is at a loss in accounting for the intensity of the behavior—an intensity that is beyond prevailing drive levels.

Theories of emotion, in contrast, appear to be capable of providing an adequate explanation of the findings. If it is assumed that acutely experienced annoyances foster retaliatory plans and that these plans can be executed at later times, it can be projected that the more intensely an annoyance is experienced, the more intense will be the retaliatory action that it eventually produces (cf. Zillmann, 1979). Clearly, such projections are based on the assumption that the intensity of annoyances and/or specific retaliatory plans are stored in memory and can be reinstated. It is conceivable that the reinstatement of annoyances carries with it a portion of the initial excitatory reaction. Data that would establish such a reinstatement of arousal are presently not available, however.

COGNITIVE CONTROL OF
AGGRESSION FACILITATION THROUGH AROUSAL

The intensification of aggression in the absence of high levels of prevailing arousal, as discussed in the preceding section, is apparently the result of cognitive processes. However, cognitive processes can exert control in the opposite direction as well: They can prevent the intensification of aggression under conditions of greatly elevated levels of arousal.

Dispositional Control

The evidence establishing the dependence of aggression facilitation through arousal on the instigation to aggression has been discussed already (e.g., Donnerstein et al., 1976, 1975; Zillmann & Bryant, 1974; Zillmann et al., 1972). As illustrated by the data displayed in Figure 1, residual excitation, even when of extreme magnitude, fails to intensify aggressive behavior in persons who are not predisposed to behave aggressively.

This failure of facilitation can be explained in two profoundly different ways. First, it can be argued that the recognition of the inappropriateness of aggressive reactions leads to the inhibition of such reactions. It should be clear that this argument (a) assigns specific-drive properties to arousal and (b) gives cognitive process the power to control drive. Second, it can be argued that response-guiding cognitive processes simply foster nonaggressive actions and that arousal feeds into these actions. Should the behavior called for be devoid of skeletal-motor operations, general motor restlessness may result. Most significantly, however, aggressive inclinations never materialize and, hence, do not have to be inhibited.

The first rationale not only involves the highly questionable assumption of an appetitive, aggressive component of arousal but also violates parsimony of explanation. It projects a force that then requires the additional projection of inhibition to account for the absence of the force's effect. This reasoning is certainly more complex than reasoning that does not entail the proposal of such a force. The second rationale, in which aggressive inclinations never become an issue, is thus to be preferred as more parsimonious. The fact that the unnecessarily complicated inhibition argument is used at all may well reflect the continued, unfounded belief that arousal is partial to aggression and that the impulses it frequently provides have to be repressed (cf. Zillmann, 1979).

Attributional Control

It appears that acutely experienced arousal that cannot be construed as deriving from provocation constitutes a further condition under which arousal fails to facilitate aggression.

Cantor, Zillmann, and Bryant (1975) observed that sexual excitement was facilitated by alien residual arousal only when subjects were no longer aware of the initial induction of arousal. As long as subjects linked the residual arousal to its actual inducer, sexual excitedness was not facilitated.

Regarding aggression, this phenomenon has been demonstrated in an investigation by Zillmann, Johnson, and Day (1974). Male subjects were provoked and performed highly strenuous exercise. The opportunity to aggress against the annoyer was provided either immediately after exertion (i.e., when excitation was at a very high level and subjects could only attribute their arousal to the exercise) or after some delay (i.e., when some excitatory recovery had taken place and subjects no longer connected residual arousal with exertion). Time between provocation and retaliation was held constant, however. Aggressive behavior was found to be facilitated by residual arousal only when the opportunity for retaliation was delayed. Immediately after exertion (i.e., when arousal was extremely high), aggression was at extremely low levels. It was, in fact, not appreciably different from preprovocation levels.

It appears, then, that whenever obtrusive intero- and exteroceptive cues of an arousal state (e.g., palpitation, hyperventilation, tremor) force the individual to attribute the state to an inducer that is not related to provocation, aggressive reactions will not be facilitated by prevailing arousal. It is conceivable that the recognition that what is felt is not anger—at least, not entirely— inhibits motivated aggressive responses. Alternatively, it is possible that the attribution of arousal to a source unrelated to provocation deprives the experience of annoyance of its emotional intensity (making anger a flat experience) and that, as a consequence, there is little urgency to aggress. Both accounts (i.e., inhibition and lack of instigation) are viable, and data that would permit the rejection of one and the acceptance of the other are not available at present.

COGNITIVE CONTROL OF AROUSAL

The most significant involvement of cognitive functioning in the facilitation of aggression through arousal appears to lie in the control of excitatory activity. Both the magnitude of excitatory reactions and the dissipation of these reactions seem greatly influenced by cognitive processes.

Interpretational Corrections

The power of cognitive processes to prevent the development of intense excitatory reactions has been demonstrated in an investigation conducted by Zillmann and Cantor (1976). Male subjects were severely provoked and later retaliated against their annoyer. In one condition, they received no information about circumstances that could have made the annoyer's behavior appear less hostile and assaultive. In the other conditions, information of mitigating circumstances was provided (the rude experimenter was said to be under a lot of stress due to exams). In one of the latter conditions, the subjects received this mitigating information prior to being mistreated; in the other, they received it after the mistreatment. Time between provocation and retaliation was kept constant across conditions.

Tracing excitatory reactions in peripheral manifestations (blood pressure, heart rate) revealed that subjects who had prior knowledge of mitigating circumstances did not become greatly aroused by the mistreatment they received. In contrast, this mistreatment led to extreme excitatory reactions in subjects without such prior knowledge. The provision of mitigating information after the mistreatment accelerated excitatory recovery, but it failed to produce prompt recovery to a level of arousal comparable to that in subjects who had prior knowledge of the mitigating circumstances. Retaliatory behavior proved to be proportional with excitatory responsiveness. All these effects are presented in Figure 2.

The findings exhibit two ways in which arousal can be modified by cognitive input. First, prior knowledge of mitigating circumstances curtailed the magni-

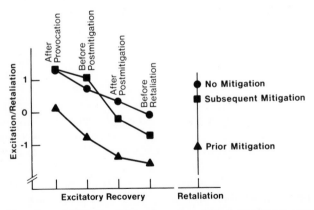

FIGURE 2 The effect of mitigating information on excitatory reactions to annoyance and on retaliatory hostility. The provision of mitigating information prior to provocation prevented intense annoyance and kept retaliation to a minimum. The subsequent provision of mitigating information accelerated the decay of excitation but failed to reduce retaliation effectively. Excitation and retaliation are expressed in z scores for ease of comparison. (Adapted from Zillmann & Cantor, 1976.)

tude of the excitatory reaction; second, the subsequent provision of the mitigating information curtailed the duration of this reaction. Both effects must have
been the result of cognitive intervention. The mechanics of this intervention
remain to be ascertained, however. In accord. .e with the three-factor theory
of emotion (cf. Zillmann, 1978, 1979), it can only be assumed that the mistreatment constituted an endangerment that triggered the excitatory reaction to
prepare the organism for fight or flight. The prior provision of mitigating information presumably fostered an interpretational correction: The treatment
could not be construed as an endangerment. It consequently did not trigger a
strong excitatory reaction that would prepare the organism for action. The later
provision of mitigating information may have fostered the same interpretational
correction. Such reinterpretation was now limited, however, to cutting off
operations that serve the maintenance of arousal. Along these lines it could be
speculated, for instance, that the release of arousal-mediating catecholamines
is directly controlled by cognitive processes that convey appraisals and that
any interpretational correction from "threat" to "nonthreat" immediately cur-
tails excessive release.

Investigations conducted by Geen (1975) and Geen and Rakosky (1973)
have shown that interpretational corrections also affect excitatory reactions in
response to witnessing the endangerment of others. Aggressive behavior believed to have actually happened triggered more intense excitatory reactions
than did the same behavior construed as fictitious, and it facilitated aggressive
responses of provoked (but not of unprovoked) male subjects accordingly
(Geen, 1975). More generally, Leventhal and his associates (cf. Leventhal,
1974) have repeatedly demonstrated that the preparedness of persons for aversive events, presumably because it removes uncertainties and thus makes these
events less threatening, curbs excitatory reactions considerably.

Interventional Corrections

The course of experiences of annoyance, it appears, depends greatly on
cognitive operations during acute annoyance. Bandura (1973) suggested that
the rumination of a provocation constitutes an optimal condition for the maintenance of annoyance and, in turn, the propensity for hostile and aggressive
behavior. Zillmann (1979) similarly proposed that the rehearsal of grievances
perpetuates the propensity for retaliatory action, but he implicated sympathetic
excitation specifically with a mediating role. This proposal assumes that the
annoyed individual, if left alone in a comparatively nondistracting environment, is likely to brood over the mistreatment he or she received and, possibly,
prepare retaliatory actions; such brooding, in turn, is expected to maintain
arousal at a high level and to foster intense reprisals accordingly. This assump-

tion, especially with regard to the behavior of males, has received support from an investigation by Sapolsky, Stocking, and Zillmann (1977).

If a minimum of diverting stimulation invites brooding over a mistreatment, extensive stimulation should distract the annoyed individual and thus impede or prevent rumination (cf. Bandura, 1973). An absorbing stimulus should disrupt the rehearsal of grievances, and this intervention should interfere with the maintenance of arousal. In other words, the intervention in arousal-maintaining cognitive activities should accelerate the decay of sympathetic excitation deriving from annoyance, annoyance should be less intensely experienced, and the propensity for hostility and aggression should diminish (cf. Zillmann, 1979).

A modification of this view has been proposed by Zillmann and Johnson (1973). These investigators suggested that the potential of a message or an activity to intervene in a state of annoyance is not merely a function of the degree to which such a message or activity normally absorbs a person but also depends on the degree to which these events relate to annoyance, anger, and aggression. Accordingly, messages and behaviors that relate to the individual's acute state of annoyance, regardless of how involving and distracting they might be under different circumstances, are expected to reinstate the experience of annoyance and thus facilitate the maintenance of arousal at high levels.

An investigation conducted by Zillmann and Johnson (1973) produced findings that are consistent with these expectations. Exposure of provoked males to stimuli unrelated to aggression proved to reduce levels of arousal and, ultimately, aggressiveness to a higher degree than did exposure to aggressive fare. Donnerstein et al. (1976) reported corroborative findings.

More definitive support for the proposal comes from an investigation by Bryant and Zillmann (1977). Stimuli that ranged from minimally to highly involving were selected in a pretest. One of two highly involving stimuli featured aggressive activities. Male subjects were provoked, exposed to these stimuli, and then provided with an opportunity to retaliate. For all nonaggressive stimuli, the decay of annoyance-induced excitation was proportional to the communications' measured intervention potential. In sharp contrast, excitation after exposure to the aggressive communication substantially exceeded what could be expected on the basis of this communication's general intervention potential. The effect on arousal achieved by this message was comparable to that achieved by a minimally involving stimulus. These findings are displayed in Figure 3. The cognitive intervention into the arousal-maintaining rehearsal of grievances, then, appears to be indeed a joint function of a stimulus' power to absorb and of its affinity with provocation and aggression. Konečni (1975a) has provided data that suggest that nonaggressive, absorbing activities (such as solving mathematical puzzles) similarly speed up the decay of annoyance-induced arousal and thereby lower the propensity for aggressive reactions.

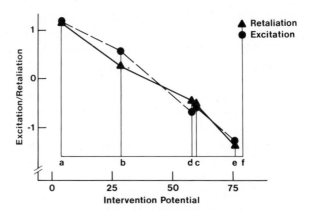

FIGURE 3 Level of excitation and retaliatory behavior as a function of the intervention potential of communications. The greater the capacity of nonhostile contents to absorb the respondent (points connected by gradients), the greater the recovery from annoyance-produced excitation (circles) and the less severe the postexposure retaliation against the annoyer (triangles). Contents featuring hostilities were absorbing to the nonannoyed subjects but failed to induce efficient recovery from excitation and failed to lower the level of retaliatory behavior in annoyed subjects (isolated points on coordinate f). The communications were: (a) a monotonous stimulus, (b) a nature film, (c) a comedy show, (d) a program featuring nonaggressive sport, (e) a quiz show, and (f) a program featuring contact sport entailing aggressive actions beyond the legitimate sports activity. Excitation and retaliation are expressed in z scores for ease of comparison. (Adapted from Bryant & Zillmann, 1977.)

LOSS OF COGNITIVE CONTROL: AROUSAL AND IMPULSIVE AGGRESSION

The preceding section has shown that cognitive processes can directly influence excitatory activity. Can excitatory activity, in turn, influence cognitive processes?

On the basis of the widely accepted inverted-U relationship between arousal and behavioral efficiency (cf. Freeman, 1940; Hebb, 1955, 1966; Malmo, 1959, 1975) and on Easterbrook's (1959) cue-utilization model, Zillmann (1979) proposed that the cognitive guidance of hostile and aggressive behaviors, because it relies on the execution of highly complex operations, is limited to an optimal range of arousal. At extreme levels of arousal, the cognitive mediation of behavior is expected to be greatly impaired, and behavior is expected to be controlled by the more basic mechanics of learning. At very high levels of excitation, then, hostile and aggressive behaviors are expected to become impulsive—that is, to become behaviors composed of learned reactions associated with great habit strength, conceivably even of unlearned defensive reactions. Berkowitz (1967, 1974a, 1974b) has directed attention to this type of aggression; he did so, however, without linking it to the particular, restrictive conditions under which it occurs.

In view of the restrictions that have to be placed on laboratory manipulations to safeguard the welfare of human subjects, experimental evidence on the proposed deterioration of cognitive response guidance under conditions of very high levels of arousal are understandably scarce. In fact, only one experiment in which this deterioration was observed has been reported (cf. Zillmann, 1979).

The provision of mitigating information has consistently been shown to reduce retaliatory behavior (e.g., Burnstein & Worchel, 1962; Cohen, 1955; Pastore, 1952; Rule, Dyck, & Nesdale, 1978). This effect can only be attributed to cognitive mediation. However, to the extent that the functioning of such cognitive control is limited to intermediate levels of arousal, the curtailment of hostile and aggressive reactions through the provision of mitigating information should not be expected under extreme excitatory conditions. This expectation was tested in an investigation conducted by Zillmann, Bryant, Cantor, and Day (1975). Male subjects were aggressively instigated, performed either a nonstrenuous task or highly demanding physical exercise, and were then provided with an opportunity to retaliate against their annoyer. Just prior to retaliation, they learned or did not learn about circumstances that made the annoyer's behavior appear less deliberately assaultive. The findings, shown in Figure 4, fully supported the predictions. As in earlier investigations, mitigating information was found to reduce retaliatory behavior when arousal was at intermediate levels. The provision of such information had no appreciable effect, however, when arousal levels were very high.

The level of sympathetic excitation, then, appears to influence the capacity for information processing. In extreme excitatory states, this capacity seems substantially impaired—at least as far as complex integration of information is concerned. There is, consequently, reason to believe that hostile and aggressive behavior will become increasingly impulsive as levels of arousal reach extreme elevations.

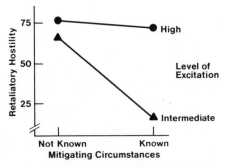

FIGURE 4 Impairment of cognitive response guidance in hostile behavior at high levels of excitation. Retaliatory hostility was measured in the subject's recommendation against his annoyer's reappointment as a research assistant. (Adapted from Zillmann, Bryant, Cantor, & Day, 1975.)

Endocrinological research is suggestive of an embodiment of the proposed negative relationship between heightened sympathetic excitation and a reduced capacity for the performance of complex cognitive operations. It has been observed, for instance, that small amounts of the catecholamines that mediate arousal in peripheral structures, especially norepinephrine, cross the brain blood barrier and affect central processes (e.g., Rothballer, 1959, 1967). Emotional stress generally has been linked to profound chemical changes in the cortex, the subcortex, the cerebellum, the hypothalamus, and the brain stem (e.g., Bliss & Zwanziger, 1966), the amines again playing a major part (e.g., Axelrod, 1959, 1971). It remains quite unclear, however, exactly what consequences any changes in the level of brain amines may have for particular forms of cognitive functioning in humans.

SUMMARY AND OUTLOOK

The relationship between arousal and aggression is apparently more complex than many investigators had imagined. Arousal is evidently *not* a universal energizer of aggression. It does *not* have appetitive properties. And if it does energize aggression, energization is *not* necessarily in proportion to prevailing levels of arousal. Rather, arousal is a potential energizer whose operation depends on a set of favorable circumstances.

Recent research has led to the identification of some, but not necessarily of all, the conditions that either prevent energization altogether or that modify the energization effect substantially. All these conditions manifest cognitive influences. Some of these influences have no apparent impact on arousal. Others achieve their effect through the modification of arousal. Finally, research suggests that arousal may influence cognitive processes.

The conditions known to exert a degree of control over the energization of hostile and aggressive behaviors through arousal can be summarized as follows:

1. The energization of aggression depends on instigation to aggression. It is not likely to occur in the absence of provocation, annoyance, and the resultant aggressive disposition.

2. The attribution of an arousal state to sources unrelated to provocation and annoyance is likely to prevent the energization of aggression.

Both 1 and 2 state *necessary* conditions for energization.

3. The magnitude of arousal reactions can be curtailed by appraisals that minimize the threat posed by an endangerment.

4. The decay of arousal can be accelerated by activities that impede the rehearsal of grievances and/or retaliatory intentions.

Both 3 and 4 state *modifying* conditions. The diminution of arousal is, of course, expected to reduce the potential for the energization of behavior.

5. It is likely that, at very high levels of arousal, the cognitive processes involved in 1–4 are impaired and that the stipulated dependencies and modifications become partly or totally defunct in impulsive hostile and aggressive behaviors.

The apparent interdependencies between cognitive and excitatory processes in impulsive aggressive behavior must be considered least understood. Clearly, the issue cannot be resolved—at least, not entirely—through experimentation. Experimental research entails a degree of risk to human subjects that is simply intolerable. Nonexperimental research approaches will have to be accepted in efforts to provide a better understanding of the mechanics of impulsive aggression.

Also, the conceptualizations and operationalizations employed in research on the arousal–aggression linkage will have to be refined. Although great progress has been made in the advancement from drive as an imaginary force to arousal that is measurable with some reliability, many facets of excitatory states have been neglected. For instance, recent research has concentrated on sympathetic activity. In terms of neuroendocrine processes, this is activity in the sympathetic-adrenal medullary system, where the secretion of the catecholamines epinephrine and norepinephrine produces the earlier discussed emergency reaction (cf. Smith, 1973; Turner & Bagnara, 1971). The potential consequences for human aggression of activity in the pituitary-adrenal cortical system, in contrast, where the secretion of corticosteroids produces longer lasting excitatory effects, have received little attention (cf. Conner, 1972; Hennessy & Levine, 1979). Furthermore, the implications of the likely covariation of brain catecholamines and indoleamines with adrenal medullary catecholamines (cf. Barchas, Ciaranello, Stolk, Brodie, & Hamburg, 1972), whose delineation might prove crucial in understanding the loss of cognitive control that is characteristic of impulsive aggression, have not been explored. Future research on the arousal–aggression linkage will have to address these neglected aspects of arousal.

REFERENCES

Axelrod, J. Metabolism of epinephrine and other sympathomimetic amines. *Physiological Reviews*, 1959, *39*, 751–776.

Axelrod, J. Noradrenaline: Fate and control of its biosynthesis. *Science*, 1971, *173*, 598–606.

Bandura, A. *Aggression: A social learning analysis.* Englewood Cliffs, N.J.: Prentice-Hall, 1973.

Barchas, J. D., Ciaranello, R. D., Stolk, J. M., Brodie, H. K. H., & Hamburg, D. A. Biogenic amines and behavior. In S. Levine (Ed.), *Hormones and behavior.* New York: Academic Press, 1972.

Berkowitz, L. The concept of aggressive drive: Some additional considerations. In L. Berkowitz (Ed.), *Advances in experimental social psychology* (Vol. 2). New York: Academic Press, 1965.

Berkowitz, L. Experiments on automatism and intent in human aggression. In C. D. Clemente & D.

B. Lindsley (Eds.), *Aggression and defense: Neural mechanisms and social patterns* (Vol. 5). *Brain function.* Berkeley: Univ. of California Press, 1967.

Berkowitz, L. The contagion of violence: An S–R mediational analysis of some effects of observed aggression. In W. J. Arnold & M. M. Page (Eds.), *Nebraska Symposium on Motivation, 1970.* Lincoln: Univ. of Nebraska Press, 1970.

Berkowitz, L. External determinants of impulsive aggression. In J. De Wit & W. W. Hartup (Eds.), *Determinants and origins of aggressive behavior.* The Hague: Mouton, 1974. (a)

Berkowitz, L. Some determinants of impulsive aggression: Role of mediated associations with reinforcement for aggression. *Psychological Review,* 1974, *81,* 165–176. (b)

Berlyne, D. E. *Conflict, arousal, and curiosity.* New York: McGraw-Hill, 1960.

Berlyne, D. E., Craw, M. A., Salapatek, P. H., & Lewis, J. L. Novelty, complexity, incongruity, extrinsic motivation, and the GSR. *Journal of Experimental Psychology,* 1963, *66,* 560–567.

Bindra, D. *Motivation: A systematic reinterpretation.* New York: Ronald Press, 1959.

Bliss, E. L., & Zwanziger, J. Brain amines and emotional stress. *Journal of Psychiatric Research,* 1966, *4,* 189–198.

Brown, J. S. *The motivation of behavior.* New York: McGraw-Hill, 1961.

Brown, J. S., & Farber, I. E. Emotions conceptualized as intervening variables—with suggestions toward a theory of frustration. *Psychological Bulletin,* 1951, *48,* 456–495.

Bryant, J., & Zillmann, D. The mediating effect of the intervention potential of communications on displaced aggressiveness and retaliatory behavior. In B. D. Ruben (Ed.), *Communication Yearbook 1.* New Brunswick, N.J.: ICA-Transaction Press, 1977.

Bryant, J., & Zillmann, D. Effect of intensification of annoyance through unrelated residual excitation on substantially delayed hostile behavior. *Journal of Experimental Social Psychology,* 1979, *15,* 470–480.

Bryson, J. B., & Driver, M. J. Conceptual complexity and internal arousal. *Psychonomic Science,* 1969, *17,* 71–72.

Burnstein, E., & Worchel, P. Arbitrariness of frustration and its consequences for aggression in a social situation. *Journal of Personality,* 1962, *30,* 528–540.

Cannon, W. B. *Bodily changes in pain, hunger, fear and rage: An account of researches into the function of emotional excitement* (2nd ed.). New York: Appleton, 1929.

Cannon, W. B. *The wisdom of the body.* New York: Norton, 1932.

Cantor, J. R., Zillmann, D., & Bryant, J. Enhancement of experienced sexual arousal in response to erotic stimuli through misattribution of unrelated residual excitation. *Journal of Personality and Social Psychology,* 1975, *32,* 69–75.

Cantor, J. R., Zillmann, D., & Einsiedel, E. F. Female responses to provocation after exposure to aggressive and erotic films. *Communication Research,* 1978, *5,* 395–411.

Cofer, C. N., & Appley, M. H. *Motivation: Theory and research.* New York: Wiley, 1964.

Cohen, A. R. Social norms, arbitrariness of frustration, and status of the agent of frustration in the frustration–aggression hypothesis. *Journal of Abnormal and Social Psychology,* 1955, *51,* 222–226.

Conner, R. L. Hormones, biogenic amines, and aggression. In S. Levine (Ed.), *Hormones and behavior.* New York: Academic Press, 1972.

Day, K. D. Short-lived facilitation of aggressive behavior by violent communications. *Psychological Reports,* 1976, *38,* 1068–1070.

Day, K. D. *The effect of music differing in excitatory potential and hedonic valence on provoked aggression.* Unpublished doctoral dissertation, Indiana University, 1980.

Deutsch, J. A., & Deutsch, D. *Physiological psychology.* Homewood, Ill.: Dorsey Press, 1966.

Dienstbier, R. A. Emotion-attribution theory: Establishing roots and exploring future perspectives. In H. E. Howe, Jr. & R. A. Dienstbier (Eds.), *Nebraska Symposium on Motivation, 1978.* Lincoln: Univ. of Nebraska Press, 1978.

Dollard, J., Doob, L. W., Miller, N. E., Mowrer, O. H., & Sears, R. R. *Frustration and aggression.* New Haven: Yale Univ. Press, 1939.

Donnerstein, E., Donnerstein, M., & Barrett, G. Where is the facilitation of media violence: The effects of nonexposure and placement of anger arousal. *Journal of Research in Personality,* 1976, *10,* 386–398.

Donnerstein, E., Donnerstein, M., & Evans, R. Erotic stimuli and aggression: Facilitation or inhibition. *Journal of Personality and Social Psychology,* 1975, *32,* 237–244.

Donnerstein, E., & Hallam, J. Facilitating effects of erotica on aggression against women. *Journal of Personality and Social Psychology,* 1978, *36,* 1270–1277.

Donnerstein, E., & Wilson, D. W. Effects of noise and perceived control on ongoing and subsequent aggressive behavior. *Journal of Personality and Social Psychology,* 1976, *34,* 774–781.

Doob, A. N., & Climie, R. J. Delay of measurement and the effects of film violence. *Journal of Experimental Social Psychology,* 1972, *8,* 136–142.

Doob, A. N., & Kirshenbaum, H. M. The effects on arousal of frustration and aggressive films. *Journal of Experimental Social Psychology,* 1973, *9,* 57–64.

Duffy, E. The psychological significance of the concept of "arousal" or "activation." *Psychological Review,* 1957, *64,* 265–275.

Duffy, E. *Activation and behavior.* New York: Wiley, 1962.

Easterbrook, J. A. The effect of emotion on cue utilization and the organization of behavior. *Psychological Review,* 1959, *66,* 183–201.

Feshbach, S. Aggression. In P. H. Mussen (Ed.), *Carmichael's manual of child psychology* (Vol. 2). New York: Wiley, 1970.

Freeman, G. L. The relationship between performance level and bodily activity level. *Journal of Experimental Psychology,* 1940, *26,* 602–608.

Geen, R. G. The meaning of observed violence: Real vs. fictional violence and consequent effects on aggression and emotional arousal. *Journal of Research in Personality,* 1975, *9,* 270–281.

Geen, R. G., & O'Neal, E. C. Activation of cue-elicited aggression by general arousal. *Journal of Personality and Social Psychology,* 1969, *11,* 289–292.

Geen, R. G., & Rakosky, J. J. Interpretations of observed violence and their effects on GSR. *Journal of Experimental Research in Personality,* 1973, *6,* 289–292.

Grossman, S. P. *A textbook of physiological psychology.* New York: Wiley, 1967.

Hebb, D. O. Drives and the C.N.S. (conceptual nervous system). *Psychological Review,* 1955, *62,* 243–254.

Hebb, D. O. *A textbook of psychology* (2nd ed.). Philadelphia: Saunders, 1966.

Hennessy, J. W., & Levine, S. Stress, arousal, and the pituitary-adrenal system: A psychoendocrine hypothesis. In J. M. Sprague & A. N. Epstein (Eds.), *Progress in psychobiology and physiological psychology.* New York: Academic Press, 1979.

Hokanson, J. E. Psychophysiological evaluation of the catharsis hypothesis. In E. I. Megargee & J. E. Hokanson (Eds.), *The dynamics of aggression: Individual, group, and international analyses.* New York: Harper & Row, 1970.

Hokanson, J. E., & Burgess, M. The effects of status, type of frustration, and aggression on vascular processes. *Journal of Abnormal and Social Psychology,* 1962, *65,* 232–237.

Hokanson, J. E., & Shetler, S. The effect of overt aggression on physiological arousal level. *Journal of Abnormal and Social Psychology,* 1961, *63,* 446–448.

Hull, C. L. *Principles of behavior: An introduction to behavior theory.* New York: Appleton, 1943.

Hull, C. L. *A behavior system: An introduction to behavior theory concerning the individual organism.* New York: Wiley, 1952.

Jaffe, Y., Malamuth, N., Feingold, J., & Feshbach, S. Sexual arousal and behavioral aggression. *Journal of Personality and Social Psychology,* 1974, *30,* 759–764.

Konečni, V. J. Annoyance, type and duration of postannoyance activity, and aggression: The "cathartic effect." *Journal of Experimental Psychology: General,* 1975, *104,* 76–102. (a)

Konečni, V. J. The mediation of aggressive behavior: Arousal level versus anger and cognitive labeling. *Journal of Personality and Social Psychology,* 1975, *32,* 706–712. (b)

Kryter, K. D. *The effects of noise on man.* New York: Academic Press, 1970.

Lacey, J. I. Somatic response patterning and stress: Some revisions of activation theory. In M. H. Appley & R. Trumbull (Eds.), *Psychological stress: Issues in research.* New York: Appleton, 1967.

Leventhal, H. Emotions: A basic problem for social psychology. In C. Nemeth (Ed.), *Social psychology: Classic and contemporary integrations.* Chicago: Rand McNally, 1974.

Lindsley, D. B. Emotion. In S. S. Stevens (Ed.), *Handbook of experimental psychology.* New York: Wiley, 1951.

Lindsley, D. B. Psychophysiology and motivation. In M. R. Jones (Ed.), *Nebraska Symposium on Motivation, 1957.* Lincoln: Univ. of Nebraska Press, 1957.

Magoun, H. W. The ascending reticular system and wakefulness. In J. F. Delafresnaye (Ed.), *Brain mechanisms and consciousness.* Springfield, Ill.: Thomas, 1954.

Malmo, R. B. Activation: A neuropsychological dimension. *Psychological Review,* 1959, *66,* 367–386.

Malmo, R. B. *On emotions, needs, and our archaic brain.* New York: Holt, 1975.

Malmo, R. B., & Bélanger, D. Related physiological and behavioral changes: What are their determinants? In S. S. Kety, E. V. Evarts, & H. L. William (Eds.), *Sleep and altered states of consciousness.* Baltimore, Md.: Williams & Wilkins, 1967.

Meyer, T. P. The effects of sexually arousing and violent films on aggressive behavior. *Journal of Sex Research,* 1972, *8,* 324–331.

Miller, N. E. The frustration–aggression hypothesis. *Psychological Review,* 1941, *48,* 337–342.

Moruzzi, G. Reticular influences on the EEG. *Electroencephalography and Clinical Neurophysiology,* 1964, *16,* 2–17.

Moruzzi, G., & Magoun, H. W. Brain stem reticular formation and activation on the EEG. *Electroencephalography and Clinical Neurophysiology,* 1949, *1,* 455–473.

Nisbett, R. E., & Schachter, S. Cognitive manipulation of pain. *Journal of Experimental Social Psychology,* 1966, *2,* 227–236.

Pastore, N. The role of arbitrariness in the frustration–aggression hypothesis. *Journal of Abnormal and Social Psychology,* 1952, *47,* 728–731.

Ross, L., Rodin. J., & Zimbardo, P. G. Toward an attribution therapy: The reduction of fear through induced cognitive-emotional misattribution. *Journal of Personality and Social Psychology,* 1969, *12,* 279–288.

Rothballer, A. B. The effects of catecholamines on the central nervous system. *Pharmacological Reviews,* 1959, *11,* 494–547.

Rothballer, A. B. Aggression, defense and neurohumors. In C. D. Clemente & D. B. Lindsley (Eds.), *Aggression and defense: Neural mechanisms and social patterns* (Vol. 5). *Brain function.* Berkeley: Univ. of California Press, 1967.

Rule, B. G., Dyck, R., & Nesdale, A. R. Arbitrariness of frustration: Inhibition or instigation effects on aggression. *European Journal of Social Psychology,* 1978, *8,* 237–244.

Rule, B. G., Ferguson, T. J., & Nesdale, A. R. Emotional arousal, anger, and aggression: The misattribution issue. In P. Pliner, K. R. Blankstein, & I. M. Spigel (Eds.), *Perception of emotion in self and others.* New York: Plenum, 1979.

Rule, B. G., & Nesdale, A. R. Emotional arousal and aggressive behavior. *Psychological Bulletin,* 1976, *83,* 851–863.

Sapolsky, B. S., Stocking, S. H., & Zillmann, D. Immediate vs. delayed retaliation in male and female adults. *Psychological Reports,* 1977, *40,* 197–198.

Schachter, S. The interaction of cognitive and physiological determinants of emotional state. In L. Berkowitz (Ed.), *Advances in experimental social psychology* (Vol. 1). New York: Academic Press, 1964.

Schachter, S., & Singer, J. Cognitive, social and physiological determinants of emotional state. *Psychological Review,* 1962, *69,* 379–399.

Smith, G. P. Adrenal hormones and emotional behavior. In E. Stellar & J. M. Sprague (Eds.), *Progress in physiological psychology*. New York: Academic Press, 1973.

Sternbach, R. *Principles of psychophysiology*. New York: Academic Press, 1966.

Tannenbaum, P. H. Studies in film- and television-mediated arousal and aggression: A progress report. In G. A. Comstock, E. A. Rubinstein, & J. P. Murray (Eds.), *Television and social behavior* (Vol. 5). *Television's effects: Further explorations*. Washington, D.C.: U.S. Government Printing Office, 1972.

Tannenbaum, P. H., & Zillmann, D. Emotional arousal in the facilitation of aggression through communication. In L. Berkowitz (Ed.), *Advances in experimental social psychology* (Vol. 8). New York: Academic Press, 1975.

Thompson, R. F. *Foundations of physiological psychology*. New York: Harper, 1967.

Turner, C. D., & Bagnara, J. T. *General endocrinology* (5th ed.). Philadelphia: Saunders, 1971.

White, L. A. Erotica and aggression: The influence of sexual arousal, positive affect, and negative affect on aggressive behavior. *Journal of Personality and Social Psychology*, 1979, *37*, 591–601.

Zillmann, D. Excitation transfer in communication-mediated aggressive behavior. *Journal of Experimental Social Psychology*, 1971, *7*, 419–434.

Zillmann, D. Attribution and misattribution of excitatory reactions. In J. H. Harvey, W. J. Ickes, & R. F. Kidd (Eds.), *New directions in attribution research* (Vol. 2). Hillsdale, N.J.: Erlbaum, 1978.

Zillmann, D. *Hostility and aggression*. Hillsdale, N.J.: Erlbaum, 1979.

Zillmann, D., & Bryant, J. Effect of residual excitation on the emotional response to provocation and delayed aggressive behavior. *Journal of Personality and Social Psychology*, 1974, *30*, 782–791.

Zillmann, D., Bryant, J., Cantor, J. R., & Day, K. D. Irrelevance of mitigating circumstances in retaliatory behavior at high levels of excitation. *Journal of Research in Personality*, 1975, *9*, 282–293.

Zillmann, D., & Cantor, J. R. Effect of timing of information about mitigating circumstances on emotional responses to provocation and retaliatory behavior. *Journal of Experimental Social Psychology*, 1976, *12*, 38–55.

Zillmann, D., Hoyt, J. L., & Day, K. D. Strength and duration of the effect of aggressive, violent, and erotic communications on subsequent aggressive behavior. *Communication Research*, 1974, *1*, 286–306.

Zillmann, D., & Johnson, R. C. Motivated aggressiveness perpetuated by exposure to aggressive films and reduced by exposure to nonaggressive films. *Journal of Research in Personality*, 1973, *7*, 261–276.

Zillmann, D., Johnson, R. C., & Day, K. D. Attribution of apparent arousal and proficiency of recovery from sympathetic activation affecting excitation transfer to aggressive behavior. *Journal of Experimental Social Psychology*, 1974, *10*, 503–515.

Zillmann, D., Katcher, A. H., & Milavsky, B. Excitation transfer from physical exercise to subsequent aggressive behavior. *Journal of Experimental Social Psychology*, 1972, *8*, 247–259.

four

The Experience of Anger as a Parallel Process in the Display of Impulsive, "Angry" Aggression

LEONARD BERKOWITZ

THE POSSIBLE ROLE OF EXPERIENCED ANGER

Thinking of Ourselves as Angry

One evening several years ago, when I was much more excitable than I am now, I returned home from my office to find a bill from my accountant for tax services I had not requested. The billing seemed entirely unjustified and, even though it was late, I grabbed the phone and quickly dialed the accountant's home number. To the best of my recollection, I was thinking only of the protest I was going to make and was not especially aware of any feelings at that moment. But then my wife, who was startled by my impulsive action, blurted out, "You're angry!" This simple statement produced a sudden change in my conscious experience and maybe in my behavior as well. I now felt angry, and my remarks to the accountant were somewhat more heated than I had original- ly intended.

I cannot be sure, of course, that my memory of this incident is accurate in every detail. Nonetheless, for our present purposes let us assume that the major features are correct: The label my wife applied to my behavior somehow led me to experience anger, and this heightened feeling seemed to intensify the hostility in my complaints to the offender. Why did this happen? What were the psychological processes that contributed to this sequence of reactions?

103

AGGRESSION
Volume 1

BODILY REACTIONS IN THE EXPERIENCE OF EMOTION

Although it is possible to classify theories of emotion in various ways (cf. Leventhal, 1980), these formulations can be organized in terms of the weight they assign to the emotionally aroused individual's cognitions. At one extreme, we might say, are those analyses that emphasize neurological and somatic responses to the comparative neglect of cognitions. Cannon's (1927) central neural theory, which held that emotional experience depends on activity in the central nervous system, is a good example of this point of view. Thalamic processes presumably determine just what specific feelings are aroused and also what expressive reactions occur. Thus, in explaining my emotional reaction to the accountant's bill, Cannon would say my cerebral cortex excited the thalamic centers of emotion and that signals from these centers then caused both my emotional feelings and my motor reactions. If my wife's remark ("You're angry!") had any effect at all, and this might be questioned, it would occur through an increased stimulation of the thalamic centers. In sum, these neurological reactions aroused my emotion, causing me to be "angry" (even though I was not consciously aware of these feelings at first) and leading me to snatch up the telephone and complain angrily to the offender.

Body reaction theories, such as William James's (1890/1950) well-known conception, take a less commonsensical position. They maintain that the emotional experience arises as the body responds to the provocative event. The outside occurrence stimulates bodily reactions, and our feelings stem from these bodily changes (especially, according to James, those in the viscera). From this perspective, then, my interpretation of the accountant's letter as unfair and unwarranted evoked a variety of reactions throughout the body, and the exact nature of these physiological changes led to my specific feelings. I felt angry only when I detected my bodily responses, perhaps because my wife's remark drew my attention to these reactions.

As most readers know, Cannon's critique of James's theory relegated this line of thought to an almost forgotten attic of psychological history for over two generations, but there has been a recent resurgence in its popularity, largely through the writings of Tomkins (1962, 1963), Izard (1977), and Leventhal (1974, 1980). Extending James's essential thesis, these theorists argue that expressive bodily reactions evoked by the exciting incident are responsible for the distinctive emotional feeling. They also agree in singling out feedback from the facial region, rather than the visceral changes emphasized by James as the major determinant of the specific experience.

COGNITIVE CONCEPTIONS OF EMOTION

Despite the growing interest in these body reaction analyses, the dominant view of emotions in contemporary social psychology insists that cognitive processes create the differentiated feelings. Greatly influenced by Schachter's (1964) cognitive theory of emotion, this formulation holds that the bodily (including neural) responses to a provocation do not in themselves give rise to a distinctive emotional experience or even to particular actions. The external occurrence presumably generates only a general arousal. What feelings people have and what they do about the event theoretically depends on their interpretation of their internal sensations. They will strike out at the source of their arousal if they label their sensations as "anger" but will experience "fear" and may run away if they think they are afraid. This cognitive conception can readily account for my response to my wife's statement. I supposedly accepted her characterization of my behavior, labeled my internal sensations as "anger," and then acted angrily.

Attribution theorizing builds on and extends this analysis. It maintains that the label given to the sensations is greatly influenced by the perceived cause of the event. So, as an extreme example, someone who had recently been insulted might conceivably believe he is not angry if he attributes his internal arousal to a sudden loud noise. Since it is the noise rather than the insult that produced his excitement (he supposedly thinks), he could not be feeling angry, and he therefore acts peacefully.

Zillmann (1979; Chapter 3, this volume) has employed a variation on this theme in his research on the consequences of physical exertion. Assuming that the individual will tend to attribute whatever excitation he feels to salient events in his environment, the young men in one of his experiments (Zillmann, Katcher, & Milavsky, 1972) were first either provoked or not provoked by their partners and then were required to work on either strenuous or easy physical tasks. Shortly afterward, when they had opportunities to punish their partners, the subjects exhibited the strongest aggression if they had been previously angered by their partners and had afterward engaged in strenuous activities. The men had presumably interpreted their relatively strong exercise-induced arousal as anger and then attacked their tormentors in accordance with this belief.

In yet another version of this general idea, Rule, Ferguson, and Nesdale (1979) have more recently argued that external cues associated with arousal affect the aggressive response by influencing the person's attributions regarding the source of his arousal and the label he applies to his feelings. So, if someone is insulted and is then exposed to arousing white noise, as in an experiment by Donnerstein and Wilson (1976), he might well attribute the noise-generated arousal to the insult he suffered. The insult is more salient to him; it commands his attention, and as a result, he interprets the added arousal created by the noise as intense anger.

Some Problems with
the Cognitive Conceptions of Emotion

The cognitive-attribution analysis just summarized continues to dominate the social psychological view of emotional behavior (e.g., Dienstbier, 1979) and is virtually taken for granted in many theoretical accounts of aggression (e.g., Ferguson & Rule, 1982; Rule & Nesdale, 1976; Zillmann, Chapter 3, this volume). Nevertheless, a mounting body of evidence indicates there is far more to emotion than is dreamt of in the cognitive formulation. Let us look at some of the more obvious problems facing this analysis.

UNDUE ENTHUSIASM

One major difficulty, largely methodological in nature, shows how this conception has been accepted so uncritically that ostensibly supporting research has not received adequate scrutiny. Consider the previously mentioned experiment by Zillmann et al. (1972) and the conceptually similar study by Konečni (1975) that are often cited as evidence for the cognitive-attribution analysis. In both of these investigations strong extraneous stimulation caused deliberately provoked subjects to be highly aggressive to their tormentor. The angered subjects had supposedly attributed the heightened arousal generated by the irrelevant stimulation to the earlier provocation and, as a consequence, presumably regarded themselves as extremely angry. An earlier experiment, by Zillmann (1971), is explained in the same fashion. In this case, male college students were first insulted by a confederate and then saw an erotic movie. When they were given an opportunity to punish their tormentor soon afterward, they displayed stronger aggression than other provoked subjects who had watched a less arousing film. Here too, supposedly because of a misattribution process, the sexual arousal had theoretically intensified "feelings of anger in the subject when he was reconfronted with his annoyer [Zillmann, Chapter 3, this volume]."

The problem with all this, as Zillmann (this volume) acknowledges, is that the attribution process was only inferred in these studies and was not assessed directly. There is no direct evidence that the extraneous arousal had heightened the provoked people's feelings of anger (or had affected their self-labeling). The cognitive theorists say the subjects' self-perception must have been influenced, because the intense arousal did not lead to greater aggression when the subjects had not been insulted. But did the irrelevant stimulation necessarily operate by strengthening the anger experience? General behavior theory, espoused by such writers as Hull, Spence, Farber, Zajonc, and others, can account for the Zillmann–Konečni findings without positing any self-labeling. This perspective maintains, quite simply, that the response an individual is set to perform can be "energized" by an irrelevant drive so that the response is carried out more strongly than otherwise would have occurred. The operative phrase here is that *the person has to be disposed to perform the action*. In the case of aggression, the individual has to be ready to attack someone before the extraneous arousal will lead to the stronger punishment.

Thus, both general behavior theory and the cognitive-attribution view of emotion lead to the same prediction for the Zillmann–Konečni experiments.

Behavior theory's advantage is that it does not confine the effect of irrelevant stimulation to instances in which people are angry. The extraneous arousal can produce a stronger reaction regardless of why the individual is set to perform that response. Anger is not required. Here we come to an interesting example of convenient neglect. Some years ago, Geen and O'Neal (1969) reported an experiment in which nonprovoked university men first watched a brief aggressive or nonaggressive scene and then delivered electric shocks to a fellow student. At the time they carried out this latter assignment, they were either exposed to a moderately arousing (but nonpainful) white noise or did not hear any sounds. In keeping with the behavior theory analysis, Geen and O'Neal found that the arousal treatment interacted with the movie condition; the men were most punitive to their peer if they had seen the aggressive film and then heard the arousing noise as they administered the shocks.

What is surprising about all this is that both Zillmann and Konečni neglect the clear theoretical implications of the Geen and O'Neal research even though they referred to this experiment in their papers. Zillmann (this volume) notes only that "the investigators attributed this difference in aggressive behavior to the arousal that probably resulted from exposure to noise. The investigators had *not* made such a statement. No behaviorally oriented theorist would have expected arousal to yield strong aggressive reactions unless a tendency to act aggressively had also been elicited in the situation. And so, Geen and O'Neal (1969) had actually concluded that "general arousal facilitates the expression of aggressive responses to aggressive cues [p. 292]." The aggressive scene had evoked aggressive inclinations—even though the observers were not angry at the time—and the arousal then intensified these reactions. This relatively simple and quite parsimonious notion has been overlooked because of an excessive and uncritical enthusiasm for the cognitive thesis.

THE SUPPOSED NEUTRALITY OF THE AROUSAL STATE

Along with Schachter (1964), cognitive-attributionists typically view the physiological arousal generated by the emotionally exciting event as being affectively neutral. The aroused person theoretically feels pleasant or unpleasant only because he has interpreted his internal sensations in a particular way. To get back to my telephone call to the accountant, the unexpected bill presumably aroused only a neutral excitement at first. However, when my wife said I was angry, I supposedly attributed my sensations to the offending bill, concluded that I had been provoked by the accountant, and only then felt bad. But is the emotional arousal state so ambiguous and highly susceptible to affective shaping by external influences? A growing body of evidence indicates the answer is no.

Some of these critical studies date back to the early 1950s. Ax (1953) and others have reported that the experiences of fear and anger are not accompanied by the same physiological patterns, whereas Izard (1977), Tomkins

(1962, 1963), and others have shown that fairly specific expressive reactions, especially in the face, are associated with particular affective states. Taken together, all this research suggests that there is a closer connection between feelings and bodily reactions than cognitive-attribution notions had initially supposed. Feedback from these bodily reactions might even dispose the individual to experience particular affects. In at least one experiment (Laird, 1974), people's moods were accentuated by manipulating their facial expression in such a way that they did not realize they were deliberately smiling or frowning.

Perhaps more compelling are the Marshall and Zimbardo (1979) and Maslach (1979) failures to replicate Schachter's initial findings. The first of these studies attempted to duplicate the essentials of Schachter's original procedure. Subjects were aroused by an injection of epinephrine and then encountered a happy peer (whose behavior was intended to influence the participants' interpretation of their sensations). However, contrary to the original results, the subject's experience was not molded by the other person's actions. Furthermore, when Marshall and Zimbardo then increased the epinephrine dosage, the participants reported having negative feelings rather than being positively euphoric as one might have expected from the Schachter formulation. Maslach's (1979) findings are equally troublesome for this analysis. Her hypnotically aroused subjects experienced negative affect whether they were exposed to an angry or euphoric confederate.

These observations have a number of implications. First, the emotionally induced arousal state apparently is not as amorphous as cognitive theorists have typically assumed. All emotional occurrences do not produce only an undifferentiated state of excitement that is easily shaped by external influences to yield the distinctive conscious feelings. Schachter and Singer (1979) evidently recognized this in their reply to Marshall and Zimbardo when they noted that intense arousal states are noxious regardless of what else might happen in the environment. Indeed, Maslach's study suggests that people experience distress whenever they are inexplicably aroused and, again, independently of the actions of the others around them. Contrary to the overly enthusiastic claims of some attribution theorists, then, we may feel bad when we encounter an aversive stimulus regardless of what we believe is the source of this stimulation. I will have more to say about this matter later when I discuss the effects of aversive stimuli on aggression.

Second, since people can recognize their feelings as either pleasant or unpleasant (at least), they may not accept some kinds of information about the possible cause of their arousal and may quickly reject certain interpretations of their sensations. In my own case, I would not have believed my wife if she had said my agitation was really due to a joke I had just heard on TV and meant I was happy (instead of angry). It is not simply that the accountant's bill was more salient to me than the TV comedian. I knew I was not happy at that time and could not be convinced that I was. Dienstbier (1979, p. 249) made just this point when he acknowledged that "the pattern of arousal" produced in a given situation can determine just what misattributions are likely to occur, and Marshall and Zimbardo essentially came to the same conclusion when they observed "that our true emotions may be . . . less susceptible to transient or whimsical situational determinants than has been suggested by Schachter and Singer [1979, p. 983]."

ANGER AS A PARALLEL PROCESS

Leventhal's Perceptual-Motor Theory of Emotion

In my view Howard Leventhal's (1980) perceptual-motor theory of emotion offers the best and most comprehensive analysis of emotional experience. While it places a great deal of emphasis on the central nervous system and information processing, I believe this formulation is entirely compatible with my own neobehaviorist position stressing associationistic processes, and I will try to integrate these two lines of thought in a general (and admittedly overly simple) fashion.

To begin, Leventhal regards emotion as "a subjective perceptual experience," so that physiological reactions (such as skin conductance and heart rate) are at best only imperfect indicators of this perception rather than the most important components of an emotion. As with other types of perception, the experience of emotion grows out of a constructive process in which a variety of elements are integrated into a concrete whole. The first stage in this process, called the perceptual-motor stage, generates the quality of the feelings comprising the emotion, while the next stage involves planning and deliberate action. We will be concerned here only with the initial stage.

When the person encounters the exciting event, whatever it might be, he detects the occurrence, interprets it, and also exhibits expressive-motor reactions to this perception. The individual's emotional experience grows directly out of this process, Leventhal says, and does not arise from any thoughtful inferences or judgments that he makes about himself on seeing the situation and observing his responses to it. The person reacts, and these spontaneous reactions (particularly in the facial region) feed back into the central nervous system as the primary generator of the distinctive emotional feeling. Leventhal believes this feeling develops only when the expressive responses are involuntary and outside of focal awareness.

A schematic or emotional memory is the second major mechanism involved in emotional processing (in addition to the expressive system). Inevitably, relatively concrete, episodic representations of earlier emotion-eliciting situations are integrated with the expressive reactions to enrich the perceptual-emotional experience. This schematic memory thus produces the subtler feelings—the experience of intimacy, envy, pride, and so on—that go beyond the perception of the immediate situation and the quick, direct reactions to it. Leventhal

(1980, pp. 172–173) emphasizes that emotional schemata are perceptual-motor memories and thus "exhibit the properties of perceptual memories in general." They operate very rapidly, as do the nonemotional schemata involved in stimulus recognition, and furthermore, like other schemata, the emotional schemata "act as selective devices, focusing attention on particular stimulus features and generating anticipations about later experience." And moreover, also like other schemata, they "play an important role in generalizing emotional experiences." These generalizations presumably take place "along dimensions that are highly characteristic of the set of concrete episodes which originally stimulated that particular class of emotional experiences."

Emotional schemata, as representations of prior emotional experiences, can be evoked by many of the same stimuli that activate the expressive motor reactions (and also, I would add, by stimuli that have been associated with these reactions in the past). Leventhal's thinking here seems to resemble Bower's (1981) network conception of the relationship between mood and memory. Both theorists posit a linkage between emotional feelings and particular thoughts so that the evocation of certain images or ideas might then elicit the feelings that had been connected with these thoughts in the past. This general notion is compatible with the suggestion I offered some years ago (Berkowitz, 1973) that words and symbols having an aggressive meaning can evoke other ideas with the same meaning and even feelings conducive to the display of aggressive behavior. Because of this associative process, a movie scene showing people fighting can elicit a variety of aggressive ideas and images in the viewers, as well as expressive reactions and feelings in their bodies, that had previously been associated with aggression.

Leventhal employs this line of thought in explaining how cognitions might influence a person's emotions without affecting the label he attaches to his sensations. "A change in cognition [can bring] a change in emotion because of the cognition's affect-eliciting properties or its past association with particular emotions. This is not the same as associating a new label with a state of general arousal [1980, p. 154]." Again, let us consider my wife's remark when she saw me pick up the telephone. Her word *angry* was connected with the expressive reactions I typically exhibited when I was enraged. Since I was either performing, or was disposed to perform, many of these reactions (inside me as well as in the nonverbal gestures I showed), the word served as a cue to intensify or evoke the pattern of anger-associated expressive responses. It also elicited images and ideas from the schematic emotional memory that were linked with the anger experience. Working together, these expressive responses, ideas, and images became strong enough so that (a) I was now aware I was angry, and (b) they intensified my verbal hostility toward the accountant. The confederate's behavior in the original Schachter and Singer experiment could have operated in a similar manner. When this person acted angrily, his behavior might have stimulated anger-associated expressive reactions, ideas, and images in the epinephrine-aroused subjects. If they were not inclined toward other actions and thoughts that were incompatible with anger, the anger-linked pattern then dominated their emotional experience and even their overt conduct.

The Experience of Anger as a Parallel Process

All this has several definite implications for the argument I am offering here. Most immediately, we should recognize that external information can influence feelings and behavior without affecting the individual's self-labeling. Contrary to Schachter, Zillmann, and others, a person does not have to think of himself as having a particular emotion if he is to experience the specific feelings or exhibit the kind of behavior that is consistent with this emotion. The label the person applies to his sensations does not in and of itself produce his differentiated feelings and actions.

This is not to say that the label has no impact whatsoever. For one thing, as I have already suggested, emotionally laden words—that the individual either receives from others or provides to himself—can evoke images, ideas, and expressive responses that may strengthen his ongoing emotional reaction. And then too, these label-elicited thoughts and expressive responses might interfere with other reactions that had also been generated by the precipitating event. This type of interference could conceivably account for the results of some of the misattribution experiments. Suppose we have just been provoked by another person in the room. The insult evokes the expressive responses and schematic memories associated with angering events in general. However, as is often the case with social interactions, the encounter might also be fairly ambiguous so that other kinds of emotional reactions are produced as well; it might also stimulate a general excitement, a loss of self-esteem, a desire to be liked, and a host of other types of expressive responses and schematic memories. What if we are then told, as in the typical misattribution study, that a drug we had taken just before has strong emotional side effects? If this information is accepted, it could generate other ideas, images, and feelings inside us, some of which might be incompatible with anger, and the anger-linked reactions are thereby weakened. In essence, the attribution defines the meaning of the incident so that ideas, images, and expressive reactions associated with this meaning are evoked and other classes of emotional responses are suppressed.

But note that the label-produced reactions only combine with the specific emotional responses elicited by the precipitating event, intensifying or weakening them. The label (or the cognition generated by it) is not the only source of these differentiated responses. To a considerable extent, then, the individual's awareness of his emotional state parallels the expressive reactions and schematic memories that had been evoked (although these reactions might also feed into the latter responses, thereby affecting them to some degree). Provocations stimulate many of the expressive reactions, images, and ideas characteristic of anger whether or not there is also an awareness of these anger-linked reactions and thoughts. If the awareness is present, it proceeds alongside these initial expressive responses, images, and ideas.

AVERSIVELY STIMULATED AGGRESSION

Going beyond Perception: Angry Aggression

Theories of emotion typically seem to stop with the emotional experience, or at least pay little attention to the overt behavior accompanying this experience, in contrast to the emphasis that is usually given to the determinants of the individual's feelings. However, since we are concerned here with aggressive behavior, and particularly the aggression displayed in the heat of anger, we obviously have to go beyond the emotional perception to account for this violent action. A comprehensive analysis of "angry" aggression obviously must discuss the origin of the angry feelings but, more than this, should also give considerable attention to the factors controlling the behavior that is actually exhibited and the relationship between the emotional experience and this behavior.

To summarize my argument on this matter, I basically hold that aversive events are the root of angry aggression. These occurrences may arouse fear and an inclination to escape or avoid the unpleasant situation (as well as a general excitement), but in addition, they presumably also elicit many of the expressive-motor reactions and schematic memories that are associated with the experience of anger. Regardless of whether the aversively stimulated person is consciously aware of these expressive responses and memories at the time, these internal reactions produce a tendency to attack the perceived source of the unpleasantness. In other words, aversive incidents create instigations to flight *and* to fight, and the emotional experiences of fear and anger (i.e., the perception of these emotionally linked bodily and ideational reactions) may accompany these instigations. Situational conditions as well as prior learning determine the comparative strengths of these emotional experiences and their associated action tendencies. And moreover, as I have also suggested (Berkowitz, Cochran, & Embree, 1981), learning might also complicate the instigation to attack so that the aversively stimulated individual is inclined to injure a suitable target. If I can again refer to my dealings with the accountant as an illustration, it is easy to put all this in commonsense terms: The accountant's bill was decidedly unpleasant—because of its amount, unexpectedness, and apparent illegitimacy. This aversive stimulus therefore evoked the expressive reactions and schematic memories characteristic of anger even before I was consciously aware of these responses, and they in turn evoked an instigation within me to attack the perceived source.

Research with Humans on
the Effects of Aversive Conditions

For obvious reasons, most of the research with humans into the effects of aversive conditions have employed unpleasant stimuli that people ordinarily avoid but that are not physically painful. Many of these studies indicate that aversive events can heighten the individual's inclination to be aggressive.

ODORS

Two experiments show that unplesant odors can provoke aggressive reactions. In one of these (Jones & Durbin, Note 1), nonsmokers were significantly more punitive to a fellow student in a Buss "aggression machine" paradigm when cigarette smoke was blown into their room than when they worked in a normal atmosphere. This occurred, furthermore, even when the subjects had not been provoked beforehand.

Rotton, Barry, Frey, and Soler (1978) conducted a more ambitious investigation. Undergraduates had to judge a stranger of their own sex either under normal air or while exposed to a foul odor (produced either by butyric acid or ammonium sulfide). The subjects' mood was reliably affected by the polluted atmosphere. They rated themselves as feeling more "aggressive" as well as "anxious," "fatigued," and "sad" in the two odor-filled rooms than in the normal atmosphere, evidently realizing they were feeling irritable as well as generally bad. Also in accord with our expectations, the subjects were also more hostile to the stranger under the aversive conditions.

HIGH TEMPERATURES

Common experience suggests that many people become irritable under high temperatures, and a growing body of research indicates that uncomfortable heat can instigate aggression. In one of the first of the recent laboratory experiments in this area, Griffitt (1970) found that his subjects' ratings of a same-sex stranger were harsher in a hot room (effective temperature = 90.6°F) than in a cooler environment (67.5°F). Their general mood was also much less pleasant in the former case. A later experiment by Griffitt and Veitch (1971) examined the effects of population density as well as room temperature, and showed that both variables independently affected the dependent measures. Again, the subjects' mood was worse and they were more hostile to the stranger when they were hot (effective room temperature = 93.5°F) and in a crowded room (12–16 people in a space 7 ft × 9 ft.) than when they were comfortably cool or in a large room.

Although this research generally supports the notion that aversive events stimulate aggressive tendencies, recent findings have also identified a number of problems that should be addressed by future investigations. These have to do with the possible victim's own emotional state and the magnitude of the aversive stimulation.

THE VICTIM'S STATE

On reviewing the body of research in this area, Kenrick and Johnson (1979) have noted that the published studies have not always obtained the same results. Several experiments found that subjects exposed to unpleasant occurrences were more strongly attracted to another person rather than being more hostile to him. This seemed to happen primarily when the subjects believed the target individual was either undergoing or would soon receive the same treatment that was being inflicted on them. Thus, in another study by Rotton et al. (1978), participants who thought the target individual was exposed to the same foul odor they were smelling tended to become friendlier, and not more hostile, to this person. In the experiment by Kenrick and Johnson (1979), undergraduate women individually rated either their female partner or a simulated stranger while they heard unpredictable bursts of noise that were either very loud (95dB) or more quieter (32dB). In comparison to the quiet condition, the aversive noise led to increased attraction for the physically present partner but decreased liking for the absent stranger.

For Kenrick and Johnson; the important characteristic that determined the research outcome had to do with whether the target individual was physically present or not; aversive events, they argued, lead to hostility toward bogus strangers only and not toward those who are actually nearby. I, on the other hand, along with several other writers (e.g., Bell and Baron, 1976), am inclined to regard shared suffering as the crucial factor. Studies of the psychology of affiliation conducted by Schachter (1959) and others have demonstrated that many of us are attracted to those who share our unhappy experience. However, these individuals become attractive to us to the extent that they seem to react as we do to the unpleasant circumstances and not because they are merely present. Thus, Schachter also reported that his frightened subjects were not drawn to others nearby who were not facing the same threat. Moreover, according to Miller and Zimbardo (1966), apprehensive persons are also not attracted to other individuals who are confronted by the same danger but who supposedly have very different personalities. Being very different kinds of people, these others conceivably might exhibit an altogether different response to the aversive event. In sum, we come to like those who (we believe) have the same emotional feelings we do when they are exposed to the same unpleasant condition (Berkowitz, 1980).

An experiment by Berkowitz and Dunand (Note 2) has yielded findings consistent with this reasoning. Half the subjects were placed in an uncomfortably hot room and then led to think that a peer, who supposedly was receiving the same treatment, was either bothered by the heat or felt quite comfortable in it. When the participants then had an opportunity to administer rewards and punishments to this person, they punished her most severely when she was not distressed by the high temperature that was bothering them and they were least punitive when she seemed to be sharing in their suffering.

This outcome shows how the available target's stimulus characteristics can affect the likelihood that he or she will be attacked. Feeling bad, those who were afflicted by aversive stimulation were inclined to be aggressive. But they were not hostile to a person having strongly positive qualities—for example, if she was fairly attractive to them because she shared in their misery.

LEVEL OF AVERSIVE STIMULATION

Does the escape tendency become stronger at higher levels of aversive stimulation? Some interesting findings suggest there may not be a linear relationship between the intensity of the aversive stimulation inflicted on a person and the strength of the resulting instigation to aggression. In their paper, Griffitt and Veitch (1971) cited some research with mice that pointed to a curvilinear relationship between temperature and aggressive behavior. Aggressive incidents increased until the environment reached about 95°F and then declined sharply. All motor activity, including assaults, decreased with the higher temperatures. Baron (1977) has emphasized this curvilinear relationship in his research. His first experiment on this topic, carried out during a hot and humid South Carolina summer (Baron, 1972), had found that uncomfortably hot temperatures (92–95°F) *reduced* the intensity of the aggression the subjects exhibited in a Buss paradigm over that shown when the participants were comfortably cool. A later experiment (Baron & Bell, 1975) complicated the picture even further. Here nonprovoked subjects were most aggressive in the same kind of paradigm when they were in a hot room (92–95°F), but people who had been insulted beforehand actually decreased the intensity of their punishment under this condition. Baron and Bell reasonably suggested that the "subjects in the hot–angry group found the experimental situation so unpleasant and aversive that escape or minimization of present discomfort became the dominant tendency in their behavior hierarchies. As a result, they may have . . . lowered the intensity of these attacks in order to avoid any delays which might result from their use of strong shocks (e.g., protests for the victim . . .) [p. 830]." In both cases, then, the high temperatures seemed to be too much for many of the subjects, either because they had already been exposed to too much heat (the South Carolina subjects) or because they were hot under the collar, so to say, as a result of the prior insult.

Baron (1977) now suggests that there is a curvilinear relationship between the intensity of the negative affect experienced by a person and his subsequent aggressiveness. Aversive experiences that make an individual feel bad dispose him to be aggressive, but very high levels of negative affect presumably lead to decreasing aggression. In keeping with this formulation, Bell and Baron (1976) reported that subjects exposed to the very unpleasant combination of (a) being in a hot room and (b) receiving a negative evaluation from (c) a confederate whose attitudes were very different from theirs were *less* aggressive to the confederate than their counterparts who either (a) were in a cooler room while dealing with the negatively evaluating, dissimilar subject or (b) were under high temperature but faced a noninsulting confederate with similar views.

These findings raise a number of important questions. It is possible, for example, that the extremely aversive situations in this research had evoked aggressive inclinations but that these tendencies were suppressed by an even stronger desire to escape from the decidedly unpleasant condition. Thus, as Baron and Bell (1975) had conjectured, their subjects feeling the very high levels of negative affect may have been reluctant to do anything, even punish someone, that could conceivably retain them in the unpleasant situation.

Pain and Aggression in Animal Research

If aversive events evoke an instigation to aggression to the extent that they are decidedly unplesant, physical pain should be particularly likely to produce such an inclination to aggression. Animal research indicates this is the case.

EXPERIMENTS WITH ANIMALS

The experiments by Azrin, Ulrich, and their associates (e.g., Ulrich, 1966; Ulrich & Azrin, 1962) have demonstrated, as an example, that physical pain can be a fairly potent stimulus to aggression in a variety of animal species. In these studies, when two animals were cooped up together in a small chamber and given painful electric shocks or physical blows, they often began to fight. Since this reaction occurred with some regularity, emerged without any prior training, and persisted even in the absence of obvious rewards, Ulrich and Azrin (1962) referred to it as reflexive. However, it is probably better to say only that the aggression is a relatively involuntary response to the painful event.

This does not mean that aggression is an inevitable reaction to pain. Some animals in pain do not show any fighting behavior unless they have had prior fighting experience; they prefer to flee unless they have learned that aggression can be rewarding. And the aggression is most likely to arise if the pained animals are close together in a small enclosure rather than apart. All these exceptions show the tenuousness of the relationship between pain and aggression; pain can have many effects and prior learning can greatly influence the nature of the response that is actually made. But still, as Moyer (1976) concluded in his review of the literature, "there can be no doubt that under certain circumstances pain can lead to an intense attack. Such behavior has been demonstrated in the monkey . . . the cat . . . the rat . . . and the gerbil . . . [p. 200]." Given the procedures used in social psychological research on this topic, it is interesting to note that Moyer has also observed that "the most effective stimulus for eliciting this kind of aggression is a sharp, sudden pain, as characterized by electric shock. Other types of aversive stimulation, such as cold, loud noises, and heat, are much less effective in producing aggression [p. 201]."

Several other points suggested by animal research are worth highlighting here because they bear on questions that must be answered if we are to obtain an adequate understanding of the relationship between pain and aggression. I will mention these matters only briefly at this time.

THE GOAL OF PAIN-ELICITED AGGRESSION

Animal experiments indicate that physical pain produces an "urge" to attack some object, as if the hurting organism specifically seeks the opportunity to aggress. In a study by Azrin, Hutchinson, and McLaughlin (1965), as a case in point, the administration of electric shocks led monkeys to pull a chain that delivered an inanimate object they could strike. But just what was the goal of this aggression? What specific class of events would reinforce their aggressive response? Some years ago, Feshbach (1964) differentiated between the inclination to hit and the inclination to hurt, implying that the provoked organism may have a specific desire to inflict injury rather than merely to perform a certain kind of response. In this vein we can ask, what kind of consequence will reinforce the pained organism's aggression—only the performance of the aggressive response or damage to the victim? While the shocked monkeys worked in order to obtain an object they could attack, would their aggressive response have been reinforced more strongly if they had learned that their victim was injured in some way?

FLIGHT OR FIGHT?

Obviously, aggression is not always the likeliest response to noxious stimulation. Animals often attempt to escape or avoid painful stimuli. What is impressive, however, is how frequently animals prefer to aggress rather than get away from the unpleasant stimulation. As Ulrich and Favell observed in their review, "animals would often fight rather than perform the escape or avoidance response [1970, p. 110]." Yet this preference is by no means invariant. Which tendency is prepotent over the other is a function of a variety of factors. "Whether an animal will fight or escape probably depends on a complex interaction of heredity, past history and the present stimulus conditions [Ulrich & Favell, 1970, p. 110]." Even the physical characteristics of the noxious stimulation might conceivably influence the comparative strengths of these two tendencies. According to Ulrich and Favell, several animal studies indicate that intermediate values of noxious stimulation are most likely to produce aggressive reactions. This observation appears to parallel Baron's (1977) previously discussed contention that there is a curvilinear relationship between the negative affect arising from aversive events and the magnitude of the resulting instigation to aggression. Can it be that the instigation to aggress is stronger than the instigation to flee at moderate levels of painful stimulation, whereas the instigation to get away becomes stronger, relatively speaking, when the pain reaches more extreme levels? As suggested earlier, both the instigation to aggress and the instigation to flee might increase in intensity as the painful stimulation mounts, but the inclination to flee could rise at a faster rate so that it overcomes the instigation to aggress at the higher levels of pain.

A PROGRAM OF RESEARCH INTO THE EFFECTS OF PAIN ON AGGRESSION

A number of years ago, I wrote an article about impulsive aggression in which I quoted an observation offered by a veteran homicide detective in Dallas, Texas. It is worth repeating his remark here because it dramatically illustrates the basic phenomenon we have to explain. The detective was talking about the murders he had encountered during the course of his career. "Murders," he said, "result from little ol' arguments about nothing at all. . . . Tempers flare. A fight starts, and somebody gets stabbed or shot (cited in Mulvihill & Tumin, 1969, p. 230]." This is impulsive aggression indeed. The violence apparently had gotten out of hand. It started with an argument "about nothing at all," but the rage evidently mounted rapidly until, finally, there was a violent outburst, probably much more extreme than was initially intended.

The research I will summarize here was designed to investigate some of the basic determinants of this type of phenomenon. While we will not consider the role of insults, fragile egos, or weak inhibitions against aggression, factors that undoubtedly play a very important part in many of these assaults, we will focus on two classes of events that, in a very general way, contribute to these violent incidents: (a) aversive occurrences that generate the instigation to aggression and (b) external cues that facilitate the translation of this instigation into open aggression.

Physical Pain as a Determinant of the Instigation to Aggression

Most of the studies I will discuss in this section inflicted physical pain on the research participants by requiring them to immerse one of their hands in a tank of cold water. While this procedure seems to be far removed from the conditions producing sudden explosions of violence in the "real world," I believe it captures one of the essential features of these occurrences: their painful nature.

From my perspective (cf. Berkowitz, 1978, 1980), frustrations and insults are apt to provoke aggression primarily because they are aversive and thus generate negative affect. This idea is not really new, of course. Researchers (e.g., Amsel, 1962; Azrin, Hutchinson & Hake, 1966; Ferster, 1957; Ulrich, 1966) have long noted that frustrative nonreward has many of the properties of punishment. In general, we attempt to avoid frustrations, undoubtedly because they are unpleasant. It is this decided unpleasantness that produces the aggression-facilitating reactions. Those factors that determine the strength of the aggressive response to some frustration—such as the intensity of the instigation that is unexpectedly blocked and the degree of interference with the goal attainment (cf. Dollard, Doob, Miller, Mowrer & Sears, 1939, p. 28)—have this capacity because they govern the magnitude of the displeasure that is experienced. We cannot say, therefore, as some psychologists have (e.g., Baron, 1977), that frustrations are relatively weak causes of aggression in comparison to personal attacks. All frustrations are not equally bothersome, and all personal attacks do not generate the same displeasure. We can be bitterly disappointed at times when we unexpectedly fail to reach some goal; on the other hand, we can easily brush off a mild criticism. It is not the exact nature of the aversive incident that is important, but how unpleasant it is. This being the case, as I suggested earlier, physical pain should be especially likely to elicit an instigation to aggression.

INTERPRETATION OF THE NOXIOUS STIMULATION

With such other neobehaviorists as Neal Miller (but in some opposition to many Skinnerians), I have long regarded a stimulus, not solely as some objective event, but rather as a construction established by the behaving person. This holds for an aversive stimulus as well. Quite frequently, it is not the stimulus' objective nature in itself that determines its aversiveness but its meaning (i.e., the associations it has for the person). The accountant's bill undoubtedly was much more unpleasant to me than it would have been to many others because of its special significance for me. Clearly, in many instances an attribution's main function is to establish the given occurrence's meaning so that this stimulus is regarded (at least) as pleasant or unpleasant. (However, let me repeat myself: Once this hedonic value is established the individual will experience pleasure or displeasure; his arousal is therefore not affectively neutral.)

Much the same kind of statement can be made about the objective events that produce physical pain. Nearly every authority has noted that the pain experience cannot be understood solely in terms of physical sensations (cf. Melzack, 1973). What the individual experiences depends to a considerable extent on how the sensory input is psychologically processed. He receives the aversive stimulation and interprets it in some way, thus determining the magnitude of the negative affect that he experiences. And it is this negative affect that evokes the instigation to aggression.

Pauline Thome and I employed a variation of a procedure that had been followed earlier by Leventhal, Brown, Shacham, and Engquist (1979) in order to test this reasoning. The undergraduate women serving as subjects were asked to keep one hand in a tank of water, supposedly as part of an investigation of the harsh environmental conditions on supervision. Two-thirds of them were to find that the water in the tank was quite cold (7° C.), whereas for the remaining participants the water was a much more pleasant 23° C. But just before they immersed their hand in the water, they were given preparatory information. The people in one of the cold water conditions and in another group about to be exposed to the warmer temperature were warned that they might feel pain. The other cold water condition was told only of the possible tingling sensations they might experience in their hand and the word *pain* was not used. Immediately after getting this information, each person as told to place her hand in the water; she was then required to evaluate her partner's ideas on a series of problems by administering rewards and punishments to her. At the end of the 6-min session, the subjects rated how they had experienced the water temperature and what their mood had been while their hand was in the water.

These latter ratings generally confirmed Leventhal's earlier findings: In general, the women reported having felt the greatest distress when they were exposed to the cold water *and* had expected to feel pain. These people apparently coded their physiological sensations as "pain" so that they then experienced strong distress. More pertinent to our present interests, they also indicated the greatest level of felt annoyance on an index composed of their ratings of "anger," "irritation," and "annoyance." But most important of all, this annoyance evidently was translated into open punitiveness. The participants exposed to the cold water who expected pain were reliably harsher to their worker than were any of the others.

TO HIT OR HURT?
THE GOAL OF AVERSIVELY STIMULATED AGGRESSION

As we have seen, a number of investigations have now demonstrated that aversive events can evoke aggressive inclinations in humans, although it is also apparent that these dispositions are not necessarily revealed in open behavior. However, this research has not shown just what is the goal of the instigation to aggression.

For some writers (e.g., Zillmann, 1979), the aversive stimulation elicits defensive aggression. The pained animal or human supposedly mistakenly attributes the unpleasant event to the salient target in the situation and then attacks this target in order to lessen his discomfort. The goal of the aggressive action, then, presumably is the lessening or termination of the aversive occurrence. It seems to me, however, that the painful stimulation does more than create a desire to escape, avoid, or terminate the unplesant event; it also evokes appetitive aggression, an instigation to attack some target. Can we reasonably assume that the unpleasantly treated subjects in the human experiments I summarized earlier had thought the person they were evaluating or punishing (depending on the study) was the source of their discomfort or that their reactions to this individual would somehow lessen their discomfort? They were hostile to an innocent bystander, someone they could not blame for their suffering.

But even assuming that the aversively stimulated persons were exhibiting appetitive aggression, were their attacks necessarily intended to injure that person? Some of the animal experiments cited earlier (e.g., Azrin et al., 1965) suggested that the pained organism can be reinforced simply by the opportunity to aggress. If we think in terms of Feshbach's (1964) differentiation between the urge to hit and the urge to hurt, it may be that these animals were instigated to "hit" a target. And similarly, the unpleasantly treated students in the human studies might also have been instigated to attack rather than to hurt the nearby stranger.

I have suggested, however, that the aversively stimulated individual does have the goal of inflicting injury. Whatever else he might want to do—lessen his discomfort, enhance his status, and so on—he presumably also seeks to hurt someone, especially but not only the source of his displeasure. Information that an aversively stimulated person has an opportunity to hurt an available target might therefore serve as an incentive to incite stronger aggression— if he wants to inflict pain. Berkowitz et al. (1981) conducted two experiments based on this possibility.

Again, as is now almost standard in the present research program, each undergraduate woman in these investigations was asked to "supervise" her partner's work by giving her rewards and punishments, while keeping one hand in a tank of water. In the first of our two experiments, this was done in three phases. First a 7-min period in which the subject had her hand in the water and listened to her partner call off 10 solutions to the two problems that had been given her. Then, after a brief intermission in which the subject's hand was out of the water, she replaced her hand in the tank and heard her partner call off another 10 ideas for solving two new problems. This also lasted 7 min. Finally, there was a third phase in which the subject as "supervisor" was not required to keep her hand in the water while making her judgments. Thus, there were 10 opportunities to reward or punish the partner in each of the three phases.

There were two experimental variations in both studies. For half of the subjects, the water in the tank was quite cold (6°C), while it was much more comfortable for the others (18°C in Study 1 and 23°C in Study 2). Orthogonal to this variation, before the sessions started, the subjects were also given information about the supposed effects of any punishment that they delivered. Half of them were told that, on the basis of earlier studies, their punishments were likely to help their partner's performance, whereas the others were informed that punishment would probably hurt the woman's work somewhat.

Questionnaire ratings made in the brief intervals between the phases indicated quite clearly in both experiments that the women exposed to the cold water found this treatment much more unpleasant than those exposed to the warmer water. Moreover, when they rated their moods, those in the cold water condition described themselves as feeling more tense, more hurt, more irritable, more annoyed, and less relaxed than the others. None of these ratings were affected by the other experimental manipulations.

The discipline the subjects administered to their partner was affected by the two experimental variations in both experiments. In particular, the water temperature interacted with punishment outcome to affect the number of rewards given the partner. Although many more rewards than punishments were given over all, the lowest number of rewards was given by the group exposed to the cold water that was informed punishment would hurt their partner. These particular people apparently were most inclined not to reward the other woman, presumably because they wanted to hurt her. If we consider the total number of rewards as the obverse of punishment, so that a low frequency of rewards is somewhat punitive, the subjects' pain-induced punitiveness evidently was facilitated by the information that they had an opportunity to injure the other individual.

Interestingly enough, the experimental treatments did not produce any significant effects at all when the subjects did not have their hands in the water. It might be that people actually have to be undergoing a painful experience at the time if they are to be instigated to aggression.

THOUGHTS OF PUNISHMENT AS A FACILITATOR OF PAIN-INDUCED AGGRESSION

In the last mentioned studies, the subjects' pain-induced inclination to aggression was most strongly translated into open punitiveness when they realized they could hurt someone. The opportunity to achieve their goal, the infliction of injury, had evidently spurred them to treat their partner relatively harshly. In the same vein, as I (Berkowitz, 1973), Leventhal (1980), and Bower (1981) probably would have predicted, other situational cues can also turn people's thought to the possibility of doing harm so that they exhibit a high level of punitiveness when exposed to aversive stimulation. Suppose, for example, that they had been asked to justify the use of punishment as they kept their hand in cold water. Being in an unpleasant situation, ideas, images, and expressive reactions conducive to aggression would be easily evoked, especially since they were thinking of punishment, and these responses might then facilitate the subsequent pain-induced aggression.

I conducted an experiment along these very lines. The subjects, this time undergraduate men, were first asked to keep one of their hands in a tank of water for 5 min while they wrote an essay on an assigned topic. (The ostensible purpose was to investigate the effects of environmental stimulation on imagination.) Half of the men were instructed to argue in favor of punishment as a disciplinary technique, whereas the others were told to write about the advantages of life in the cold northern states as against life in the sunbelt. At the end of the 5 min, each participant was placed in our standard "supervisory" role and required to administer rewards and punishments to a fellow student as evaluations of that person's problem solutions. As usual, there were 10 opportunities to deliver these rewards and punishments during the 6-min session.

The essay task interacted significantly with the aversiveness of the water temperature to affect the severity of the subjects' treatment of their partner ($p <$ .01). By and large, the men required to think of punishment while their hand was in the painfully cold water administered the greatest number of punishments to the other person, reliably more than that given in either of the two warm water groups. Other findings we cannot go into here argue against a demand characteristics interpretation of these results and also tend to contradict the possibility that the punishment essay had merely lowered the subjects' restraints against being punitive. Instead, the data suggest that it was fairly easy for the people exposed to the 6°C water to write about punishment and that they even enjoyed this assignment to some extent. Thoughts of punishment evidently came readily to mind for them. These thoughts, and the semantically associated ideas about aggression then may have facilitated the aggressive reactions elicited by the aversive stimulation.

The Role of Environmental Stimuli

Over the years, virtually since my first book on aggression (Berkowitz, 1962), I have given special attention to the way certain environmental stimuli (called aggressive cues) can enhance the likelihood that a suitably disposed individual will attack an available target (also cf. Berkowitz, 1964, 1974). These cues are especially important in impulsive acts of aggression, such as homicidal assaults. If we think back to the enraged people discussed by the Dallas detective I quoted earlier, we might wonder why it is that the violence had gotten out of control in so many instances. Many of the murderers had wanted to strike, and even hurt, their victims. But in some cases, at least, they had not wanted to kill these persons. Why had their attack been so extreme or so strong? I suggest, in keeping with the Geen and O'Neal (1969) findings I discussed earlier, that the aggressors may have been affected by stimuli in their surroundings. The aversive event they had experienced (a humiliation, insult, or frustration) had produced the expressive reactions and schematic memories characteristic of anger. They might have been able to restrain themselves, to some extent at least, if they had not been stimulated further by the aggressive cues in the situation. These stimuli intensified the expressive responses, ideas, and images within them that were associated with aggression and thus evoked the violent assault.

WEAPONS AS AGGRESSIVE CUES: THE WEAPON EFFECT

Guns are a good example of such a stimulus. Imagine a husband and wife in the midst of a furious argument and also that the husband has had several drinks so that his inhibitions are relatively weak. Then let us suppose that the husband happens to glance at a nearby table and sees an open drawer containing a pistol. The mere sight of the weapon might elicit ideas, images, and expressive reactions that had been linked with aggression in the past so that the man's aggressive inclinations are strengthened. He grabs the pistol, and without thinking, points the gun at his wife and pulls the trigger.

This possibility is supported by the results in the experiment by Berkowitz and LePage (1967). Deliberately provoked university men were more aggressive toward their tormentor if two guns were lying nearby than if only two neutral objects were present. When the men saw the weapons and thought of them as aggressive objects (i.e., used to intentionally injure someone or something), the guns presumably served as aggressive cues to elicit internal, aggression-enhancing responses that increased the strength of their attacks; the evoked impulsive responses rode along with the instrumental components of the subjects' behavior, intensifying their aggression.

This analysis attracted some attention for several years, partly because of our national concern about the domestic violence that seemed to be tearing at the fabric of our society and also (I believe) because it held that we sometimes react mindlessly and impulsively to features of our environment. Other behavioral scientists then sought to replicate my original experiment (with LePage) that demonstrated the weapons effect. Their efforts met with mixed success. Indeed, several investigators (e.g., Page & Scheidt, 1971) failed to duplicate our findings, so that critics then argued that the original results were due to "demand cues" in the experiment. According to them, the subjects in our study had caught on to what we wanted of them when they saw the weapons on the laboratory table and then exhibited a high level of aggressive behavior only because they wanted to confirm our hypothesis. There really was no good evidence, the critics maintained, that the trigger could pull the finger.

Later studies have refuted this objection fairly well. Much of this positive evidence has been summarized by Turner, Simons, Berkowitz, and Frodi (1977), but nevertheless, since this paper and many of the other confirming investigations have not been published in mainstream journals, the current status of the weapons effect research is not well known.

The first matter we should take up in this brief review has to do with the possible role of demand cues. Did the experimental subjects regard the nearby weapons only as a signal that they ought to be highly aggressive if they wanted to be good subjects? Charles Turner, along with his associate Lynn Simons

(Turner & Simons, 1974), addressed this question. Their reasoning was quite straightforward. If many of the participants in the earlier experiments had caught on to why the guns were present in the room, and had then given the experimenter the high level of aggression they believed he wanted, other subjects who also become aware of the weapons' experimental importance should then also exhibit a good deal of laboratory aggression. Turner and Simons tested this demand prediction by having a confederate, posing as a student who had just finished serving in the experiment, give the waiting naive subject some prearranged information. In the condition intended to create a relatively high awareness of the experimenter's purpose, the confederate "revealed" that the subject would see weapons on a table and that they were probably meant to change his reactions. By contrast, in the medium awareness condition, the naive subject was told only that the study probably involved some deception. Later, when each participant was given an opportunity to deliver shocks to another person, the greater his awareness of the importance of the guns on the table the *fewer* the shocks he tended to administer.

In other words, the subjects' knowledge of the experimenter's interest in the weapons led them to restrain their aggression rather than to exhibit a high level of this behavior as the demand idea would have us expect. A later experiment by Simons and Turner (1976) corroborated this finding. All in all, these studies (as well as several other investigations) indicate that the display of aggression in the experimental laboratory is apt to come about in spite of the subjects' suspicions rather than because of their awareness of the experimental hypothesis. The reason, of course, is that the participants do not want to act in a socially disapproved fashion. If they think the researcher is watching their aggression, they are likely to hold back and not show this antisocial behavior.

These observations can help us explain many of the negative results obtained by Buss and others (see Turner et al., 1977). Their subjects might have detected the experimenter's interest in their responses to the nearby weapons or they conceivably might have become apprehensive about the aggressive inclinations they felt, and so they restrained themselves. But whatever the exact reason for the inhibitions against aggression, it is clear that these restraints are all too apt to exist in the laboratory. We are unlikely to see the stimulating effects of the mere presence of guns unless the subjects are relatively uninhibited at the time (and also, keep in mind, assign an aggressive meaning to the weapons).

All this is not to say there have been no other experimental demonstrations of the weapons effect after my original 1967 experiment. Indeed, other researchers have obtained comparable findings in a variety of settings and with a broad range of research participants. For example, Frodi (1975) showed that Swedish high school students gave relatively many shocks to the available target after being exposed to a weapon. This occurred, moreover, even when the subjects were not angry at the time. (In my original study, the weapons effect was obtained only if the participants had been insulted beforehand.)

Frodi's youngsters probably were sufficiently uninhibited for some reason, so that their heightened aggressiveness was revealed even when they had not been provoked by the target person. Anger arousal is not necessary for the weapons effect; it probably only makes it more likely that this gun-evoked stimulation will appear in open behavior.

Leyens and Parke (1975) have reported an interesting extension of this phenomenon with Belgian university students, although the effect was significant in their study only when the subjects were angry. Instead of exposing the men to actual weapons, the researchers asked the participants to look at slides while ostensibly waiting for their partners. These slides had been chosen so that they were either high, moderate, or low in aggressive meaning as rated by another group of judges. Soon afterward, when the subjects could select the intensity of the punishment they wanted to give their partners, the provoked men who had seen the pictures of the highly aggressive objects (guns) were reliably more punitive than the people in the other conditions. Pictures of weapons as well as movies portraying aggression can also elicit aggression-facilitating reactions in susceptible viewers.

Like their real-life brothers, toy guns are not entirely neutral and can also increase the chances of aggression. Turner and Goldsmith (1976) observed 4- and 5-year-old children in a nursery setting who played either with their usual toys, with such novel toys as planes, or with toy weapons. In keeping with somewhat similar findings obtained by other investigators, Turner and Goldsmith found that the play with the make-believe guns was followed by a significant increase in verbal and physical antisocial behavior. It is important to note here that the measure of antisocial behavior did not include actions that were appropriate for toy pistols (such as saying, "Bang, bang, you're dead!") but had more to do with pushing, shoving, and hitting. Finally, I will mention just one more study dealing with what seems to be make-believe aggression but that also points to the aggression-stimulating consequences of weapons. In this research (see Turner et al., 1977), Simons and his associates investigated the behavior of young men at a college spring carnival. Taking advantage of one of the carnival booths that invited the students to throw wet sponges at a live clown, the psychologists placed a rifle conspicuously near the front of the booth for some players and removed the gun for others. The participants did not know they were involved in an experiment, but they still threw more sponges at the available target when they were exposed to the rifle. And here, too, this happened even when the students were not angry with their victim.

The weapons effect seems real, but why does it occur—when it does? In my original formulation, I likened the weapon to a conditioned stimulus; to the extent that it had aggressive associations (i.e., an aggressive meaning), it was capable of evoking other reactions that were also associated with aggression and that could therefore facilitate aggressive behavior. More recently, however, Turner and Layton (1976) have published a study of the weapons effect that is entirely compatible with Leventhal's (1980) analysis of emotions. Recall that in Leventhal's theory the emotional occurrence stimulates both expressive re-actions and memories and that the latter are presumably largely schematic images. Situational stimuli that evoke these emotional images should therefore elicit the expressive reactions and feelings that are linked with them and thus enhance overt aggression. In the Turner and Layton experiment, subjects learned a list of words that had either an aggressive or a neutral meaning and that were also either high or low in imagery value. Immediately afterward, when they were required to punish a fellow student for mistakes on an assigned task, those who had learned aggressive words high in imagery value gave their partner the strongest shocks. These words evidently evoked easily imagined and vivid memories associated with aggression, and the associated responses then facilitated the performance of overt aggression.

ASSOCIATIONS WITH POSITIVE REINFORCEMENTS FOR AGGRESSION

So far, I have suggested that an external stimulus is apt to elicit aggression-facilitating reactions to the extent that this stimulus is associated with the notion of aggression (i.e., has aggressive meaning). Thus, people might be-come more inclined to act aggressively after they see a violent movie, simply because they regard the persons on the screen as trying to hurt each other (Berkowitz & Alioto, 1973). However, there is a question as to whether the aggressive reactions are evoked because the stimuli have this general aggres-sive meaning or because they have more specific associations. Several years ago, I hypothesized that the crucial aspect of an aggressive cue is its linkage with positively reinforced aggression (Berkowitz, 1974). In this sense, weapons might promote violence because they are frequently connected with successful aggression. They signify aggression that works and not merely aggression in general. Turner and Layton (1976) offered a variation on this possibility when they noted that guns could function as retrieval cues reminding many persons of earlier aggressive scenes, especially episodes in which aggression paid off.

A number of studies have pointed to the importance of these associations with positively reinforced aggression. At the animal level, several experiments have demonstrated that a previously neutral stimulus can elicit overt attacks after it has been paired with rewards for fighting (cf. Berkowitz, 1974, p. 170). Geen and Stonner (cf. Berkowitz, 1974, p. 170) have obtained comparable results with adult humans. And moreover, the research on pain cues with angered college students can be looked at in the same light. In these investiga-tions, provoked men attack their tormentor more strongly on learning that the punishment they are delivering is painful to this person (cf. Baron, 1977; Berkowitz, 1974). The information about the provocateur's suffering indicates that they are approaching their aggressive goal (the infliction of an appropriate degree of injury); being associated with this mounting success, it evokes still stronger aggression.

ASSOCIATIONS WITH AVERSIVE EVENTS

At the opposite end of the conceptual spectrum, environmental stimuli that are linked to aversive events can also stimulate aggressive responses. This has also been documented by both animal and human experiments. Thus, the presentation of stimuli that had been paired with unpleasant occurrences can start animals fighting (Hutchinson, 1972; Hutchinson, Renfrew, & Young, 1971). In much the same vein, experiments by Fraczek and his associates in Poland have demonstrated that associations with aversive events can affect the intensity of human aggression. Some of the university students in one of his studies (Fraczek, 1974) were taught to associate the color green with the receipt of electric shocks. Soon afterward, when all the students were asked to punish someone else, half the people found that the apparatus they were to employ in administering the punishment was painted green, whereas for the others, the "weapon" apparatus was a different color. The most punitive subjects were those whose "weapon" had the color-mediated connection with their earlier suffering.

These pain-related associations obviously need not be confined to similarities in color or other physical characteristics. People who have a name-mediated connection with earlier frustraters are apt to evoke relatively strong attacks from those who are disposed to be aggressive at the time (Berkowitz & Knurek, cited in Berkowitz, 1973). In other words, a target can facilitate the aggression that is directed against it by being associated with earlier aversive events, occurrences that had previously produced an instigation to aggression.

This reasoning can be extended even further. Consider those who are handicapped in a very unfortunate way or who are afflicted with some terrible disease. We might sympathize with these people, feeling sorry for the suffering they are undergoing. However, as a great many writers have noted, there is a good chance that we will also, at the same time, experience some distaste for them. In Goffman's (1963) terminology, these persons are stigmatized. They have an undesirable physical characteristic, and we may want to get away from them. Several studies have obtained evidence of this inclination to withdraw from those who are crippled or disfigured in some way (e.g., Kleck, Ono, & Hastorf, 1966). At least one investigation (Piliavin, Piliavin, & Rodin, 1975) has even found that there may well be a considerable reluctance to help someone who is stigmatized in this manner. Thus, we are often ambivalent toward those who are handicapped or ill, feeling sorry for them and also finding them aversive (Katz, Glass, Lucido, & Farber, 1977).

There are a good many reasons why these stigmatized persons are aversive to us. For one thing, we may be threatened by their affliction. The analysis I have been offering raises one possible explanation: Those who are ill or handicapped are associated with unpleasantness, with suffering, and perhaps even with pain. To a considerable extent, they are aversive because of this connection. Assuming this is the case, then, physically stigmatized people should tend to draw hostility from those who are disposed to be aggressive and whose restraints against aggression happen to be weak on that occasion.

Frodi and I (Berkowitz & Frodi, 1979) have reported two experiments with undergraduate women showing that targets with undesirable physical characteristics tend to receive relatively strong punishment. In the second of these investigations, the women first watched a televised interview between the experimenter and a 10-year-old boy whom they were later to supervise. Unknown to the subjects, the interview had been videotaped earlier and the child was made up so that he was either good-looking or fairly unattractive in appearance. And furthermore, cross-cutting this variation, in half the cases the youngster stuttered, whereas in the other instances he spoke normally.

At the close of the interview, the child worked on his assigned task with the TV monitor turned off. The subject-as-supervisor was informed each time the boy made a mistake and had to punish the child by giving him a blast of noise that he would hear over his earphones. However, the subject could select the intensity of the punishment she delivered on a 10-step scale ranging from quite weak to fairly intense. It is important to note that each woman had another job to perform as she "supervised" the boy, so that she was somewhat distracted at the time and not fully aware of what she was doing.

Our findings generally supported our expectations. Combining all 10 of the opportunities that the subjects had to punish the youngster, the women were significantly more punitive to the unattractive-looking than to the good-looking boy. The most intense punishment of all, as we had predicted, was administered to the child who was both "funny looking" and had the speech impediment. This unfortunate youngster was doubly stigmatized: in appearance and with his speech handicap. Being twice afflicted, he evoked the strongest attacks upon him.

CONCLUSION

The approach I have taken here should not be misunderstood. I certainly have not been arguing that an emotionally aroused person's cognitions do not have any influence on his actions. His interpretation of the precipitating event undoubtedly has a considerable impact on what he feels and how he will act. He might regard the occurrence as unpleasant so that he experiences negative affect and is then instigated to aggression, or he could think of the very same incident in neutral terms and have relatively little feeling at all. Moreover, his understanding of what happened could determine the perceived cause of the event, and thus, the person he is most likely to attack if he is disposed to be aggressive, or it might lead him to restrain his aggression because such behavior seems dangerous or morally wrong.

My point is not that cognitions have no effect but that they need not be all-important, especially after the individual has experienced strong displeasure.

Once these negative feelings arise, for whatever reason, the person presumably will be instigated to aggression and may even attack any available target, particularly if the potential victim has appropriate stimulus characteristics. In other words, the person does not have to think of himself as angry in order to display emotional, "angry" aggression. The expressive reactions and emotional memories generated by the negative affect can stimulate aggressive responses within him that create, at least, a fairly strong disposition to aggression. (To repeat myself, however, the evoked instigation may not be revealed in open behavior if the individual's interpretation of the situation engenders a strong desire to flee from the encounter or if he believes his ends will best be served by restraining his aggression.)

Cognitions can also affect the characteristics that determine whether a given external stimulus is capable of evoking the involuntary reactions that can intensify aggressive behavior. In many instances, it is the meaning that the individual assigns to the stimulus that determines what associations it will have for him. He might think of a gun as an aggressive object that is intended to hurt others, or he might regard it as something terrible and even morally reprehensible so that the sight of it elicits more fear and anxiety than aggressive tendencies. Interpretations probably play a very important part in affecting the audience's reaction to scenes of violence and even to contact sports. Is the clash of the opponents on the athletic field an *aggressive* encounter, or are they only competing in a skillful and determined fashion? The spectators who view the game in the former manner are more likely to be stimulated aggressively by it (Berkowitz & Alioto, 1973). Similarly, thought processes create the semantic networks that link feelings, images, and ideas and that determine whether a particular stimulus can evoke the emotional memories and expressive responses that facilitate emotional behavior.

Again, however, whatever factors have influenced the characteristics of the external stimulus, this environmental detail often acts in a largely automatic fashion to produce the impulsive behavior. This is especially likely if the person is already disposed to perform that action for some reason. We can easily understand why an enraged individual is so apt to strike at somebody in an apparently irrational manner. His intensely unpleasant experience generates the internal reactions that make him highly susceptible to the operation of external aggressive cues. His thoughts are fairly simple at the time, establishing the meaning of the incident and of the stimuli in his surroundings. But in the heat of his passion, he probably is not engaging in the sort of analyses envisioned by the cognitive-attribution theories of emotion.

REFERENCE NOTES

1. Jones, J. W., & Durbin, M. J. The effects of secondary cigarette smoke on aggressive behavior of non-smokers. Presented at summer meetings of the Illinois Alliance of Nonsmokers, Chicago, Illinois, 1978.

2. Berkowitz, L., & Dunand, M. Misery wants to share the misery. Unpublished data, 1981.

REFERENCES

Amsel, A. Frustrative nonreward in partial reinforcement and discrimination learning: Some recent history and a theoretical extension. *Psychological Review,* 1962, *69,* 306–328.

Ax, A. The physiological differentiation between fear and anger in humans. *Psychosomatic Medicine,* 1953, *15,* 433–442.

Azrin, N., Hutchinson, R., & Hake, D. Extinction-induced aggression. *Journal of the Experimental Analysis of Behavior,* 1966, *9,* 191–204.

Azrin, N. H., Hutchinson, R. R., & McLaughlin, R. The opportunity for aggression as an operant reinforcer during aversive stimulation. *Journal of Experimental Analysis of Behavior,* 1965, *8,* 171–180.

Baron, R. A. Aggression as a function of ambient temperature and prior anger arousal. *Journal of Personality and Social Psychology,* 1972, *21,* 183–189.

Baron, R. A. *Human aggression.* New York: Plenum, 1977.

Baron, R. A., & Bell, P. A. Aggression and heat: Mediating effects of prior provocation and exposure to an aggressive model. *Journal of Personality and Social Psychology,* 1975, *31,* 825–832.

Bell, P. A., & Baron, R. A. Aggression and heat: The mediating role of negative affect. *Journal of Applied Social Psychology,* 1976, *6,* 18–30.

Berkowitz, L. *Aggression: A social-psychological analysis.* New York: McGraw-Hill, 1962.

Berkowitz, L. Aggressive cues in aggressive behavior and hostility catharsis. *Psychological Review,* 1964, *71,* 104–122.

Berkowitz, L. Words and symbols as stimuli to aggressive responses. In J. F. Knutson (Ed.), *Control of aggression: Implications from basic research.* Chicago, Ill.: Aldine-Atherton, 1973.

Berkowitz, L. Some determinants of impulsive aggression: Role of mediated associations with reinforcements for aggression. *Psychological Review,* 1974, *81,* 165–176.

Berkowitz, L. Whatever happened to the frustration–aggression hypothesis? *American Behavioral Scientist,* 1978, *32,* 691–708.

Berkowitz, L. *A survey of social psychology* (2nd ed.). New York: Holt, 1980.

Berkowitz, L., & Alioto, J. The meaning of an observed event as a determinant of its aggressive consequences. *Journal of Personality and Social Psychology,* 1973, *28,* 206–217.

Berkowitz, L., Cochran, S., & Embree, M. Physical pain and the goal of aversively stimulated aggression. *Journal of Personality and Social Psychology,* 1981, *40,* 687–700.

Berkowitz, L., & Frodi, A. Reactions to a child's mistakes as affected by her/his looks and speech. *Social Psychology Quarterly,* 1979, *42,* 420–425.

Berkowitz, L., & LePage, A. Weapons as aggression-eliciting stimuli. *Journal of Personality and Social Psychology,* 1967, *7,* 202–207.

Bower, G. H. Mood and memory. *American Psychologist,* 1981, *36,* 129–148.

Cannon, W. B. The James-Lange theory of emotions: A critical examination and an alternative theory. *American Journal of Psychology,* 1927, *39,* 106–124.

Dienstbier, R. A. Emotion-attribution theory: Establishing roots and exploring future perspectives. In R. A. Dienstbier (Ed.), *1978 Nebraska Symposium on Motivation.* Lincoln: Univ. of Nebraska Press, 1979.

Dollard, J., Doob, L., Miller, N., Mowrer, O. & Sears, R. *Frustration and aggression.* New Haven: Yale Univ. Press, 1939.

Donnerstein, E., & Wilson, D. W. Effects of noise and perceived control on ongoing and subsequent aggressive behavior. *Journal of Personality and Social Psychology,* 1976, *34,* 774–781.

Ferguson, T. J., & Rule, B. G. An attributional perspective on anger and aggression. In R. G. Geen & E. Donnerstein (Eds.), *Aggression: Theoretical and empirical reviews.* New York: Academic Press, 1982.

Ferster, C. B. Withdrawal of positive reinforcement as punishment. *Science,* 1957, *126,* 509.

Feshbach, S. The function of aggression and the regulation of aggressive drive. *Psychological Review,* 1964, *71,* 257–272.

Fraczek, A. Informational role of situation as a determinant of aggressive behavior. In J. de Wit & W. W. Hartup (Eds.), *Determinants and origins of aggressive behavior*. The Hague: Mouton, 1974.

Frodi, A. The effect of exposure to weapons on aggressive behavior from a cross-cultural perspective. *International Journal of Psychology*, 1975, *10*, 283–292.

Geen, R. G., & O'Neal, E. C. Activation of cue-elicited aggression by general arousal. *Journal of Personality and Social Psychology*, 1969, *11*, 289–292.

Goffman, E. *Stigma: Notes on the management of spoiled identity*. Englewood Cliffs, N.J.: Prentice-Hall, 1963.

Griffitt, W. Environmental effects on interpersonal affective behavior: Ambient effective temperature and attraction. *Journal of Personality and Social Psychology*, 1970, *15*, 240–244.

Griffitt, W., & Veitch, R. Hot and crowded: Influence of population density and temperature on interpersonal affective behavior: Ambient effective temperature and attraction. *Journal of Personality and Social Psychology*, 1971, *17*, 92–98.

Hutchinson, R. R. The environmental causes of aggression. In J. K. Cole & D. D. Jensen (Eds.), *Nebraska Symposium on Motivation, 1972*. Lincoln: Univ. of Nebraska Press, 1972.

Hutchinson, R. R., Renfrew, J. W., & Young, G. A. Effects of long-term shock and associated stimuli on aggressive and manual responses. *Journal of the Experimental Analysis of Behavior*, 1971, *15*, 141–166.

Izard, C. E. *Human emotions*. New York: Plenum, 1977.

James, W. *The principles of psychology* (Vol. 2). New York: Dover, 1950. (Originally published, 1890.)

Katz, I., Glass, D. C., Lucido, D. J., & Farber, J. Ambivalence, guilt, and the denigration of a physically handicapped victim. *Journal of Personality*, 1977, *45*, 419–429.

Kenrick, D. T., & Johnson, G. A. Interpersonal attraction in aversive environments: A problem for the classical conditioning paradigm? *Journal of Personality and Social Psychology*, 1979, *37*, 572–579.

Kleck, R., Ono, H., and Hastorf, A. H. The effects of physical deviance upon face-to-face interaction. *Human Relations*, 1966, *19*, 425–436.

Konečni, V. J. The mediation of aggressive behavior: Arousal level versus anger and cognitive labeling. *Journal of Personality and Social Psychology*, 1975, *32*, 706–712.

Laird, J. D. Self-attribution of emotion: The effects of expressive behavior on the quality of emotional experience. *Journal of Personality and Social Psychology*, 1974, *29*, 475–486.

Leventhal, H. Emotions: A basic problem for social psychology. In C. Nemeth (Ed.), *Social Psychology*. Chicago: Rand McNally, 1974.

Leventhal, H. Toward a comprehensive theory of emotion. In L. Berkowitz (Ed.), *Advances in experimental social psychology* (Vol. 13). New York: Academic Press, 1980.

Leventhal, H., Brown, D., Shacham, S., & Engquist, S. The effects of preparatory information about sensations, threat of pain, and attention on cold pressor distress. *Journal of Personality and Social Psychology*, 1979, *37*, 688–714.

Leyens, J. P., & Parke, R. D. Aggressive slides can induce a weapons effect. *European Journal of Social Psychology*, 1975, *5*, 229–236.

Marhsall, G. D., & Zimbardo, P. G. Affective consequences of inadequately explained physiological arousal. *Journal of Personality and Social Psychology*, 1979, *37*, 970–985.

Maslach, C. Negative emotional biasing of unexplained arousal. *Journal of Personality and Social Psychology*, 1979, *37*, 953–969.

Melzack, R. *The puzzle of pain*. New York: Basic Books, 1973.

Miller, N., & Zimbardo, P. Motives for fear induced affiliation: Emotional comparison or interpersonal similarity? *Journal of Personality*, 1966, *34*, 481–503.

Moyer, K. E. *The psychobiology of aggression*. New York: Harper, 1976.

Mulvihill, D. J., & Tumin, M. M. (Eds.). *Crimes of violence* (Vol. 2). *Staff Report to the National Commission on the Causes and Prevention of Violence*. Washington, D.C.: U. S. Government Printing Office, 1969.

Page, M., & Scheidt, R. The elusive weapons effect: Demand awareness, evaluation and slightly sophisticated subjects. *Journal of Personality and Social Psychology,* 1971, *20,* 304–318.

Piliavin, I. M., Piliavin, J. A., & Rodin, J. Costs, diffusion, and the stigmatized victim. *Journal of Personality and Social Psychology,* 1975, *32,* 429–438.

Rotton, J., Barry, T., Frey, J., & Soler, E. Air pollution and interpersonal attraction. *Journal of Applied Social Psychology,* 1978, *8,* 57–71.

Rule, B. G., & Nesdale, A. R. Emotional arousal and aggressive behavior. *Psychological Bulletin,* 1976, *83,* 851–863.

Rule, B. G., Ferguson, T. J., & Nesdale, A. R. Emotional arousal, anger and aggression: The misattribution issue. In P. Pliner, K. R. Blankenstein, & I. M. Spigel (Eds.), *Perception of emotion in self and others.* New York: Plenum, 1979.

Schachter, S. *The psychology of affiliation.* Stanford, Cal.: Stanford Univ. Press, 1959.

Schachter, S. The interaction of cognitive and physiological determinants of emotional state. In L. Berkowitz (Ed.), *Advances in Experimental social psychology* (Vol. 1). New York: Academic Press, 1964.

Schachter, S., & Singer, J. E. Comments on the Maslach and Marshall-Zimbardo experiments. *Journal of Personality and Social Psychology,* 1979, *37,* 989–995.

Simons, L. S., & Turner, C. W. Evaluation apprehension, hypothesis awareness, and the weapons effect. *Aggressive Behavior,* 1976, *2,* 77–87.

Tomkins, S. S. *Affect, imagery, consciousness* (Vol. 1). *The positive affects.* New York: Springer, 1962.

Tomkins, S. S. *Affect, imagery, consciousness* (Vol. 2). *The negative affects.* New York: Springer, 1963.

Turner, C. W., & Goldsmith, D. Effects of toy guns and airplanes on children's antisocial free play behavior. *Journal of Experimental Child Psychology,* 1976, *21,* 303–315.

Turner, C. W., & Layton, J. F. Verbal imagery and connotation as memory induced mediators of aggressive behavior. *Journal of Personality and Social Psychology,* 1976, *33,* 755–763.

Turner, C. W., & Simons, L. S. Effects of subject sophistication and evaluation apprehension on aggressive responses to weapons. *Journal of Personality and Social Psychology,* 1974, *30,* 341–348.

Turner, C. W., Simons, L. S., Berkowitz, L., & Frodi, A. The stimulating and inhibiting effects of weapons on aggressive behavior. *Aggressive Behavior,* 1977, *3,* 355–378.

Ulrich, R. E. Pain as a cause of aggression. *American Zoologist,* 1966, *6,* 643–662.

Ulrich, R. E., & Azrin, N. H. Reflexive fighting in response to aversive stimulation. *Journal of the Experimental Analysis of Behavior,* 1962, *5,* 511–520.

Ulrich, R. E., & Favell, J. E. Human aggression. In C. Neuringer & J. L. Michael (Eds.), *Behavior modification in clinical psychology.* New York: Appleton, 1970.

Zillmann, D. Excitation transfer in communication-mediated aggressive behavior. *Journal of Experimental Social Psychology,* 1971, *7,* 419–434.

Zillmann, D. *Hostility and aggression.* Hillsdale, N.J.: Erlbaum, 1979.

Zillmann, D., Katcher, A. H., & Milavsky, B. Excitation transfer from physical exercise to subsequent aggressive behavior. *Journal of Experimental Social Psychology,* 1972, *8,* 247–249.

five

Social Influence Theory and Aggression
JAMES T. TEDESCHI

The title of this chapter refers to a theory of aggression, but the word *aggression* as used here departs from the usual understanding of the term. The theory deals with aggression in terms of the reasons why an actor uses coercive power, particularly when those around him consider the action to be antinormative or wrong. The word *aggression* does not denote any one kind of human action, but instead it is a label applied by observers when they perceive the actor as possessing an intent to do harm to one or more other persons and there is no explanation that legitimizes the action. Strictly speaking, then, the study of aggression is reserved as a special case of person perception or implicit personality theory. Thus, a theory of coercive power is not just another theory of aggression but instead attempts to redefine entirely what it is we are studying.

This is not the place to review the many analyses that have been made of the definitions of aggression. The unanimous opinion of all recent writers on the topic is that the term has insurmountable difficulties. However, the perspective here offers a conclusion different than heretofore. Instead of finally accepting some inadequate definition of aggression, it is suggested that we exorcize the term altogether from the lexicon of descriptors of human behavior.[1] The chap-

---

[1] The detailed arguments for this conclusion may be found in Tedeschi, Melburg, and Rosenfeld (1981).

AGGRESSION
Volume 1

Copyright © 1983 by Academic Press, Inc.
All rights of reproduction in any form reserved.
ISBN 0-12-278801-X

ter will begin by explaining why this choice was made. This requires some discussion of definitional problems.

The social influence perspective is based on a radical critique of biological, psychoanalytic, and learning approaches to the study of aggression. This critique will be briefly summarized, establishing the need for a fresh approach to the phenomena of interest to social psychologists. Then a typology of coercive power will be offered as a basis for describing behaviors, some of which might be labeled as aggressive by observers of them. This terminology is believed to be both more discriminative and as more value free than are various definitions of aggression.

A theory of coercive power is then offered to explain why people use various forms of threats and punishments against one another. Two questions are involved in explaining why a source uses coercive power: Why is a particular target chosen, and why is coercive power rather than some other mode of influence chosen? A cost/gains analysis is applied to both these questions. These are decisions made by a source, and it is not surprising that a decision theory approach would be applied to them. One advantage claimed for this approach is that it focuses the theorist's attention on the interpersonal dynamics underlying actions that are associated with harm doing, and it tends to discount intrapsychic theories that rely on such mediating mechanisms as instincts, Thanatos, aggressive energy, tension, and arousal. More will be said about this shift in perspective later.

Sometimes the use of coercive power leads observers to label the actor as aggressive, a label carrying generally negative connotations in American society. This labeling has important consequences for the actor. The prospect of being labeled as aggressive may inhibit the use of coercion. If coercion is nevertheless used, the actor may attempt to legitimize or excuse the use of coercion and thus change observers' impressions of him. Should these impression management tactics fail to convince observers that they have mislabeled the actor, the latter may engage in other actions to mitigate the negative reactions expected from others. Thus, the label of aggression plays an important role in the understanding of actions and reactions of persons when coercive power is the mode of influence used by an actor. We will consider these interpersonal dynamics in more detail because they clarify the distinction made between descriptions of behavior in terms of coercive power and the conditions under which such behavior will be labeled as aggressive by observers.

DEFINITIONS OF AGGRESSION

An evaluation of basic definitions in an early period of science often involves an assessment of how well concepts capture the commonsense designation of relevant events. Furthermore, if these definitions are vague or include implicit value judgments of the scientist, and the concepts are central to theory construction, then derivations from the theory will be similarly vague and indeterminant. Examination of concepts of aggression reveals that each is inadequate in either or both of these respects (Baron, 1977; Johnson, 1972; Kaufmann, 1970; Tedeschi, Smith, & Brown, 1974).

The behavioristic definition of aggression as harm-doing behavior clearly does not capture the domain of actions that the term carries in vernacular language. The behavioristic definition includes responses that would not usually be considered aggressive and excludes responses that almost everyone would agree are aggressive. Accidents, mistakes, or otherwise inadvertent harm toward others are not usually considered aggressive. On the other hand, actions that do no harm but lead observers to infer that the actor intended to do harm are considered aggressive. While Buss (1961) has tried to rescue the behavioristic definition by excluding all harm doing that is accidental or culturally legitimized, the problem of how we determine what is accidental and what is not, and what is really legitimate and what only appears legitimate is not seriously considered. Of course, what is accidental may be a technical question having little to do with psychology, and what is legitimate and what is not is a value judgment made by an observer about which there can be considerable disagreement. Thus, the behavioristic definition, constructed to avoid questions of intent and value judgments, ultimately includes both.

Widespread dissatisfaction with the behavioristic definition led some social psychologists to accept an attributional definition of aggression as the intent to do harm. If this concept is meant to refer to a set of observable behaviors, it is clearly inadequate. One does not perceive intentions directly. The class of events designated by the attributional concept of aggression is indeterminant because to date no rules have been provided about how one infers intentions from a set of observations. It is left to each scientist to make his own attributions, and as a consequence, the designation of an event as "aggression" requires a subjective judgment by each researcher.

Bandura's (1973) view is that aggressive behavior consists of skills that are acquired and then used to harm others. When one reviews studies showing modeling of aggression by children, who hit or shoot dart guns at Bobo the Clown, it becomes clear that Bobos are seldom harmed. It also seems unreasonable to attribute intent to do harm to such young children. After all, they witnessed an adult fail to damage Bobo and could hardly expect to surpass the model's performance. Indeed, criminal law does not recognize the ability to form intent in young children. Thus, neither a behavioristic nor an attributional definition would identify such Bobo-directed behavior as "aggressive." The reason Bandura views this behavior as aggressive is because learning such skills as punching or shooting guns creates the potential to harm others.

Reflection suggests that almost all human behavior has the potential to harm others, and hence Bandura's definition includes too wide a scope of behaviors. For example, learning to control one's fingers (usually in the cradle) is a skill that could eventually lead a person to push buttons that electrocute another person or to release a barrage of intercontinental ballistic missiles. Learning how to talk provides a person with a set of skills that allows him to spread vicious rumors about another person, to mediate direct social punishments, and to conspire against others. Actually, we are less interested in how people acquire skills than what motivates them to want to harm others. Presumably, given sufficient desire to harm others, a person will find some way to do so.

Value judgments tend to creep into all definitions of aggression, because harm doing, intent to do harm, and potential to do harm are not considered aggression if the action in question is excusable or justifiable. If a stranger came to your home in the middle of the night and knocked down your front door with an ax, almost everyone would agree that harm was done, it was intended, and it was aggression. However, if that same stranger came on a fire truck, wore the proper firefighter's attire, and had reason to believe that the action was necessary (even if it was not), no one would consider the action as aggression. Thus, it is not the action or the intent (to knock down the door) that identifies the action as aggression, but rather the lack of justification that does so. Apparently, the labeling of an action as aggression must include perceptions, attributions, and value judgments. The distinction between angry and instrumental aggression alludes to the goals of the actor. But such factors clearly take us into the realm of person perception and implicit personality theory, and away from the problem of developing a theory of clearly designated behaviors.

While many writers have noted one or more of these problems with various definitions of aggression, they tend to shrug their shoulders and comment that we all know what we want to study (e.g., Bandura, 1973, p. 8) and then settle for one or the other inadequate concept. The present approach is to reject every definition of aggression as inadequate and to provide an alternative way of conceptualizing the relevant behaviors. Concepts of coercive power appear to offer descriptive categories for behavior that avoid the problems noted here for concepts of aggression. Of course, it is recognized that coercive power may or may not be perceived as aggression, but that is a separate question from why people use this mode of influence. On the other hand, almost all behaviors referred to as aggression take the form of one or another type of coercive power. Furthermore, questions of intent and justification can be explicitly considered, particularly when considering how observers characterize the person who uses coercion. The present approach separates coercive actions from the labeling of them by observers, whereas past views of aggression often required identification of the relevant behaviors made privately and implicitly by the scientists. Thus, confusion of action and judgment of the action contained in previous approaches to the study of aggression is avoided by a social influence approach, which discriminates between the action and its labeling.

BIOLOGICAL, PSYCHOANALYTIC, AND LEARNING APPROACHES TO AGGRESSION

Traditional approaches to the study of aggression are replete with unsupported assumptions, false analogies, and inappropriate generalizations. Also, there has been a tendency to focus on intraorganismic processes to the exclusion of social factors in a search for the causes of "aggression." Although it is not possible here to document these statements thoroughly (see Tedeschi & Lindskold, 1976; Tedeschi et al., 1974), the basic arguments can be summarized.

Biological View of Aggression

J. P. Scott (1958) has identified predatory behavior, which refers to approach, attack, and kill responses between two different species, and agonistic behavior, which refers to threat and fighting responses within a species of animals. It is clear that in nature many animals have genetically prewired, stereotyped predatory behavior patterns. It is equally clear that humans do not have instinctual predatory behavior patterns. In fact, few humans ever kill anything larger than a mosquito, except by accident. Biological bases of agonistic behavior patterns, such as dominance hierarchies and territoriality, have also been found among many species of animals. Superficial similarities in human and animal behavior led some writers to suggest that similar biological factors regulate the agonistic behavior patterns of both. For example, many groups of animals develop dominance hierarchies or peck orders. The analogy is often made between this behavior and hierarchical status arrangements created in human groups. However, dominance hierarchies among other-than-human primates are affected primarily by size, strength, sex, age, and hormonal factors, whereas status hierarchies among humans are determined by wealth, kinship, friendship, expertise, and other social factors. Furthermore, human status arrangements must be rationalized by a set of symbols or else members of the group will not accept the superordinate–subordinate relations as legitimate. Whereas a high position in a dominance hierarchy among other primates allows for early selfish access to food, territory, and mating, leaders in human groups are primarily focused on the solution of group problems, although status and other rewards may be accrued thereby. The bases and functions of dominance and status hierarchies among animals and humans are not the same. There is clear evidence that human status hierarchies are based primarily on social factors and serve social purposes, and there is no evidence that humans are genetically programmed or predisposed to develop status hierarchies.[2]

[2]There are instances of course where dominance in human groups is determined by fighting behavior (e.g., children, gangs). However, cross-cultural differences in such behavior suggest cultural and learning factors, not biological ones, as primary determinants of what may appear to some to represent biological continuities. (See Rajecki and Flanery, 1981, for an opposing view.)

Animals have a number of biologically based drives, such as hunger, thirst, and sex, that have characteristic deprivation and satiation cycles. For example, food deprivation will activate the organism to find and ingest food. When the animal has eaten sufficient amounts of nutrients, this activity ceases. This go–stop sequencing is biologically based and in fact may be regulated from a particular brain center or circuit. Some ingenious experiments have attempted to demonstrate that a go–stop system in the brain controls stereotyped response sequences associated with predatory aggression. Predatory behavior can be elicited by electrode stimulation of brain centers, but only when appropriate environmental stimuli are present. Far from proving that there are brain centers for aggression in humans, this evidence appears to indicate that there is no innately generated biological energy that must be released in the form of aggressive behavior. Furthermore, humans do not possess stereotyped response patterns that can be easily identified as aggression, as, for example, occurs in cats, monkeys, and bulls. Thus, while internal physiological factors may dampen or intensify responses, current evidence does not support the view that biological factors cause the behavior to occur.

It is easy to be misinterpreted when one makes categorical statements. Let me be clear about what I am not saying. The biological approach seems clearly appropriate to the study of aggression among subhuman organisms, and to the extent that internal factors affect the intensity of such behavior among humans, it also has an important contribution to make there. Nevertheless, the considerably greater complexity of human social behavior, which is attributable primarily to the development of language and tools, requires that we shift from a biological to a more social–cultural perspective.

Psychoanalytic Theory

Freud proposed two very different views of aggression. His later view (Freud, 1950) opposed Eros, or positive energy, against Thanatos, or destructive energy. These forces were assumed to be biologically based and to require overt expression. We have already noted that there is no biological evidence for this kind of assumption. Freud's earlier discarded view of frustration and aggression has survived and remains an important theory in experimental psychology. We will examine the frustration–aggression view as reformulated in learning theory.

Learning Theory

The major problem of interest to learning theory is how organisms acquire new responses. When learning theory is applied to the study of aggression, it is necessary to be able to identify a response as an instance of aggression. Without a satisfactory observational construct of aggression, such identification is not possible.

Frustration– aggression theory (Dollard, Doob, Miller, Mowrer, & Sears, 1939) is a learning theory adaptation of Freud's early ideas on aggression. It is still a widely influential theory 40 years after its publication.[3] According to this theory, aggressive behavior serves the function of reducing arousal built up through experience of frustration. When organisms learn inhibition of prepotent responses, the built-up energy persists and requires release. Displacement refers to a shift by the organism from a prepotent to a substitute response or from one target to another. A demonstration of displaced aggression attended by catharsis of pent-up energy would be supportive of the frustration–aggression theory.

Several reviewers of the research on catharsis (Berkowitz, 1962; Bramel, 1969; Weiss, 1969) concluded that the evidence for such a process is weak at best. Geen and Quanty (1977) concluded from their more recent review that aggressive behavior does reduce physiological arousal but that there is no parallel reduction in aggressive behavior. Surprisingly enough, there is no available recent review of research on displacement. I am in the process of reviewing the displacement literature. Surprisingly, fewer than 50 studies on displacement have been done with human subjects, and a number of these suffer from methodological problems. Further, sometimes researchers find a strong displacement effect, and sometimes they fail to find any. However, the data can be interpreted in a way that makes sense of the total body of evidence. Experiments that show displacement effects can be interpreted as allowing for the operation of other social psychological processes, such as generalized reciprocity, social comparison, or negative equity (cf. Nacci and Tedeschi, Note 1). Studies that inadvertently control for these extraneous processes and allow only the operation of frustration and inhibitory forces fail to find displacement effects. The conclusion appears to be that displacement does occur, but not for the reasons that Dollard et al. (1939) postulate. That is, displacement is not a response whose function is to release built-up tension.

The lack of strong evidence for catharsis and the weak evidence for tension-produced displacement undermine the attempt by Dollard et al. to avoid the problems associated with the behavioristic and attributional definitions of aggression. That is, there is no reliable way of determining if a response does release aggressive energy. As a consequence, it is impossible to designate the class of responses that are to be considered aggressive.

Once again, it may be helpful to state what I am not saying. Learning theorists have produced evidence and postulated processes that are important to the study of harm-doing behavior. No attempt will be made here to examine all learning theories or empirical findings of related research. Clearly, people

---

[3]There have been modifications of the basic theory (e.g., Berkowitz, 1962), but the basic functions of frustration and learning have remained the focus of revisionist theories.

are inhibited from behaving in certain ways by the potential costs of so doing, and displacement effects do occur, though perhaps for reasons other than those proposed by learning theorists. When considering the use of coercive power, we will assume that such behavior is often learned either by reinforcement histories or by modeling, although the performance of such behavior will depend primarily on situational factors, including the behavior of other persons. Like biological and psychoanalytic approaches, learning theory is inadequate to explain those actions that are labeled as aggression by most observers in Western cultures. The recognition of the limitations of these traditional approaches to the study of aggression led me to reinterpret the phenomena of interest with concepts of coercive power.

USE OF COERCIVE POWER

I was studying threats in conflict situations long before it occurred to me that the topic had anything to do with human aggression. It is interesting to note that researchers studying threats and political scientists whose specialty is the study of deterrence, threats, and force seldom use the term *aggression*. For example, I have just read a draft of a book on threats by a social psychologist who has strong interdisciplinary experience, and I do not recall a single instance of the use of the term *aggression*. Coercive power covers a greater data domain than is represented by the phenomena referred to as aggression by biologists, psychoanalysts, and learning theorists. Again, to make the latter statement clear requires that one remembers that the present approach refers to actions as coercion and reserves the term *aggression* as a subjective label sometimes placed on such actions by observers. While some acts of coercion are perceived as aggressive, there are many coercive acts that are not so labeled.

A set of observational constructs of coercion has been proposed (Tedeschi, 1970), and a costs–gains theory has been proposed for explaining why coercion is used by an actor (Tedeschi, Schlenker, & Lindskold, 1972). Both these papers were published before it occurred to me that we had discovered an alternative interpretation to phenomena heretofore referred to by the generic (but imprecise) term *aggression*. It will be worthwhile to summarize these papers here and then relate theory on coercive power to the topic of aggression.

Constructs of Coercive Power

According to Webster's dictionary definition, to coerce is to restrain or constrain by force, to curb or to compel, and to enforce. That is, coercion is conceptualized as a form of influence. Of course, there are many other forms of influence that depend on information or rewards rather than force. Tedeschi and Bonoma (1977) stated that "when a person cannot persuade, bribe, manipulate, or otherwise induce a target to comply to his demands, then the success of influence may depend upon the source's ability to restrain, transport, immobilize, injure, or destroy the target [p. 228]." In addition to direct influence of another in terms of deterrence, compellent threats, or constraint, coercive power may also be used for self-defense, revenge, reciprocity, and self-presentation.

Psychologists do not use the notion of force in their technical language, but instead refer to such terms as *threats, negative reinforcements,* and *punishments*. Various definitions have been given to each of these terms in the literature, and so it is important for us to be explicit about the meaning to be given to them here. A threat is a communication and as such may be considered an objective environmental event. Identification of a threat communication is rather easy when the message is explicitly encoded in language. A contingent threat is a message that includes a demand and a statement that punishment will follow noncompliance. The demand may be specific and ask that a response not be performed (deterrence) or require that a response be performed (compellence). On the other hand, the message may leave the demand ambiguous or implicit. Similarly, the punishment to be administered should the target choose to defy the threatener may be specified in the threat communication or the type and magnitude of punishment may be left unspecified.

A source may intend to send threats that are not verbally encoded and are not perceived as threats by target persons, and targets may perceive threats that are neither intended nor encoded by a source. These failures at communication should not lead us as scientists to conclude that no objective, value-free definition of threats is possible. It is well known that communication is not the same thing as language and that many forms of communication may take place nonverbally. To identify threats that are not explicitly put into language may require an analysis of the cultural and social contexts within which persons are interacting, the history of relations between actors, the nonverbal cues emitted, the environmental props available, and the verbal context of the action taking place. On the other hand, it is rather simple to identify types of explicit verbal threats for the purposes of testing scientific theories in the laboratory.

An empirical definition of punishment has served psychologists well since Thorndike introduced it into scientific usage in the nineteenth century: A punishment is any stimulus that the organism will seek to avoid and do nothing to attain. The intensity of avoidance actions generally corresponds to magnitudes of punishments. The result of this way of defining punishments is that they are viewed as primarily quantitative and not varying in quality. I have argued (Tedeschi 1970) that targets react differently to various kinds of punishments, and for this reason, it is important to distinguish between them. My proposed typology included noxious stimulation, deprivation of existing resources, denial of promised rewards, and social punishers.

Noxious forms of punishment include all stimuli that when applied to one's body produce unpleasant sensations or tissue damage. Electric shocks, heat, cold, pressure, acidic tasting substances, explosions, gunshots, knife pricks, punches to various parts of the body, and many other stimuli are noxious in their effects. Deprivation of resources occurs when a person loses a resource to which access had been readily available. Such deprivation may involve the loss of material possessions or money; the loss of influence resources, such as prestige or status; or separation from another person who is a source of rewards. Denying a person promised rewards typically follows a sequence in which a promise of reward is made and then withdrawn for reasons that have no relationship to the specifics of the original promise. For example, if a young person shovels the snow off a driveway after consulting with the head of the household and the latter then changes his or her mind and refuses to pay the young worker, the young person is likely to become angry. Unfulfilled expectations are believed to underlie many social upheavals, including revolutions. Social punishers take the form of name calling, ostracism, insults, denial of group membership, stigma, degradation ceremonies, and so on.

Any form of threat may include one or more kinds of punishments, and the magnitude of punishment may be specified in the threat message. Thus, many kinds of threats can be discriminated. Threats may be contingent or noncontingent; they may be demand specific or nonspecific and, if specific, may take a deterrent or compellent form. The threat may also refer specifically to a punishment or remain nonspecific and, if specific, may indicate the kind but not the magnitude of punishment or may indicate both the kind and magnitude. In addition, threats may be nonverbal or implicit, such as may be conveyed by a vigorous upward movement of the right arm. Of course threats may be made without the use of subsequent punishments, and punishments may be delivered without making prior threats.

Constructs of Coercive Power and Forms of Aggression

One important test of the adequacy of the coercive power terminology for reinterpreting the area heretofore referred to as aggression is how well the new language captures the distinctions that have been found necessary by researchers in the area of aggression. The distinctions that have been made with regard to threats and punishments appear not only to capture the various categories of aggression that have been proposed but also to make much finer and objectively discriminable ones.

The behavioristic definition of aggression appears to be translatable into the various types of punishment. A distinction between angry and instrumental aggression has been made because some actions seem to have the goal of harming the victim and others harm the victim only incidently or as a means of gaining some other goal. The identification of these forms of aggression requires an analysis of the intentions and motives of the actor in addition to the observation that some form of coercive power was used by her. For example, cultural values requiring reciprocity or justifying self-defense may allow the observer to attribute the intent to harm the victim or merely to avoid or deter harm from the victim. The separation of the description of the action from the analysis of intentions and motives allows the scientist to avoid the problems that are attendant to the attributional definition of aggression.

Aggression theorists often refer to arbitrary and nonarbitrary forms of frustration, with the former, but not the latter, eliciting aggression. These frustrations refer to events that harm the interests of the actor in some way, but either the interference with goal-related activity can or can not be explained, excused, or justified in a manner that satisfies the actor. Thus, the distinction between kinds of frustration requires an analysis of the kinds of explanations that can be offered to the actor and the values, norms, or motives that lead her to accept such accounts. While this is surely an important theoretical enterprise, no one has seriously pursued it. The language of coercive power focuses attention on the social nature of the phenomena referred to by an inadequate concept of aggression. When we ask why a person uses coercion or why the kind of coercion used is chosen, the analysis is automatically turned to an analysis of reasons, explanations, accounts, intentions, and motives. The language of frustration and aggression has typically led investigators in the past to posit internal tension states that give rise to the relevant behavior. A social influence approach focuses on social determinants of behavior, whereas traditional approaches look to physical and environmental and/or internal and physiological factors. Of course, neither necessarily excludes the other. However, it will be argued that many of the most important determinants of the use of coercive power by human actors are social in origin.

A Theory of Coercive Power

According to the political scientist Morgenthau (1960), an instance of power occurs when one person, by any means, is at least a partial causal agent in affecting another person's thoughts, plans, attitudes, intentions, motives, or actions. Influence may be intentional or unintentional, and the source may or may not be aware that influence has occurred (Dahl, 1957). A social scientist should be able to discern whether influence has occurred and by what means, whatever the intentions or states of consciousness that exist among the participants to interaction.

Tedeschi, Schlenker, and Linkskold (1972) and Tedeschi, Schlenker, and Bonoma (1973) proposed a general theory of influence that focuses on explicit influence attempts made by a source. According to this theory, the rewards of people are interdependent and can be attained only by coordinated actions. Each person typically has a set of wants or values to be implemented and furthered. For each reward that is desired (or punishment to be avoided), there is a set of other people who can through cooperative action help attain it. The problem for the actor is to decide which people to influence and how to bring about the cooperative behavior. Assuming that all potential targets can mediate the same value for the source, the most important considerations for choosing a target and an influence mode would be the probability and value of success and the probability and value of any costs that might be accrued by attempting influence.

The source might be thought of as first choosing a target out of the population of potential targets and considering how likely it is the target would engage in the desired behavior if a persuasive communication of a particular type were directed toward him. Of course, the potential costs of attempting persuasion with the chosen target must also be considered. The source might then consider the probability of success and the potential costs of delivering a contingent promise to the chosen target. The source might consider the subjective expected value (SEV) of each influence mode that might be chosen to gain compliance from the target. The source might then select another target from the population of potential targets (those who have or can mediate the relevant value) and generate a set of SEVs for this second potential target. The source is likely to discontinue this kind of predecision information processing whenever the SEV associated with attempting influence is sufficiently good (a "satisficing" criterion, Simon, 1957). Of course the SEV associated with maintaining solitude and withdrawing from social interaction may be greater than any alternative of attempting influence.

How the individual decides what people to include in a population of potential targets is not clear. The target must be directly or indirectly capable of satisfying some desire of the source. The population of targets may be capable of mediating some rewards or decreasing or removing some punishments. Perhaps there is only one potential target, as is the case when a source seeks revenge. Potential targets are normally those who are accessible to the decision maker.

The question of most concern to us here is why a source chooses to use coercive power rather than some other form of influence. Among the factors that contribute to the source's decision to use coercive power are lack of self-confidence, time perspective and failure to perceive costs, fear, self-presentation and face saving, maintenance of authority, conflict intensity, norms of self-defense and reciprocity, modeling and learning, and perceived injustice. Let us examine each of these factors more carefully.

LACK OF SELF-CONFIDENCE

When a person does not believe she can be successful in gaining interpersonal objectives by using other modes of influence, she may choose to use threats and/or punishments to gain her way with others. Any number of factors may undermine a person's confidence in the effectiveness of noncoercive influence modes. The potential influencer may believe she does not possess many of the characteristics that increase the likelihood of successful influence, such as expertise, status, prestige, and attractiveness. Inarticulateness, inadequate education, and low self-esteem contribute to a person's sense of powerlessness and makes it more likely that she will rely on coercive means of influencing others. A good example of this dynamic is Jake LaMotta, a prize fighter in the 1950s and the Raging Bull of the motion picture. He indicated in a television interview that when he was a boy he knew he was not very bright and could not argue effectively with others, so he tried to solve every argument through fighting.

Ransford (1968) has found that people who feel powerless and isolated are perceived by acquaintances as more aggressive than are more self-confident persons. This supports the view that the use of coercion is related to a person's feeling that he cannot be successful by using other means of influence. Indeed, persons who are internal control oriented are more apt to use positive modes of influence, whereas persons who are external control oriented more frequently use threats and punishments (Goodstadt & Hjelle, 1973). Also, subjects who indicated lack of self-confidence used more coercion than those who exuded confidence (Lindskold & Tedeschi, 1970).

A person who successfully uses coercion may become more reliant on this mode of influence on future occasions. Threatening and punishing others earns the actor the enmity and distrust of the target and others who witness the action. Benign modes of influence, such as persuasion, promises, and moral suasion, can be effective only when the target trusts the source. Given the lessened effectiveness of positive modes of influence, the coercer must again rely on threats and punishments on future influence occasions.[4] When a person of low self-esteem or self-confidence gets into this kind of vicious cycle, it is very difficult to extricate himself. As a result, the person falls into a pattern that may be referred to as a coercive influence style.

TIME PERSPECTIVE AND FAILURE TO PERCEIVE COSTS

All theories of aggression take into account factors that inhibit the organism from performing the relevant behaviors. Political scientists and military strategists elaborate intricate theories of nuclear deterrence, and sociologists, criminologists, and politicians argue about the effectiveness of capital punishment as a deterrent to homicide. Deterrence or inhibition may not occur if the actor's

---

[4]It is possible that the use of coercion leads to fear and that fear motivates compliance with other forms of influence. Lindskold and Bennett (1973), for example, have shown that possession and use of threats and punishments made a source's promises more effective in controlling the behavior of a target. In such instances, the threat of punishment must be maintained or the fear-induced compliance to other forms of influence will be withheld by the target.

time perspective is contracted to the existential moment. In such a case, the actor would not consider the future consequences of his action and any costs that might accrue through performing it. Strong emotions, such as anger and fear, alcohol consumption, and the use of drugs are some of the factors known to have the effect of reducing the person's time perspective, and all are known to be associated with suicide, homicide, child abuse, spouse abuse, physical assault, and automobile fatalities.

The failure to consider the risk of retaliation, social disapproval, or other forms of punishment may cause the person to ignore ethical or normative standards of conduct. Should this condition be combined with low self-esteem and a situation that encourages dehumanizing the target person, assaultive and criminal behavior may be the result. Most murders appear to be based on short-lived and impulsive motives, often involving domestic arguments over money, children, and alcohol. It should not be surprising, then, that a majority of murder victims are friends, lovers, or relatives of the murderer (Zimring, Note 2).

When inhibitory factors have been removed by pharmacological agents (including alcohol), the availability of weapons can increase the amount of harm done to others. According to the FBI (1968), about 63% of all homicides in 1967 were due to shootings. In a country in which there are over 9 million alcoholics and drug addicts and 115 million privately owned guns, it is not surprising that there is such a high incidence of violence.

FEAR

Another factor affecting a person's use of coercion is fear. The cognitive component of fear is the anticipation of harm. The response to fear is to avoid, escape, or somehow remove or control the source of anticipated harm. Coercive power may be used to deter, control, or destroy the fear-inducing party. The development of powerful arsenals of weapons serves as a deterrent for fearful nations, and the acquisition of skills, such as the martial arts, may be based on the anticipation of a need to defend oneself against attack. Fear can bring about the very situation parties may seek to avoid. Thus, when a nation arms to deter others, arming produces fear and stimulates others to arm, which produces fear in the first nation and increased acquisition of arms. This dynamic of an arms race has led to many wars in the past. A similar dynamic can occur between individuals.

Expectations and a state of preparedness can cause a person to misinterpret cues emitted from others as signs of imminent attack and lead to a preemptive strike. The actor may interpret the situation as a case of get her before she gets you. Toch (1969) found that prison inmates reliably displayed violence in reaction to particular and specific cues emitted by others. Certain kinds of facial expressions, verbal statements, and skeletal movements have apparently been associated with potential danger by these men, and they react violently to preempt the attacks they expect from others. There is a great deal of variability in the interpretation of cues as indicating the intent to do harm by others. Actions that appear innocent to one person may be interpreted as threatening by another. Of course, if the individual's reaction appears to be totally baseless, he is said to be suffering from feelings of persecution or paranoia.

SELF-PRESENTATION AND FACE SAVING

A great deal of coercion is used in the service of fostering various identities in front of others. Building a reputation for being manly and tough is referred to as "macho" and may take the form of belligerence and apparently senseless violence. In order to win the respect of fellow gang members, a young teenager may steal a car, deface property, or pick fights with others who have done that person no harm. A reputation for being tough can be very functional for a person who interacts with others in particular subcultures. It may prevent others from attempting to use coercion against him and may facilitate the effectiveness of his own use of coercion.

The use of punishments may occur because the source feels it is necessary to establish credibility for herself. If the source demands compliance from a target and the target refuses to comply to the threat, the source is placed in a put-up or shut-up position. Punishing the target may not bring about after-the-fact compliance, but it will at least establish that the source means what she says and that in the future her word can be believed. Failure to establish credibility for threats may be costly in future interactions, particularly when deterrence or other influence objectives require the effective use of coercion. Thus, the source may be quite reluctant to punish a target and it may actually be costly to carry out the punishment, but nevertheless the source may feel compelled to do so. A good example of this reluctant form of punishment is often observed in a parent who punishes a dearly loved child.

An otherwise inexplicable act of violence might be understood when it serves the purpose of affirming the actor's very existence. A person who has a history of ineffectual interpersonal relations and is lonely, unsuccessful, and perhaps unemployed may dedicate himself to some cause or commit some action to bring attention to himself and hence assume some notoriety. When a person has an impact on events, it affirms that he is in some sense important. Thus, the smirk on Arthur Bremer's face when he was led away from the shooting of Governor George Wallace indicated his pleasure at the notoriety of his action. He even asked arresting officers how much they thought he would receive for his memoirs. Investigation established that Bremer had stalked George McGovern, Richard Nixon, Hubert Humphrey, and Wallace. He apparently did not care which one he killed, just so it was someone who had national attention. A presidential commission's report on political assassinations concluded that presidential assassins are characterized by a need to bring public attention to themselves (Kirkham, Levy, & Crotty, 1970).

Tedeschi, Gaes, and Rivera (1977) suggest that assaultive behavior in school playgrounds may follow a similar pattern. They provide an example of a "child who is dominated by his parents in the home and derogated or ignored by his teachers and peers. Friendless and alone, full of self-doubt and anxiety, perceiving others as hostile, and believing that no one cares about him, the child lashes out and assaults a victim. Now he may be punished, but he will not be ignored [p. 113]." A similar dynamic may occur when a child is told to stay in bed when company is in the home; he may rather take a chance on being spanked than being ignored.

A person may assume costs to protect a positive identity against insult or attack from another person. Brown (1968) found that subjects would engage in costly retaliatory action when such action would serve to reestablish a positive identity following an incident where they had been embarrassed in front of an audience. Direct insults in the course of an argument tend to escalate the conflict, sometimes to the point where things get out of control. Felson (1981) reported that victims of homicide had more frequently engaged in identity attacks, threats, and noxious punishments than had victims of physical assaults. Thus, the interaction of the antagonists rather than premeditation, prior learning, and instrumental goals may be the main determinant of the course of events.

MAINTENANCE OF AUTHORITY

Not only does insubordination disrupt the functioning of a group or interfere with the accomplishment of some particular task, but it also serves as an example, which, if widely followed, would undermine the legitimacy of the authority Attempts to accommodate the dissident may be perceived as weakness and may legitimize her behavior. A public display of punishment serves the purpose of showing that the authority cannot be disobeyed without costs and bolsters the prestige of the authority. The use of coercion may also force the subordinate to submit to the authority. Kipnis (1974) found that authorities do use coercion when faced with insubordination.

The deference received by an authority may be dependent to some degree on a reputation for toughness. This may be true of basketball referees who maintain tight control over a game, and it may also be important to a police officer. Once a police officer issues an order to someone, he may feel it is necessary to enforce it even if the legitimacy of the order is at best doubtful. Toch (1969) found assaults against police often followed an escalation cycle in which an officer issues an order to someone to move on or to go home, the target person resists the order as illegitimate, and the officer than becomes belligerent, issuing threats of arrest. The offender may become angered by what he perceives as arbitrary use of power by the officer, and an altercation may result. The police defend their actions by indicating that they have a tough job, dealing with all kinds of people, and if their word is not believed, the consequences would be detrimental to their work and perhaps to their well-being.

CONFLICT INTENSITY

When the goals of two or more people are interdependent and incompatible and neither is willing to defer to the other, the potential for coercion exists. For example, if two men love the same woman, it is unlikely that either can persuade, bribe, or promise something to get the other to give up the contest. The goal is simply too important for either to defer voluntarily to the other. Withdrawal, bargaining and compromise, and other noncoercive modes of conflict resolution will not be considered by either party, and hence each may attempt to use coercion to make the other person withdraw. The critical factor in this example is the scarcity of the desired resource. Conflicts over territorial boundaries, rights to fishing and hunting areas, decisions over which television program will be watched, and many other situations create conflicts of greater or lesser intensity between persons, institutions, and nations.

Conflict breeds suspicion and distrust regarding the intentions and motives of the adversary. This distrust reduces the effectiveness of promises, persuasive communications, statements of fact, and moral exhortations. This process makes it more likely that threats will be used and believed by each party. The tendency is for each party to also assume a righteous position as the defender against a malevolent and illegitimate adversary. As Deutsch, Canavan, and Rubin (1971) have shown, the greater the intensity of conflict, the more probable the use of threats and punishments.

Escalation cycles in conflict situations are to some degree moderated by norms and institutional constraints. However, when a confluence of factors occur, such as loss of face, fear, lack of self-confidence, and heavy drinking, the presence of a third party can be an important factor in either resolving a conflict or making it worse. If the third party acts as a mediator and defuses insults and fear, then the conflict may be resolved. However, if the third party only increases the person's sense of embarrassment or fear, legitimizes a grievance, or takes sides with the adversary, the conflict may escalate to the point that someone is harmed.

NORMS OF SELF-DEFENSE AND RECIPROCITY

A national survey of adult American men revealed a strong norm of self-defense (Blumenthal, Kahn, Andrews, & Head, 1972). More than 60% of American males considered it a right to kill another human being in defense of family, property, and self. This norm is expressed in courses on the history of the United States in school and in all the mass media. Television has often been criticized for the amount of violence presented to the viewer, but it should be noted that the norm of self-defense is frequently used to legitimize the coercion wielded by the hero or heroine of the program. The police officer, private investigator, marshal, cowboy, and passerby may fight, shoot, or otherwise immobilize and fend off the bad person who threatens to harm or is harming the weak or defenseless victim.

Young males are taught to retaliate when attacked and to stand up to bullies. There is strong social pressure to use threats and punishments as a mode of defense when challenged. The norm of self-defense does not have the same legitimizing function for the use of coercion by women in our society; however, women have developed an increasing interest in the martial arts for purposes of self-defense, and the norm may soon apply equally to both sexes.

The negative norm of reciprocity affirms a basic dictum of the Old Testament of an eye for an eye. This norm affirms the person's right to exact revenge from a harm doer. But reciprocity does not justify disproportionate retaliation. An individual's desire for revenge may conflict with a legal code that transfers the right of punishment from the individual to the state. Thus, a California woman who entrapped and shot a man who had raped her was prosecuted for carrying out her premeditated revenge. However, as might be expected, the crime done against her served to mitigate the punishment meted out by the judicial process.

The power, attractiveness, and sex of the attacker may affect the level of retaliation by the victim. If the attacker is very powerful, the victim may be inhibited from retaliating, and if the attacker is very attractive, the amount of retaliation may be lowered somewhat (cf. Tedeschi & Linkskold, 1976). Furthermore, the norm in American middle-class society that men should not physically harm women appears to mute retaliation with noxious stimulation (Shortell & Miller, 1970). People also differ in their willingness to deliver noxious stimulation to others (Pisano & Taylor, 1971), but what factors contribute to such individual differences are not well documented. Finally, cues that produce physiological arousal tend to accentuate the level of retaliation by the victim, but such arousal does not provoke the individual to launch unprovoked attacks against others (Zillmann, 1971).

MODELING AND LEARNING

The well-known work of Bandura and his associates (cf. Bandura, 1977) has established that humans learn much through observing models, including language rules, self-sacrificial behavior, and moral judgments. It is probable that the use of coercion is also learned through modeling and the individual's history of reinforcements. The present approach would make a finer analysis than is usual in the modeling literature by examining whether specific forms of coercion are learned by observing others. For example, an individual's mother may frequently use threats involving the withholding of love against members of the immediate family and by so doing gain compliance from them (i.e., is rewarded). A child observing this exercise of power may subsequently imitate the use of similar threats, but there may be no generalization to other kinds of threats—say, those involving the use of physical punishments. If the home is characterized by conflicts and resolution is typically achieved through various forms of coercion, the child may learn to adopt a coercive influence style. What has worked successfully in the home to resolve conflicts is the method the child will come to adopt when facing conflicts outside the home. Of course, more positive forms of influence may be modeled in the home and by significant others, and the individual may therefore learn not to use coercion against others.

PERCEIVED INJUSTICE

There are a number of conditions that cause an individual to feel resentment, disappointment, unhappiness, anger, and unjustly treated by others. These subjective reactions are not independent of the principles and values of both the individual and relevant social groups. Among the principles adopted by human groups are standards for allocating or dividing rewards to group members. For example, rewards may be divided equally or they may be distributed according to the contribution the individual members made toward achieving group goals. The latter principle of equity is common in individualistic cultures, whereas the former is more typical of collectivist societies (Leung & Bond, Note 3). A sense of injustice may accompany the failure to adhere to such distributive standards. For example, if a person believes in standards of equity and receives an equal share of the rewards (which represents negative equity), the reaction may be one of disappointment and anger. Studies of relative deprivation indicate that the fate of comparison others may contribute to resentment (Stouffer, Suchman, DeVinney, Star, & Williams, 1949). Thus, even if the person receives rewards that are greater in magnitude than those obtained in other social groups, she may be resentful because other members of her own group have received greater rewards than she has.

Resentment and anger may under certain conditions lead the person to take coercive action against another person, a class of persons, a group, or an institution believed to be responsible for the unfair treatment. The individual may attempt to reestablish equity in a group by imposing costs on a relatively advantaged other person, even when the target is in no way responsible for the injustice (Nacci & Tedeschi, Note 1). Coercive action may be taken as a show of the depth of anger experienced by the person. For example, although there may be political motives, a desire to obtain material possessions, and attempts to gain revenge against a class of other persons, much of the behavior in a property riot may on occasion be a spontaneous expression of the depth of anger that a group experiences—a kind of threat or warning to others meant to deter future unjust behavior. The series of riots that occurred throughout the United States following the assassination of Martin Luther King, Jr., appeared to be motivated primarily by anger.

Perceptions that social norms have been violated often serve to justify or legitimize collective violence. Atrocities committed on the battlefield, lynchings by mobs, and brutal behavior by arresting police officers are frequently perceived as just punishment for the victim because of his alleged brutality and inhumanity. Terrorism may also be calculated to intimidate subordinate groups and spur activities directed toward economic, political, or social change. Riots in the 1960s were often precipitated by police incidents in ghetto areas of urban centers. Police are greatly resented not only because of individual incidents but also as symbols of an unjust social system. If there is no political outlet for remedying the situation, coercion is often the mode of action taken.

Use of Coercion and Perceived Aggression

The concept of aggression may be important as a label used by observers to characterize an actor or his or her actions. However, not all coercion is perceived as aggressive. It is important to understand when the use of coercion will be perceived as aggressive, because being labeled in this way has repercussions for the actor. The source of coercion may be quite aware of these negative consequences and hence may engage in behaviors meant to avoid being labeled as aggressive or to mitigate the negative consequences associated with such a label. The determinants of perceived aggression, the consequences for the actor of being labeled as aggressive, and the posttransgression behaviors that the actor may perform are typically topics for the area of person perception and may be considered apart from the reasons why people use coercion.

PERCEIVED AGGRESSION

Not all uses of coercion are perceived as aggression. A parent who disciplines a child, a vice-principal who expels an adolescent from school, a police officer handcuffing a suspect, a fireman knocking down a front door with an ax use some form of coercion, but none would be said to be committing aggression. The determinants of perceived aggression include the observer's attribution to the actor of intent to do harm and a judgment that there is no explanation for the action to justify it (Tedeschi et al., 1974). Thus, there are three components to perceived aggression: (a) some action (usually but probably not always a form of coercion) is observed; (b) an intent to do harm is inferred; and (c) the action is judged to be antinormative. Under these circumstances the actor will typically be blamed, disapproved, and perhaps punished (cf. Rule & Nesdale, 1976).

An interesting question is whether the actor ever perceives her behavior as aggression at the time it is performed. Typically actors believe they have adequate reasons for their behavior or presumably it would not occur. If an action must be perceived as illegitimate to be labeled as aggression, then it would follow that actors would normally not characterize any of their own actions as aggression. However, there are occasions, as when Gary Gilmore senselessly murdered a gas station attendant and a motel clerk, when the actor has no justification for what is being done and on such occasions the actor would perceive the act as one of aggression (Mailer, 1979). In retrospect we can all come to view our actions differently either by inventing post hoc justifications or by judging prior explanations to be insufficient justifications.

LABELING EFFECTS ON THE ACTOR

Being labeled as aggressive with the corresponding judgments of responsibility and blame entails costs to the actor. Various reactions may be associated with blame, such as lowered attraction, avoidance by others, such social punishments as disapproval and stigma, fear, and legal sanctions and other forms of retribution. Anticipation of these costs may be sufficient to deter the actor from using coercive modes of influence. When the goal is very valuable, however, the actor may be willing to incur these costs, particularly if he believes he can avoid or mitigate them.

Moral judgments are defeasible. Just as lower court decisions can be appealed to a higher court, the first impressions of observers may be changed by additional information. Actors do not passively allow others to make whatever judgments they want but actively attempt to manipulate information to either produce desired impressions or at least avoid or mitigate negative ones. Among the impression management tactics that the actor may use are verbal explanations or accounts consisting of excuses and justifications (Austin, 1961; M. R. Scott & Lyman, 1968). An excuse is a verbal explanation that denies that the actor is responsible for a negative action. There are three general types of excuses: denial of intention, denial or volition, and denial of agency (Tedeschi & Riess, 1981b).

Denial of intention asserts that the negative effects of an action were not planned. It may be alleged that the event involved an accident, mistake, or inadvertancy, or that the failure to foresee the consequences was due to lack of information, poor judgment, distraction by other events, misrepresentation of events by others, or lack of time for deliberation.

Denial or volition asserts that the actor lacked control over her own body. This lack of control may be alleged because of physical causes, such as drugs, alcohol, physical illness, or exhaustion, or it may be attributed to psychological causes, such as mental illness, uncontrollable emotions, coercion by others, hypnosis, brainwashing, or somnambulism. When failure to act leads to negative consequences, the actor may state that he lacked authority to act in the situation.

Denial of agency may take the form of an alibi or an assertion of mistaken identity. A direct denial may only be implied, as when a person claims amnesia for a critical period of time. In any case, the individual basically states that she did not commit the act in question.

If the excuses are accepted by the listener, the actor will be absolved of responsibility and blame for the relevant action or the amount of blame will be mitigated. That is, the acceptance of the actor's excuses by others lowers the costs of the previous action. Contemplation by the actor prior to the critical event that she will have an acceptable excuse may facilitate the performance of the negative action. A person who is drinking alcoholic beverages may be more prone to violent behavior, for example, both because of shortened time perspective and the knowledge that others may attribute her conduct to the effects of alcohol and to some extent mitigate the degree of blame that might otherwise be ascribed to her.

Justifications are explanations for behavior that accept responsibility for the outcomes but assert the positive motives or values that led to the behavior. Justifications attempt to reverse or neutralize initial negative impressions formed by observers, have the interpersonal function of avoiding blame and associated negative reactions of others, and align the actor with the norms or rules that govern conduct in the group (Stokes & Hewitt, 1976). Although there are numerous specific justifications, Tedeschi and Riess (1981b) proposed a typology including appeals to higher authority, ideology, norms of self-defense and justice, loyalties, humanistic values and self-fulfillment, statements that the effect was misrepresented, and social comparisons. Of course, if justifications are found acceptable by observers, they will reverse or mitigate initial judgments of blame.

In addition to accounts, a wide range of other posttrangression responses are available to the actor for the purpose of deflecting or reducing the negative reactions of others to him. Among such responses are expressions of guilt and remorse, self-punishment, and apologies. For example, Schwartz, Kane, Joseph, and Tedeschi (1978) found that expressions of remorse reduced the perceived aggressiveness of a transgressor and the level of punishment considered appropriate for him. It is widely known that judges will impose a greater penalty on a convicted felon if he shows no remorse for what he has done. Presumably guilt and remorse reveal that the individual possesses the appropriate societal values and suggests that the condemned behavior was based on some temporary or environmental factor. Assuming that punishment serves to rehabilitate a person and is not merely an act of societal revenge on the criminal, expressions of guilt and remorse suggest that the individual needs less punishment than those who do not already possess the correct standards.

LEGITIMIZATION AND COERCION

Legitimated use of coercion is often an extremely effective form of influence as well as a tactic preventing others from forming negative impressions of the source. For these reasons, the availability of justifying norms and values facilitates and encourages the use of coercion. One would expect and of course finds wide cultural variation in the frequency and kinds of violence manifested by people. In a cross-cultural study, Textor (1967) reported a positive relationship between glorification of the military and the incidence of personal crimes. Justifications based on the organization of the society and its underlying values (however contradictory they may be) serve to facilitate or inhibit the use of certain kinds of coercion, particularly the threat of noxious punishments.

The more traditional approaches to the study of aggression refer to the effects of legitimation in terms of arbitrary and nonarbitrary frustration. Illegitimate uses of coercion by others brings about legitimate retaliation by the victim. The mass media, schools, churches, primary groups, and others contribute to socialization and thus the individual's readiness to use coercion as a legitimate form of influence. Modeling, instrumental learning, reinforcement history, and other forms of learning surely contribute to this socialization process and may even predispose the individual to a particular influence style (cf. Tedeschi et al., 1977). Middle-class parents tend to discuss failings with children, whereas lower-class parents may be more prone to employ noxious forms of punishment in gaining compliance. In general, it could be expected that a class difference would occur in influence style, with middle-class people more inclined to use persuasion and moral suasion and lower-class persons more likely to use coercion.

LABORATORY RESEARCH ON AGGRESSION

Social psychological experiments on aggression typically involve a planned attack on the subject by a confederate in the form of either an insult or the mediation of noxious stimulation. The experimenter then legitimizes the subsequent use of punishment by the subject against the attacker. Subjects are told to produce stress for another person because the scientist's interest is on the effects of stress on performance (Holmes, 1972), or the purpose of the study is to examine the effects of punishments upon learning (Buss, 1961), or shocks are being used as a way of evaluating performance (Berkowitz, 1962). Generally, it is found that subjects deliver about as much punishment to the attacker as the latter had administered to them or that attackers are given more punishments than nonattackers.

There are two points to be made here about this kind of research. First, in terms of how naive persons would perceive the behavior of subjects in these situations, it is clear that the use of punishments is justified by both the behavior of the attacker and the norms established by the experimenter. As we have seen, the legitimate use of coercion is not perceived as aggression. Kane, Joseph, and Tedeschi (1976) examined the essay evaluation paradigm invented by Berkowitz and found that the kinds of behavior referred to as aggression by researchers is not labeled as aggressive by naive observers. This poses a problem because no satisfactory observational definition of aggression has been proposed by scientists, and as we have seen, they wish to exclude culturally acceptable behaviors from the set identified as aggression (see Buss, 1961). As Kane et al. (1976) demonstrated, delivery of different numbers of shocks was not perceived as more or less aggressive, but a subject who delivered six shocks without justification was perceived as more aggressive than a subject who delivered six shocks to a victim who had previously attacked the subject. Thus, it is not the number of punishments or even their magnitude that leads observers to view coercive behavior as aggression, but the violation of norms or lack of justification that does.

The second point is a caution against generalizing from findings regarding the antecedents of defensive and legitimized forms of coercion to the causes of antinormative or illegal forms of coercion. The kinds of behavior observed in a laboratory, where the individual knows she is under surveillance and may be concerned about presenting herself as normal, intelligent, average, and good (see Tedeschi & Riess, 1981a), are certainly motivated by different factors than are the behaviors of rapists, murderers, and armed robbers. This caution should not be interpreted as saying there is no association between legitimate and antinormative actions. As was indicated earlier, an actor who uses coercion antinormatively may believe she has justification for acting as she does. While the basis of justification may be different for the laboratory subject and the criminal, once the behavior has been justified for the actor, the factors contributing to the use of coercion may be very similar. Whether legitimazation has this releasing effect on the tendency to use coercion must be established by future research.

Research on modeling of aggression has had a prominent place in the field. Yet, it is a situation in which the actors are typically small children, no harm is actually done (hitting an inanimate object made specially to be durable through such treatment), and it is unreasonable to attribute to the children intentions to do harm. In fact, Joseph, Kane, Nacci, and Tedeschi (1977) found that naive observers did not label a child as aggressive if he imitated destructive behavior of an adult model. Presumably, the adult acts as a legitimizer of conduct for a child, and when the child engages in imitative behavior, his conduct is not perceived as antinormative or as intending harm. If this interpretation of modeling is correct, then it is probable that a child's imitative behavior would generalize to similar situations only when the behavior is interpreted by him as permissable or "correct." Models may also serve to legitimize the behaviors of adult subjects in laboratory studies. Insofar as the researcher in the area of aggression is primarily interested in antinormative behavior, the relevance of modeling studies to such deviant conduct is at least questionable.

From a social influence viewpoint, future research should focus on factors that lead participants in laboratory experiments to use coercion even when they believe observers (e.g., the experimenters) will view such behavior as aggression. Some excuses and justifications may be more potent than others in disinhibiting such behavior, and future research should investigate legitimating factors that facilitate the use of coercion. The associations between different forms of coercion would also be of great interest. For example, does a person who learns to use threats of social punishments tend also to use threats of noxious stimulation? We also need to know a great deal more about the contributions of the attribution process, implicit personality theory, and labeling on the course of human interactions, particularly when the result involves severe personal harm to one or more individuals.

CONCLUSIONS AND IMPLICATIONS

The social influence approach to the kinds of problems formerly conceptualized as aggression focuses on the use of various forms of threats and punishments by the individual in behalf of various interpersonal objectives. The use of coercion may be perceived as aggression when it is not legitimized by social norms and values. Being labeled as aggressive is tantamount to being blamed for an antinormative action, and social costs may be incurred by the actor. Consideration of the probability and value of such costs may serve to inhibit the actor from using coercion; however, if these values are low or the goal is very valuable, the actor may nevertheless use coercion. Various impression management tactics may serve to absolve the actor of responsibility or mitigate the degree of blame and retribution ascribed to him. The availability of justifications for using coercion and the economic and political organization of society appear to be directly related to the frequency of coercive acts in a culture. Because legitimization increases the effectiveness of coercion and removes the negative impressions associated with its use, availability of justifications tends to facilitate or inhibit the individual in issuing threats and punishing others.

The language system employed in this chapter provides a new perspective for the study of actions formerly labeled as aggression. It avoids the difficulties associated with the various definitions of aggression and provides a rather precise observational language of threats and punishments. The description of the relevant actions can be made without making inferences about intentions or legitimizing reasons for actions, although these are important considerations for understanding when coercive actions will be labeled as aggression. A social influence theory focuses on the social motives for interpersonal conduct, rather than on intrapsychic factors, such as instincts, brain centers, aggressive energy,

Thanatos, and tension, which have been postulated by traditional theorists in the area. While certain aberrations in behavior may occasionally be determined by biological factors, by far the greater incidence is attributable to interpersonal goals of the actor.

The perspective presented here should make it clear that most social psychological research has been focused on legitimized uses of coercion. Typically, subjects are attacked, insulted, or otherwise harassed by confederates and then given a legitimized opportunity to retaliate. By the norms of American soceity, subjects would be justified in responding with proportionate punishments, and they do.

A coercive power perspective cautions the investigator against making generalizations from laboratory studies of legitimized uses of coercion to societal problems involving illegitimate forms of threats and punishments. Similarly, the very small correlation between viewing television violence and the viewer's tendency to engage in illegitimate forms of coercion may be attributable to the social norms such programming teaches the young. These norms are also taught by radio, books, schoolteachers, parents, and clergy. Television is an important mass media, but it communicates within the context of a value system. The basis of violence is in the legitimizing values of society, and television is merely one way these values are communicated.

In conclusion, a social influence perspective dissociates the study of social behavior from biological origins and the learning processes involved in acquiring skills and values. Biological and learning approaches to antinormative social actions have been insensitive to implicit value judgments related to "good" and "bad" uses of coercion. Punishing a child for misbehavior is not considered aggression by anyone in American society, unless child abuse is at issue. Yet, it is a form of coercion. The separation of normatively justified from illegitimate behavior has been implicitly made by social scientists, but they have not always been explicitly aware of making such a distinction. Social influence theory asks why a person uses coercion, and considers the probable gains and probable costs associated with such action. Whether the action is considered as aggression is a question of person perception and moral judgments. Thus, the range of behaviors to be included under the rubric of social influence theory is much greater than traditionally thought necessary, and the explicit consideration of attributions of intentions, moral judgments, and impression management tactics of the actor to avoid negative typifications enlarges the range of phenomena required to understand the process formerly lumped under the various versions of frustration—aggression theory.

REFERENCE NOTES

1. Nacci, P., & Tedeschi, J. T. A social psychological interpretation of the displacement of aggression literature. Unpublished manuscript, State University of New York at Albany, 1977.

2. Zimring, F. Is gun control likely to reduce violent killings? Unpublished study, Center for Studies in Criminal Justice, University of Chicago Law School, 1968.
3. Leung, K., & Bond, M. H. How Chinese and Americans reward task-related contributions. Unpublished manuscript, Chinese University of Hong Kong, 1981.

REFERENCES

Austin, J. L. *Philosophical papers.* New York: Oxford Univ. Press, 1961.
Bandura, A. *Aggression: A social learning analysis.* Englewood Cliffs, N.J.: Prentice-Hall, 1973.
Baron, R. A. *Human aggression.* New York; Plenum, 1977.
Berkowitz, L. *Aggression: A social psychological analysis.* New York: McGraw-Hill, 1962.
Blumenthal, M., Kahn, R. L., Andrews, F. H., & Head, K. B. *Justifying violence: Attitudes of American men.* Ann Arbor, Mich.: Institute for Social Research, 1972.
Bramel, D. The arousal and reduction of hostility. In J. Mills (Ed.), *Experimental social psychology.* Toronto: Macmillan, 1969.
Brown, B. R. The effects of need to maintain face in interpersonal bargaining. *Journal of Experimental Social Psychology,* 1968, *4,* 107–122.
Buss, A. H. *The psychology of aggression.* New York: Wiley, 1961.
Dahl, R. A. The concept of power. *Behavioral Science,* 1957, *2,* 201–218.
Deutsch, H., Canavan, D., & Rubin, J. The effects of size of conflict and sex of experimenter upon interpersonal bargaining. *Journal of Experimental Social Psychology,* 1971, *7,* 258–267.
Dollard, J., Doob, N., Miller, N. E., Mowrer, O. H., & Sears, R. R. *Frustration and aggression.* New Haven: Yale Univ. Press, 1939.
Federal Bureau of Investigation. *Uniform crime reports.* Washington, D.C.: U.S. Government Publications Office, 1968.
Freud, S. [*Beyond the pleasure principle*] (J. Strachey, trans.). New York: Liveright, 1950.
Geen, R. G., & Quanty, M. B. The catharsis of aggression: An evaluation of a hypothesis. In L. Berkowitz (Ed.), *Advances in experimental social psychology* (Vol. 10). New York: Academic Press, 1977.
Goodstadt, B. E., & Hjelle, L. A. Power to the powerless: Locus of control and the use of power. *Journal of Personality and Social Psychology,* 1973, *27,* 190–196.
Holmes, D. S. Aggression, displacement and guilt. *Journal of Personality and Social Psychology,* 1972, *21,* 296–301.
Johnson, R. N. *Aggression in man and animals.* Philadelphia: Saunders, 1972.
Joseph, J. M., Kane, T. R., Nacci, P. L., & Tedeschi, J. T. Perceived aggression: A re-evaluation of the Bandura modeling paradigm. *Journal of Social Psychology,* 1977, *103,* 277–289.
Kane, T. R., Joseph, J. M., & Tedeschi, J. T. Person perception and an evaluation of the Berkowitz paradigm for the study of aggression. *Journal of Personality and Social Psychology,* 1976, *33,* 663–673.
Kaufmann, H. *Aggression and altruism.* New York: Holt, 1970.
Kipnis, D. The powerholder. In J. T. Tedeschi (Ed.), *Perspectives on social power.* Chicago: Aldine, 1974.
Kirkham, J. S., Levy, S., & Crotty, W. J. (Eds.), *Assassination and political violence.* New York: Praeger, 1970.
Lindskold, S., & Bennett, R. Attributing trust and conciliatory intent from coercive power capability. *Journal of Personality and Social Psychology,* 1973, *28,* 180–186.
Lindskold, S., & Tedeschi, J. T. Self-confidence, prior success, and the use of power in social conflicts. *Proceedings of the 78th Annual Convention of the American Psychology Association,* 1970, *5,* 425–426. (Summary)
Mailer, N. *The executioner's song.* Boston: Little, Brown, 1979.

Morgenthau, H. *Politics among nations* (3rd ed.). New York: Knopf, 1960.

Pisano, R., & Taylor, S. P. The reduction of physical aggression: The effects of four strategies. *Journal of Personality and Social Psychology*, 1971, *19*, 237–243.

Rajecki, D. W. & Flannery, R. C. Social conflict and dominance in children: A case for a primate homology. In M. E. Lamb & A. Brown (Eds.), *Advances in developmental psychology.* Hillsdale, N.J.: Erlbaum, 1981.

Ransford, H. E. Isolation, powerlessness, and violence: A study of attitudes and participation in the Watts riot. *American Journal of Sociology*, 1968, *73*, 581–591.

Rule, B. G., & Nesdale, A. R. Moral judgment of aggressive behavior. In R. G. Geen & E. C. O'Neal (Eds.), *Perspectives on aggression.* New York: Academic Press, 1976.

Schwartz, G., Kane, T., Joseph, J. M., & Tedaschi, J. T. The effects of remorse on reactions to a harm-doer. *British Journal of Social and Clinical Psychology*, 1978, *17*, 293–297.

Scott, J. P. *Aggression.* Chicago: Univ. of Chicago Press, 1958.

Scott, M. R., & Lyman, S. M. Accounts. *American Sociological Review*, 1968, *33*, 46–62.

Shortell, J. R., & Miller, H. B. Aggression in children as a function of sex of subject and of opponent. *Developmental Psychology*, 1970, *3*, 143–144.

Simon, H. *Models of man.* New York: Wiley, 1957.

Stokes, R., & Hewitt, J. P. Aligning actions. *American Sociological Review*, 1976, *41*, 838–849.

Stouffer, S. A., Suchman, E. A., DeVinney, L. C., Star, S. A., & Williams, R. M., Jr. *The American soldier* (Vol. 1) *Adjustment during army life.* Princeton, N.J.: Princeton Univ. Press, 1949.

Tedeschi, J. T. Threats and promises. In P. Swingle (Ed.), *The structure of conflict.* New York: Academic Press, 1970.

Tedeschi, J. T., & Bonoma, T. V. Measures of last resort: Coercion and aggression in bargaining. In D. Druckman (Ed.), *Negotiations: Social psychological perspectives.* Beverly Hills, Cal.: Sage, 1977.

Tedeschi, J. T., Gaes, G. G., & Rivera, A. M. Aggression and the use of coercive power. *Journal of Social Issues*, 1977, *33*, 101–125.

Tedeschi, J. T., & Lindskold, S. *Social psychology: Interdependence, interaction, and influence.* New York: Wiley, 1976.

Tedeschi, J. T., Melburg, V., & Rosenfeld, P. Is the concept of aggression useful? In P. Brain & R. Benton (Eds.), *Aggression: A multidisciplinary view.* London: Academic Press, 1981.

Tedeschi, J. T. & Riess, M. Identities, the phenomenal self, and laboratory research. In J. T. Tedeschi (Ed.), *Impression Management Theory and social psychological research.* New York: Academic Press, 1981. (a)

Tedeschi, J. T., & Riess, M. Verbal tactics of impression management in predicaments. In C. Antaki (Ed.), *Ordinary language explanations of social behavior.* London: Academic Press, 1981. (b)

Tedeschi, J. T. Schlenker, B., & Bonoma, T. V. *Conflict, power, and games.* Chicago: Aldine, 1973.

Tedeschi, J. T., Schlenker, B. R., & Lindskold, S. The exercise of power and influence: The source of influence. In J. T. Tedeschi (Ed.), *The social influence processes.* Chicago: Aldine, 1972.

Tedeschi, J. T., Smith, R. B., III, & Brown, R. C., Jr. A reinterpretation of research on aggression. *Psychological Bulletin*, 1974, *81*, 540–563.

Textor, R. B. *A cross-cultural summary.* New Haven: Human Resources Area Files Press, 1967.

Toch, H. H. *Violent men: An inquiry into the psychology of violence.* Chicago: Aldine, 1969.

Weiss, W. Effects of the mass media of communication. In G. Lindzey & E. Aronson (Eds.), *Handbook of social psychology* (Vol. 5). Reading, Mass.: Addison-Wesley, 1969.

Zillmann, D. Excitation transfer in communication-mediated aggressive behavior. *Journal of Experimental Social Psychology*, 1971, *7*, 419–425.

six

Implications of an Escape–Avoidance Theory of Aggressive Responses to Attack

H. A. DENGERINK
M. K. COVEY

INTRODUCTION

During the past two decades, research on aggressive behavior has clearly and repeatedly demonstrated that such behavior occurs readily following attack from another person. Persons who have been insulted or physically attacked are likely to respond with verbal abuse (James & Mosher, 1967) or with physical counterattack (Baron, 1972; Berkowitz, 1974). Further, the intensity of aggression depends on the intensity of the attack (Epstein & Taylor, 1967; O'Leary & Dengerink, 1973). The consistency of this relationship has prompted Bandura (1973) to conclude that "if one wished to provoke aggression, the most dependable way to do so would be simply to physically assault another person, who would then be likely to oblige with a vigorous counterattack [p. 153]."

The observed importance of attack in eliciting aggression suggests that aggressive behavior should be conceputalized as occurring within an ongoing exchange between attackers and aggressors. Aggressive responses to attack constitute consequences for the attacker's behavior and attack for the person originally identified as the attacker. The counterattack then may instigate further attack, which in turn may instigate additional counterattack. Some authors have suggested that this dynamic process of aggressive interchange may imply an intent on the part of the aggressor to maintain social equity (Walster,

163

Berscheid, & Walster, 1973) or to promote self-aggrandizement (Chadwick-Jones, 1976) within the aggressive interchange. Another related notion has been proposed by Buss (1961), who suggested that aggressive responses to attack may be reinforced by termination of the pain experienced from the attack. That is, aggressive responses to attack may be viewed as instrumental attempts to terminate or modify the behavior of the attacker. These notions, thus, suggest that aggresive responses to attack are, at least in part, behaviors with some purpose rather than reflexive reactions to some aversive event.

Buss's suggestion that aggressive responses to attack may be reinforced by termination or abatement in the behavior of the attacker also suggests that the consequences of aggressing may modify subsequent aggressive behavior. If aggressive responses to attack are successful in modifying the attacker's behavior, then such aggressive responses to attack may be expected to continue or to increase in frequency with subsequent attack. Alternatively, if aggressive responses to attack are not successful in achieving escape form attack, then these aggressive responses may be expected to decrease in frequency, at least eventually.

This notion, that aggressive responses to attack are instrumental attempts to modify the behavior of another person, may have many important implications for understanding such behavior. Differing histories of reinforcement may be responsible for differences in the use of aggressive behaviors by different individuals. It may also provide an explanation for differences in aggression caused by aggressive cues and other situational variables or by other subject behaviors, such as attribution of intent. It may also predict changes in the aggressive behavior, including changes in frequency, alterations in intensity, modifications in form, and acquisition or fading of instigating stimuli and the choice of target.

Despite its potential importance, the possibility that aggressive responses to attack are instrumental attempts to modify the behavior of the attacker has received relatively little attention in the aggression literature. This lack of attention may stem, first of all, from the kinds of research procedures that have achieved predominant acceptance (see Bertilson, Chapter 8, this volume). Repeated exchanges of attack and counterattack are not permitted in these procedures. The influence on aggression by the context of repeated and ongoing exchange is thus left to conjecture or specifically eliminated in most procedures.

Two other sets of laboratory procedures have been devised that do permit repeated exchanges of attack and counterattack. These are the competitive reaction-time task devised by Taylor (Epstein & Taylor, 1967) and the minimal social situation adopted by Hokanson (Hokanson, Willers, & Koropsak, 1968). Additionally, the more recently devised procedures for continuous observation of naturally occurring interactions (Gottman, 1979; Patterson & Cobb, 1973; Hops, Wills, Patterson, & Weiss, Note 1) have provided data from repeated exchanges of both aversive and positive behaviors (see Bertilson, Chapter 8, this volume). These various procedures have begun to provide results that are more relevant to the notion that aggressive responses to attack are instrumental attempts to modify the behavior of the attacker.

Another impediment to recognizing the potential importance of avoidance/ escape motivation for aggression has been the proclivity for many authors to develop classifications of aggressive behavior that incorporate mutually exclusive categories. One of the most frequent classifications has been that of instrumental aggression. This class of aggressive acts has been defined as "acts which are reinforced by nonaggressive goals [Feshbach, 1976, p. 270]." It is not clear what constitutes "nonaggressive goals." It appears, however, that Feshbach would include such outcomes as money, self-esteem, social status, and self-preservation (p. 258). The last example implies that reduction in or termination of the attack may be included. Typically, however, instrumental aggression appears to be conceptualized as being controlled via consequences (generally positive ones) that are only incidental to the aggressive act and to the aggressive exchange. The other classes of aggression have included expressive aggression, in which aversive stimuli elicit motivation for some form of behavior (aggression) rather than motivation for any particular outcome (Feshbach, 1964). Another class is hostile (Feshbach, 1964) or impulsive (Berkowitz, 1974) aggression which is viewed as being controlled by associative processes and reinforced by the victim's pain, not by changes in the victim's behavior. Most authors do concede that "expressive, hostile and instrumental functions are interwoven in most aggressive acts [Feshbach, 1964, p. 270]." The mutually exclusive classification schemes have, however, permitted primary attention to the stimulus control of aggression and to motives other than escape– avoidance.

The potential role of escape–avoidance has been described by some authors. Bandura (1973) has placed considerable emphasis on instrumental controls, including the processes of escape and avoidance, for the acquisition of aggressive behavior. It has also been explicitly recognized by Tedeschi, Smith, and Brown (1974), whose concept of the defensive use of "coercive power" appears similar to the position taken here (see Tedeschi, Chapter 5, this volume).

The current chapter suggests that aggressive responses to attack may be complexly motivated and controlled, but that one important aspect of these multiple controls is the motivation for escape–avoidance from the attack that instigated it. Further, it is suggested that the attention to such motivation may greatly increase the explanation and prediction of several aggressive phenomena over that which is permitted by selective attention to stimulus controls and to pain of the victim as the major reinforcer. The basic propositions of this notion, derived from an operant theory of negative reinforcement, will be outlined and reviewed. The implications of these propositions for various aspects of aggressive behavior will also be explored.

Patterson (1979) has described the role of negative reinforcement in main-

taining aggressive interchanges in families that include young children, particularly aggressive boys. This chapter will not attempt to incorporate a review of
the observational findings reported by Patterson. Rather, it will attempt to
apply a negative reinforcement theory to the aggressive behavior of adults that
has been examined in the laboratory by the current authors and by others.[1]

NEGATIVE REINFORCEMENT PREDICTIONS OF AGGRESSIVE BEHAVIOR

The first set of propositions for the proposed escape–avoidance theory of
aggressive responses to attack are derived from an operant theory of negative
reinforcement. Negative reinforcement refers to a process of terminating some
event that has the effect of increasing the frequency of the behavior upon
which termination of that event was contingent. Thus, the first prediction is that
termination of aversive events (in this case, attack) will have the eventual effect
of increasing the frequency of aggressive responses to attack.

Conceivably, negative reinforcement could occur with the termination of a
variety of events, both aversive and nonaversive. For practical purposes, and
particularly as it applies to attack-instigated aggression, it will be assumed here
that this process involves withdrawal of aversive events. That is, these are
events that, if applied (rather than withdrawn) contingent upon some behavior,
would function as punishers.

Negative reinforcement processes, then, have special properties among instrumental or operant conditioning procedures. They require that the processes
involve discrimination learning. That is, an aversive stimulus must be applied
or presented and then terminated only when the specified behavior is emitted.
Termination of the attack, then, while providing reinforcement, also eliminates
the stimulus that instigated that behavior. Thus, one would predict that termination of attack would be followed initially by the termination or abatement of
aggression if that behavior has been acquired via negative reinforcement. The
second prediction of this escape–avoidance theory of aggressive performance
is that termination of the attack will result in an immediate termination of the
aggression.

Behavior that is acquired via negative reinforcement is subject to extinction
just as is behavior acquired via other reinforcement processes. Thus, one
would anticipate that failing to terminate attack when aggression is emitted will
eventually result in a reduction or cessation of aggressive responses to attack.
This is the third prediction.

While the eventual effect of maintaining attack (negative reinforcement ex-

---

[1]Gerald Patterson, Ph.D., contributed considerably to the formulation of the ideas expressed
here. Without his willingness to share data and to critique ideas, this chapter would not have been
written.

TABLE 1
Immediate and Eventual Effects of Escape–Avoidance on Aggression Behavior Predicted by a
Negative Reinforcement Theory

	Immediate effects	Eventual effects
Escape–Avoidance	Decrease in aggression	Increase in aggression
No escape–Avoidance	Increase in aggression	Decrease in aggression

tinction) may be a reduction in aggression, the immediate effect may be a
maintenance or even an escalation of the aggressive responses. Repeating or
maintaining the attack maintains or re-presents the stimulus condition that
instigates aggression. The fourth prediction derived from a negative reinforcement theory is that the immediate effect of continuing the attack will be maintenance or escalation of the aggression. These four predictions are summarized
in Table 1.

It should be pointed out that the research on aggression that does address
issues of ongoing interaction have seldom been designed to test these hypotheses directly. Rather, the majority of the related evidence involves reinterpreta-
tions of results gathered for other purposes.

Immediate Effects of Terminating or Reducing Attack

The immediate effect of terminating or reducing attack has been examined
most often with the aid of the competitive reaction-time task designed by
Taylor (Taylor & Epstein, 1967). In that task, each member of a pair of subjects
competes for the faster reaction time in order to avoid receiving an electric
shock of an intensity chosen by the other. However, the two subjects do not
actually compete. The frequency of winning and losing and the intensity of the
feedback are determined by the experimenter.

Using these procedures, O'Leary and Dengerink (1974) programmed the
opponent to provide one of four different kinds of attack. In one condition the
opponent selected attack that was initially at or near maximum (4.5 on a 5-
point scale) but then decreased gradually across trials to 1.5. In another condition the opponent chose the maximum or near maximum (4.5) on all trials,
while in another the opponent chose only mild levels (mean 1.5) on all trials.
In a fourth condition the opponent chose shocks that increased from mild (1.5)
to maximal (4.5). Of primary interest for the current purposes is the observation
that the decreasing attack condition resulted in counterattack that decreased
across successive trial blocks. This effect is illustrated in Figure 1. A reduction
in the intensity of attack is followed by a reduction in the intensity of counterattack.

The decrement in aggression with termination of the attack is more clearly

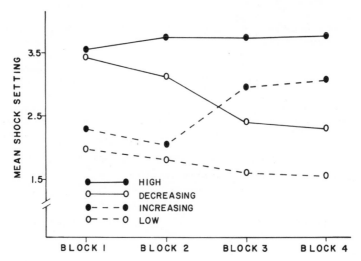

FIGURE 1 Aggressive counterresponses as a function of the intensity and pattern of attack.
(From O'Leary & Dengerink, 1974.)

demonstrated in a study by Dengerink and Bertilson (1974). Using the competitive reaction-time task, these authors first provided subjects with the highest possible intensity of shock. The subjects responded in kind by delivering maximal intensity shocks of their own. Then the opponent was programmed to adopt one of three strategies to reduce the aggression that he had just instigated. In one condition the opponent adopted a strategy of delivering (or choosing) only the least intense possible shock. As Figure 2 indicates, this "withdrawal" strategy was markedly effective in reducing the intensity of counterattack. When the opponent withdrew to a nonaggressive strategy, the subject did so as well. Further, this strategy was more effective in reducing aggression than was a matching strategy or a yoked strategy.

The immediate effect of terminating attack is even more clearly demonstrated by Dengerink, Schnedler, and Covey (1978), utilizing a modification of the Hokanson procedures (Hokanson et al., 1968). In these modified procedures subjects were asked to interact with another subject in a situation that, limited them to interactional behaviors that delivered one of five different intensity shocks to the other person or delivered no shock (zero intensity). In their procedures (Experiment 2), the subject first received a series of maximum-intensity shocks. When the subject responded by delivering the maximum-intensity shock, the opponent then chose the zero intensity on the subsequent few trials. The opponent later reinitiated the attack and then withdrew contingent upon the maximum choice by the subject and continued for a total of six such cycles. Dengerink et al. (1978) report that shock intensities chosen by the subject decreased markedly during all six no-attack periods compared to

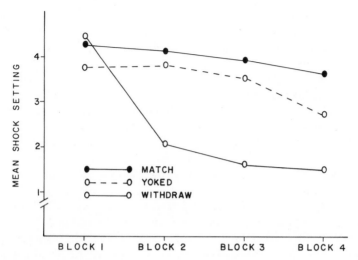

FIGURE 2 Aggressive counterresponses as a function of strategies to reduce aggression. (From Dengerink & Bertilson, 1974.)

periods of attack, even though the opponent continued to reinitiate maximum-intensity attack.

Thus, it appears that termination of the attack will result in an immediate reduction or termination of counterattack. Such effects have been replicated by Bertilson, Wonderlich, Blum, and Lien (Note 2) with differing frequencies of actually delivering the shock to the subject. Similar effects have been noted in observational studies of ongoing interactions between mothers and their children.

Observational research procedures rely on coding ongoing interactions among persons without the injection of such intrusive procedures as reaction-time competition, interaction task boards, or electric shock. They must rely, however, on the observation of behaviors that are far less aggressive, including such minor annoyances as whining, disapproval, and other forms of verbal aggression, and it is often impossible to control for important variables. Despite such major differences from laboratory procedures, observational studies have confirmed the findings noted in laboratories.

Patterson (1976), for example, reported one experiment in which mothers of aggressive children were asked to play with their children following instructions from the experimenter. During one 10-min interval, they were asked to engage in those behaviors that had been previously identified as aversive (Patterson, 1974) and that would increase the likelihood of whining (e.g., disapproving of something the child did). During that period, the probability that the child would whine during any given 6-sec interval was .32. That is, when the mothers engaged in aversive behaviors, their children whined approximately once every 18 sec. During the subsequent 10-min interval, mothers were asked to refrain from those behaviors that were known to elicit a child's whining. During that period, the probability that the child would whine decreased to .04 for any given 6-sec interval. Thus, the likelihood that the child would whine decreased markedly and quickly when the mother terminated her behavior that was aversive to the child.

Patterson (1974) also reported that more precise observations in homes indicated similar effects of escape–avoidance. For one child who was observed extensively, the probability that he would continue acting hostilely (whining, disapproving, yelling) during the 6-sec period was .08 if the mother did not respond to him. On the other hand, if his mother complied with a request that accompanied his hostile behavior, the probability that he would continue behaving hostilely during the succeeding 6 sec was only .008. If the mother complied with the child's demands, she could be assured of a 10-fold decrement in the likelihood that the hostility would continue. Patterson (1976) replicated these findings. Such maternal behaviors may constitute double reinforcement, both positive and negative. Still, these results in combination with those reported from laboratory studies indicate that, within both laboratory-created and existing behavioral systems, termination of aversive events will curtail aggressive behavior.

The prediction of a reduction in aggression upon termination of attack is a particularly important one for an escape–avoidance theory of attack-instigated aggression. First, it is one that has not been specifically included or even necessarily implied in previous writings concerning impulsive or hostile aggression. Second, it is one prediction that has been solidly supported both in laboratory and in observational research. Third, it is a phenomenon that may have some major implications for ongoing interactions among aggressive persons. If one terminates aggression as soon as the attack is terminated, then doing so also provides negative reinforcement for the person who terminated the attack. Providing such negative reinforcement for the attacker may assure the aggressor of avoiding attack or of more rapid termination of attack on future occasions. That is, terminating attack may have some utility for the attacker, but terminating the counterattack contingent on terminating the attack may have utility for the aggressor as well.

Eventual Effects of Avoiding–Escaping Attack

While the immediate effect of terminating attack may be a reduction in aggression, the eventual effect may be an increase in the likelihood of aggressive responses to attack. This is the basic prediction of an operant learning theory of negative reinforcement. It has received considerable attention in studies of the acquisition of aggressive behavior, particularly on the part of animals. It has received relatively little attention, however, in considerations of aggression by persons who may be assumed to have already acquired aggressive skills. Still, it is possible that persons who are displaying aggression at less than maximal rates may increase the likelihood of aggressing if doing so permits them to terminate attack. Particularly in combination with shaping procedures, such a process may lead either to escalation in the intensity of aggression or to aggressive reactions to less potent eliciting stimuli.

One series of studies that is relevant to this prediction involves the minimal social situation (Hokanson et al., 1968). As noted earlier, this set of procedures permits pairs of subjects to interact by either delivering electric shock or illuminating a light labeled "reward" for the other person. In their earlier studies, the experimenters were concerned only with the responses chosen by the subject after receiving electric shock from the other person. They reported that during baseline conditions, when the opponent's choices of shock or reward were not contingent upon the subject's choices, females responded to attack (shock) by delivering shock, on the average, 59% of the time. Later, they programmed the opponent to deliver shock only 10% of the time after subjects responded to the attack by delivering shock, and 90% of the time when the subject responded by delivering reward. During this conditioning phase, when subjects could avoid receiving shock by reacting aggressively, they gradually increased the probability of responding to shock with shock to an average of 78% of the time. Subsequently, Knott, Lasater, and Shuman (1974) reported similar results for subjects who reported themselves to be low on a measure of aggression guilt.

These results support the notion that avoidance or escape conditioning procedures may result in an increase in aggressive responses (delivering electric shock) following attack (receiving electric shock). Unfortunately, they are confounded with the possibility of positive reinforcement as well. If the subjects in these procedures did not receive shock, they received feedback from the person in the form of an illuminated light that was labeled "reward." While this positive reinforcement may be viewed as extremely mild, it is still possible that such positive reinforcement, rather than negative reinforcement, was responsible for the increases in aggressive responses to attack.

Dengerink et al. (1978) have modified the procedures adopted by Knott et al. by eliminating the reward alternative and substituting a zero-intensity or no-shock alternative. In the previous section, it was reported that subjects who received blocks of trials that alternated between maximum-intensity attack and no attack continued to reduce the intensity and frequency of their shock choices when the opponent provided trials of no attack. Half of the subjects in that experiment experienced onset of the no-attack trials contingent on their choosing the maximum-intensity shock for the opponent. The remaining half of the subjects were yoked with the first half and experienced reductions in attack that were not contingent upon their own aggressive responses to attack. Experimental subjects, despite continuing to reduce the intensity and frequency of their shock responses during periods of no attack, delivered shock more frequently and of higher intensity than the yoked subjects during the later blocks of no attack. Dengerink et al. concluded that the increase in aggressive responding to no attack may have represented attempts to avoid rather than merely curtail attack on the part of the experimental subjects. Although similar differences between experimental and yoked subjects during the periods of high attack were in the expected direction (the average probability of delivering shock was .84 and .71, respectively), these differences were not significant. Such responses to maximum-intensity attack may have been too near ceiling levels to permit conditioning effects.

The notion that negative reinforcement may increase attempts to avoid rather than merely terminate attack suggests that the escape contingencies may promote escalation of aggression. That is, after conditioning, aggressive responses to no attack were more likely and more intense than before conditioning. Escalation of human aggression from mild to more severe forms (e.g., from verbal to physical) has not been examined as a function of negative reinforcement. It should be pointed out, however, that Straus (1979) reports sizable positive correlations between self-reports of verbal and physical aggression. Further, Kelly (1976) reported that 72% of homicides occurred following arguments, not during felonious activities. Thus, the possibility that negative reinforcement can result in escalation of aggression from verbal abuse to physical violence warrants attention.

Increments in aggressive behavior as a function of avoidance contingencies have also been reported in observational field studies. For example, Devine (1971) asked mothers to ignore their children—a condition that frequently results in children's engaging in aversive behaviors (cf. Patterson, 1976)—and to respond to them only when they showed objectionable behaviors. Within as few as four trials, these children evidenced dramatic increases in the duration and intensity (decibel level) and decreases in the latency of their aversive behaviors. These laboratory and observational studies thus suggest that escape or avoidance contingencies can increase the likelihood and intensity of aggressive behaviors.

The combination of the immediate and eventual effects of terminating attack may be particularly insidious. Well-meaning attempts to terminate another's aggressive behavior may be particularly effective if these involve the elimination of aversive antecedents. In attempting to achieve immediate change, however, one may unknowingly increase the likelihood that the aggressive behavior will occur in similar later situations. Alternatively, persons who employ aggressive means of controlling another's aversive behavior may find that successful use of such tactics are ultimately self-corrupting.

Immediate Effects of Continued Attack (No Escape)

If aggressive responses to attacks have been previously acquired via negative reinforcement, then the attacker's failure to terminate the attack should be followed, at least temporarily, by a continuation or even an increment in the aggression. The reptition of the attack–counterattack phenomenon has been noted frequently. Several authors have reported that subjects who experienced continued high-intensity attack respond with maintained high-intensity aggression. Epstein and Taylor (1967), for example, employed the competitive reaction-time task and presented subjects in some conditions with attack that remained maximal across trials. They reported that subjects responded with continued high-intensity aggression. Similar results have been reported by Dengerink, O'Leary, and Kasner (1975). O'Leary and Dengerink (1974) further supported the possibility of increased aggression in response to continued attack following aggression. In their study, which also employed the competitive reaction-time task, one group of subjects competed with an opponent who chose maximum and near maximum shocks across all trials. A second group received attack that increased across trials until it equaled the intensity set by the opponent in the high-intensity attack condition. During the last block of trials, when subjects in these two conditions were receiving equally intense shock, those in the high-intensity condition chose shocks for the opponent that were somewhat more intense than those chosen by subjects in the increasing condition (see Figure 1).

The clearest evidence for this phenomenon in observational research comes from studies of the effects of punishment on children's aversive behavior. Patterson's observational procedures consist of coding the behavior of a subject according to a predetermined complex code every 6 sec. Additionally, the behavior of persons with whom the subject is interacting is coded during each 6-sec period. The list of possible codes includes 29 different behaviors that Patterson has grouped into various categories on empirical bases. The two categories that are of greatest interest here have been labeled "Hostile" and "Social Aggression." He reported (Patterson, 1976) that the base rate–probability for normal children to continue behaving in a similar fashion during the succeeding 6-sec period, after having engaged in that behavior during the preceding 6 sec, was .29 for Hostile and .20 for Social Aggression. If the parents had punished the child during the first observation period, these probabilities decreased only to .23 and .12, respectively. Thus, punishment resulted in only a slight suppression. Among children who had been identified as requiring clinic services for aggressive behavior, the base rates of continuing the behaviors were .31 for Hostile and .29 for Social Aggression. If the parents punished the child, these conditional probabilities were .41 and .29, respectively. Thus, parental punishment for these children either did not alter the probability of persisting (Social Aggression) or increased it (Hostile). These findings provide both laboratory and field observational support for the prediction that persons will continue to be aggressive or will increase that behavior if they fail to achieve termination of another's aversive behavior.

The immediate effect of repeated or continued counterattack with representation of the attack may have some important implications. The reoccurrence of counterattack, until termination of the attack occurs, suggests that such behavior is likely to occur in close proximity to the reinforcement. This close proximity may ensure more rapid and more thorough acquisition of aggressive counterresponses than may be the case for positively reinforced behaviors. Persons who have investigated negative reinforcement in other contexts have concluded that this process does result in more rapid acquisition than does positive reinforcement (cf. Logan & Ferraro, 1978, p. 247).

If aggressive behavior has been frequently followed by rapid termination of attack, then the aggressor may come to expect such rapid changes in another's behavior as a function of his or her behaving in that fashion. Consequently, it may be appropriate to predict that persons will be most likely to employ aggressive means of controlling another's behavior when immediacy of the change is most important. Tedeschi et al. (1974) have made such a prediction explicit. They state that aggression "is predicted to be more likely . . . the greater the time pressure on the [person] for reaching his goals [p. 553]." The authors are unaware of research that has tested this prediction directly. One study, however, is relevant. One characteristic of the coronary-prone (Type A) personality is a sense of time urgency or impatience. Carver and Glass (1978) reported that such persons were likely to use more intense electric shocks than non-coronary-prone persons in attempts to modify the behavior of another person in the Buss (1961) aggression procedures.

Eventual Effects of Continued Attack (No Escape)

If aggressive responses to attack do occur as instrumental attempts to terminate the attack, then the repeated failure to achieve this end should result in eventual abatement of that behavior. Investigations of negative reinforcement extinction for adult human aggression have not yet employed enough trials to demonstrate convincing changes. Some findings, however, provide tangential or suggestive support.

In a study described earlier, Hokanson et al. (1968) reported that during a baseline condition males responded to the receipt of shock by delivering shock at an average of 74% of the time. During the subsequent conditioning phase, these subjects received shock 90% of the time after delivering shock and only 10% of the time after responding positively. Hokanson et al. reported that these subjects decreased the probability of responding aggressively to shock to 66%. In another study, Knott et al. (1974) reported that similar contingencies significantly decreased both the probability and intensity of aggressive responses to shock for high-guilt persons. As noted before, however, the no-shock consequence was a positive one. Thus, it is not clear whether the process of extinction, avoidance–escape contingencies, or positive reinforcement contingencies were responsible for the observed decrements.

An interesting modification of the minimal social situation was adopted by Stone and Hokanson (1969). In addition to the alternatives of delivering shock or reward to the other person, their subjects could deliver a lesser intensity shock to themselves (three-fourths the intensity of shock the other person delivered to them). During the 80 experimental trials, subjects were given the more intense shock 90% of the time when they delivered shock or reward to the opponent. If they delivered a shock to themselves, the subjects received reward 90% of the time. The proportion of trials on which subjects delivered shock after receiving it from the other person declined from .64 during baseline to .48 during the experimental phase.

Stone and Hokanson's (1969) findings point to the possibility that any behavior, whether aggressive or not, will be adopted if it has utility for avoiding attack from another person. That is, aggressive responses to attack may occur because of their functional value, not because of any inherent relationship between attack and aggression. Further, if persons will adopt self-punitive behaviors in order to avoid more intense punitive behaviors of another person, then such avoidance–escape procedures may be particularly powerful ones for engendering or modifying human aggressive behavior.

Several studies have examined extinction processes without the confounding influences of positive reinforcement. Dengerink and Bertilson (1974) and Bertilson et al. (Note 2) programmed the bogus opponent in the competitive reaction-time task first to provide a series of maximum-intensity attacks and then to match the intensity chosen by the subject over a longer series of trials. Similarly, Pisano and Taylor (1971) selected highly aggressive subjects (who chose high-intensity shocks on the first trial, before any feedback from the opponent) and attempted to reduce their aggression via a matching strategy. This matching strategy provides continued punishment or extinction for aggressive responses and permits avoidance for nonaggressive responses in degrees that are proportional to the degree of aggression. In all cases, the matching strategy resulted in a gradual decrement in the intensity of the aggressive behavior (see Figure 2).

A matching strategy provides for the possibility of reduced attack only if the subject first reduces the intensity of his or her attack, and only to the degree that the subject reduces it. Maintenance (either complete or partial) of the aggression ensures re-presentation of the attack. The matching strategy would thus appear to be effective only if the subject is aware that the opponent is choosing shock intensities contingent on his or her own. The reaction-time task may obscure any awareness of the contingencies. In these procedures, the subject receives feedback at the end of one trial that is contingent upon the shock chosen by the subject at the beginning of the previous trial. Thus, two whole trials elapse between the subject's response and the feedback that was contingent on that response. The procedures adopted by Hokanson et al. (1968) may be more useful for investigating the efficacy of a matching strategy. Since the subjects alternate with their partners, feedback occurs during the second half of the trial, rather than at the end of the subsequent trial. Contingencies may thus be more apparent to the subject.

Bertilson *et al.* (Note 2) explored the possibility that the matching strategy would be more effective in reducing attack-instigated aggression in the minimal social situation than in the reaction-time task. They modified the Hokanson task to permit several shock intensities and a zero or no-reward option. Subjects tested with this procedure were compared with those tested with the competitive reaction-time task, which was also modified to include a zero alternative. The programmed opponent first provided high-intensity attack and then matched the aggressiveness of the subject who had chosen high-intensity counterattacks. They reported that reductions in aggression were more rapid in the minimal social situation than in the reaction-time task. Further, in a second experiment, Bertlilson *et al.* reported that, while the withdrawal strategy resulted in more rapid reductions in aggression than the matching strategy, these did not differ in the low level eventually reached when the minimal social interaction paradigm was employed.

The findings reported here do not provide conclusive evidence that extinction procedures will result in the eventual reduction of aggressive responses to attack. In all cases, the extinction procedures have been obscured by the potential operation of other processes, such as avoidance for nonaggressive responses. These results do indicate, however, that extinction *may* occur. They also provide the encouraging conclusion that aggressive responses to attack may be reduced with the appropriate arrangement of contingencies.

COROLLARIES

The hypotheses outlined in the preceding discussion were derived primarily from an operant theory of negative reinforcement—that is, from processes assumed to occur if aggressive responses were acquired via contingencies that permit the person to terminate attack. They do not include related predictions that may be logically derived or that are based on related theories, such as social learning theory. In the pages that follow, three such corollaries will be discussed. The first describes the stimulus control of aggression. The second describes the potential role of individual differences in previous learning history. The third discusses the role of perceived effectiveness (expectations of success).

Stimulus Control in the Instigation of Aggression

In the preceding pages, the relationship of aggressive behavior to attack stimuli has been emphasized. Implied in the notion that aggressive behavior may have been acquired in large part via the process of negative reinforcement is the possibility that aggression is under greater stimulus control than are other behaviors. It is not clear that there is a good index of the degree of stimulus control. The existing data suggest, however, that aggression is under consider-able stimulus control and that this stimulus control is greater than for other behaviors. Dengerink et al. (1978) report that, over several conditions, the average probability that subjects would respond to attack with a counterattack was .71. Similar probabilities for male subjects have been reported by Hokan-son et al. (1968) and Knott et al. (1974). It should also be pointed out that Patterson (1979) reports a similar probability (.80) of aversive behaviors being observed after aversive antecedents. Thus, the reciprocity of aversive behaviors is not simply a laboratory phenomenon limited to the exchange of electric shocks. In contrast, Dengerink et al. (1978) report that the probability of sub-jects delivering shock after receiving no shock was .24.

Similarly, subjects appear to match the intensity of their counterattacks to the intensity of the attack. This conclusion is strongly supported in a study by O'Leary and Dengerink (1974) described earlier (see Figure 1). Their findings do not indicate a perfect matching of attack and counterattack; as noted ear-lier, some cumulative effects occur as well. Nevertheless, O'Leary and Den-gerink concluded that the best predictor of the intensity of aggression was the intensity of the immediately preceding attack.

The possibility that pleasuring interactions were governed by a similar norm of reciprocity was investigated by Bergstrom (Note 3). He employed a minimal social situation, similar to that of Hokanson et al. (1968), that permitted sub-jects to interact by choosing to deliver a pleasurable stimulus or not to respond to another subject. The single pleasurable alternative permitted subjects to press a button that would activate a massage pad upon which the other partici-pant was sitting. Subjects were tested in cross-sexed pairs, and the subject received the pleasurable stimulus (the intensity of the vibration was that judged as most pleasurable before the trials began) according to a predetermined schedule. Subjects received the pleasurable stimulus frequently (80%), infre-quently (20%), with increasing frequency (from 20% to 80% across blocks), or with decreasing frequency (from 80% to 20% across blocks).

The frequency of pleasuring across blocks for these four conditions is plotted in Figure 3. This figure illustrates that the frequency of delivering pleasure did vary across the groups. The discrimination among groups, however, is not as clear as that reported by O'Leary and Dengerink, which is illustrated in Figure 1. Bergstrom failed to observe any significant decrement in pleasuring by the group given decreasing stimulation. The group given increasing pleasure did evidence more pleasuring in the last than in any other block, but no other comparisons were significant for that group. Furthermore, the probability that subjects would deliver pleasure after receiving pleasure was .67. The proba-bility that they would deliver pleasure after receiving no pleasure was .61. The comparable probabilities for shock to shock and shock to no shock were .71 and .24, as noted earlier. These figures suggest that pleasure begets pleasure and that attack begets counterattack, and that, although the absence of attack assures an absence of aggression, an absence of pleasure does not preclude

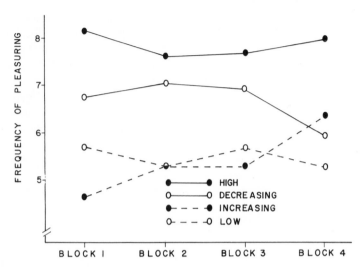

FIGURE 3 Frequency of delivering pleasure as a function of the frequency and pattern of receiving pleasure. (From Bergstrom, Note 3.)

pleasuring. It may thus be appropriate to conclude that aggressive behavior is governed by a norm of reciprocity to a greater extent than is pleasuring behavior.

While attack appears to be a frequent instigator of aggression, attack may be repeatedly paired with other stimuli, and via such conditioning, other stimuli may come to instigate aggression as well. Alternatively, in terms of social learning theory (Rotter, 1972), subjects may respond aggressively when they expect that attack will occur. If one responds aggressively to potential attack and the attack does not ensue, then one may have avoided rather than merely curtailed the aversive behavior of the other person. Such avoidance may have even greater importance than escape. Bandura (1973) more specifically states, "Defensive aggression is sustained to a greater effect by anticipated consequences than by its instantaneous effects [p. 201]."

The phenomenon of potential attack has been addressed in a study by Taylor, Shuntich, and Greenberg (1979). In the first experiment, subjects competed with an opponent in the reaction-time task on three different occasions. Experimental subjects competed with opponents (different ones on each session) who were highly aggressive during the first two sessions, but nonaggressive during the third session. Control subjects competed with an opponent who was nonaggressive during all sessions. Of particular importance are the shocks chosen by the subject on the first trial. These choices occurred before any feedback was received about the intensity of shocks chosen by the opponent. Taylor et al. reported that subjects in the experimental condition increased the intensity of shocks (first trial) chosen over the three sessions, whereas control subjects did not increase the intensity. Further, the experimental subjects were more aggressive toward the unmitigating opponent during the second than the first session on trials after the first one. Experimental subjects were also more aggressive than controls in the final session, when the opponent was nonaggressive. A second experiment revealed similar effects in a group that observed another subject interact with an aggressive opponent for the first two sessions and then compete with a nonaggressive opponent during the third session. While Taylor et al. do not report assessing their subjects' expectations concerning the opponent's behavior, these findings may suggest that expectations of high-intensity attack, rather than the attack itself, will facilitate subsequent aggression.

A related phenomenon is that of attribution of intent. Epstein and Taylor (1967) as well as Nickel (1974) report that subjects were aggressive when they believed that the person with whom they were interacting intended to harm them but was unable to do so. Additionally, subjects were not aggressive (in the Nickel study) if the other person caused the subject some discomfort but the subject believed this to have been an accident. These findings led these authors and Dengerink (1976) to conclude that attribution of intent may be more important in eliciting subsequent aggression than is the attack that generates the attribution. Beyond describing this process, however, these authors have not explained why attribution of intent may overshadow the actual attack. One important possibility is that attributions of aggressive intent lead a potential aggressor to believe that the attack will continue unless he or she intervenes. Beliefs that an attack was accidental, however, may lead one to predict that such attacks will abate even without aggressive intervention.

Other aggressive cues may also be considered in this light. If one assumes that various aggressive cues regulate aggressive behavior (Berkowitz, 1974), then one may assume that these cues are conditioned stimuli that regulate aggression in a predictable but noninstrumental fashion. Alternatively, one could argue that these cues have some important functional (rather than merely associative) relationship to the aggressive behavior. The latter possibility has not been directly investigated but is suggested here. Specifically, aggressive cues of a broad variety may convey information to a potential aggressor concerning the likelihood that aggressive behavior will be effective in terminating attack. Such cues may also indicate whether maximal aggression is necessary or whether a mild counterattack is sufficient. Cues that indicate that an attacker is highly aggressive or competitive may lead a potential aggressor to believe that maximal attack is necessary to modify the other's behavior. If one's attacker has been described as a college boxer, then one may assume that, because of pain tolerance or aggressive ability, that particular attacker may require more intense counterattack to modify his behavior than would a person described as a speech major. Such differences in expectation may be particularly true if one has just witnessed a film of a boxer inflicting and tolerating pain (see Berkowitz, 1974). Similarly, if one's attacker were female, one may anticipate that less intense counterattack is necessary than if the attacker were male (Taylor & Epstein, 1967).

The effect of such cues, however, will depend, as Berkowitz (1974) suggests, on the potential aggressor's interpretation of the aggression-related cues. The information value of any particular set of stimuli will vary with the associations applied by the person reviewing such cues. The effect of aggression-related cues emitted by the victim of one's counterattack, rather than those supplied by the procedures, may also function in this fashion. If a victim's expressions of pain are interpreted as indicating that the counterattack is sufficiently intense to produce change in the attacker-victim's behavior, then such cues may aid in maintaining or reinforcing aggression. Such effects of witnessing a victim's pain have been reported (see Berkowitz, 1974, for review).

Alternatively, expressions of pain from a victim may lead one to anticipate that the attacker-victim is being provoked by the subject's actions and may likely increase the attack. In such cases, one may anticipate that witnessing a victim's pain may lead to inhibited counterattack. The inhibiting effect of victim's pain cues has also been reported by Baron (1974) and Geen (1970). Such marked differences in results of a victim's pain cues are confusing if one considers the pain to be an end in itself. If, however, one views such pain cues as a means of predicting the usefulness of aggressive counterresponses, then these differing results are potentially predictable. We suggest that the underlying motivation is one of escape or avoidance rather than the infliction of pain. Pain may, for some persons, become an end in itself with repeated conditioning, but in Bandura's terms, "the alleviation of aversive treatment from an injured oppressor rather than his suffering may be the *primary* source of satisfaction [1973, p. 198, emphasis added]."

If aggressive cues have varying meaning, then one would anticipate that this variation would be predictable via a number of methods. First, certain types of persons, such as highly anxious individuals, would be more likely to fear excess provocation than to believe pain indicated successful intervention (cf. Dengerink, 1971). Alternatively, one would anticipate that some situations would facilitate the belief that the victim's pain indicates a counterattack's value and others would suggest the opposite. Previous experience that has associated a victim's pain with escape or avoidance may promote aggressive responding to pain cues. A study by Swart and Berkowitz (1976) found such an effect. Other situations, such as those that permit or promote the possibility of repeated attacks from the attacker-victim, may lead to the inhibiting effect of victim pain cues on counterattack.

In this vein, a study by Savitsky, Izard, Kotsch, and Christy (1974) is relevant. They asked subjects to shock a learner who was visible via a closed-circuit television monitor. When the learner received shock, he either smiled, indicated anger, was neutral, or indicated fear. Savitsky et al. reported that, if the victim was neutral or indicated fear, the intensity of shock chosen by the subjects did not change over trials. If the victim smiled after receiving shock, the subjects chose shocks that increased in duration and intensity across trials. If the victim indicated anger, then the subjects chose shocks that decreased, particularly in duration, across trials. These findings suggest that the victim's expression of pain per se is minimally relevant. Instead, the kind of emotion expressed by the victim may lead to very different effects.

Individual Differences in Aggressive Habit Strength

To suggest that aggression is stimulus controlled is not to suggest that such behavior is an invariant function of the stimulus. Indeed, aggressive responses to attack may vary markedly from person to person. These differences, as discussed elsewhere (Dengerink, 1976), may arise for a variety of reasons, including variations in such cognitive variables as expectations, variations in emotional arousal, and variations in socialization history. For the present purposes, variations in socialization history may be most germane. While it may be argued that most persons have adequate opportunity to acquire aggressive skills (Patterson, 1976), it is undoubtedly true that there are major variations in the degree to which such opportunities have occurred, the degree to which aggression has been reinforced, and the degree to which it has been punished. In Hullian learning terms, it may be appropriate to conclude that individuals vary in aggressive habit strength.

One manifestation of these differences may be the likelihood that persons will be aggressive in the absence of attack. Earlier, it was pointed out that the termination of attack was followed by a rapid and major reduction in aggression. There is an important exception to that finding, however. Pisano and Taylor (1971) selected subjects who were highly aggressive (chose high-intensity shock) before any feedback from the opponent in the competitive reaction-time task. Pisano and Taylor exposed these subjects to a variety of procedures designed to reduce aggression. A matching strategy was partially effective, but passivity, choosing only mild-intensity shocks for the subjects, was clearly ineffective for these persons.

Another indication of aggressive habit strength may be self-reports of engaging in violent behavior during real-life attempts to resolve conflicts. In a recent study, Gully and Dengerink (1983) used the Conflict Tactics Scale (Straus, 1979) to assess the frequency of subjects directing physical aggression or violent behaviors toward siblings and acquaintances during the past year. These subjects were then recalled in heterosexual pairs and asked to role play resolution of a problem while being videotaped. The pairs were formed by matching violent history males with violent history females, violent males with nonviolent females, nonviolent males with violent females, and nonviolent males with nonviolent females. The videotaped interaction was then coded by trained observers, who used the Marital Interaction Coding System (Hops et al., Note 1). They found that persons who reported violent histories were more frequently negative than were those who reported nonviolent histories. Further, when conditional probabilities were calculated, violent history females interacting with violent history males were more likely than nonviolent history females to respond negatively to positively coded behaviors of their partners. That is, violent history persons responded in ways that are likely to contribute to the development and escalation of aversive interactions, by presenting more aversive stimuli and punishing positive behaviors.

Efficacy of the Aggressive Response

Rotter (1972) has suggested that behavior is a function, in part, of the person's expectation that the behavior will achieve some desired end. In this vein, it may be predicted that aggressive responses to attack will occur only if the potential aggressor expects that such aggression will be effective in terminating or avoiding attack. When one chooses to aggress against an attacker, one may be able to terminate the attack but may also provoke that person to even more intense attack. One situation that may lead a person to believe that aggression is ineffective is one in which the other person has greater aggressive ability than the potential aggressor. Shortell, Epstein, and Taylor (1970) and Dengerink and Levendusky (1972) reported that subjects were less aggressive when the other participant in the reaction-time task was able to deliver more intense shock than was the subject. Even under high levels of attack, those who had less aggressive ability were less intensely aggressive than those who were equal to or greater than the other participant in aggressive ability.

If a balance of power not in the person's favor inhibits his or her behavior, then the person may expect that a balance of power in his or her favor, could inhibit the other person's behavior. That is, if excessive aggressive ability on the part of the attacker inhibits counterattack, then greater aggressive ability on the part of the counterattacker may be expected to inhibit attack. Dorsky (1972) did report such an effect for some subjects. He employed the competitive reaction-time task and increasing attack over a series of trials. During a final block of trials, the subject could deliver shock that was twice as intense as the shock the opponent could deliver. Dorsky reported that persons who had previously described themselves as being nonanxious increased their counterattack during the last block and delivered the maximum shock intensity over twice as often (23.3%) as persons who described themselves as anxious (9.5%). It thus appears that some persons, notably nonanxious ones, will utilize a balance of power that is in their favor.

This notion of perceived efficacy may be particularly important in explaining other situational variations in aggressive behavior. Patterson (1976) has reported that children who have been identified as being excessively aggressive are much less likely to act aggressively toward their fathers than toward their mothers. He suggests that this difference occurs because the fathers are more likely than the mothers to provide extreme consequences for noxious behaviors on the part of their sons. Further, Patterson, who has devised clinic procedures to alter rates of aggressive behavior by aggressive children, suggests that the program is effective in large part because the parents begin consistently to use more appropriate and more aversive consequences (time-out and loss of privileges rather than verbal disapproval).

This latter observation suggests that the balance of power may depend on one's willingness to employ extreme consequences rather than on physical or structural characteristics. Thus, the balance of power notion suggests that moderate attack is likely to lead to counterattacks and moderate counterattack is likely to lead to repeated attack. If one or the other of the participants, however, exerts aggressive power and delivers severely intense attack (or counterattack), then the other person, if lacking the extreme ability or willingness to use it, will terminate the counterattack. Such an effect has been reported by Dorsky (1972) for highly anxious subjects.

The effects of anxiety reported by Dengerink (1971) and Dorsky (1972) suggest that the predictors of successful versus unsuccessful aggression may lie within the individual rather than within the situation. That is, regardless of the situation, some persons may expect their behaviors to be successful in modifying their environment, whereas others will expect the opposite. Dengerink and Myers (1977) exposed subjects either to repeated failure or to repeated success prior to an aggression task. The prior failure or success was designed to teach subjects that they could or could not successfully influence their environment. These authors reported that depressed persons who had experienced prior failure were less aggressive than those who experienced prior success (see Figure 4). In another experiment, Dengerink et al. (1975) tested subjects who

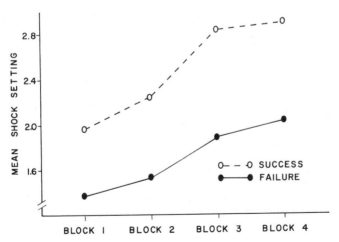

FIGURE 4 Aggressive counterresponses as a function of prior success or failure and increasingly intense attack. (From Dengerink & Myers, 1975.)

expressed generalized expectancies of being able or unable to influence their environment (cf. Rotter, 1972). They reported that persons with an external locus of control failed to discriminate in their aggressive responses among intense, moderate, and mild attack. That is, persons with an external locus of control did not conform to the usual pattern of responding more aggressively to more intense attack. Subjects with an internal locus of control, on the other hand, evidenced marked differences in their responses to the differing levels of attack (see Figure 5). Dengerink et al. concluded that the subjects with an internal locus of control were more aggressive in response to intense attack because they believed that by being so they could influence the other person's behaviors.

The perceived efficacy of aggressive responses to attack may also relate to one's history of socialization for aggression. A commonly expressed notion is that persons who are reared in violent environments will eventually become violent themselves. Seldom are such statements followed by qualifiers concerning the kind of experiences that engender the use of violence. One study, however, suggests that the kind of experience with violence that a person has may be most important.

Gully, Dengerink, Pepping, and Bergstrom (1981) asked college subjects to complete the Conflict Tactics Scale (Straus, 1979) several different times: to report observing violence between parents, between siblings, and between siblings and parents; to report being violent toward parents and toward siblings; to report being a victim of violence from parents and from siblings; and finally to report directing violence toward nonfamily members during the past

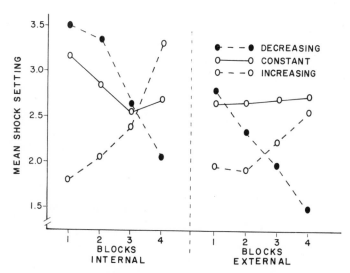

FIGURE 5 Aggression counterresponses as a function of the pattern of attack by internal and external locus of control subjects. (From Dengerink, O'Leary, & Kasner, 1975.)

12 months. Taken together, the family experience variables did significantly predict violence toward nonfamily members during the past 12 months. When overlapping variance was partialled out, however, being violent toward one's siblings was clearly the best predictor, and a discriminant analysis retained that variable as the only significant positive predictor. Further, being a *victim* of sibling violence was a significant suppressor variable. These findings suggest that having a chance to practice violence may be the clearest method of facilitating violence. Being punished by siblings, on the other hand, may inhibit the use of such coercive behaviors.

Other Corollaries

Earlier, it was suggested that persons may weigh the perceived cost and benefits of aggressive responses to attack and that such perceptions may vary with personal characteristics, such as anxiety. Rotter (1972) suggests that, in addition to such outcome expectancies, judgments of reward value will also moderate one's behavior. Such variables have not, to our knowledge, been investigated in relationship to negative reinforcement for aggression. It may be appropriate to suggest, however, that if aggression has been partially acquired via negative reinforcement, then one may be more likely to use such behavior when change in another's behavior is most important. Thus, persons may be most likely to respond aggressively to attack from persons with whom they must continue to interact or from persons whose behavior has import beyond isolated exchanges of aggressive behaviors. In this vein, it is interesting to note that most homicides occur in the context of ongoing multifaceted relationships, such as marriages and friendships (Prosterman, 1972).

The notions discussed in this chapter suggest several strategies for modifying aggressive behavior. First, it is suggested that any nonaggressive behaviors that also achieve termination of attack may be considered as an appropriate substitutes. Other behaviors that permit emotional expression but have no functional value in modifying another's behavior are unlikely as acceptable substitutes. Substitution of other means of avoiding another's aversive behaviors is an important part of the marital therapy procedures proposed by such persons as Gottman (1979). A second important strategy may be to modify the aggressive person's interpretations of aggression-related cues, including perhaps one's own anger level. A third potential focus of intervention, particularly when parents are being taught to modify their children's behavior, is attention of those persons to the immediate versus the eventual effects of interventions.

Finally, these notions suggest that one means of producing an immediate change in violent behavior is to terminate the attack. Eliminating the attack or source of it is a major part of the procedures developed by Bard (1971) for police officers who must control violent exchanges among family members.

CONCLUSION

The major position taken in this chapter is that aggressive behaviors, particularly in response to attack, may be instrumental attempts to terminate or avoid aversive behaviors of another person. This is hardly a new suggestion, but it is one that has received relatively little attention in the aggression literature. The current formulation relies primarily on a series of predictions arising from a negative reinforcement theory. Second, the currently proposed escape– avoidance theory of aggression relies on some propositions of social learning theory. It is hoped that these notions will serve to stimulate more directly relevant research and the thinking of future theorists.

It is suggested that understanding of an avoidance–escape motivation may have important implications for explaining a number of aggression-related phenomena. These include attribution of intent, aggressive cues, escalation, expectations of control, and some situational variations. It is further suggested that such a motivation may have major implications for procedures to control aggression and for understanding such behavior as it occurs both in the laboratory and in naturally occurring interactions.

We do not suggest that avoidance–escape phenomena exclusively influence aggression. Rather aggression is a multifaceted and multiply controlled behavior. Aggression that occurs in differing contexts may require differing explanations, and each aggressive act may be the end result of numerous processes. One potentially very important set of processes, however, may be those involving escape–avoidance motivation. In particular, such a motivation may be an important explanatory system for Western cultures that emphasize individual responsibility and self-determination. It may be of less value for other cultures that emphasize fatalistic concepts of one's experience.

REFERENCE NOTES

1. Hops, H., Wills, T., Patterson, G. R., & Weiss, R. L. Marital interaction coding system. Unpublished manuscript, University of Oregon, 1974.
2. Bertilson, H. S., Wonderlich, S. A., Blum, M. W., & Lien, S. K. Opponents' strategies in reducing attack-instigated aggression. Unpublished manuscript, Weber State College, 1981.
3. Bergstrom, D. A. Reciprocity and global impressions of the other in interpersonal physical pleasuring. Unpublished master's project, Washington State University, 1979.

REFERENCES

Bandura, A. Aggression: A social learning analysis. Englewood Cliffs, N.J.: Prentice-Hall, 1973.
Bard, M. The study and modification of intra-familial violence. In J. L. Singer (Ed.), The control of aggression and violence: Cognitive and physiological factors. New York: Academic Press, 1971.

Baron, R. Reducing the influence of an aggressive model: The restraining effects of peer censure. *Journal of Experimental Social Psychology*, 1972, *8*, 266–275.

Baron, R. Aggression as a function of victim's pain cues, level of prior anger arousal, and exposure to an aggressive model. *Journal of Personality and Social Psychology*, 1974, *29*, 117–124.

Berkowitz, L. Some determinants of impulsive aggression: Role of mediated associations with reinforcements for aggression. *Psychological Review*, 1974, *81*, 165–176.

Buss, A. *The psychology of aggression*. New York: Wiley, 1961.

Carver, C. S., & Glass, D. C. Coronary-prone behavior pattern and interpersonal aggression. *Journal of Personality and Social Psychology*, 1978, *36*, 361–366.

Chadwick-Jones, J. K. *Social exchange theory: Its structure and influence in social psychology*. London: Academic Press, 1976.

Dengerink, H. A. Anxiety, aggression, and physiological arousal. *Journal of Experimental Research in Personality*, 1971, *5*, 223–232.

Dengerink, H. A. Personality variables as mediators of attack instigated aggression. In R. G. Green & E. O'Neal (Eds.), *Perspectives on Aggression*. New York: Academic Press, 1976.

Dengerink, H. A., & Bertilson, H. S. The reduction of attack instigated aggression. *Journal of Research in Personality*, 1974, *8*, 154–162.

Dengerink, H. A., & Levendusky, P. G. Effects of massive retaliation and balance of power on aggression. *Journal of Experimental Research in Personality*, 1972, *6*, 230–236.

Dengerink, H. A., & Myers, J. D. The effects of failure and depression on subsequent aggression. *Journal of Personality and Social Psychology*, 1977, *35*, 88–96.

Dengerink, H. A., O'Leary, M. R., & Kasner, K. H. Individual differences in aggressive responses to attack and no attack. *Journal of Personality*, 1975, *9*, 191–199.

Dengerink, H. A., Schnedler, R. S., & Covey, M. K. The role of avoidance in aggressive responses to attack and no attack. *Journal of Personality and Social Psychology*, 1978, *36*, 1044–1053.

Devine, V. T. *The coercion process: A laboratory analogue*. Unpublished doctoral dissortation, State University of New York at Stony Brook, 1971.

Dorsky, F. *The effects of social and physical anxiety on human aggressive behavior*. Unpublished doctoral dissertation, Kent State University, 1972.

Epstein, S., & Taylor, S. P. Instigation to aggression as a function of degree of defeat and perceived aggressive intent of the opponent. *Journal of Personality*, 1967, *35*, 265–289.

Feshbach, S. The function of aggression and the regulation of aggressive drive. *Psychological Review*, 1964, *71*, 257–272.

Geen, R. Perceived suffering of the victim as an inhibitor of attack-induced aggression. *The Journal of Social Psychology*, 1970, *81*, 209–215.

Gottman, I. M. *Marital interaction: Experimental investigations*. New York: Academic Press, 1979.

Gully, K., & Dengerink, H. A. The dyadic interaction of persons with violent and nonviolent histories. *Aggressive Behavior*, 1983.

Gully, K. Dengerink, H. A., Pepping, M., & Bergstrom, D. Sibling contribution to the acquisition of violence: A research note. *Journal of Marriage and the Family*, 1981, *42*, 333–339.

Hokanson, J. E., Willers, K. R., & Koropsak, E. The modification of autonomic responses during aggressive interchange. *Journal of Personality*, 1968, *26*, 386–404.

James, P., & Mosher, D. Thematic aggression, hostility-guilt, and aggressive behavior. *Journal of Projective Techniques*, 1967, *3*, 61–67.

Kelly, C. M. *Uniform crime reports for the United States*. Washington, D.C.: U.S. Government Printing Office, 1976.

Knott, P. D., Lasater, L., & Shuman, R. Aggression-guilt and conditionability for aggressiveness. *Journal of Personality*, 1974, *41*, 332–334.

Logan, F. A., & Ferraro, D. P. *Systematic analysis of learning and motivation*. New York: Wiley, 1978.

Nickel, T. W. The attribution of intention as a critical factor in the relation between frustration and aggression. *Journal of Personality*, 1974, *41*, 482–492.

O'Leary, M. R., & Dengerink, H. A. Aggression as a function of the intensity and pattern of attack. *Journal of Research In Personality,* 1973, *41,* 482–492.

Patterson, G. R. A basis for identifying stimuli which control behavior in natural settings. *Child Development,* 1974, *45,* 900–911.

Patterson, G. R. The aggressive child: Victim and architect of a coercive system. In L. A. Hamerlynck, L. C. Handy, & E. J. Mach (Eds.), *Behavior modification and families. I. Theory and research.* New York: Brunner/Mazel, 1976.

Patterson, G. R. A performance theory for coercive family interactions. In R. Cairns (Ed.), *Social interaction: Methods, analysis, and illustration.* Hillsdale, N.J.: Erlbaum, 1979.

Patterson, G. R., & Cobb, J. A. Stimulus control for classes of noxious behavior. In J. F. Knutson (Ed.), *The control of aggression.* Chicago: Aldine, 1973.

Pisano, R., & Taylor, S. P. Reduction in physical aggression: The effects of four different strategies. *Journal of Personality and Social Psychology,* 1971, *19,* 237–242.

Prosterman, R. L. *Surviving to 3000.* Belmont, Cal.: Duxbury Press, 1972.

Rotter, J. B. An introduction to social learning theory. In J. B. Rotter, J. E. Chance, & J. Phares (Eds.), *Application of a social learning theory of personality.* New York: Holt, 1972.

Savitsky, J. C., Izard, C. E., Kotsch, W. E., & Christy, L. Aggressor's response to the victim's facial expression of emotion. *Journal of Research in Personality,* 1974, *7,* 346–357.

Shortell, J., Epstein, S., & Taylor, S. P. Instigation to aggression as a function of degree of defeat and capacity for massive retaliation. *Journal of Personality,* 1970, *38,* 313–328.

Stone, L. J., & Hokanson, J. E. Arousal reduction via self-punitive behavior. *Journal of Personality and Social Psychology,* 1969, *12,* 72–79.

Straus, M. Measuring intrafamily conflict and violence: The conflicts Tactics (C.T.) Scale. *Journal of Marriage and the Family,* 1979, *41,* 75–88.

Swart, C., & Berkowitz, L. The effects of a stimulus associated with a victim's pain on later aggression. *Journal of Personality and Social Psychology,* 1976, *33,* 623–631.

Taylor, S. P., & Epstein, S. Aggression as a function of the interaction of the sex of the aggressor and the sex of the victim. *Journal of Personality,* 1967, *35,* 474–486.

Taylor, S., Shuntich, R., & Greenberg, A. The effects of repeated aggressive encounters on subsequent aggressive behavior. *Journal of Social Psychology,* 1979, *107,* 199–228.

Tedeschi, R. E., Smith, R. C., & Brown, R. C. A reinterpretation of research on aggression. *Psychological Bulletin,* 1974, *81,* 540–562.

Walster, E., Berscheid, E., & Walster, G. W. New directions in equity research. *Journal of Personality and Social Psychology,* 1973, *25,* 151–176.

seven

Animal Aggression:
Implications for Human Aggression[1]

D. W. RAJECKI

A chapter on animal behavior in a book written by social psychologists is something of a curiosity, because nonhuman animals are all but invisible in the mainstream social psychological literature. Rajecki (1977) examined the contents of salient journals in the period from 1971 to 1975 and determined that, of 1,353 papers in the *Journal of Personality and Social Psychology, Journal of Experimental Social Psychology, Journal of Applied Social Psychology, Representative Research in Social Psychology,* and *Journal for Theory of Social Behavior,* a scant 3 (less than 1%) dealt with the behavior of nonhumans. More recently this picture has not changed: Of 192 papers appearing in the *Journal of Personality and Social Psychology* in 1979, only 1 (less than 1%) was on nonhumans. Even when nonhumans are taken seriously, some social psychologists feel that there is a tremendous gulf between our behavior and theirs. To take an example, Zillman (1979) concluded that the aggression seen in humans is discontinuous with that seen in other organisms, so that any comparisons would be quite useless.

However, before one can correctly conclude that cross-species comparisons

---

[1]Portions of this chapter were presented at the meeting of the American Psychological Association, Montreal, September 1980 (Rajecki, Note 1). Some of the numerical values in these two reports are slightly different, because certain results discussed in the 1980 version were based on experimentation still in progress.

189

of aggression are or are not useful, it is necessary to first establish the very correctness of the meaning or usage of concepts by which comparisons can be attempted. Currently, the most widely used concepts in this endeavor are *homology, analogy,* and *model.* Homology and analogy are more than figures of speech and cannot be treated loosely if they are to retain their utility. These terms come to us from biology, in which field they have very special meanings. Similarly, the term *model,* as used here, comes from biomedical research and also has a special meaning. Social psychologists may and should use these concepts, since they represent powerful analytic tools. But like any tool, their improper use can be damaging.

My purpose in this chapter is to elaborate on the notions of homology, analogy, and model in social behavior. I will argue that these particular approaches offer a framework in which we can use nonhuman data in conjunction with human data to meaningfully inform and illuminate our understanding of aggression. In the sections to follow, homologies, analogies, and animal models of human behavior will be discussed in turn, and evidence will be presented to support the claim that such comparisons are relevant to mainstream social psychology. I will proceed by offering definitions and illustrations of each.

BEHAVIORAL HOMOLOGIES

Definition

The concept of homology comes from biological systematics, wherein organisms are classified as to their taxonomic position. Homologies are taken to be genetically based resemblances between members of various species that are traceable to a common ancestor. Such a method of comparison is extremely valuable in following lines of evolutionary descent, speciation, or hybridization, because this approach enables genetic relationships to be established in the absence of direct genetic data. Thus, biologists are able to use fossil or morphological records to infer genetic links.

Regarding resemblances of structure, the rules for establishing homologies are quite explicit and clear. Atz (1970) has outlined the principle criteria proposed by the biologist A. Remane:

> *Criterion of position:* Homology results from the same position in comparable systems of structures. (That is, structures that occupy the same position within comparable anatomical units are likely to be homologous.)
> *Criterion of special quality:* Similar structures can be homologized, without regard to position, if they agree in several unusual characteristics. The greater the complexity and degree of correspondence, the more likely the homology.
> *Criterion of constancy or continuity:* Even dissimilar and differently located structures can be considered homologous if intermediate, connecting forms can be shown to

exist, so that Criterion 1 or 2 can be met by comparing the adjacent forms. The connecting forms may be ontogenetic stages or members of taxonomic groups [p. 57].

For an illustration of the application of one of these criteria to structure, we can turn to the evidence supplied by Washburn and Avis (1958). These writers discussed special sensory features that are common in monkeys, apes, and humans, and some of these are listed in Table 1. As Washburn and Avis (1958) point out, a great change in special senses occurred between the prosimians of the Eocene and the more recent forms of primates. Whereas prosimians explore the world with olfactory equipment located in a muzzle, monkeys, apes, and humans explore with the hands and eyes, with the latter three primate forms receiving basically the same sensory impressions. In short, one can argue that the similarities noted in Table 1 are to be considered homologous through an appeal to Remane's second criterion of special quality. Certain sensory features of monkeys, apes, and humans in the Holocene agree in several unusual characteristics; thus, these resemblances can be attributed to genetic similarity and common ancestry.

Therefore, it is a relatively straightforward matter to apply one or another of Remane's criteria to *structural* comparisons. However, in attempting to apply these rules to establish *behavioral* homologies, one quickly encounters certain difficulties. For example, Atz (1970) insisted that, whereas structural elements have precise boundaries and are thus easy to compare, behavior in his view is immaterial, evanescent, and continuous, and thus difficult to compare. Moreover, Atz reminded us that behavior itself does not fossilize; hence, we have no precise record of our extinct ancestors' social behavior. Still, Atz (1970) did acknowledge that, of the three criteria specified here, the second standard—that of special quality—was the most likely candidate for use where behavioral comparisons were concerned. On the basis of this recommendation, Rajecki and Flanery (1981) attempted to establish a series of comparisons of nonhuman and human primate behavior that focused on agreement in special features or

TABLE 1
Sensory Characteristics in Agreement across Monkeys, Apes, and Humans[a]

	Primate groupings		
Sensory characteristic	Monkeys	Apes	Humans
Loss of tactile hairs?	Yes	Yes	Yes
Reduced sense of smell?	Yes	Yes	Yes
Loss of primitive muzzle?	Yes	Yes	Yes
Stereoscoptic color vision?	Yes	Yes	Yes
Loss of mobility of external ears?	Yes	Yes	Yes

[a]After Washburn & Avis, 1958.

unusual characteristics, with particular reference to social conflict and dominance behavior.

Illustration

NONHUMAN BEHAVIOR

Social conflicts and acts of dominance within most nonhuman primate
groups occur in the context of a social structure or a dominance hierarchy. In
their survey, Rajecki and Flanery (1981) identified several varieties of behavior
involved in aggression at one or another level of behavioral organization: fine
motor movements of individuals, gross motor movements between individuals,
and behavior patterns at the group level. At the level of relatively fine motor
movement, monkeys and apes reveal their aggressive disposition or motivation
via expressions. Dominant animals often take the initiative in social conflicts
and engage in threats (see Deag, 1977). This category of social signal involves
configurations of facial musculature and posture. (For a demonstration of these
more or less subtle displays in monkeys, refer to Wickler, 1967, and for apes,
see van Lawick-Goodall, 1968.)

At the next level of behavioral organization, that of rather more gross movements between individuals, threats from dominant members often elicit appeasement signals from subordinates, and conflict episodes might well end
there. But at times, more violent forms of behavior erupt, involving anything
from the displacement of the subordinate to downright mauling. Nonhuman
primates get involved in chasing, grappling with, pinching, pulling, and biting
one another. Animals on the receiving end of such abuse cower, scream, or
flee. Interestingly enough, losers among both apes and monkeys sometimes
seek the aid of third parties in attempting to deal with their attacker!

In the remaining category of behavioral organization, behavior patterns at
the group level, aggression and dominance are clearly implicated in the dynamics of such groups. Rajecki and Flanery report on a number of these
patterns, including the following.

The social monitoring of one another within groups of nonhuman primates is
related to rank and dominance. Subordinates are much more likely to pay
attention to dominant members than vice versa. In fact, when there is an abrupt
change in the social hierarchy, the shift in an animal's rank is accompanied by
a shift in the amount of attention paid to him or her.

Social rank in a group of nonhumans is related to the allocation of scarce
resources, with high-ranking individuals generally having priority of access to
the resource (e.g., food, sexual partner) in question.

Environmental demands or stresses—such as those generated by captivity or
artificial provisioning of food—generally result in an intensification of aggressive behavior or in a rigidification of the dominance structure of the group.

Table 2 provides a sampler of references in support of the contentions made in the preceding paragraphs. Recall that the aim is to compare the behavior of various species, here lumped into the categories of monkeys and apes. According to the literature, there is a good deal of agreement in special or unusual characteristics across these categories. For example, the stare or glare is appar-

TABLE 2
Sampler of Unusual or Special Characteristics Involved in Social Conflict and Dominance That Are in Agreement across Monkeys, Apes, and Humans[a]

Characteristic	Primate groupings		
	Monkeys	Apes	Humans
Fine Motor Movement of Individuals			
Details of threatening facial expressions: lowered brow, face thrust, stare?	Yes: Hinde & Rowell (1962) Yes: Rowell (1972)	Yes: Schaller (1963) Yes: van Hooff (1967)	Yes: Grant (1969) Yes: Blurton Jones (1972)
Gross Motor Movements between Individuals			
Dominant behavior: hit, bite, steal objects?	Yes: Fedigan (1976) Yes: Deag (1977)	Yes: van Lawick-Goodall (1968, 1972)	Yes: Abramovitch & Strayer (1978) Yes: Camras (1977)
Subordinate behavior: appease (grimace), scream, cower, seek aid?	Yes: Fedigan (1976) Yes: Deag (1977)	Yes: van Lawick-Goodall (1968, 1972)	Yes: Abramovitch & Strayer (1978) Yes: Ginsburg (1980)
Behavior Patterns at the Group Level			
Dominance and attention structure: dominant members monitored more than subordinates?	Yes: Haude, Graber, & Farres (1976) Yes: Keverne, Leonard, Scruton, & Young (1978)	Yes: Bauer (1980) Yes: van Lawick-Goodall (1972)	Yes: Abramovitch (1976) Yes: Omark & Edelman (1976)
Dominance and allocation of resources: dominant members have priority of access?	Yes: Christopher (1972) Yes: Richards (1974)	Yes: Wrangham (1974)	Yes: Smith & Green (1975) Yes: Strayer & Strayer (1978)
Structural reaction to environmental stress: social conflict and dominance patterns intensified?	Yes: Gartlan (1968) Yes: Southwick, Siddiqi, Farooqui, & Pal (1976)	Yes: Wrangham (1974)	Yes: Smith (1974) Yes: Strayer & Strayer (1978)

[a] After Rajecki & Flanery, 1981.

ently a universal element in threat signals (see Camras, 1980, for a review). Second, dominance behavior is clearly distinguishable from subordinance behavior, and agreement in many details exists across monkeys and apes. Finally, there is general agreement between the various species at the level of behavior patterns of the group. Attention structure, allocation of resources, and reactions to environmental demands are all bound up in the social structure of these groups in much the same way across monkeys and apes. Therefore, if agreement in special characteristics can be taken as evidence for homology of structure (see Table 1), the argument can be extended to the agreement of special characteristics seen in Table 2, which can be taken as evidence for homologies of behavior in monkeys and apes.

HUMAN BEHAVIOR

Having established the levels and phenomena for comparisons across nonhuman primates, it becomes a relatively straightforward matter to seek records of human behavior for further comparison. Admittedly, much of this information will come from the study of preschool and school-age children, but the available evidence is by no means restricted to this developmental span. As it happens, data are in from studies of adolescents (e.g., Savin-Williams, 1979) and adults (e.g., Austin & Bates, 1974), the results of which are compatible with the findings on children.

How does the aggressive behavior of children in natural groups compare with that of other primates? According to the right-most column in Table 2, very closely indeed. Good evidence is available that many details of children's threatening facial expressions are similar to those seen in nonhumans. Further, there are clear parallels between the dominance and subordinance patterns in children and the patterns seen in groups of other kinds of primates. They threaten, hit, bite, and steal objects from others, and the recipients of such treatment appease, cower, scream, or seek aid from third parties, just as monkeys and apes do. Finally, behavior patterns at the level of children's groups are much like those seen in groups of nonhumans. Attention structure, allocation of resources, and structural reaction to environmental demands in relation to conflict and dominance are well documented in human groups, as they are in those of nonhumans.

Conclusions on Behavioral Homologies

We have just encountered marked resemblances in the behavior of monkeys, apes, and humans in an important area of everyday life: social conflict and dominance in the group (see Table 2). What should we make of such evidence? Some writers argue that this sort of information may (or may not) be useful in making "*generalizations* from animal to human behavior" or in drawing *"inferences* about aggression from animals to man" (Zillman, 1979, p. 3, emphasis added). Quickly note, however, that a theorist generalizes[2] or draws inferences only when information is missing or inaccessible, and that missing or inaccessible information is not at issue here. We know about nonhuman and human primate behavior, and the question is not *if* it is similar, but *why* it is similar. Drawing inferences about known behavior is as unnecessary as drawing inferences from nonhuman primates concerning the possibility that humans have lost the primitive primate muzzle or the mobility of our external ears (see Table 1). One need not draw inferences about such possibilities when one can simply look in a mirror.

Why are there such clear parallels in social conflict and dominance between nonhuman primates and, in this case, human children? Socialization practices may account for some of the behavior seen in spontaneous interaction between human peers, but certainly not for all, and perhaps not most. Who on earth decided that children should act like monkeys and apes? Moreover, why on earth would we want our children to act like monkeys and apes? The more probable answer to the question of behavioral parallels between nonhumans and humans is that these similarities are homologous. Our human behavior takes these forms precisely because we are human primates, and therefore closely related to the rest of the primates. We are structurally homologous to other primate forms, and thus it should come as no surprise that we should act like them to a considerable extent. The overall comparative picture seen in Table 2 is complex yet coherent, and on the whole, one would be hard pressed to account for it with an explanation other than homology.

If this conclusion is correct, it reveals something of an irony. Social psychologists have generally ignored nonhuman behavior, presumably for the sake of uncovering our strictly human nature. The irony here is that in some instances we must look simultaneously at the behavior of humans and nonhumans to get a truer picture of our own human condition. When biologists were able to

---

[2]The word *generalization* itself deserves elaboration in this context, because it has common definitions that are somewhat contradictory. One definition is that to generalize is "to give general applicability to" (a law, for instance). This is the definition that seems to be in the mind of the social psychologist, since in many cases he or she wishes to extend (give) an interpretation based on a controlled set of factors (such as in a laboratory) to an uncontrolled set of factors (such as in the real world). Here the scientist makes extrapolations or draws inferences.

Another definition is that to generalize is "to derive or induce (a general conception or principle) from particulars." (Both quotes come from *Webster's Seventh New Collegiate Dictionary*.) Here one need not extend, extrapolate, or infer, because points of comparison are available (that is, are particulars).

Regarding the current issue, if one had *only* nonhuman data or *only* human data, then cross-species generalization in the former sense is suspect and too easily leads to anthropomorphism or zoomorphism, depending on what type of data are lacking. However, if one has both nonhuman *and* human data, then generalization in the latter sense can yield general conceptions or principles. For example, Table 1 yields the principle of homology of structure in certain primate taxa, and Table 2 yields the principle of homology of behavior in certain primate taxa.

arrive at traditional taxonomies based on morphological and fossil evidence, humans no longer had unquestionable grounds for claiming to be on the side of the angels, for they were clearly on the side of the apes. Therefore, biological systematics are fundamental in showing humanity's place in the biological scheme of things. If social psychologists are to arrive at a deeper understanding of our human aggression and its place in the scheme of things, sooner or later they must look beyond themselves and establish such relationships as behavioral homologies. In addition to the search for homologies, the discovery of behavioral analogies will also permit these scientists to look beyond their own kind, and it is to analogies that we now turn.

BEHAVIORAL ANALOGIES

Definition

If one can assume that environmental pressures influence the physical forms that evolution produces, then one can seek and compare resemblances across species even without the additional assumption of genetic relationships. That is, widely disparate species (or forms) may evolve in roughly the same fashion under the force of the same environmental demands, a process known as convergent evolution. The resultant similarities of structure or movement are termed analogies or convergences. For an example of structural analogy, sharks (elasmobranch fishes) and dolphins (small, toothed whales) are quite unrelated genetically speaking, yet they bear a striking resemblance to one another. One infers that the external shapes of sharks and dolphins are similar because of convergent evolution. In a sense, a streamlined shape is those species' "solution" to the problems of efficient movement within the same relatively dense aquatic environment.

The identification of analogies or convergences is therefore important for two reasons. First, since such resemblances are presumably due to evolutionary solutions to environmental problems, the identification of a biological analogy reveals something fundamental about the organism, as was the case with homology. Second, since analogies or convergences do not depend on genetic links, humans have license to compare themselves with any animal form within reason.

Alas, there is the rub, for as yet there are no formal rules for separating "true" analogies from those that are "false." Lorenz (1974) identified this problem when he pointed out that, whereas ethologists are sometimes accused of drawing false analogies between human and nonhuman behavior, no such thing as a false analogy exists. This is so because an analogy is merely more or less detailed, and therefore more or less informative. Given this consideration, the analogy between the wing of a bird and the wing of an airplane is as true as the analogy between the wing of a bird and the wing of a bat. Unfortunately, it must be doubted whether much would be learned about birds from the study of winged aircraft. Apparently, the only brake on the offering of uninformative analogies is common sense (cf. Hodos & Campbell, 1969; Lockard, 1971), and thus we must utilize the concept of behavioral analogy with discretion.

Even so, social psychologists should be interested in environmental pressures that foster the evolution of social behavior, and especially in the forms that such behavior might take. Since most animals live in some kind of society (see Wilson's 1975 discussion of the kinds and degrees of sociality), it would be informative to search for analogies on a fairly broad basis. One interesting aspect of the social life of our species is that *not* everyone is welcome to any given group. A sharp distinction is usually drawn between companions and strangers. Encounters with unfamiliar individuals are likely to produce fearful or aggressive reactions, commonly termed xenophobia. For some writers, xenophobia is identified as a "universally encountered fact" (Eibl-Eibesfeldt, 1979). Accordingly, the next section will deal with analogies in xenophobic reactions.

Illustration

Rajecki and Nerenz (Note 2) reviewed a large amount of comparative material on xenophobia. In some cases, hostile reactions to the approach of an unfamiliar conspecific (species mate) on the part of a resident group can be dramatic indeed. For instance, Southwick, Siddiqi, Farooqui, and Pal (1974) attempted to introduce (add) a number of unfamiliar conspecifics to various free-ranging groups of monkeys in India, with the result that 100% of juvenile and adult strangers were completely driven off by the residents or killed on the spot!

Why would a strange animal evoke such abusive treatment? One answer proposed by Rajecki and Nerenz (Note 2) is that, since many animal and human groups are hierarchically organized, individuals therein can control or predict the behavior of others. Further, even in groups where a strict hierarchy is less salient, members are still familiar with one another and thus can predict what each might do. However, strangers are unknown elements who are not necessarily controllable or predictable, and are therefore alarming. Xenophobic reactions, including aggression toward the stranger, serve to reduce his or her alarming nature by expulsion (or destruction), assignment to a subordinate rank or status, or sheer familiarization.

NONHUMAN BEHAVIOR

If unfamiliarity—and, hence, unpredictability—underlies xenophobic reactions, then the strongest of such reactions should occur on initial contact. If contact is maintained, familiarity between individuals would increase, and aggressive or fear responses should diminish. In light of this simple hypothesis, Rajecki and Nerenz (Note 2) sought what might be analogous behavior patterns in fish, precocial birds, rodents, nonhuman primates, and ultimately humans. The patterns of xenophobia they discovered were quite interesting.

Fish. A variety of fish have been tested for changes over time in aggressive responses (e.g., displaying, butting) toward a variety of strangers, including live conspecifics, dummies or pictures of conspecifics, and the "stranger" represented by a fish's own mirror image. In all cases, response strength or rate was generally highest early in the test sequence and subsequently declined.

It is important to point out that this pattern of waning is not attributable solely to fatigue. Peeke and Veno (1973), observing sticklebacks, found the typical decline over time of aggressive attacks toward a given stranger. These researchers then either replaced the original stranger with another test fish, changed the site of presentation of the original stranger, or instituted both changes. It was found that each independent change produced a resurgence of aggression in the resident, that changing the fish had a greater effect than changing the site of presentation of the original intruder, and that the combination of changes had an additive effect. Such resurgence effects, therefore, seem to rule out the explanation that the original decline in aggressiveness over time toward the first stranger was due primarily to fatigue.

Precocial Birds. Young precocial birds show fairly rapid declines in xenophobic reactions over time. For formerly isolated ducklings, fear reactions to conspecifics were replaced by aggressive responses (pecking), which in turn were supplanted by filial behavior, all within about an hour's continuous exposure (Hoffman, Ratner, Eiserer, & Grossman, 1974, Figure 2). Further, chick cage mates separated for a 3-day period showed most social pecking on the first day of reunion and a marked decrease thereafter (Rajecki, Lamb, & Suomi, 1978). Similarly, repeated brief exposures are known to reduce birds' adverse reactions to strangers. Chickens that had been socially isolated from hatching to about 1 month of age initially failed to imitate the food pecking of trained exemplars, but after four 5-min exposures over 4 days, these birds matched the exemplars' feeding responses at the level of normal, socially reared birds (Rajecki, Suomi, Scott, & Campbell, 1977).

Rodents. The xenophobic reactions of rodents to conspecifics generally conform to the time-dependent profiles already seen in other animal forms, with a diminution of one or another xenophobic response (e.g., vigorous investigation, biting) over an extended period of observation. There is evidence that these downward shifts are not necessarily due to fatigue. Blanchard, Blanchard, and Takahashi (1978) tested the same resident and stranger twice in a colony situation, with several days intervening between tests. The resident's rate of *initial* attack in the second test was the same as the *terminal* level of the first test (see their Figure 1).

Nonhuman Primates. The typical finding is that the stranger to nonhuman primate groups is quickly recognized. This recognition is summarily followed by some form of aggression, and then this aggressive behavior is rapidly reduced. For example, in the field study cited earlier, Southwick et al. (1974) estimated that every rhesus stranger they released was recognized as such by residents within 15 min at maximum. Similarly, for captive monkeys the introduction of a stranger usually results in a peak of aggressive responding in the first hour or so, with an abatement thereafter (rhesus: Bernstein, 1964; pigtails: Bernstein, 1969). Rapid decreases in fighting with strangers have also been observed in talapoin monkeys (Scruton & Herbert, 1972) and squirrel monkeys (Rosenblum, Levy, & Kaufman, 1968). Finally, this sort of quick outbreak and rapid drop in aggression has been recorded when unfamiliar groups are introduced to one another (mangabeys: Bernstein, 1971).

In sum, xenophobic responses are on record for a variety of animal types, and there is evidence that such behavior follows a specific time line. The most intense or frequent fear or aggressive responses occur early in a meeting with a stranger and decline thereafter if contact is maintained.

HUMAN BEHAVIOR

Violent reactions of humans to strangers in our modern world are perhaps less frequent than those of other animal types, but there is no reason to think that strangers are not worrisome to people or that they would not be met with violence under the right circumstances. Rather dangerous reactions to strangers are on record for humans in hunter–gatherer societies. Tindale (1974) provides illustrated examples (see his Plates 56–67) of such xenophobic behavior in cases where unfamiliar Aboriginal tribes come into contact. Such meetings of human strangers obviously produce much concern and tension, and can involve impressive displays of weaponry and martial capacities. However, while the examples of naturalistic human xenophobia available in Tindale (1974; see also Peterson, 1975) are impressive, these observations were not made with our hypothesis in mind, and precise information as to the time line in this behavior is not discussed. The impression is that tribes' fear and aggressive responses terminated rather quickly, but for the moment, we must turn to laboratory research for better estimates. Happily, several such studies are on hand.

Adults seem more uneasy early in their contact with a stranger than later on, as reflected by the number of times they look at the person (Patterson, Mullens, & Romano, 1971; Rajecki, Ickes, & Tanford, 1981) or by their anxiety as indicated by time-dependent shifts in filled pauses (e.g., the sounds "uh" or "um") in speech (Lalljee & Cook, 1973). Even the behavior of chronically hospitalized mental patients was markedly influenced by the presence of a stranger sitting passively in the ward dayroom. Early in the test day, 96% of the patients actively avoided the stranger, but only 42% did so later in the same test day (Hershkowitz, 1962). Human babies also seem most wary of strangers early in the test session and less so later on (Eckerman & Whatley, 1975; Ross, 1975), and related findings have been reported for preschoolers (Connolly & Smith, 1972). Eckerman and Whatley (1975) observed resurgence effects in babies' wariness of strangers, so initial declines are not solely attributable to fatigue or simple uninterest.

It happens that close comparison of some of the Eckerman and Whatley, and the Rajecki, Ickes, and Tanford human data yield an interesting result. The first 5-min period in each study was quite similar: A baby in the former case and an adult in latter were confronted with an adult stranger, and their behavior was covertly recorded. It is noteworthy that both the infant and adult subjects spontaneously looked and smiled at the unfamiliar person. Perhaps more noteworthy and of some theoretical significance is the finding that the two vastly different demographic classes of subjects apportioned these two types of responses in about the same way (see Figure 1) and showed proportional decreases in looking and smiling (viewed here as a propitiatory kind of behavior) over the same period of time.

Conclusions on Behavioral Analogies

If Eibl-Eibesfeldt (1979) was correct in his assertion that xenophobia is universal among humans, how much more interesting it is that this phenomenon is widespread throughout the animal kingdom. We are therefore at about the

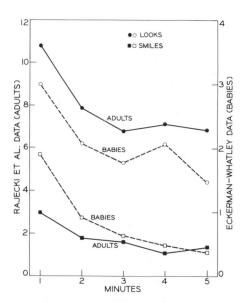

FIGURE 1   Change over time in rate of looks and smiles at a stranger by babies (after Eckerman & Whatley, 1975) and adults (after Rajecki, Ickes, & Tanford, 1981)

same stage that was reached at the conclusion on homology: The question is not whether human and nonhuman behavior is similar in some respect, but why it is similar. Xenophobic reactions in various animal forms, including humans, are too alike to escape our critical attention, yet we do not presume that they satisfy the criteria for homology. Admittedly, the responses in question are different. Fish butt, rodents bite, birds peck, nonhuman primates hit and chase, and humans wave weapons at strangers, but these various responses stem from the subjective experience of xenophobia, which we take to be biologically or psychologically analogous. That is, xenophobia is evident in all these disparate organisms presumably because such a social adaptation is a successful "solution" to some environmental pressure or problem. It seems plausible that in the long run xenophobia would enhance the survival of the group and hence be of benefit to individual group members.

We gain some sense of the importance of these convergent forms of behavior in animal and human societies when we look to a distinction provided by Wilson (1975, p. 25). Wilson argued that analogies can be divided into two sorts, roughly those that are *deep* versus those that are *shallow*. Deep analogies (or deep convergences) are highly complex and of extensive influence in the organism's entire way of life. For Wilson, the eye of the vertebrate and the eye of the cephalopod mollusk would serve as an example of a deep analogy. It follows that shallow analogies are less complex and less extensive in the organism's entire way of life. By Wilson's standards, cross-species similarities in xenophobia would be a shallow analogy. Thus, analogy's place in Wilson's (1975) scheme is a basis on which to judge its significance, which, by implication, means that analogies *have* significance.

As things stand, one can say at least the following about the utility of seeking analogies and comparing human aggressive behavior with that of only remotely related species. First, the resemblances *are* there. Second, the concept of analogy (convergence) *is* respectable, and has found acceptance in other sciences of behavior, such as sociobiology (Wilson, 1975). Third, we *can* take precautions against uninformative analogies if we remain aware that a glib analogy is not false; it is merely counterproductive and worse than no analogy at all. Great care must be taken to ensure that variables and behavior compared in this fashion are well documented and actually part of the mundane social lives of the species in question. This concern is also central to the issue of animal models of human aggressive behavior, to which consideration we now turn.

ANIMAL MODELS OF BEHAVIOR

Definition

In many areas of scientific discourse, the term *model* means something of an abstraction. Physicists and biologists use oversize assemblages to depict the structures of molecules and proteins, for example, and mathematicians use symbolic formulas to represent many kinds of material phenomena. Behavioral scientists also use models in the sense of flowcharts, decision trees, or computer programs that are meant to be theories or reflections of experience and interaction. But there is yet another meaning to the word *model,* and one that is more concrete: The phrase "animal model of human behavior" can be paraphrased to mean "animal *substitute* for human behavior." Some researchers are simply not in a position to use human subjects all the time, so animals are studied in their stead. Presumably, the information gained from the animal model will have some bearing on human concerns. In fact, valuable information is very often gathered in this fashion, as seen in programs of drug and poison evaluation. It is common to find containers of diet foods that bear the following warning:

Use of this product may be hazardous to your health. This product contains saccharine, which has been determined to cause cancer in laboratory animals.

This information probably came from a rodent model of cancer.

How does one choose such a model? Models of this sort are not defined by theory, but rather are determined by empirical method. Scientists who are in need of such a model (a substitute for humans) simply must search until they find one—that is, until they find an animal subject (species) that can provide somehow useful results. In the area of psychopathology, a number of animal models have been established, including those for addiction, catatonia, depression, hyperkinesis, learned helplessness, obesity, psychosomatic disorders, and schizophrenia (cf. Maser & Seligman, 1977; Serban & Kling, 1976). Perhaps more familiar to social psychologists are the animal models that were employed in the research on the drive theory of social facilitation effects (see Zajonc, 1965). Beginning in the 1930s, the social facilitation literature has been strongly influenced by data from ants, cockroaches, chickens, dogs, monkeys, rats, and other animal forms. In that literature, there was little question of homologous or analogous relationships, but only interest that the animals' behavior informed social facilitation theory.

Illustration

I wish to suggest a way in which such animal models might be informative where human aggression is concerned. Let us begin with the example of an imaginary medical researcher who is ignorant but curious about the effect of the ingestion of saccharine on health. He or she might ask, "Does saccharine cause cancer in humans?" Or the question might be, "Does saccharine cause cancer in rodents?" These are obviously two different questions, but if it turned out that the answer to the latter was affirmative, the researcher would doubtless be that much more motivated to seek an answer to the former.

Returning to our concerns, let us recognize that much of what we claim to know about human or nonhuman aggression comes from laboratory research and that for the most part the methods employed in these facilities are highly contrived and artificial. Next imagine that we are ignorant but curious about the behavior that goes on in these unlikely situations, thus we ask, "What do humans look like in the typical laboratory situation?" Or the question might be, "What do rats look like in the typical laboratory situation?" These are obviously two different questions, but it may be that the answer to the latter might make us very eager to try to answer the former. Let us take a look, then, at the behavior of some rats.

NONHUMAN BEHAVIOR

The single most widely used technique for controlling the onset of animal aggression in the laboratory is the irritable aggression paradigm (see Blanchard & Blanchard, 1977). The behavior seen in this paradigm has also been variously labled shock-induced aggression or pain-induced aggression. In a typical version of the irritable aggression approach, two rats are confined in a restricted area and electrical shock is administered to their feet via a grid floor. The effects of this simple procedure are rapid and dramatic. The rats will quickly begin to maul one another, sometimes to the point of severe tissue damage. But despite its wide use, one cannot take for granted that the irritable aggression paradigm is the most desirable way to study animal aggression, or that it is suitable at all. To make an evaluation, it is only necessary to compare the actual behavior of animals in more ordinary circumstances, such as the colony situation. Blanchard and Blanchard (1977) make a convincing case that patterns of fighting in the colony, especially where strangers are concerned (see earlier section on xenophobia), are essentially the same in the laboratory and the wild.

Illustrations of aspects of colony fighting can be found in a number of reports (cf. Adams, 1976; Blanchard et al., 1978). The picture that emerges is quite clear. The home rat engages in bite-and-kick attacks on the intruder's back, or it shows an offensive side (lateral attack) posture. Residents also show piloerection on these occasions. The intruder, for its part, does not do these things, but rather shows an upright (i.e., boxing) stance or a submissive posture. In short, the resident undertakes attack, whereas the intruder engages in defense (Blanchard & Blanchard, 1977).

With this picture of colony fighting clearly in mind, let us now turn to a direct comparison of such fighting with the activity seen in the shock situation. This sort of comparison is provided by Blanchard et al. (1978). These researchers tested the same pair of rats three times: once in the colony situation, next in a shock situation, and then once again in the colony situation. Results of these tests are listed in Table 3 where it can be seen that the two test settings produced vastly different results. In the colony tests, the resident and intruder

TABLE 3
Attack and Defense Responses of Resident and Intruder Rats in Tests in a Colony Situation and a Shock Situation

Measure (percentage time)	Resident			Intruder		
	First colony test	Shock test	Second colony test	First colony test	Shock test	Second colony test
Piloerection	97.25	11.00	97.35	.00	.00	.00
Lateral attack[b]	19.25	.03	10.46	.12	.00	.18
Upright boxing	4.51	72.50	1.99	30.41	53.73	12.08
Submissive posture	.06	.00	.00	22.52	17.51	25.41
Freezing	.00	15.38	.00	16.41	19.31	38.14

aAfter Blanchard et al., 1978.
bThis measure corresponds to Adams's (1976) measure of attack.
Note: The percentages in the above columns need not sum to 100.

behaved as expected, with the former showing offense (attack) and the latter defense. However, in the shock situation *both* animals reverted to a defensive posture!

The findings of Blanchard et al. (1978) shown in Table 3 are therefore quite instructive. They clearly indicate that intruders act self-protectively. This means that an intruding rat that is at a severe territorial disadvantage, and that is strenuously trying to protect itself, cannot be said to be engaging in aggression or attack in any manner equivalent to that of the attacking resident. By extension, I cannot imagine that any rat in a shock situation is behaving aggressively at all, since the topography of that reaction matches the pattern seen in the hapless intruder. The shock situation does not induce attack; it induces self-protection in this species.

HUMAN BEHAVIOR

What, then, do humans look like in a typical human laboratory setup? Doubtless, the most widely used approach here is some variant of an "aggression machine" procedure (see Baron, 1977, Chapter 2). Since these techniques are probably familiar to the reader, I shall proceed directly to an accounting of a recent pilot study. I (Rajecki, Note 1) replicated a standard human aggression procedure whereby about half of my subjects were in an "angry" condition, wherein they were informed that they were to have received 7 shocks as assigned by an adversary. The other half of my subjects were in a "not angry" condition, wherein they were informed they were to have received only 1 shock as assigned by the adversary. Such a procedure is already known to elicit "aggression," in that "angry" subjects generally retaliate by delivering more return shocks to their adversary than do "not angry" subjects (see Schuck &

Pisor, 1974). Indeed, I too was able to produce the expected pattern of returned shocks: In my total sample, "angry" subjects retaliated with a total of 5.00, whereas those who were "not angry" returned only 1.46, a well-known effect.

But what was unique about my pilot study was that I covertly photographed people's faces while they delivered the retaliatory shock, and managed to get photographic records of seven persons in the angry condition and nine individuals in the not angry group. I later had these photographs evaluated by naive judges. Some of the judges ($N = 81$) were asked to estimate the emotional state revealed in the subjects' faces on an eight-point bipolar scale ranging from angry–hurtful to friendly–helpful. Other judges ($N = 60$) were asked to estimate how many shocks (1–10) persons wearing such faces would deliver. In addition to the pictures of my subjects, I had the same sets of judges evaluate some of the original Frois-Wittmann faces, including smiles (Numbers 70, 71, and 72), scowls (Numbers 39, 59, and 60), and neutral expressions (Numbers 14, 43, and 49) (see Schlosberg, 1954) The Frois-Wittmann pictures served as anchor points for the judgments of the subjects' faces.

The reader can sense, of course, what all this is leading up to. The question of what human subjects look like in the laboratory when they are behaving "aggressively" need no longer be rhetorical. Recall that I used a standard laboratory technique and observed the standard pattern wherein "angry" subjects delivered five shocks while their "not angry" counterparts delivered fewer than two. But what about those faces? How much of a difference in "aggression," "anger," or whatever did my judges detect across the two experimental treatments? The answer is that they detected *no* difference at all, as indicated in Table 4. While it is clear that the judges could make appropriate discriminations between the Frois-Wittmann categories, they could not tell the so-called angry versus not angry subjects apart. Allowing the reader to have a look, literally, at the subjects' faces would also be useful here. Figure 2 presents a sampler of portraits of people who served as subjects. Can the reader

TABLE 4
Judges' Average Estimates of Emotional States, and Number of Shocks Hypothetically Given by Persons Depicted in Photographs[a]

Measure	Frois-Wittmann pictures			Subjects' pictures	
	Smiling	Neutral	Scowling	Not angry	Angry
Emotion?	7.15[b]	4.33	1.42	5.16	5.23
Shocks given?	2.22[c]	4.86	9.28	3.90	3.87

[a]After Rajecki, Note 1.
[b]The emotion scale ranged from 1 (angry-hurtful) to 8 (friendly-helpful).
[c]Judges estimates could range from 1 to 10 shocks delivered.

FIGURE 2 Photographs of persons in the act of pushing a shock assignment button in a typical aggression machine study. Half the persons are in an "angry" condition, and half are in a "not angry" condition.

distinguish between the subgroups? That is, which people in Figure 2 were "angry" and which were "not"? The answer to this problem can be found at the end of the text.

FIGURE 2 (continued)

Conclusion on Animal Models of Behavior

I wish to make an informative digression by alluding to the writing of Gould (1977), who outlines a controversy that took place in eighteenth-century biology. The question then was how an organism as complex as a baby could result from something as undifferentiated and formless as an egg. On one side of the issue, the epigeneticists believed what they saw of embryonic development and argued that a baby's ultimate parts were formed sequentially by some sort of force. In their ignorance of ontogenetic mechanisms, however, those epigeneticists had to take refuge in vitalism or mysticism to account for such forces. On the other side, preformationists believed that the final human form was always present, even from the very germ stage, but that this preformed homunculus could not be seen at first because it was simply too tiny or too transparent. According to Gould (1977, p. 18), this latter position avoids the dilemma of mystic forces, *"but it compels us to postulate what we do not perceive* [emphasis added]."

It seems to me that researchers who use certain methods to study aggression are also in the unfortunate position of having to postulate what we do not perceive. According to the evidence discussed here, rats in the artificial shock situation are acting to *protect* themselves, yet we have uncritically labeled these special postures as "attacks" (for example, see Zillmann, 1979, p. 80). Similarly, humans in the artifical setup look anything but angry, yet we have been willing to interpret their laboratory responses as due to their being angry or not (for example, see Baron, 1977, p. 131). That is, when we take a close look at human behavior, or what we have termed an animal model of such behavior, we do *not* perceive what we postulate. Human beings and rats do not necessarily exhibit or engage in aggression simply because a researcher assumes he or she is studying aggression by some conventional operational definition.

GENERAL CONCLUSION

I am not so presumptuous as to instruct social psychologists to become comparative psychologists; let them compare if they care to. But a decision to compare on the one hand, or to reject comparisons on the other, demands that we correctly appraise the concepts of behavioral homology, analogy (convergence), and model, and that we employ them properly. Homologies, analogies, and models can always be dismissed out of hand, of course, but only by those who do not understand them.

(Note: The people in the left half of Figure 2 were in the "angry" condition; those in the right half were in the "not angry" group.)

REFERENCE NOTES

1. Rajecki, D. W. Comparative social psychology: Homology, analogy, or model? Paper presented at the meeting of the American Psychological Association, Montreal, September 1980.

2. Rajecki, D. W., & Nerenz, D. R. Xenophobia. Unpublished manuscript, 1979.

REFERENCES

Abramovitch, R. The relation of attention and proximity to rank in preschool children. In M. R. A. Chance & R. R. Larsen (Eds.), *The social structure of attention.* New York: Wiley, 1976.

Abramovitch, R., & Strayer, F. Preschool social organization: Agonistic, spacing, and attentional behaviors. In L. Krames, P. Pliner, & T. Alloway (Eds.), *Aggression, dominance, and individual spacing.* New York: Plenum, 1978.

Adams, D. B. The relation of scent-marking, olfactory investigation, and specific postures in the isolation-induced fighting of rats. *Behaviour,* 1976, *56,* 286–297.

Atz, J. W. The application of the idea of homology to behavior. In L. R. Aronson, E. Tobach, D. S. Lehrman, & J. S. Rosenblatt (Eds.), *Development and evolution of behavior.* San Francisco: Freeman, 1970.

Austin, W. T., & Bates, F. L. Ethological indicators of dominance and territory in a human captive population. *Social Forces,* 1974, *52,* 447–455.

Baron, R. A. *Human aggression.* New York: Plenum, 1977.

Bauer, H. R. Chimpanzee society and social dominance in evolutionary perspective. In D. R. Omark, F. F. Strayer, & D. G. Freedman (Eds.), *Dominance relations.* New York: Garland STMP Press, 1980.

Bernstein, I. S. The integration of rhesus monkeys introduced to a group. *Folia Primatologica,* 1964, *2,* 50–63.

Bernstein, I. S. Introductory techniques in the formation of pigtail monkey troops. *Folia Primatologica,* 1969, *10,* 1–19.

Bernstein, I. S. The influence of introductory techniques on the formation of captive mangabey groups. *Primates,* 1971, *12,* 33–44.

Blanchard, R. J., & Blanchard, D. C. Aggressive behavior in the rat. *Behavioral Biology,* 1977, *21,* 197–224.

Blanchard, R. J., BLanchard, D. C., & Takahasi, L. K. Pain and aggression in the rat. *Behavioral Biology,* 1978, *23,* 291–305.

Blurton Jones, N. G. Non-verbal communication in children. In R. A. Hinde (Ed.), *Non-verbal communication.* London: Cambridge Univ. Press, 1972.

Camras, L. A. Facial expressions used by children in a conflict situation. *Child Development,* 1977, *48,* 1431–1435.

Camras, L. A. Animal threat displays and children's facial expressions: A comparison. In D. R. Omark, F. F. Strayer, & D. G. Freedman (Eds.), *Dominance relations.* New York: Garland STMP Press, 1980.

Christopher, S. B. Social validation of an objective measure of social dominance in captive monkeys. *Behavior Research Methods and Instrumentation,* 1972, *4,* 19–20.

Connolly, K., & Smith, P. K. Reactions of pre-school children to a strange observer. In N. Blurton Jones (Ed.), *Ethological studies of child behaviour.* London: Cambridge Univ. Press, 1972.

Deag, J. M. Aggression and submission in monkey societies. *Animal Behaviour,* 1977, *25,* 465–474.

Eckerman, C. O., & Whatley, J. L. Infants' reactions to unfamiliar adults varying in novelty. *Developmental Psychology,* 1975, *11,* 563–566.

Eibl-Eibesfeldt, I. Human ethology—concepts and implications for the sciences of man. *Behavioral and Brain Sciences,* 1979, *2*(1), 1–26.

Fedigan, L. M. A study of roles in the Arshiyama West troop of Japanese monkeys (*Macaca fuscata*). In F. S. Szalay (Ed.), *Contributions to primatology* (Vol. 9) Basel: Karger, 1976.

Gartlan, J. S. Structure and function in primate society. *Folia Primatologica,* 1968, *8,* 89–120.

Ginsburg, H. J. Playground as laboratory: Naturalistic studies of appeasement, altruism, and the omega child. In D. R. Omark, F. F. Strayer, & D. G. Freedman (Eds.), *Dominance relations.* New York: Garland STMP Press, 1980.

Gould, S. J. *Ontogeny and phylogeny.* Cambridge, Mass.: Belknap Press, 1977.

Grant, E. C. Human facial expressions. *Man,* 1969, *4,* 525–536.

Haude, R. H., Graber, J. G., & Farres, A. G. Visual observing by rhesus monkeys: Some relationships with social dominance rank. *Animal Learning & Behavior,* 1976, *4,* 163–166.

Hershkowitz, A. Naturalistic observations on chronically hospitalized patients. I. The effects of "strangers." *Journal of Nervous and Mental Diseases,* 1962, *135,* 258–264.

Hinde, R. A., & Rowell, T. Communication by postures and facial expressions in the rhesus monkey (*Macaca mulatta*). *Proceedings of the Zoological Society of London,* 1962, *138,* 1–21.

Hodos, W., & Campbell, C. B. G. *Scala Naturae:* Why there is no theory in comparative psychology. *Psychological Review,* 1969, *76,* 337–350.

Hoffman, H. S., Ratner, A. M., Eiserer, L. A., & Grossman, D. A. Aggressive behavior in immature ducklings. *Journal of Comparative and Physiological Psychology,* 1974, *86,* 569–580.

Keverne, E. B., Leonard, R. B., Scruton, D. M., & Young, S. K. Visual monitoring in social groups of Talapoin monkeys (*Miopithecus talapoin*). *Animal Behaviour,* 1978, *26,* 933–944.

Lalljee, M., & Cook, M. Uncertainty in first encounters. *Journal of Personality and Social Psychology,* 1973, *26,* 137–141.

Lockard, R. B. Reflections on the fall of comparative psychology: Is there a message for us all? *American Psychologist,* 1971, *26,* 168–179.

Lorenz, K. Z. Analogy as a source of knowledge. *Science,* 1974, *185,* 229–234.

Maser, J. D., & Seligman, M. E. P. (Eds.), *Psychopathology: Experimental models.* San Francisco: Freeman, 1977.

Omark, D. R., & Edelman, M. S. The development of attention structures in young children. In M. R. A. Chance & R. R. Larsen (Eds.), *The social structure of attention.* New York: Wiley, 1976.

Patterson, M. L., Mullens, S., & Romano, J. Compensatory reactions to spatial intrusion. *Sociometry,* 1971, *34,* 114–121.

Peeke, H. V. S., & Veno, A. Stimulus specificity of habituated aggression in the stickleback (*Gasterosteus aculeatus*). *Behavioral Biology,* 1973, *8,* 427–432.

Peterson, N. Hunter–gatherer territoriality: The perspective from Australia. *American Anthropologist,* 1975, *77,* 53–68.

Rajecki, D. W. Ethological elements in social psychology. In C. Hendrick (Ed.), *Perspectives on social psychology.* Hillsdale, N.J.: Erlbaum, 1977.

Rajecki, D. W., & Flanery, R. C. Social conflict and dominance in children: A case for a primate homology. In M. E. Lamb & A. Brown (Eds.), *Advances in developmental psychology* (Vol. 1) Hillsdale, N.J.: Erlbaum, 1981.

Rajecki, D. W., Ickes, W., & Tanford, S. Locus of control and reactions to strangers. *Personality and Social Psychology Bulletin,* 1981, *7,* 282–289.

Rajecki, D. W., Lamb, M. E., & Suomi, S. J. Effects of multiple peer separations in domestic chicks. *Developmental Psychology,* 1978, *14,* 379–387.

Rajecki, D. W., Suomi, S. J., Scott, E. A., & Campbell, B. Effects of social isolation and social separation in domestic chicks. *Developmental Psychology,* 1977, *13,* 143–155.

Richards, S. M. The concept of dominance and methods of assessment. *Animal Behaviour,* 1974, *22,* 914–930.

Rosenblum, L. A., Levy, E. J., & Kaufman, I. C. Social behaviour of squirrel monkeys and the reaction to strangers. *Animal Behaviour,* 1968, *16,* 288–293.

Ross, H. S. The effects of increasing familiarity in infants' reactions to strangers. *Journal of Experimental Child Psychology,* 1975, *20,* 226–239.

Rowell, T. E. *The social behavior of monkeys.* Baltimore: Penguin, 1972.

Savin-Williams, R. C. Dominance hierarchies in groups of early adolescents. *Child Development,* 1979, *50,* 923–935.

Schaller, G. B. *The mountain gorilla.* Chicago: Univ. of Chicago Press, 1963.

Schlosberg, H. The dimensions of emotion. *Psychological Review,* 1954, *61,* 81–88.

Schuck, J., & Pisor, K. Evaluating an aggression experiment by the use of simulated subjects. *Journal of Personality and Social Psychology,* 1974, *29,* 181–186.

Scruton, D. M., & Herbert, J. The reaction of groups of talapoin monkeys to the introduction of male and female strangers of the same species. *Animal Behaviour,* 1972, *20,* 463–473.

Serban, G., & Kling, A. (Eds.), *Animal models in human psychobiology.* New York: Plenum, 1976.

Smith, P. K. Aggression in a preschool playgroup: Effects of varying physical resources. In J. de Wit & W. W. Hartup (Eds.), *Determinants and origins of aggressive behavior.* The Hague: Mouton, 1974.

Smith, P. K., & Green, M. Aggressive behavior in English nurseries and play groups: Sex differences and response of adults. *Child Development,* 1975, *46,* 211–214.

Southwick, C. H., Siddiqi, M. F., Farooqui, M. Y., & Pal, B. C. Xenophobia among free-ranging rhesus groups in India. In R. L. Holloway (Ed.), *Primate aggression, territoriality, and xenophobia.* New York: Academic Press, 1974.

Southwick, C. H., Siddiqi, M. F., Farooqui, M. Y., & Pal, B. C. Effects of artificial feeding on aggressive behaviour of rhesus monkeys in India. *Animal Behaviour,* 1976, *24,* 11–15.

Strayer, J., & Strayer, F. F. Social aggression and power relations among preschool children. *Aggressive Behavior,* 1978, *4,* 173–182.

Tindale, N. B. *Aboriginal tribes of Australia.* Berkeley: Univ. of California Press, 1974.

van Hooff, J. A. R. A. M. The facial displays of the catarrhine monkeys and apes. In D. Morris (Ed.), *Primate ethology.* London: Weidenfeld & Nicolson, 1967.

van Lawick-Goodall, J. The behaviour of free-living chimpanzees in the Gombe Stream Reserve. *Animal Behaviour Monographs,* 1968, *1,* 161–311.

van Lawick-Goodall, J. A preliminary report on expressive movements and communication in the Gombe Stream chimpanzees. In P. Dolhinow (Ed.), *Primate patterns.* New York: Holt, 1972.

Washburn, S. L., & Avis, V. Evolution of human behavior. In A. Roe & G. G. Simpson (Eds.), *Behavior and evolution.* New Haven: Yale Univ. Press, 1958.

Wickler, W. Socio-sexual signals and their intra-specific imitation among primates. In D. Morris (Ed.), *Primate ethology.* London: Weidenfeld & Nicolson, 1967.

Wilson, E. O. *Sociobiology.* Cambridge, Mass.: Belknap Press, 1975.

Wrangham, R. W. Artificial feeding of chimpanzees and baboons in their natural habitat. *Animal Behaviour,* 1974, *22,* 83–93.

Zajonc, R. B. Social facilitation. *Science,* 1965, *149,* 269–274.

Zillman, D. *Hostility and aggression.* Hillsdale, N.J.: Erlbaum, 1979.

eight

Methodology in the Study of Aggression
H. S. BERTILSON

Hermann Ebbinghaus asserted that understanding mental life presents the greatest difficulty to scientific investigation—that mental processes change so unceasingly and are dependent on so many hidden but influential factors that it is difficult to gain insight into their causal connections (Ebbinghaus, cited in Zimbardo & Maslach, 1977). These comments by Ebbinghaus in earlier days of scientific psychology seem apt today for such areas of study as human aggression. Research into aggression has been described by contemporary investigators as being fraught with difficulties in interpretation and understanding (e.g., Tedeschi & Lindskold, 1976). Fundamentally, the issue is one of both theory and research methodology.

The purpose of this chapter is to discuss human aggression research methodology. Such a section on methodology can be quite useful, since it allows the discussion of research issues within a narrow, and therefore relatively clear, set of integrations and comparisons. One must, of course, not lose sight of theory and data—theory and empirical data are inextricably tied to methodology (e.g., Boring, 1950; Kuhn, 1970; McGuire, 1973; Mischel, 1973; Newcomb, 1953). This chapter will proceed by discussing some of the methodological issues of research in human aggression and then describe and give examples of the more common methods of research (see Table 1 at end of this chapter).

AGGRESSION
Volume 1

METHODOLOGICAL ISSUES

Concept Validity

The recognition that passive observation of spontaneous happenings of nature is not adequate by itself to understand human social interaction has led to the experimental method—the setting up of special conditions in order to bring about events of interest (Hull, 1943). "But even in deliberate experiments it is often extraordinarily difficult to determine with which among a complex of antecedent conditions a given consequence is primarily associated; in this way arise a complex maze of control experiments and other technical procedures [p. 2]." The task facing the investigator, to paraphrase Kerlinger (1973), is to construct an efficient research design that (a) maximizes primary variance; (b) controls extraneous or secondary variance; and (c) minimizes error variance. However, control also refers to dependent as well as independent variables (Campbell & Stanley, 1963; Shontz, 1965). Dependent variable measurement is regulated and limited by the type of subject behavior that is possible in a situation and by restrictions of the measurement process itself. The issues of control and measurement are particularly troublesome because aggression is not a unitary phenomenon, either in the laboratory or in the world at large. A further complication is that, although a massive amount of research has been done on aggression, little work has been done in search of valid dependent variables (Geen, 1976).

Concept validity (Crano & Brewer, 1973) involves the adequacy of the researcher's operational definitions (Bridgman, 1945) and theoretical constructs. The extensive discussions of definitions found in the literature on aggression is an example of this issue (e.g., Bandura, 1973; Baron, 1977; Berkowitz, 1962; Buss, 1961; Dollard, Doob, Miller, Mowrer, & Sears, 1939; Tedeschi, Gaes, & Rivera, 1977). Complex treatments, such as those used in aggression research, are characterized by what Aronson and Carlsmith (1968) call "multiple meaning"; that is, subjects' behaviors are determined by many factors inherent in the treatment that are extraneous to the important theoretical variables of interest. Confidence in interpretation is enhanced when a series of experiments operationalize the conceptual variable in different ways, thus removing the confound of extraneous factors.

Multiple Operationalism

The following review of aggression methodology seems to indicate that investigators use an impressive variety of research approaches. The effects of multiple approaches should be salubrious, since individual research studies are subject to multiple interpretations (e.g., Boring, 1954, 1969; Campbell,

1969). Such multiple interpretations may be untangled by holding the conceptual variables constant while varying research operations. Such a process of multiple approaches was called "spiral approximation" of adequate operational definitions by Bridgman (1945), "converging operations" by Garner, Hake, and Eriksen (1956), and "eliminating plausible rival hypotheses" by Campbell (1957, 1969). Hicks (1971) has elaborated the notion of converging operations by describing Venn diagrams of the overlap of the work of several researchers and several situations as the way researchers converge on the understanding of conceptual variables. More recently, Crano and Brewer (1973) have called this process "multiple operationalism."

Internal Validity

Much has been written in recent years regarding threats to validity extant in individual experiments. These issues relate to internal and external validity (Campbell, 1957). *Internal validity* refers to the ability to attribute the observed changes in dependent variables to treatment effects rather than to uncontrolled sources of variance. *External validity* refers to the generalizability of research findings to other populations, settings, treatment variables, and measurement variables (Campbell, 1957; Campbell & Stanley, 1963). The concept of external validity has been controversial both in general and in its application to research on human aggression. Berkowitz and Donnerstein (1982) reviewed the external validity criticisms of laboratory experiments in psychology. These criticisms are that laboratory research on aggression is not representative of events in the world at large. In Brunswik's (1955) terms, they lack "ecological" validity. Berkowitz and Donnerstein answered these criticisms in two ways. First, the validity of a theory depends on internal validity, not on representativeness; and second, the meaning subjects assign to their psychological situation is what is crucial, not mere surface resemblance of the environmental variables to events in the world at large. The arguments presented by Berkowitz and Donnerstein are consistent with the positions of a number of theoreticians and methodologists in social psychology (e.g., Aronson & Carlsmith, 1968; Festinger, 1953). In keeping with this argument, methodological issues related to internal validity and theory building will be emphasized in the following discussion.

Major threats to internal validity have been described by Campbell (Campbell, 1957, 1969; Campbell & Stanley, 1963). Six of Campbell's threats to internal validity seem directly applicable to contemporary research on human aggression. The argument will be made that the artifacts that Campbell originally labeled as "reactive arrangements" pose a threat to internal validity as well. Finally, the present review of aggression research suggests a further threat to internal validity, which I have called "personal involvement."

TESTING

In some research designs, assessment is administered before application of treatment procedures. The effectiveness of treatment is analyzed in these cases by comparing posttest assessment to pretest assessment. The pretest is considered "reactive" when it causes subjects to alter their responses to the posttest because of their pretest experience. This threat to internal validity Campbell (1957) has labeled "testing." When this type of reactivity produces a main effect, it may be a serious problem in clinical assessment (e.g., Kazdin, 1979a). Such a main effect may cause fewer interpretative problems in laboratory research when the principal comparisons are between groups that have all responded to the same pretest measure. However, the testing artifact may pose a serious problem to field and laboratory research to the extent that it interacts with independent variables.

AWARENESS OF EXPERIMENTATION

Demand characteristics (Orne, 1969), evaluation apprehension (Rosenberg, 1969), the Hawthorne effect (Roethlisberger & Dickson, 1939), expectancy effects (Kazdin, 1979b; Rosenthal & Rosnow, 1969), and suspiciousness of experimenter's intent (McGuire, 1969) were originally labeled by Campbell (1957) as reactive arrangements and were discussed in the context of external validity. More recently, Campbell (1969) has discussed these artifacts in the context of experimental control under the label of "awareness of experimentation." As such, these artifacts appear to the present author to be a threat to internal validity as well as to external validity. This interpretation seems consistent with Aronson and Carlsmith's (1968, p. 24) observation that internal validity may suffer when the subject sees through the experiment or responds "like a subject." Awareness of experimentation may involve the treatment procedures and context of the setting as well as reactivity to the experimenter. Taylor, Shuntich, & Greenberg (1979), for example, have shown that prior experience with actual or vicarious aggressive interactions may increase subsequent aggression, at least when using the Taylor (1965) reaction-time procedures to investigate aggression in the laboratory.

In their discussion of these artifacts, Aronson and Carlsmith (1968) described the importance of "experimental realism": An experiment is said to have high experimental realism when the treatment procedures "have a real impact upon subjects"—that is, force them to attend to the experimentally controlled stimuli. The Taylor (1965) reaction-time procedures seem to have this effect. Subjects are often seen pounding their fists on the table and asserting to themselves that they will "get" the opponent next time. Such experimental realism is believed to elicit behavior that is less self-conscious, thus producing less artificiality and results that are more likely valid. This concern about validity is that self-consciousness may both artifactually inhibit aggressive behavior as well as artifactually elicit it (Simons & Turner, 1976).

PERSONAL INVOLVEMENT

Whereas awareness of experimentation refers to various artifactual reactions to being testing, personal involvement refers to the general degree or intensity of involvement in the questionnaire, interview, or experimental stimuli. Aronson and Carlsmith (1968, p. 24), for example, have observed that the subject must take the questionnaire seriously. If he or she does not, internal validity is threatened. Experimental realism is expected to attenuate this artifact as well as awareness of experimentation. Another example of potential personal-involvement reactivity in the laboratory is the use of mirrors or one-way vision screens. A number of studies (e.g., Dengerink & Bertilson, 1974) have used a one-way vision screen to observe subjects during testing. It has been shown, however, that being aware of one's self via reflections in mirrors and one-way vision screens increases aggressive responses in some situations (Carver, 1974) and decreases aggressive responses in other situations (Scheier, Fenigstein, & Buss, 1974). Should this effect interact with treatment variables, it would also be a threat to internal validity.

HISTORY

Events occurring between measurements, in the field or the laboratory, that artifactually alter independent variables pose a threat to internal validity. Several of the aggression research paradigms involve the use of shocks to the wrist as independent variables of attack (e.g., Epstein & Taylor, 1967). Tursky, in a series of investigations (e.g., Tursky, 1974), has systematically evaluated shock as a pain stimulus and has recommended certain procedures that reduce the potential for changes in pain sensation across a series of trials. Tursky recommends that the skin be rubbed briskly with abrasive electrode paste before applying the shock electrode. This procedure removes some of the scaly epidermis and produces uniform pain sensation across trials.

INSTRUMENT DECAY

The problem of "instrument decay" artifactually influencing dependent measures is also important in aggression research. Dependent measures, for example, may be differentially affected by treatment conditions when humans are part of the measuring process as judges, observers, raters, and coders. Rater "drift" and related problems have received a great deal of attention (e.g., Patterson, 1977).

STATISTICAL REGRESSION

Statistical regression (regression toward the mean) may occur when experimental procedures are used to produce scores and these scores are compared to later scores. When groups of subjects are selected on the basis of extreme scores (e.g., Dengerink, O'Leary, & Kasner, 1975; see aslo Dengerink, 1976), shifts toward the mean may occur that are due to random imperfections in the measuring instrument or random instability in the population. Such a main effect may lead experimenters to believe they have selected a greater contrast between groups than they actually have, producing a weaker design than intended.

Statistical regression may also occur when experimental procedures are used to produce pre- and postexperimental data for comparison. Thibaut and Coules (1952), for example, measured interpersonal hostility in their study by having their subjects write personality sketches about their opponent before and after instigation to hostility. The slope of the curves in their data may reflect to some extent a regression of postexperimental hostility toward the mean, thus understating the magnitude of their effect.

BIASED SELECTION

Biased selection refers to bias resulting in differential selection of subjects for comparison groups. Biased selection is a particular weakness in the static group comparison in which randomization is not a possible control. In this design, the experimental group is selected because it has already experienced a treatment of interest. The control group is selected because it has not received the treatment of interest. Often in these studies (e.g., Gelles, 1974), control subjects are matched on theoretically relevant variables in order to provide some comparability. However, comparability cannot be assured by matching alone. Unknown factors are not controlled, thus permitting the two groups to differ before the treatment occurred.

EXPERIMENTAL MORTALITY

Even when groups are equivalent before the experiment, an equal amount of data among groups may not be available by the end of the experiment. Some subjects may not be located for follow-up interviews, or data collected on them may be incomplete. Some subjects may have decided to drop out because certain treatment levels, such as attack, were considered unpleasant. In the McCord, McCord, and Howard (1961) study of the familial correlates of aggression, for example, data from 476 of the original sample of 650 were eliminated—262 because the information was insufficient, 74 were known delinquents and judged atypical of the intended subject pool, 70 had died or moved from Massachusetts, and 70 matched mates were omitted from the control group. As a result of such "mortality," data from the remaining subjects may not be representative of the subject pool before the research began, that is, data from a particular category of subjects may be omitted, thus obscuring an otherwise evident interaction (a threat to internal validity).

From Discovery to Justification

Theory building can be conceptualized as a dimension reaching from the context of discovery, a descriptive process, to the context of justification, a theory-testing process (Reichenbach, 1938). The following discussion of research methods in aggression is organized along such a dimension. At one extreme, the case history and interview methods contain mundane realism and operate to a greater degree in the context of discovery than in the context of justification. At the other extreme, the laboratory method emphasizes experimental realism and internal validity, and operates to a greater extent in the context of justification than in the context of discovery. The laboratory method does contribute to the context of discovery as well. (See Henshel, 1980, for an elaboration of the context of discovery in the laboratory setting.) Between these extremes are some of the clinical methods with extensive attention to control and validity and, in some cases, both mundane and experimental realism. In conducting effective research, there is an "active relationship between laboratory experimentation and the study of real-life situations [Festinger, 1953, p. 140]." The hypotheses, hunches, and recognition of important variables emerge more often from measures of real life (the context of discovery), whereas the verification and elaboration of these hypotheses and hunches more often occurs in the laboratory (the context of justification). From the standpoint of multiple operationalism, these disparate methods of control and description converge in the process of theory building.

AGGRESSION METHODOLOGY

Case Study

The clinical approach to aggression frequently relies on case studies during the early stages of the context discovery. The one-shot case study approach involves observation of behavior only after exposure to the treatment conditions, so that no formal comparisons are possible (Campbell, 1957; Shontz, 1965). One such approach was the historical review of prison administration views about restraint and force in prisons at each nationally reported prison riot from the Civil War until Attica in 1971 (Garson, 1972). Another example of this approach is the Bach-Y-Rita, Lion, Climent, and Ervin (1971) summarization of case studies from 130 violent patients. The report is rich in possible research

hypotheses in implicating, for example, unconsciousness due to injury or illness, electroencephalogram abnormalities, and childhood histories of
hyperactivity.

The survey method may be thought of as the accumulation of case study
materials from a large number of subjects for the purpose of describing general
nomothetic trends. When the survey data are reduced to numerical expressions
and statistically analyzed, Shontz (1965) refers to it as the actuarial method. This
approach may be particularly useful in the context of discovery, as in Austin
and Bayer's (1971) analysis of antecedents to disruptive campus protests during
the 1968–1969 academic year. Gully, Dengerink, Pepping, and Bergstrom
(1981) have used a variation of the survey method in approaching the problem
of family interactions as possible antecedents to later aggression. College students responded to a three-part questionnaire: (a) the type and degree of violent behavior they had directed toward people outside their family during the
preceeding 12 months; (b) the type and amount of violent behavior they directed toward their parents and siblings, and the type and amount of violent
behavior they observed among their parents and siblings; and (c) predictions
by subjects about their potential for violent behavior in three different, highly
stressful hypothetical situations. Comparisons between 108 students who had
engaged in some violent behavior during the last 12 months and 108 students
who had not engaged in violent behavior during the same period were evaluated by means of multiple regression and factor analysis procedures. Recollec-
tions of familial violence, especially with siblings, were significant predictors
of both self-reported violence and self-predicted violence in the three hypothetical situations. Although restricted to inferences about self-reports, this type
of research seems to be powerful methodology in suggesting subsequent research in the context of justification.

Interview

Crano and Brewer (1973) conceptualize the research interview as a form of
observational technique that uses linguistic data as the primary dependent
measure. It permits the reconstruction, albeit imperfectly, of a pattern of interactions and attitudes in the natural environment. The mere presence of the
interviewer may get the subject to pay heed to the questions to a greater extent
than is the case when the subject checks off alternatives on a questionnaire
(Aronson & Carlsmith, 1968). The Sears, Maccoby, and Levin (1957) study of
379 New England mothers is a classic example of this approach. The interviews were somewhat unstructured in style, with 72 principal, open questions
and a series of follow-up probes. Extensive attention was given to interview
nuances—face-saving statements, assessing the existence of negatively valued
behavior, making a wide range of answers appear socially acceptable, and
pitting two stereotyped values against each other. Transcriptions from the inter-

views were scored into 188 dimensions of child-rearing attitudes, behaviors, and responses to child-rearing practices. Questions concerning aggression included parental permissiveness for aggression among siblings, toward parents, and toward other children, and parents' demands for aggressiveness toward other children "at appropriate times." Interview research must, of course, be integrated with other sources of information since there are questions about the objectivity of parents' observations, the fidelity of their memories, and their ability to recall information for the interviews (Eron, Banta, Walder, & Laulicht, 1961; Wenar, 1961).

In-depth, unstructured interviews with members of 80 families were used to collect data on intrafamilial violence by Gelles (1976, 1977). Forty families suspected of using violence were selected for the study—20 from the files of a private social service agency and 20 from police booking records of cases in which the police had been called in to break up a violent dispute. The control comparison was provided by selecting an additional 40 families—one neighboring family for each family from agency or police records. The methodology, sampling procedure, and interview instruments are described in detail in Gelles (1974). The study must be considered in the context of discovery, not justification. The data are retrospective recall of a small number of people of unknown representativeness. Comparisons between experimental and control groups must be viewed tentatively, because rough matching instead of random assignment was used to obtain comparability that is probably imperfect. However, the methodology seems well suited to investigations into new areas. The unstructured interview format, general in scope, permitted analyses of factors not anticipated when the study was originally designed. During the process of data analysis, for example, information was accumulated concerning reasons given by abused women for remaining with their husbands. This data analysis was not anticipated but was available and was used to prepare the Gelles (1976) research report.

Another extensive interview program was the Institute for Social Research interviews of 1400 males during the summer of 1969. The interviews focused on attitudes pertaining to student disturbances, ghetto riots, and violence in general. The measured attitudes were then related to such background variables as religion, race, and income; such psychological variables as values and beliefs; and justification beliefs for violence (Blumenthal, Kahn, Andrews, & Head, 1972). The Owens and Straus (1975) study of the relationship between experience with violence as a child and attitudes toward the use of violence as an adult is also interesting methodologically since it was a reanalysis of a nationwide sample survey. Data from this analysis were obtained from interviewing conducted by Louis Harris and associates for the National Commission on the Causes and Prevention of Violence (Baker & Ball, 1969).

The Eron, Walder, Toigo, and Lefkowitz (1963) study was an interesting combination of interviews, assessment of punishment techniques, peer ratings, and socioeconomic background information. The use of multiple methods allows strengthened conclusions and "converging operations" (Bridgman, 1945). Aggression scores were derived from a peer-rating procedure in the form of a guess-who game in which each child rated every other child in his class on 10 aggressive behaviors. These aggression scores were then related to scores from a 286-item objective, precoded, personal interview; a 24-item punishment scale; and socioeconomic class information. The punishment scale asked for the likely response of a parent to different kinds of aggressive behavior on the part of the child toward the parent and toward other children.

Personality Assessment

The personality assessment method of studying aggression and the effects of aggression may be illustrated by the social learning research of Kilpatrick, Veronen, and Resick (1979a, 1979b). The Kilpatrick et al. (1979a) study compared the responses of rape victims to a 120-item fear scale with the responses of carefully matched nonvictims (a) 6–10 days after rape; (b) 1 month after rape; (c) 3 months after rape; and (d) 6 months after rape. Results from these comparisons were used in the context of justification to confirm hypotheses that (a) victims exhibit greater amounts of fear and anxiety than nonvictims; (b) fear responses shift over time from rather specific rape cues to more generalized fear of subsequent attack; (c) fear patterns related to interactions with the criminal justice system persist; and (d) fear and anxiety responses represent relatively long-term problems for the victims. Only 45% of those contacted agreed to participate, thus producing a threat to validity that the 45% of the population that agreed to participate may be a biased subset of rape victims.

Investigatory interest in causes of child abuse has been high in recent years. One illustrative study used the Michigan Screening Profile of Parenting (Helfer, Schneider, & Hoffmeister, 1977) to investigate personality differences between abusing and nonabusing mothers. Three groups of abusing mothers (adjudicated abusers, spouses of adjudicated abusers, and mothers convicted of child neglect) were compared to three groups of nonabusing mothers selected from a college student population, a middle socioeconomic level, and a lower socioeconomic level. The comparison of three experimental groups to three control groups permitted more generalization than would a one-to-one comparison (Spinetta, 1978).

The Megargee (1966) monograph on undercontrolled and overcontrolled personality types represents an extensive analysis of aggressive behavior based on case history, interview, observational, and assessment methods. Case history data from probation officers' reports were rated on a 10-point aggression scale in order to dichotomize subjects as extremely assaultive and moderately assaultive. Behavior checklists were used to quantify the observational data. A series of 28 predictions was prepared, all testing the general hypothesis that the extremely assaultive subjects would be lower on measures of aggression and higher on measures of control than would other subjects—thus permitting hypothesis testing and the context of justification.

Behavioral Assessment

The development of direct-observation methods has been a relatively recent contribution to psychological methodology (Jones, Reid, & Patterson, 1975). Such techniques involve the direct recording of behavior by trained observers who use rigorous rules and procedures for recording actual, ongoing behavior. Coincident has been the development of sophisticated and effective methodologies and a better understanding of the methodological issues (Gottman, Markman, & Notarius, 1977; Jones et al., 1975; Kazdin, 1977; Mash & Terdel, 1976; Sanson-Fisher, Poole, Small, & Fleming, 1979). The McCord, McCord, and Howard (1961) study of familial correlates of aggression was long term (observations were made in the homes over an average of 5 ¾ years) and presented evidence to rule out a "halo effect" (Thorndike, 1920) that may have contributed to spurious relationships between the boys' aggression and the aggression observed of other members of the families.

The historical development of one type of behavioral coding system is discussed by Patterson (1977). Behaviorally oriented clinicians became aware of problems with the use of parent ratings, structured personality inventories, and child self-report scales that did not yield the kinds of specific behavioral information necessary for changing behavior. Follow-up studies confirmed the existence of major discrepancies between interview reports and actual behavior during home observations. Patterson interpreted the problem in eliciting satisfactory parent report data as due to two factors. First, it seemed that parents were not tracking and storing relevant information. Second, the parents tended to underestimate rates of deviant child behavior and to overestimate improvement in these behaviors. The Oregon Social Learning Center then proceeded to develop an extensive behavior coding system of 28 behavior categories in abbreviated form. Each 6 sec these codes are assigned and associated with specific actors in order to describe a continuous stream of behavior. "For example, if the father made a request of his son, and the child complied with the request, the code looks like this: 3CM–1CO, or in other words, father commands son, son complies [Patterson, 1977, p. 311]." Examples of these behavior categories are "tease," "compliance," "command," "ignore," "physical negative," and "destructiveness." The Patterson (1977) article presents evidence for validity and reliability of the behavioral coding system including first half–second half reliability, interobserver reliability, reactive effects of being observed, possible observer bias, and content, concurrent, and construct validity. The Oregon Social Learning Project has reported both theoretical analyses and 1-year follow-up data from eight research projects over a 10-year period (Patterson & Fleischman, 1979). Although this type of research investigates behaviors that when taken alone are relatively minor, findings from this research tend to confirm the findings reported in laboratory research on aggression (see Dengerink & Covey, Chapter 6, this volume). Indeed the present discussion of behavioral assessment has been expanded to give the reader examples of concept validity, internal validity, and context of justification in a nonlaboratory area of research that is methodologically and theoretically related to laboratory research on aggression.

Psychologists from the Oregon Research Institute and the University of Oregon have performed a series of laboratory and clinical studies concerning the antecedents of and treatment for marital conflict. The theoretical focus of these studies is on the "coercion process" (Patterson & Cobb, 1973; Patterson & Reid, 1970). The Patterson, Hops, and Weiss (1975) study used procedures that are fairly typical of the research program. Moderately distressed couples participated in a 2-week baseline study, followed by the treatment program. Videotapes of couples' attempts to solve problems were coded for each 30-sec interval into 30 categories designed to identify problem-solving skills, positive and aversive stimuli, and more subtle actions used by people to facilitate or sidetrack problem solving.

The Marital Interaction Coding System (Hops, Wills, Patterson, & Weiss, Note 1) is a behavioral coding system (Weider & Weiss, 1980) extensively employed in these studies of marital conflict, and the coding system is reported to have a good track record for discriminating between distressed and non-distressed marital interactions (e.g., Vincent, Friedman, Nugent, & Messerly, 1979). A number of studies have been performed to answer questions about reliability, validity, and generalizability. For example, Weider and Weiss (1980) systematically analyzed video and audio-only samples of 14 clinic couples obtained on two occasions and independently coded by four coders. Components of variance analyses indicated that the majority of variance in both video and audio-only samples was accounted for by valid sources (differences among couples and cross-situational differences within couples). Evidence was not found for invalid sources of variance, such as observer drift or coder biases, across couples or occasions.

Similar marital distress programs exist. For example, Jacobson (1979) reports a series of six single-subject (couple) experiments using the Spouse Observation Checklist (R. L. Weiss, Hops, & Patterson, 1973), Marital Interaction Coding System (Hops et al., Note 1), Areas-of-Change Questionnaire (R. L. Weiss et al., 1973), and Marital Adjustment Scale (Locke & Wallace, 1959). The use of multiple baselines in this study reduced the likelihood that the apparent effects of problem-solving training was due to demand characteristics. Conclusions about treatment effects were strengthened by a reported correspondence between couples' ratings in the home and both the self-report and observer-coded data collected in the laboratory.

In contrast to the approach used by the Oregon Research Institute of repeated measures across baseline and treatment sessions, the Koren, Carlton, and

Shaw (1980) study of marital conflict was limited to one interaction session, providing a kind of snapshot view of conflict. Sixty couples were classified as distressed or nondistressed per the Locke-Wallace Marital Adjustment Scale (Locke & Wallace, 1959) and were required to participate in six 10-min laboratory interaction tests. One methodological concern with clinical observation procedures has been with the reactivity of the observational situation in the home (e.g., Patterson, 1977) and the laboratory (e.g., Freedman, 1969). Koren et al. (1980) may have decreased reactivity in this experiment by increasing both experimental realism and mundane realism while each couple participated in the interaction tests. Mundane realism was enhanced by requiring couples to role play common problem situations. Experimental realism was enhanced by providing spouses with information that slanted the issues in their favor. The interactions were audiotaped and then transcribed verbatim into typescripts. Separate groups of coders analyzed typescripts for influence, inquiry, and responsiveness behaviors and attainment of resolutions. Subjects also responded to questions about satisfaction with the outcomes, representativeness of their behavior in these situations, and the relative frequency of certain behaviors in the laboratory situations and in everyday interactions at home.

Both Bandura (1973) and Toch (1969) concluded that many aggressive persons respond aggressively to aggression-eliciting situations because they tend to be deficient in alternate social skills, such as "positive assertiveness." Kirchner, Kennedy, and Draguns (1979) pursued this issue by assessing assertive and aggressive behavior through role-playing and self-report techniques in groups of convicted offenders. Control comparisons were provided by testing demographically similar people from a vocational retraining program who had histories of inadequate or irregular employment. The role-playing task required subjects to respond to eight interpersonal conflict situations, two situations designed to elicit positive assertive behaviors, and one situation that began as a positive situation and changed to one of conflict. Ratings of videotaped role-playing responses were made for aggression, assertiveness, positive expressiveness, noncompliance, persistence, latency, deviation, eye contact, attack statements, behavioral requests, and speech dysfluencies. Self-report measures included positive assertiveness, conflict assertiveness, aggression, hostility, anxiety and distress from the Adult Self-Expression Scale (Gay, Hollandsworth, & Galassi, 1975), Buss-Durkee Hostility Inventory (Buss & Durkee, 1957), and the Social Avoidance and Distress Scale (Watson & Friend, 1969). Results were interpreted to indicate that offenders asserted their feelings and wants in a more aggressive manner than did nonoffenders. Nonoffenders behaved just as assertively as offenders but without being as aggressive. These procedures illustrate control of reactivity by conservative arrangement (Campbell, 1969). The aggressiveness of offenders emerged even though the role-playing situation in the prison led offenders to perceive a demand for socially appropriate behavior.

The role-playing method was used with various experimental controls by

Hull and Schroeder (1979) as an initial step in differentiating the perception of aggression from the perception of assertiveness. Subjects and confederates were asked to respond verbally through four role-played situations. Two situations represented request situations (e.g., returning a poorly cooked steak in a crowded restaurant) and two situations represented refusal situations (e.g., refusing to work overtime). A female confederate posed as another subject and behaved nonassertively with one-third of the subjects, assertively with another third, and aggressively with the final third of the subjects. A separate manipulation-check study confirmed that the confederate was consistently perceived as nonassertive, assertive, and aggressive in the appropriate experimental conditions.

Field Experiments

Field experiments (French, 1953) have frequently been employed in research on human aggression (Baron, 1977). French (1953) has defined a field experiment as a "theoretically oriented research project in which the experimenter manipulates an independent variable in some real social setting in order to test some hypotheses [p. 101]." Baron (1976), in an oft-cited field study of the arousal of incompatible response tendencies on annoyance-aroused aggression, used horn honking, verbal comments, and facial expressions as dependent measures of aggression. (For additional discussion of horn honking as a measure of aggression, see Baron, 1976, 1977; Turner, Layton, & Simons, 1975). In the Baron study, annoyance was aroused by stalled vehicles in an intersection and incompatible response tendencies were aroused by empathy, humor, and sexual arousal dress and behavior of a confederate. Two control conditions, distraction and no treatment, were used as an aid in ruling out competing interpretations. "The use of adequate control groups is especially important in most field experiments because the real-life setting is both complex and changing, with many uncontrolled factors at work [French, 1953, p. 114]." Harris (1974) studied frustration and aggression in waiting lines at stores, banks, restaurants, ticket windows, and airport passenger check-in stands. Frustration was varied by having the experimenter step in line in front of the person standing either third or twelfth in line. The dependent measure was a combined index of verbal and nonverbal responses to the intrusion.

Time-series models have been used in field research to evaluate the effects of police patrol strategies (Schnelle, Kirchner, McNees, & Lawler, 1975). In this research, the effects of police saturation patrolling was evaluated by multiple control comparisons across a series of time samples. One type of control comparison was to *nonequivalent control groups*—patrol zones randomly chosen from zones in which burglaries were not as frequent. Another type of comparison was to *nonequivalent dependent variables*—the incidence of burglaries in the target patrol zones at hours when saturation patrols were not in operation.

Miller and Bugelski (1948) performed a pretest–posttest field experiment to evaluate the effects of frustration on aggressive attitudes toward outgroups. Attitudes were measured by asking young men to indicate the presence or absence of 10 desirable and 10 undesirable traits in an average Japanese or Mexican foreigner. The validity of these measures in discriminating responses to frustration had been confirmed in earlier research. Half the subjects rated Japanese before the frustration and Mexicans after the frustration. The remaining subjects rated Mexicans first and Japanese later. Alternating the target population between pretest and posttest does reduce the effect of prior experience during pretest upon posttest responses, but it does not eliminate those effects. A comparison group with pretest and posttest without frustration would have helped obtain less ambiguous results. In general, the pretest–posttest design has the additional shortcoming that it frequently telegraphs the experimenter's hypothesis to the subject and may therefore be reactive (Aronson & Carlsmith, 1968).

Laboratory Research

The laboratory experiment may be defined as one in which the investigator creates a situation with the exact conditions he or she wants to have and in which he or she controls some variables and manipulates others (Festinger, 1953, p. 137). The hallmark of the effective laboratory experiment is that the effects of the independent variables on the dependent measures can be clearly seen under the special conditions created. These special conditions include both sufficient control and systematic variation (Festinger, 1953). One of the marks of progress in science according to Festinger is the extent to which such laboratory manipulations can be refined and specified. On the basis of this criteria, it may be seen that research on human aggression has progressed to a sophisticated and productive level. The following discussion gives brief examples of seven principal laboratory research methodologies. The flexibility with which these procedures can be applied to diverse questions will be evident to the reader.

VERBAL HOSTILITY

Such studies as Miller and Bugelski (1948), described earlier, are examples of verbal hostility measured in the field (see also Harris & Samerotte, 1975). There is some evidence that verbal measures of hostility respond to stimuli in a manner that is similar to physically aggressive responses (Berkowitz, 1962; Berkowitz & Geen, 1967). However, Baron (1977, p. 47) suggested a distinction between those investigations in which the subjects' evaluations of another person can potentially inflict harmful consequences on that person (e.g., Berkowitz, Corwin, & Heironimus, 1962) and those in which they can not. The former Baron would treat as expressions of aggression, whereas the latter he would treat as expressions of subjects' current emotional arousal. The following are some of the ways verbal aggression and hostility have been measured: as fantasy aggression to thematic apperception test cards (Hokanson & Gordon, 1958) and specially designed pictures (Kagan, 1956), indirect questionnaire measure (Berkowitz et al., 1962), Siegel's (1956) Manifest Hostility Scale (Kaufmann, 1966; Rosenbaum & Stanners, 1961), the Buss-Durkee Hostility Inventory (Buss & Durkee, 1957), attribution of traits to groups of people (Miller & Bugelski, 1948), personality sketches of another person (e.g., Rosenbaum & deCharms, 1960; Thibaut & Coules, 1952), prison sentences (Kaufmann, 1966), evaluations of a target person that were to be sent to that person's supervisor and have an impact on his future (Berkowitz et al., 1962), and oral responses to instigation (Harris & Huang, 1974). The Buss and Durkee (1957) research is noteworthy for its attention to subclasses of hostility and to methods to control social desirability (e.g., Edwards, 1957). The Berkowitz et al. (1962) study is an example of research with attention to control procedures, confirmation of effectiveness of manipulations, and the multiple measurement of conceptual dependent variables.

PLAY BEHAVIOR

Play behavior in the study of aggression is similar to the behavioral assessment method discussed earlier. These two methods are discussed in separate sections of this chapter in order to juxtapose behavioral assessment with its clinical tradition and play behavior with its laboratory research tradition. Although Baron (1977, p. 47) has limited his definition of "play measures of aggression" to assaults by individuals against inanimate objects, a more inclusive definition of play behavior in aggression research would include childrens' games designed to elicit physical aggression. Davitz (1952) trained half the children in his study to play aggressively and half to play "constructively" and then compared the effects of this differential training on aggressive play following frustration. The experimental procedure followed four steps: (a) a free-play before measure; (b) a series of training sessions; (c) the frustration (the stopping of a film at a climactic point and taking away of candy from the children without explanation); and (d) a free-play after measure. The free-play measures were recorded on moving picture film and transferred to written protocols for scoring by two observers. Aggressive training took place during a series of games designed to produce competition and aggression. One such game was "Cover the Spot." The children were told that the person standing on the X on the floor at the end of the game would win. There were no other rules, and aggressive behavior was praised. In contrast, constructive training included cooperative and constructive activities, such as the drawing of pictures on a large wall mural.

Walters and Brown (1963) used two of the aggressive games from Davitz (1952) in order to measure the effects of reinforcement of aggression against a Bobo doll on subsequent interpersonal aggression. The Bobo doll was an automated toy that when struck by the child, lit up lights in its eyes and in a flower in its buttonhole. Punching the clown in the stomach also provided the child with colored glass marble reinforcers. The effects of continuous reinforcement, FR6, and no reinforcement of Bobo doll aggression were measured during free play after the children had been arbitrarily frustrated. Lovaas (1961) studied the effects of symbolic (film) aggression on doll aggression. A pair of dolls, 6 in. high and 3 in. apart, were used for the dependent measure. Depression of a lever would swing one of the doll's arms down, striking the other doll with a stick.

Perhaps the best-known play behavior studies, though, are the Bandura, Ross, and Ross (1961, 1963a, 1963b) imitative aggression ones. Unlike in the previous play behavior studies, subjects were not reinforced for play with the Bobo doll. Instead, the Bobo doll provided the opportunity, during free play, for the child to reveal incidental learning. The Bandura et al. (1961) study progressed through three experimental stages—model exposure, aggression arousal, and test for delayed imitation. During the aggressive model condition, the adult model engaged in distinctive aggressive acts against a 5-ft. inflated Bobo doll. The model punched it, sat on it, struck it with a mallet, kicked it, and emitted a series of verbally aggressive responses, such as "Sock him in the nose," "Kick him," and "Pow." In the nonaggressive condition, the model assembled tinker toys in a quiet subdued manner, ignoring the Bobo doll. Mild arousal was manipulated in order to ensure some instigation to aggression and was accomplished by tempting the children with attractive but prohibited toys. The test for delayed imitation occurred in a separate room, which was furnished with a variety of toys—some that tended to elicit nonaggressive responses and others, such as mallets and a 3-ft. Bobo doll, that tended to elicit aggressive responses. The 20-min test for delayed imitation was divided into 5-sec intervals for scoring by an observer. Half the sessions were scored by a second observer in order to obtain interscorer agreement measures. Aggression was scored in specific categories, such as mallet aggression, as well as in categories for imitative verbal aggression and nonimitative physical and verbal aggression (aggressive responses different from those directly modeled). This basic paradigm has been used to investigate a number of conceptual variables, including the effects of the aggressive model, the sex of the subject, and the sex of the model (Bandura et al., 1961, 1963a), live versus symbolic film model (Bandura et al., 1963a), and effects of reinforcement and punishment of the model on subsequent imitative aggression (Bandura et al., 1963b). There is some controversy regarding interpretation of assaults against inanimate objects as aggressive behavior. These issues are reviewed in Baron's (1977, pp. 47–51) chapter on methodology in human aggression and may be summarized by indicating suggestive evidence in support of such an interpretation. However, the evidence seems stronger for assaults against inanimate objects as important in learning of aggression, while there is less agreement for such assaults being adequate dependent measures of aggressive performances (Bandura, 1973, pp. 82–88; Baron, 1977).

AGGRESSION MACHINE

The Buss (1961) "aggression machine" has supplied the basic procedure in a large number of laboratory studies on human physical aggression (Baron, 1977), including such diverse areas of investigation as the effects of objective self-awareness (Carver, 1974), the effects of alcohol on human aggression (Bennett, Buss, & Carptenter, 1969), and the physiological arousal of psychopaths during an aggressive task (Dengerink & Bertilson, 1975). The aggression machine procedures create a situation in which a subject may deliver various intensities and durations of shock (Buss, 1963), irritating noise (Fitz, 1976), or excessive heat (Liebert & Baron, 1972) to a target person without being aware that aggressive behavior is the purpose of the investigation.

Early studies with the aggression machine were presented to the subject and a confederate as a study of the effects of punishment on learning. A lottery drawing controlled by the experimenter is usually used to designate the confederate as the learner and the subject as the teacher. The subject is asked to present a pattern of lights or other codes to the confederate as elements of a series of problems to be solved. Whenever the confederate makes a correct response, the subject is instructed to signal the "correct" indicator light to the confederate. Whenever the confederate makes an incorrect response, the subject is instructed to choose among available shock intensities for delivery to the confederate's wrist (Buss, 1963).

More recent investigations have used the same basic procedures with several variations. Berkowitz and Powers (1979) required the subject first to be the learner before exchanging places with the confederate and being the teacher. According to Berkowitz and Powers, this treatment may heighten the subject's willingness to shock the confederate. Baron and Eggleston (1972) have presented evidence that the motive for setting high shocks may actually be to help the confederate learn, as much as it is to hurt the confederate. As such, Baron has adopted more neutral instructions in which the purpose of the experiment is explained to the subject as an examination of the effects of shock upon physiological reactions (e.g., Baron & Bell, 1975). Donnerstein has described the situation to the subjects as a study of performance under stress and has apparently increased the experimental realism as well by using closed-circuit TV to display the confederate to the subject, to present aggressive or neutral films, and to project visually the multiple-choice questions to the confederate (Donnerstein, Donnerstein, & Barrett, 1976).

Baron (1977) reviewed the evidence for the validity of laboratory methods of studying aggression. According to his review, relatively few investigations have tested whether these methods actually produce valid measures of overt aggression. More evidence has been gathered concerning the aggression machine procedures than other procedures, and these studies do indicate that the aggression machine procedures seem to be valid and useful measures of physical aggression (e.g., Wolfe & Baron, 1971). Less evidence, albeit some, has been gathered concerning the validity of the other human aggression laboratory procedures.

EVALUATION PROCEDURES

Attack is known to be an important determinant of aggression (e.g., Geen & Stonner, 1973; O'Leary & Dengerink, 1973) and has been studied in several ways. One commonly employed method to study attack has been to place the subject and a confederate into a situation that requires the confederate to evaluate the subject and later requires the subject to evaluate the confederate (e.g., Berkowitz, 1962, 1964). The confederate's evaluation of the subject may serve as the attack variable, and the subject's subsequent evaluation of the confederate serves as the dependent variable measure of aggression. The McDaniel, O'Neal, and Fox (1971) study may be used to represent this paradigm. The task was presented to the subject as a study of the effects of stress on problem solving. The subject and confederate were both given a problem to solve, and at the end of 5 min, the solutions were picked up and exchanged— the subject receiving a standard programmed solution. Each participant was allowed 1 min to review the other person's solution, and then the confederate was asked to evaluate the subject's solution by depressing a toggle switch several times. One response would signify that the solution was very good; seven responses would indicate that the solution was judged to be very poor. Numbers in between would indicate levels of performance between very good and very poor. Attack was systematically varied by having half the confederates respond with high attack (six responses) and half the confederates respond with low attack (two responses). Modality of attack was also systematically varied. In a completely crossed design, half the subjects received shocks to the wrists from the confederate, whereas the other half received visual messages of two or six on a digital counter.

This basic paradigm permits a number of variations in procedures (e.g., Berkowitz, 1965; Berkowitz & Geen, 1966). One such variation is to study the effects of aggressive models on anger-aroused subjects (e.g., Perry & Perry, 1976; Turner & Berkowitz, 1972). In the Perry and Perry study, evaluations (shock) delivered by the confederate for solutions prepared by the subject served as the anger-arousal manipulation. An aggressive model was introduced by showing the boxing sequence from the film *The Champion*. Three independent variables were systematically investigated within this basic set of procedures.

1. Whether the subject was encouraged to identify with the loser or the winner in the fight scene. In order to help them focus their attention on the

loser or the winner, subjects were asked to press a switch whenever the victor hit the victim (or in the victim condition, whenever the victim was hit by the victor).

2. Crossed within the levels of identification was a self-verbalization variable. This permitted systematic evaluation of implicit verbalizations as mediators of aggression. One-half the subjects in each group were instructed to engage in covert verbalizations each time they pressed the button. It was suggested that subjects in the victor condition might say, "Hit him" or "Kill him," that subjects assigned to the victim condition might say such things as "Ow" or "Uh," and that subjects in control condition say, "Now."

3. Finally, justification of the victim's aggression was systematically varied. All subjects received a brief summary of the prize-fight scene at the same time that the film was introduced. For one-half the subjects, the summary indicated that the victim deserved the beating he got. For the rest of the subjects, the summary implied that the beating was unjustified. Aggression was measured as the total number and duration of shocks administered to the confederate by the subject as an evaluation of the confederate's performance on a task—in this case, the evaluation of ideas for a promotional campaign. Questionnaires were used to evaluate the success of the experimental manipulations and deceptions and to assess reactions to the film and experimental tasks, thus ruling out competing explanations and permitting reasonably strong inferences about cause and effect among these variables.

COMBINATION PROCEDURES

The Berkowitz (1962, 1964) evaluation of performance and the aggression machine procedures have been combined in some studies. Geen and Stonner (1974) studied the effects of attributed revenge motive on observed violence. Before the teaching task was to begin, the experimenter allegedly wished to assess a potentially important variable on teaching—similarity of attitudes between teacher and learner. That explanation was used to justify the independent variable manipulation of attack, which was accomplished via the evaluation of performance procedures. In the attack condition, the confederate gave the subject moderately strong shocks on 8 of the opinion statements, mild shocks after 2 opinion statements, and no shocks on the other 2. In the no-attack condition, the confederate gave the subject mild shocks after 2 opinion statements and no shocks after the other 10. A manipulation check was performed at this point in order to ascertain how angry the procedures had made the subjects, in order to rule out alternative explanations and permit reasonably strong inferences.

Next, a movie was introduced that contained information for subsequent testing. The movie was a 6-min sequence from the Hollywood production *The Return of the Seven,* which contained considerable gunplay among gunfighters and outlaws. The short introductory narrative presented to subjects before the film provided the attribution-of-motive manipulation. A fourth of the subjects in each attack condition were told that gunfighters were assisting villagers out of their motive of vengence—to avenge the outlaws for killing several of the gunfighters. Another quarter of the subjects were told that the gunmen were professionals hired by the villagers. Another fourth of the subjects were told that the gunmen's motives were solely altruistic. The last quarter of the subjects were given no introductory narrative. After the film, the teacher was given a set of letter codes for use with the aggression machine in the learning task. The experiment ended with a final questionnaire assessing the subject's mood and perceptions of the film and the confederate. Blood pressure was taken at three points during the experiment as a manipulation check on the effectiveness of physiological arousal manipulations.

Research in recent years seems to be asking more complex questions and, therefore, has used elaborate experimental manipulations. The likelihood of competing explanations for research findings may increase with the increase in experimental complexity. As such, the use of a series of manipulation checks on the success of altering intervening processes, as was done by Perry and Perry (1976) and Geen and Stonner (1974), becomes important (Aronson & Carlsmith, 1968, pp. 17–18).

Yoked control procedures have been used in an application (Geen, 1978) of the combined performance evaluation task followed by the aggression machine procedures to investigate the effects of uncontrollable noise on attack-instigated aggression. The yoked control procedure is a particularly powerful method of ruling out competing explanations. With this technique, control subjects receive the same stimulation as experimental subjects, except that the experimental subjects have actual or perceived control over the stimulation and the yoked subjects do not. When subjects are randomly assigned to the experimental and yoked control group, the experimenter may reasonably conclude that there is only one systematic difference between the two groups—control over stimuli. As with other experimental designs, random assignment to experimental and yoked control groups is necessary in order to rule out unknown but potentially systematic biasing of subject samples. There are cases in the literature of probable biasing due to nonrandom assignment of subjects—for example, the Brady "executive monkey" studies (Brady, Porter, Conrad, & Mason, 1958) as analyzed by Weiss in a series of follow-up studies (e.g., J. M. Weiss, 1968, 1971). Typically in yoked control designs, each experimental subject is permitted to make choices that determine such environmental outcomes as the pattern of shocks or noise administered to the experimental subject. A control subject who is not permitted to control the environment is yoked to the same environmental conditions (e.g., Dengerink & Bertilson, 1974).

In the Geen (1978) study, experimental subjects were provided with predictability over bursts of randomly occurring noise by being yoked to subjects in the control condition who chose when to turn off the noise. Subjects were told that in order to maintain absolute conncentration during the problem-solving task, a masking noise would occur in order to block out external distractions. Five variations in control over the noise and predictability of noise were tested in the first experiment.

1. The control group was given control over the noise. Control subjects were told that a switch on the panel could be used to turn off the noise but that the experimenter would prefer that the subject leave the noise on for a while.

2. The experimental group was given predictability but no control over the noise. Each experimental subject was yoked to a subject in the control condition and was told before the beginning of the task when the noise would be terminated. Three additional control groups were used to assist in ruling out alternative explanations.

3. Subjects in the no-control condition were told nothing about termination of the noise, although the yoking procedure also determined when their random noise was turned off.

4. A fourth group received random noise for the full length of the aggression task.

5. The fifth group was told nothing about noise and received no noise.

A follow-up experiment permitted Geen to demonstrate that facilitation of attack-instigated aggression was most likely due to subjects inaccurately attributing increased arousal from the noise to the physical attack.

The standard aggression machine procedures, discussed earlier, permit time-series measurement of aggressive responses. In the Buss (1963) study, for example, subjects were required to administer 46 shocks during the course of the experiment. While the aggression machine procedures permit the investigation of numerous variables, such as frustration and instrumentality, they are not easily used to investigate attack. The standard evaluation procedures permit an attack while the confederate evelutes the subject's performance and an aggression response while the subject evaluates the confederate. The combination procedures using evaluations of subjects followed by the aggression machine permit one attack followed by a series of aggressive responses. Aggressive events in the home or on the street, however, are often a series of interactions. Indeed, Bandura (1977) has argued that aggressive behavior is produced by what he calls reciprocal determinism—that "counter-influences undergo reciprocal adjustments in ongoing sequences of interaction [p. 199]." (See also Dengerink & Covey, Chapter 6, this volume.) The clinical procedure of Patterson, Weiss, and their colleagues are designed to measure the very dynamics that Bandura is speaking of, but the laboratory procedures reviewed so far do not.

TAYLOR REACTION TIME PROCEDURES

A principal advantage of the Taylor (1965) reaction-time procedures is that it measures a series of interactions among aggressive responders. In these procedures, the subject interacts with an opponent in a competitive reaction-time task. The task is described as one in which the person with the slowest reaction time on each trial loses that trial and receives a shock to the wrist. (One variation of this procedure uses noise instead of shock; e.g., Shortell & Biller, 1970; Kimble, Fitz, & Onorad, 1977). Typically, four events occur during each trial. The "set" light signals subjects to set a shock level for their opponents to receive should their opponents lose the competition on that trial. Next the "press" light signals subjects to press down on the reaction-time key. At the onset of the "release" light, subjects are to release their thumbs from the reaction-time key as rapidly as possible. At the onset of the "feedback" light, subjects receive feedback in two forms. On every trial, a light on the response panel indicates what shock level opponents had set for the subjects. On those trials in which the subjects' reaction times were slower than the opponents', the subjects also receive a 1-sec shock to the wrist at the intensity set by their opponents. There is in fact no opponent, although some uses of these procedures have involved the indepndent testing of two subjects simultaneously as a means to strengthen experimental realism (e.g., Dengerink & Myers, 1977). Winning or losing and the opponent's shock settings are programmed by the experimenter and often serve as one of the principal experimental variables (e.g., Epstein & Taylor, 1967). Although subjects receive indicator lights and shock to the wrist as feedback, Geenwell and Dengerink (1973) have shown that subjects' aggressive responses are controlled more by the symbolic aggression through indicator lights than by variations in physical shock to the wrist.

Baron (1977) has described several advantages of the reaction-time procedures. First, a series of attack and counterattack interactions can be and usually are studied. Second, the responses of the opponent may be systematically investigated so that the effects of such variations on subjects' responses can be determined (e.g., O'Leary & Dengerink, 1973; Pisano & Taylor, 1971). Finally, the influence of a wide variety of variables—for example, degree of defeat (Epstein & Taylor, 1967), personality differences (Dengerink, O'Leary, & Kasner, 1975), third-party instigation of aggression (Gaebelein & Hay, 1975), alcohol (Shuntich & Taylor, 1972), and failure experiences (Dengerink, & Myers, 1977)—on responses during aggressive interactions can be readily explored. As attractive as the Taylor paradigm is in these respects, there are several limiting factors. First, findings using these procedures may in some ways be limited to aggression emitted as part of competitive situations (Baron, 1977). Second, research using the yoked control design led to the suggestion that the exact contingencies between the shock settings of subjects and those of their opponents may be masked by the reaction-time events (Dengerink & Bertilson, 1974); this will be discussed later. Finally, direct evidence for the validity of these procedures is sparse, although indirect evidence is available in the form of "face validity." As expected, such variables as attack (Borden, Bowen, & Taylor, 1971; O'Leary & Dengerink, 1973) and low anxiety (Dengerink, 1971) do lead to increases in shock settings.

MINIMUM SOCIAL SITUATION

There is another set of laboratory procedures that have not often been used but that provide some of the advantages of the Taylor procedures without its limitations. This is the minimum social situation, in which subjects exchange shocks and reward signals with a confederate (Dengerink, Schnedler, & Covey, 1978; Hokanson, Willers, & Korospak, 1968; Knott, Lasater, & Shuman, 1974; Sidowski, Wyckoff, & Tabory, 1956). These procedures permit the alternation or exchange of responses—first the subject, then the confederate, then the subject, and so on. The reaction-time procedures do not permit such a direct exchange of aggressive responses. The reaction-time procedures seem quite sensitive to trends in shock settings over trials, but they may not be as sensitive to trial-by-trial interactions between the subject and the confederate (Bertilson & Lien, 1982; Dengerink & Bertilson, 1974). The reaction-time procedures require subjects and confederates to set shocks simultaneously and then simultaneously wait for feedback before simultaneously making another response. When studying the effects of a matching strategy by an opponent, the four steps of set, press, release, and feedback must be repeated twice before the matching contingency can become apparent to the subject—for example, (a) assume that during Trial 1 the subject sets a 3 for the opponent, while the opponent sets a 4; and then (b) during Trial 2 the opponent matches the subject's Trial 1 response with a 3, while the subject is setting perhaps a 4. In contrast, the minimum social situation permits a more direct interaction of the matching strategy: (a) the subject sets a 3, and (b) the opponent matches with a 3. In addition, the minimum social situation does not convey the competitive atmosphere that the reaction-time procedures do. On the other hand, it may be easier for subjects to guess that the minimum social situation is actually a study of human aggression and because of that knowledge respond in a socially desirable (Edwards, 1953, 1957) rather than veridical manner. Thorough debriefing interviews can help detect this type of reactivity, but perhaps the best overall method is to answer research questions with several different research procedures. As was done by Bertilson, Wonderlich, and Blum (1982; 1983) and Dengerink and Bertilson (1974), using both the reaction-time and the minimum social situation procedures.

GAMES AND SIMULATIONS

A number of laboratory procedures other than these seven have been used for studying human aggression. For example, Zillmann, Johnson, and Day (1974) used a series of battleship games to study the effects of aggression among athletes. Subjects were assigned the task of producing deceptive feedback to delay a hit by one's opponent. Both positive and negative feedback were available for this purpose. Negative feedback consisted of noxious noise through the headphones to one of the opponent's ears at levels of intensity from low to very intense and quite painful. Positive feedback consisted of graded removal of a moderately intense, unpleasant noise that was otherwise continuously administered to the opponent's other ear. The positive and negative feedback were the dependent measures of aggression. Before the second game began, a provocation manipulation was introduced. While the intercom was open for an exchange between the confederate and experimenter, the confederate was heard to make an arbitrary, unwarranted insult demeaning the subject's ability in the game. In the no-provocation condition, the confederate was heard only to ask how many trials it took him to find the subject's battleship. A minute later, the second game commenced; immediately following that, the third game occurred.

A rather extensive literature on bargaining games has accumulated (e.g., Black & Higbee, 1973; Deutsch & Krauss, 1962; Horai & Tedeschi, 1969; Shure, Meeker, & Hansford, 1965; Swingle, 1970). In some cases (e.g., Pisano & Taylor, 1971; Tedeschi et al., 1977), conceptual bridges have been made between bargaining games and aggression research. Probably much more of that type of integration could be done. One way to accomplish such a goal would be to develop research methodology that would integrate the procedures of both areas of investigation.

CONCLUSION

Theory and philosophy of science have been reviewed that suggest several criteria for successful research in social psychology. Multiple meanings result when viewing single investigations in isolation and as such pose a threat to concept validity. The process of multiple operationalism is used by the researchers to untangle these multiple interpretations by holding conceptual variables constant while varying research operations. It has been argued that this process of multiple operationalism is not limited to laboratory research but includes investigations using case study, research interview, personality assessment, and field experiments as well.

Particular attention is placed on the establishment of internal validity in individual investigations in order to support systematic theory building. Examples of threats to the internal validity of research in aggression were discussed. It was shown that awareness of experimentation poses a threat to internal as well as external validity. Personal involvement was added to Campbell's original list of threats to internal validity. Finally, it was shown that the various methods of research common to the study of human aggression could be conceptualized as a dimension extending from the context of discovery to the context of justification, although considerable overlap is evident. Case history, research interview, and personality assessment methods may contribute more to the context of discovery, whereas the behavior assessment, field experiments and laboratory research methods may contribute more to the context of

TABLE 1
Representative Methods of Research in Human Aggression

Method	Comments	Uses	Examples
Case study	Observation of behavior only after treatment	Context of discovery—no formal comparisons	Bach-Y-Rita et al., 1971
Survey	Case study material from large number of people	Context of discovery—describe general trends	Gully et al., 1981
Research interview	Observational technique with linguistic data	Context of discovery—reconstruct memories	Sears et al., 1957; Gelles, 1977
Combination	Interviews, peer-ratings, assessment, socio-economic	Converging operations	Eron et al., 1963
Personality assessment	Individual differences	Relate personality constructs to behavior	Kilpatrick et al., 1979a; Helfer et al., 1977
Combination	Assessment, case history, interview, observational	Converging operations	Megargee, 1966
Behavioral assessment	Direct observation	Valid and reliable measurement	Patterson, 1977; Patterson et al., 1975
Role playing	Experimental control	Hypothesis testing	Kirchner et al., 1979
Field experiments	Experimental control in the field	Internal and external validity	Baron, 1976
Time series	Experimental control in the field	Comparisons across time samples	Schnelle et al., 1975
Laboratory research	Experimental control	Internal validity	
Verbal hostility		Verbal and nonverbal communication	Berkowitz et al., 1962
Play behavior		With children	Bandura et al., 1961
Aggression machine		Physical aggression	Buss, 1963
Evaluation		Effects of anger and attack	McDaniel et al., 1971
Combination		Anger, attack, and series of responses	Geen & Stonner, 1974
Reaction time		Series of interactions	Epstein & Taylor, 1967
Minimal situation		Direct interactions without a masking task	Dengerink et al., 1978
Games and simulations		Meets various needs	Zillmann et al., 1974

justification. However, all these methods are seen as important to the multiple operationalism necessary to adequate theory building.

A sample of the research methods and illustrative citations are summarized in Table 1. The review of research methods in this chapter, as capsulized in the table, seems to indicate that multiple operationalism does exist. Such multiple operations thereby provide the opportunity to rule out threats to internal validity and to build systematic theories of human aggression.

REFERENCE NOTE

1. Hops, H., Wills, T. A., Patterson, G. R., & Weiss, R. L. Marital Interaction Coding System. Unpublished manuscript, University of Oregon and Oregon Research Institute, 1972.

REFERENCES

Austin, A. W., & Bayer, A. E. Antecedents and consequents of disruptive campus protests. *Measurement and Evaluation in Guidance*, 1971, *4*, 18–30.

Aronson, E., & Carlsmith, J. M. Experimentation in social psychology. In G. Lindzey & E. Aronson (Eds.), *The handbook of social psychology* (Vol. 2). *Research methods*. Reading, Mass.: Addison-Wesley, 1968.

Bach-Y-Rita, G., Lion, J. R., Climent, C. E., & Ervin, F. R. Episodic dyscontrol: A study of 130 violent patients. *American Journal of Psychiatry*, 1971, *127*, 1473–1478.

Baker, R. K., & Ball, S. J. *Mass media and violence: A report to the National Commission on the Causes and prevention of Violence*. Washington, D. C.: U.S. Government Printing Office, 1969.

Bandura, A. *Aggression: A social learning analysis*. Englewood Cliffs, N.J.: Prentice-Hall, 1973.

Bandura, A. *Social learning theory*. Englewood Cliffs, N.J.: Prentice-Hall, 1977.

Bandura, A., Ross, D., & Ross, S. A. Transmission of aggression through imitation of aggressive models. *Journal of Abnormal and Social Psychology*, 1961, *63*, 575–582.

Bandura, A., Ross, D., & Ross, S. A. Imitation of film-mediated aggressive models. *Journal of Abnormal and Social Psychology*, 1963, *66*, 3–11. (a)

Bandura, A., Ross, D., & Ross, S. A. Vicarious reinforcement and imitative learning. *Journal of Abnormal and Social Psychology*, 1963, *67*, 601–607. (b)

Baron, R. A. The reduction of human aggression: A field study of the influence of incompatible reactions. *Journal of Applied Social Psychology*, 1976, *6*, 260–274.

Baron, R. A. *Human aggression*. New York: Plenum, 1977.

Baron, R. A., & Bell, P. A. Aggression and heat: Mediating effects of prior provocation and exposure to an aggressive model. *Journal of Personality and Social Psychology*, 1975, *31*, 825–832.

Baron, R. A., & Eggleston, R. J. Performance on the "aggression machine": Motivation to help or harm? *Psychonomic Science*, 1972, *26*, 321–322.

Bennett, R. M., Buss, A. H., & Carpenter, J. A. Alcohol and human physical aggression. *Journal of Studies on Alcohol*, 1969, *30*, 870–876.

Berkowitz, L. *Aggression: A social psychological analysis*. New York: McGraw-Hill, 1962.

Berkowitz, L. Aggressive cues in aggressive behavior and hostility catharsis. *Psychological Review*, 1964, *71*, 104–122.

Berkowitz, L. Some aspects of observed aggression. *Journal of Personality and Social Psychology*, 1965, *2*, 359–369.

Berkowitz, L., Corwin, R., & Heironimus, M. Film violence and subsequent aggressive tendencies. *Public Opinion Quarterly,* 1962, *27,* 217–229.

Berkowitz, L., & Donnerstein, E. External validity is more than skin deep: Some answers to criticisms of laboratory experiments (with special reference to research on aggression). *American Psychologist,* 1982, *37,* 245–257.

Berkowitz, L., & Geen, R. G. Film violence and the cue properties of available targets. *Journal of Personality and Social Psychology,* 1966, *3,* 525–530.

Berkowitz, L., & Geen, R. G. Stimulus qualities of the target of aggression: A further study. *Journal of Personality and Social Psychology,* 1967, *5,* 364–368.

Berkowitz, L., & Powers, P. C. Effects of timing and justification of witnessed aggression on the observers' puntiveness. *Journal of Research in Personality,* 1979, *13,* 71–80.

Bertilson, H. S., & Lien, S. K. Comparison of reaction time and interpersonal communications tasks to test effectiveness of a matching strategy in reducing attack-instigated aggression. *Perception and Motor Skills,* 1982, *55,* 659–665.

Bertilson, H. S., Wonderlich, S. A., & Blum, M. W. Withdrawal, matching, withdrawal-matching, and variable-matching strategies in reducing attack-instigated aggression. *Aggressive Behavior,* 1982, *8,* in press.

Bertilson, H. S., Wonderlich, S. A., & Blum, M. W. Withdrawal and matching strategies in reducing attack-instigated aggression. *Replications in Social Psychology,* 1983, in press.

Black, T. E., & Higbee, K. L. Effects of power, threat, and sex on exploitation. *Journal of Personality and Social Psychology,* 1973, *27,* 383–388.

Blumenthal, M. D., Kahn, R. L., Andrews, F. M., & Head, K. B. *Justifying violence: Attitudes of American men.* Ann Arbor: Univ. of Michigan, 1972.

Borden, R. J., Bowen, R., & Taylor, S. P. Shock setting behavior as a function of physical attack and extrinsic reward. *Perceptual and Motor Skills,* 1971, *33,* 563–568.

Boring, E. G. *A history of experimental psychology* (2nd ed.). New York: Appleton, 1950.

Boring, E. G. The nature and history of experimental control. *Journal of Psychology,* 1954, *67,* 573–589.

Boring, E. G. Perspective: Artifact and control. In R. Rosenthal & R. L. Rosnow (Eds.), *Artifact in behavioral research.* New York: Academic Press, 1969.

Brady, J. V., Porter, R. W., Conrad, D. G., & Mason, J. W. Avoidance behavior and the development of gastroduodenal ulcers. *Journal of Experimental Analysis of Behavior,* 1958, *1,* 69–72.

Bridgman, P. W. Some general principles of operational analysis. *Psychological Review,* 1945, *52,* 246–249.

Brunswik, E. Representative design and probalistic theory in functional psychology. *Psychological Review,* 1955, *62,* 193–217.

Buss, A. H. *The psychology of aggression.* New York: Wiley, 1961.

Buss, A. H. Physical aggression in a relation to different frustrations. *Journal of Abnormal and Social Psychology,* 1963, *67,* 1–7.

Buss, A. H., & Durkee, A. An inventory for assessing different kinds of hostility. *Journal of Consulting Psychology,* 1957, *21,* 343–348.

Campbell, D. T. Factors relevant to validity of experiments in social settings. *Psychological Bulletin,* 1957, *54,* 297–312.

Campbell, D. T. Prospective: Artifact and control. In R. Rosenthal & R. L. Rosnow (Eds.), *Artifact in behavioral research.* New York: Academic Press, 1969.

Campbell, D. T., & Stanley, J. C. Experimental and quasi-experimental designs for research on teaching. In N. L. Gage (Ed.), *Handbook on research on teaching.* Chicago: Rand McNally, 1963.

Carver, C. S. Facilitation of physical aggression through objective self-awarness. *Journal of Experimental Social Psychology,* 1974, *10,* 365–370.

Crano, W. D., & Brewer, M. B. *Principles of research in social psychology.* New York: McGraw-Hill, 1973.

Davitz, J. R. The effects of previous training on postfrustration behavior. *Journal of Abnormal and Social Psychology,* 1952, *47,* 309–315.

Dengerink, H. A. Anxiety, aggression, and physiological arousal. *Journal of Experimental Research in Personality,* 1971, *5,* 223–232.

Dengerink, H. A. Personality variables as mediators of attack-instigated aggression. In R. G. Geen & E. C. O'Neal (Eds.), *Perspectives on aggression.* New York: Academic Press, 1976.

Dengerink, H. A., & Bertilson, H. S. The reduction of attack-instigated aggression. *Journal of Research in Personality,* 1974, *8,* 254–262.

Dengerink, H. A., & Bertilson, H. S. Psychopathy and physiological arousal in an aggressive task. *Psychophysiology,* 1975, *12,* 682–684.

Dengerink, H. A., & Myers, J. D. The effects of failure and depression on subsequent aggression. *Journal of Personality and Social Psychology,* 1977, *35,* 88–96.

Dengerink, H. A., O'Leary, M. R., & Kasner, K. H. Individual differences in aggressive responses to attack: External locus of control and field dependence–independence. *Journal of Research in Personality,* 1975, *9,* 191–199.

Dengerink, H. A., Schnedler, R. W., & Covey, M. K. Role of avoidance in aggressive responses to attack and no attack. *Journal of Personality and Social Psychology,* 1978, *36,* 1044–1053.

Deutsch, M., & Krauss, R. M. Studies of interpersonal bargaining. *Journal of Conflict Resolution,* 1962, *6,* 52–76.

Dollard, J., Doob, L., Miller, N., Mowrer, O. H., & Sears, R. R. *Frustration and aggression.* New Haven: Yale Univ. Press, 1939.

Donnerstein, E., Donnerstein, M., & Barrett, G. Where is the facilitation of media violence: The effects of nonexposure and placement of anger arousal. *Journal of Research in Personality,* 1976, *11,* 386–398.

Edwards, A. L. The relationship between the judged desirability of a trait and the probability that the trait will be endorsed. *Journal of Applied Psychology,* 1953, *37,* 90–93.

Edwards, A. L. *The social desirability variable in personality assessment and research.* New York: Dryden, 1957.

Epstein, S., & Taylor, S. P. Instigation to aggression as a function of degree of defeat and perceived aggressive intent of the opponent. *Journal of Personality,* 1967, *35,* 265–289.

Eron, L. D., Banta, T. J., Walder, L. O., & Laulicht, J. H. Comparison of data obtained from mothers and fathers on childrearing practices and their relation to child aggression. *Child Development,* 1961, *32,* 457–472.

Eron, L. D., Walder, L. O., Toigo, R., & Lefkowitz, M. M. Social class, parental punishment for aggression, and child aggression. *Child Development,* 1963, *34,* 849–867.

Festinger, L. Laboratory experiments. In L. Festinger & D. Katz (Eds.), *Research methods in the behavioral sciences.* New York: Holt, 1953.

Fitz, D. A revised look at Miller's conflict theory of aggressive displacement. *Journal of Personality and Social Psychology,* 1976, *33,* 725–732.

Freedman, J. L. Role playing: Psychology by consensus. *Journal of Personality and Social Psychology,* 1969, *13,* 107–114.

French, J. R. P., Jr. Experiments in field settings. In L. Festinger & D. Katz (Eds.), *Research methods in the behavioral sciences.* New York: Holt 1953.

Gaebelein, J. W., & Hay, W. W. The effects of verbal and behavioral noncompliance on third party instigation of aggression. *Journal of Research in Personality,* 1975, *9,* 113–121.

Garner, W. R., Hake, H. W., & Eriksen, C. W. Operationalism and the concept of perception. *Psychological Review,* 1956, *63,* 149–159.

Garson, G. D. Force versus restraint in prison riots. *Crime and Delinquency,* 1972, *18,* 411–421.

Gay, M. L., Hollandsworth, J. G., & Galassi, J. P. An assertiveness inventory for adults. *Journal of Counseling Psychology,* 1975, *22,* 340–344.

Geen, R. G. The study of aggression. In R. G. Geen & E. C. O'Neal (Eds.), *Perspectives on aggression.* New York: Academic Press, 1976.

Geen, R. G. Effects of attack and uncontrollable noise on aggression. *Journal of Research in Personality*, 1978, *12*, 15–29.

Geen, R. G., & Stonner, D. Context effects in observed violence. *Journal of Personality and Social Psychology*, 1973, *25*, 145–150.

Geen, R. G., & Stonner, D. The meaning of observed violence: Effects on arousal and aggressive behavior. *Journal of Research in Personality*, 1974, *8*, 55–63.

Gelles, R. J. *The violent home: A study of physical aggression between husbands and wives.* Beverly Hills: Sage, 1974.

Gelles, R. J. Abused wives: Why do they stay. *Journal of Marriage and the Family*, 1976, *38*, 659–668.

Gelles, R. J. No place to go: The social dynamics of marital violence. In M. Roy (Ed.), *Battered women: A psychosociological study of domestic violence.* New York: Van Nostrand-Reinhold, 1977.

Gottman, J., Markman, H., & Notarius, C. The topography of marital conflict: A sequential analysis of verbal and nonverbal behavior. *Journal of Marriage and the Family*, 1977, *39*, 461–477.

Greenwell, J., & Dengerink, H. A. The role of perceived versus actual attack in human physical aggression. *Journal of Personality and Social Psychology*, 1973, *26*, 66–71.

Gully, K. J., Dengerink, H. A., Pepping, M., & Bergstrom, D. Research notes: Sibling contribution to violent behavior. *Journal of Marriage and the Family*, 1981, *43*, 333–337.

Harris, M. B. Mediators between frustration and aggression in a field experiment. *Journal of Experimental Social Psychology*, 1974, *10*, 561–571.

Harris, M. B., & Huang, L. C. Aggression and the attribution process. *Journal of Social Psychology*, 1974, *92*, 209–216.

Harris, M. B., & Samerotte, G. The effects of aggressive and altruistic modeling on subsequent behavior. *Journal of Social Psychology*, 1975, *95*, 173–182.

Helfer, R. E., Schneider, C., & Hoffmeister, J. K. *Manual for use of the Michigan Screening Profile of Parenting.* East Lansing: Michigan State Univ., 1977.

Henshel, R. L. The purposes of laboratory experimentation and the virtues of deliberate artificiality. *Journal of Experimental Social Psycholgy*, 1980, *16*, 466–478.

Hicks, R. G. Converging operations in the psychological experiment. *Psychophysiology*, 1971, *8*, 93–101.

Hokanson, J. E., & Gordon, J. E. The expression and inhibition of hostility in imaginative and overt behavior. *Journal of Abnormal and Social Psychology*, 1958, *57*, 327–333.

Hokanson, J. E., Willers, K. R., & Korospak, E. Modification of autonomic responses during aggressive interchange. *Journal of Personality*, 1968, *36*, 386–404.

Horai, J., & Tedeschi, J. T. Effects of credibility and magnitude of punishment on compliance to threats. *Journal of Personality and Social Psychology*, 1969, *12*, 164–169.

Hull, C. L. *Principles of behavior.* New York: Appleton, 1943.

Hull, D. B., & Schroeder, H. E. Some interpersonal effects of assertion, nonassertion, and aggression. *Behavior Therapy*, 1979, *10*, 20–28.

Jacobson, N. S. Increasing positive behavior in severely distressed marital relationships: The effects of problem-solving training. *Behavior Therapy*, 1979, *10*, 311–326.

Jones, R. R., Reid, J. B., & Patterson, G. R. Naturalistic observation in clinical assessment. In P. McReynodls (Ed.), *Advances in Psychological Assessment* (Vol. 3). San Francisco: Jossey-Bass, 1975.

Kagan, J. The measurement of overt aggression from fantasy. *Journal of Abnormal and Social Psychology*, 1956, *52*, 390–393.

Kaufmann, H. Hostility, perceived similarity, and punitivity under arousal condition. *Journal of Personality*, 1966, *34*, 538–545.

Kazdin, A. E. Artifacts, bias and complexity of assessment: The ABC's of reliability. *Journal of Applied Behavior Analysis*, 1977, *10*, 141–150.

Kazdin, A. E. Unobtrusive measures in behavioral assessment. *Journal of Applied Behavior Analysis*, 1979, *12*, 713–724. (a)

Kazdin, A. E. Nonspecific treatment factors in psychotherapy outcome research. *Journal of Consulting and Clinical Psychology*, 1979, *47*, 846–851. (b)

Kerlinger, F. N. *Foundations of behavioral research* (2nd ed.) New York: Holt, Rinehart and Winston, 1973.

Kilpatrick, D. G., Veronen, L. J., & Resick, P. A. Assessment of the aftermath of rape: Changing patterns of fear. *Journal of Behavioral Assessment*, 1979, *1*, 133–148. (a)

Kilpatrick, D. G., Veronen, L. J., & Resick, P. A. The aftermath of rape: Recent empirical findings. *American Journal of Orthopsychiatry*, 1979, *49*, 658–669. (b)

Kimble, C. E., Fitz, D., & Onorad, J. R. Effectiveness of counteraggression strategies in reducing interactive aggression by males. *Journal of Personality and Social Psychology*, 1977, *35*, 272–278.

Kirchner, E. P., Kennedy, R. E., & Draguns, J. G. Assertion and aggression in adult offenders. *Behavior Therapy*, 1979, *10*, 452–471.

Knott, P. D., Lasater, L., & Shuman, R. Aggression-guilt and conditionability for aggressiveness. *Journal of Personality*, 1974, *42*, 332–344.

Koren, P., Carlton, K., & Shaw, D. Marital conflict: Relations among behaviors, outcomes, and distress. *Journal of Consulting and Clinical Psychology*, 1980, *48*, 460–468.

Kuhn, T. S. *The structure of scientific revolutions* (2nd ed.). Chicago: Univ. of Chicago Press, 1970.

Liebert, R. M., & Baron, R. A. Some immediate effects of televised violence on children's behavior. *Developmental Psychology*, 1972, *6*, 469–475.

Locke, H. J., & Wallace, K. M. Short marital adjustment and prediction tests: Their reliability and validity. *Marriage and Family Living*, 1959, *21*, 251–255.

Lovaas, O. I. Effect of exposure to symbolic aggression on aggressive behavior. *Child Development*, 1961, *32*, 37–44.

Mash, E. J., & Terdal, L. G. *Behavior-therapy assessment: Diagnosis, design, and evaluation.* New York: Springer, 1976.

McCord, W., McCord, J., & Howard, A. Familial correlates of aggression in nondelinquent male children. *Journal of Abnormal and Social Psychology*, 1961, *62*, 79–93.

McDaniel, J. W., O'Neal, E., & Fox, E. S. Magnitude of retaliation as a function of the similarity of available responses to those employed by attacker. *Psychonomic Science*, 1971, *22*, 215–217.

McGuire, W. J. Suspiciousness of experimenter's intent. In R. Rosenthal & R. L. Rosnow (Eds.), *Artifact in behavioral research*. New York: Academic Press, 1969, Pp. 13–57.

McGuire, W. J. The Yin and Yang of progress in social psychology: Seven Koan. *Journal of Personality and Social Psychology*, 1973, *26*, 446–456.

Megargee, E. I. Undercontrolled and overcontrolled personality types in extreme antisocial aggression. *Psychological Monographs*, 1966, *80*, (3, Whole No. 611).

Miller, N. E., & Bugelski, R. Minor studies of aggression: II. The influence of frustration imposed by in-group on attitudes expressed toward out-groups. *Journal of Psychology*, 1948, *25*, 437–442.

Mischel, W. Toward a cognitive social learning reconceptualization of personality. *Psychological Review*, 1973, *80*, 252–283.

Newcomb, T. M. The interdependence of social-psychological theory and methods: A brief overview. In L. Festinger & D. Katz (Eds.), *Research methods in the behavioral sciences*. New York: Holt, 1953. Pp. 1–12.

O'Leary, M. R., & Dengerink, H. A. Aggression as a function of the intensity and pattern of attack. *Journal of Research in Personality*, 1973, *7*, 61–70.

Orne, M. T. Demand characteristics and the concept of quasi-control. In R. Rosenthal & R. L. Rosnow (Eds.), *Artifacts in behavioral research*. New York: Academic Press, 1969.

Owens, D. J., & Straus, M. A. The social structure of violence in childhood and approval of violence as an adult. *Aggressive Behavior,* 1975, *1,* 193–211.

Patterson, G. R. Naturalistic observation in clinical assessment. *Journal of Abnormal Child Psychology,* 1977, *5,* 309–322.

Patterson, G. R., & Cobb, J. A. Stimulus control of classes of noxious behaviors. In J. F. Knutson (Ed.), *The control of aggression: Implications from basic research.* Chicago: Aldine, 1973. Pp. 144–199.

Patterson, G. R., & Fleischman, M. J. Maintenance of treatment effects: some considerations concerning family systems and follow-up data. *Behavior Therapy,* 1979, *10,* 168–185.

Patterson, G. R., Hops, H., & Weiss, R. L. Interpersonal skills training for couples in early stages of conflict. *Journal of Marriage and the Family,* 1975, *37,* 295–303.

Patterson, G. R., & Reid, J. B. Reciprocity and coercion: Two facets of social systems. In C. Neuringer & J. L. Michael (Eds.), *Behavior modification in clinical psychology.* New York: Appleton, 1970. Pp. 133–177.

Perry, D. G., & Perry, L. C. Identification with film characters, covert aggressive verbalization, and reactions to film violence. *Journal of Research in Personality,* 1976, *11,* 399–409.

Pisano, R., & Taylor, S. P. Reduction of physical aggression: The effects of four strategies. *Journal of Personality and Social Psychology,* 1971, *19,* 237–242.

Reichenbach, H. *Experience and prediction.* Chicago: Univ. of Chicago Press, 1938.

Roethlisberger, F. J., & Dickson, W. J. *Management and the worker.* Cambridge, Mass.: Harvard Univ. Press, 1939.

Rosenbaum, M. E., & deCharms, R. Direct and vicarious reduction of hostility. *Journal of Abnormal and Social Psychology,* 1960, *60,* 105–111.

Rosenbaum, M. E., & Stanners, R. F. Self-esteem, manifest hostility, and expressions of hostility. *Journal of Abnormal and Social Psychology,* 1961, *63,* 646–649.

Rosenberg, M. J. The conditions and consequences of evaluation apprehension. In R. Rosenthal & R. L. Rosnow (Eds.), *Artifact in behavioral research.* New York: Academic Press, 1969. Pp. 279–349.

Rosenthal, R., & Rosnow, R. L. (Eds.). *Artifact in behavioral research.* New York: Academic Press, 1969.

Sanson-Fisher, R. W., Poole, A. D., Small, C. A., & Fleming, I. R. Data acquisition in real time— An improved system for naturalistic observations. *Behavior Therapy,* 1979, *10,* 543–554.

Scheier, M., Fenigstein, A., & Buss, A. H. Self-awareness and physical aggression. *Journal of Experimental Social Psychology,* 1974, *10,* 264–273.

Schnelle, J. F., Kirchner, R. E., McNees, M. P., & Lawler, J. M. Social evaluation of two police patrolling strategies. *Journal of Applied Behavior Analysis,* 1975, *8,* 353–365.

Sears, R. R., Maccoby, E. E., & Levin, H. *Patterns of child rearing.* New York: Harper & Row, 1957.

Shontz, F. C. *Research methods in personality.* New York: Appleton-Century-Crofts, 1965.

Shortell, J. R., & Biller, H. B. Aggression in children as a function of sex of subject and sex of opponent. *Developmental Psychology,* 1970, *3,* 143–144.

Shuntich, R. J., & Taylor, S. P. The effects of alcohol on human physical aggression. *Journal of Experimental Research in Personality,* 1972, *6,* 34–38.

Shure, G. H., Meeker, R. J., & Hansford, E. A. The effectiveness of pacifist strategies in bargaining games. *Journal of Conflict Resolution,* 1965, *9,* 106–117.

Sidowski, J. B., Wyckoff, L. B., & Tabory, L. The influence of reinforcement and punishment in a minimal social situation. *Journal of Abnormal and Social Psychology,* 1956, *52,* 115–119.

Siegel, S. M. The relationship of hostility to authoritarianism. *Journal of Abnormal and Social Psychology,* 1956, *52,* 368–372.

Simons, L. S., & Turner, C. W. Evaluation apprehension, hypothesis awareness, and the weapons effect. *Aggressive Behavior,* 1976, *2,* 77–87.

Spinetta, J. J. Parental personality factors in child abuse. *Journal of Consulting and Clinical Psychology,* 1978, *46,* 1409–1414.

Swingle, P. G. Exploitive behavior in non-zero-sum games. *Journal of Personality and Social Psychology,* 1970, *16,* 121–132.

Taylor, S. P. The relationship of expressed and inhibited hostility to physiological activation. Unpublished doctoral dissertation, University of Massachusetts, 1965.

Taylor, S. P., Shuntich, R. J., & Greenberg, A. The effects of repeated aggressive encounters on subsequent aggressive behavior. *Journal of Social Psychology,* 1979, *107,* 199–208.

Tedeschi, J. T., Gaes, G. G., & Rivera, N. Aggression and the use of coercive power. *Journal of Social Issues,* 1977, *33,* 101–125.

Tedeschi, J. T., & Lindskold, S. *Social psychology: Interdependence, interaction, & influence.* New York: Wiley, 1976.

Thibaut, J. W., & Coules, J. The role of communication in the reduction of interpersonal hostility. *Journal of Abnormal and Social Psychology,* 1952, *47,* 770–777.

Thorndike, E. L. A constant error in psychological ratings. *Journal of Applied Psychology,* 1920, *4,* 25–29.

Toch, H. *Violent men.* Chicago: Aldine, 1969.

Turner, C. W., & Berkowitz, L. Identification with film aggression (Covert Role Taking) and reactions to film violence. *Journal of Personality and Social Psychology,* 1972, *21,* 256–264.

Turner, C. W., Layton, J. F., & Simons, L. S. Naturalistic studies of aggressive behavior: Aggressive stimuli, victim visibility, and horn honking. *Journal of Personality and Social Psychology,* 1975, *31,* 1098–1107.

Tursky, B. Physical, physiological, and psychological factors that affect pain reaction to electric shock. *Psychophysiology,* 1974, *11,* 95–112.

Vincent, J. P., Friedman, L. C., Nugent, J., & Messerly, L. Demand characteristics in observations of marital interaction. *Journal of Consulting and Clinical Psychology,* 1979, *47,* 557–566.

Walters, R. H., & Brown, M. Studies of reinforcement of aggression: III. Transfer of responses to an interpersonal situation. *Child Development,* 1963, *34,* 563–571.

Watson, D., & Friend, R. Measurement of social-evaluation anxiety. *Journal of Consulting and Clinical Psychology,* 1969, *33,* 447–457.

Weider, G. B., & Weiss, R. L. Generalizability theory and the coding of marital interactions. *Journal of Consulting and Clinical Psychology,* 1980, *48,* 469–477.

Weiss, J. M. Effects of coping responses on stress. *Journal of Comparative and Physiological Psychology,* 1968, *65,* 251–260.

Weiss, J. M. Effects of coping behavior in different warning signal conditions on stress pathology in rats. *Journal of Comparative and Physiological Psychology,* 1971, *77,* 1–13.

Weiss, R. L., Hops, H., & Patterson, G. R. A framework for conceptualizing marital conflict, a technology for altering it, some data for evaluating it. In L. A. Hammerlynck, L. C. Handy, & E. J. Mash (Eds.), *Behavior change: Methodology, concepts and practice.* Champaign, Ill.: Research Press, 1973. Pp. 309–342.

Wenar, C. The reliability of mothers' histories. *Child Development,* 1961, *32,* 491–500.

Wolfe, B. M., & Baron, R. A. Laboratory aggression related to aggression in naturalistic social situation: Effects of an aggressive model on the behavior of college students and prisoner observers. *Psychonomic Science,* 1971, *24,* 193–194.

Zillmann, D., Johnson, R. C., & Day, K. O. Provoked and unprovoked aggressiveness in athletes. *Journal of Research in Personality,* 1974, *8,* 139–152.

Zimbardo, P., & Maslach, C. *Psychology for our times.* Glenview, Ill.: Scott, Foresman, 1977.

A Concluding Comment

One conclusion warranted by the chapters of the present volume is that they reflect many of the theoretical developments of the 1970s, representing a major step in sophistication from those included by Geen and O'Neal (1976) in their earlier book on the subject. By the end of the 1960s most of the major concepts in human aggression had been formulated: imitative, reactive, and angry aggression; inhibition and disinhibition; instrumental aggression; arousal; and many others. Theorizing in the 1960s consisted of the development of several informative but constricted viewpoints that explained some types of aggression under some circumstances. The present volume reflects at least two more recent developments on the theoretical level that go beyond the stage of the minitheory. First, higher levels of theoretical integration are now being attained than was formerly the case. Second, this integration reveals more and more explanation in terms of general psychology, rather than strictly social psychology.

The developments are desirable. If the psychology of aggression is a viable concept, it must be founded on underlying sets of constructs that not only give form to the several approaches that psychologists take but also connect with the constructs of more general psychological theory. An empirical law (such as the law of effect) gives a valid explanation for a phenomenon only if it systematically explains other phenomena as well. Furthermore, it must be embedded within a larger nomological network, however rudimentary. In the psychology

AGGRESSION
Volume 1

of aggression we have many empirically derived constructs (e.g., anger, frustration, inhibition, arousal), which subsume many specific behaviors. Constructs of a theory must be held together by a syntax, however. The simple construct systems that we have built in search of that syntax constitute the traditional theories of aggression, the frustration–aggression hypothesis being one of the oldest and best known. The theoretical developments of the 1960s all took place on this level. By taking the next step and tying the various minitheories to construct systems of general psychology—emotional, cognitive, motivational, physiological, genetic—aggression theorists are availing themselves of syntactic relations that are already relatively well established. Theories of aggression will continue to develop to the extent that they are grounded in general psychological theories.

The first part of the book shows this trend clearly. Bandura's chapter allows us to see how his now-familiar conclusions on modeled and imitative aggression fit into a more broadly conceived model of cognitive learning and control. Ferguson and Rule have constructed a sequential model of anger and aggression that is based on current concepts from attribution theory and, through the latter, on the more general notions of cognitive expectancy. Zillmann, after first examining the concept of arousal in general terms, offers an interpretation of cognitive control of aggressive arousal. Finally, in a chapter that provides a counterpoint to the heavy cognitive emphasis that precedes it, Berkowitz builds a case for aggression as a reaction to aversive stimulation that requires no cognitive intervention. In so doing, he shows connections between his own research and theorizing and the general approach to emotion now articulated by Leventhal and his associates.

The chapter by Tedeschi and Melburg represents a break with the theoretical assumptions of the papers that precede it. These authors prefer to think of "aggression" primarily as a label attached by observers to acts of coercive power. Thus, aggression, or at least what is usually called by that name, is regarded as instrumental behavior carried out in an interpersonal context. The same interpersonal emphasis characterizes the contribution of Dengerink and Covey, who review the evidence on aggression as a means of escaping or avoiding attack. These two chapters convey an impression of aggression as social behavior to a greater degree than the ones that preceded it, in which the emphasis was mainly on internal cognitive and motivational determinants of aggressive behavior. The chapter by Rajecki points toward an even broader conceptualization of aggression by suggesting human–animal comparisons. He thereby challenges the assuption often made by social psychologists that the study of lower animals provides little useful information about aggression in humans. In so doing, he reminds us of the correct meanings of homolog and analog, and their significance for cross-species comparison. Rajecki's views articulate well with those of Berkowitz, and less well with those of the more cognitively oriented psychologists.

The chapter by Bertilson on methodology in the study of aggression could have been included at the beginning of Volume 2 in which research evidence is reviewed. Its inclusion in Volume 1 highlights the close relationship between theories and the research generated by predictions derived from theoretical premises. Theory construction ends with the specification of semantic relationships between constructs and observable operations or measurements. Research beings with predictions derived from theory. Thus methodology, which concerns operations, procedures, and measurements, provides the bridge between the formal and the empirical aspects of psychological theory.

Author Index

Subject Index